THEY ALSO FLEW

THEY ALSO FLEW

THE ENLISTED
PILOT LEGACY
1912-1942

LEE ARBON

SMITHSONIAN INSTITUTION PRESS

WASHINGTON AND LONDON

The paper used in this publication meets the minimum
requirements of the American National Standard for
Permanence of Paper for Printed Library Materials
Z39.48-1984

Library of Congress Cataloging-in-Publication Data

Arbon, Lee.
They also flew : the enlisted pilot legacy, 1912–1942 /
Lee Arbon.
        p.   cm.
Includes bibliographical references and index.
ISBN 1-56098-108-3 (alk. paper)
1. United States. Army. Air Corps—History. 2. Air pilots,
Military—United States—History. I. Title.
UG633.A82   1992
358.4'13'0973—dc20   91-32814
                                                   CIP

A paperback reissue (ISBN 1-56098-837-1) of the original
cloth edition

Printed in the United States of America
03 02 01 00   5 4 3

For permission to reproduce individual illustrations
appearing in this book, please correspond directly with the
owners of the images, as stated in the picture captions. The
Smithsonian Institution Press does not retain reproduction
rights for these illustrations individually or maintain a file
of addresses for photo sources.

Publisher's note: The descriptions of otherwise
undocumented personal incidents and the recollections of
episodes and persons are entirely the author's. Every effort
has been made to verify details and insure correctness;
inaccuracy if it occurs is regretted.

Logo: courtesy J. H. MacWilliam

To Peggy

CONTENTS

FOREWORD

THIS VOLUME FILLS A VOID. IT IS ONE of what I hope will be a host of documentaries about common men and women who have contributed to the heritage of the American people.

It is a military history, to be sure. But it is a humanistic volume written from within by an unaffected author who marched within the ranks.

The sergeant pilot legacy is a personal history written from the inside out. It is the story of a few brave men who wanted to experience the exhilaration of flight—from the cockpit. These young men did more than wonder about the mysteries of flying. They gravitated to fragile aircraft in search of unfettered flight. Initially, most were swept up in the excitement afforded by aerial demonstrations at county fairs, by written accounts of air combat over France in World War I, or by the barnstorming pilots of the 1920s.

That enlisted men—noncommissioned officers—were permitted to fly was an accident in the first place. After all, in the eyes of official Washington, enlisted men were routinely uneducated and, hence, not considered intelligent enough to fly.

Congress ultimately provided limited opportunities for enlisted aviators. Those who were able to take advantage of the programs were not formally educated. They were motivated, challenged, inquisitive young men in search of adventure, who would not be limited by economic deprivation or the absence of a college degree.

To be sure, this legacy evolved incidentally. Enlisted pilots were an accident of the birth of flight, men caught up in the passion, challenge, and romance of flight. Some were simply at the right place at the right time; others had to wage a concerted effort to win their wings.

Yet, once anointed as pilots, they were cast adrift in a bureaucratic sea of uncertainty. Their status as noncommissioned pilots provided the military with a dilemma. After all, pilots were commissioned officers, members of a uniformed caste system that was a throwback to the Old World.

It is fitting and proper, albeit overdue, that enlisted pilots get their just rewards. This year, a half century after America's entry into World War II, our common, everyday enlisted airmen are finally being recognized for their contributions to aviation history.

Some of those contributions are recognized in the pages that follow. To be sure, this is a historical document replete with references and appendices. More important, though, it is a story of real people and colorful characters who truly went above and beyond the call of duty.

These men have been overlooked and ignored in official histories. Yet, in many cases, their contributions were invaluable, especially when America needed trained pilots for one emergency or another. And, for that chance to fly, for their turn in the cockpit, they performed a host of other, more mundane duties. In looking back, most of them remember with reverence that "they also flew."

GEORGE HICKS
Director
Airmen Memorial Museum
Suitland, Maryland

INTRODUCTION

THIS BOOK IS A FIRST. NOWHERE ELSE has there been such a compilation of enlisted pilot contributions to the development of air power. From the earliest, uncertain days of aerial flight to the American-dominated skies of World War II, the legacy of these stripe-wearing pilots spans nearly a half-century of resplendent courage, daring feats, and heroic sacrifices.

Yet so little is known about them. Like millions of others who were unaware of the facts, I grew up believing that only officers—through some mysterious, secret transformation that occurred upon commissioning—were capable of performing military aerial flight. That myth has been dispelled—shattered by this book and the saga of a little-known band of men, noncommissioned officers all, who flew in an era of aviation that will never be replicated.

The history of enlisted contributions to the development of American air power are many and, if compared to precious stones, would be like jewels in a crown. Among the shiniest of the jewels in the crown of U.S. aviation achievements is that of the legacy of the sergeant pilots.

They Also Flew is *the* definitive chronology of the enlisted pilots and their achievements. It provides crucial material for filling in the details of a missing chapter in U.S. military aviation history. It is an integral part of our heritage, and we must know about it. Thankfully, Lee Arbon provides us a magnificent opportunity through this book.

CHIEF M. SGT. WAYNE L. FISK
U.S. Air Force
Washington, D.C.

PREFACE

WHILE THE HISTORY OF THE UNITED STATES Air Force as a separate and independent component of the Department of Defense did not officially begin until September 1947, its roots went back to August 1907, when its parent, the Army, began to concern itself with aeronautics.

Understandably proud of its new status, the Air Force had to look to its future. Only recently has it begun to reflect on its earlier, humbler beginnings—beginnings that included a small number of enlisted pilots.

Those of us who served their nation as enlisted pilots, even if for a little while, have found it humbling to learn that few ever knew we served. When the term *enlisted pilot,* or *sergeant pilot,* is introduced into any appropriate conversation today, and draws only a blank response, an accounting seems overdue.

I have undertaken this writing to place the legacy of this small number of pilots into the literature, and to inform its readers that from 1912 to 1942 enlisted pilots also flew.

I have chosen to use the terms *aeroplane* and *airplane* in their contemporary context, that is, aeroplane, 1903–17, and airplane, 1917–42.

A caveat in closing: Since I am neither a writer nor a historian, my reconstruction of the sergeant pilot story, drawn from documents forty-five to eighty-two years old as well as from the recollections of individuals years after the events, is bound to be flawed by time and bias. It is, however, as careful and honest an account as I can construct. Readers who discover such flaws would do this account a favor by bringing them to the author's attention.

ACKNOWLEDGMENTS

AS ONE MIGHT SUPPOSE, THE QUEST FOR material in this book has demanded a fervor and persistence akin to that of a bastard child in search of a legitimate connection to his or her family tree. At the same time, it has been great fun. Those institutions and individuals I have called upon for help have responded with open doors and minds, making my search a pleasure.

The long effort to reconstruct the history of the enlisted pilot has left me beholden to many. This is my opportunity to acknowledge their contributions, my chance to be an unabashed name-dropper.

I consider my friend and cohort, James H. MacWilliam, a collaborator on this book. MacWilliam spurred the creation of an association of former sergeant pilots which, in turn, became a network for the reconstruction of their honorable and noble service. That network has furnished this author and J. H. MacWilliam some very important ingredients: encouragement and freely given personal stories, diaries, documents, and photographs, far more than one volume could contain. This accumulation of documents became our "Sergeant Pilot Archives," and has recently been donated to the USAF Historical Research Center at Maxwell Air Force Base. Interested persons may find them under call number 16.6-63. From such material, MacWilliam has compiled as complete an accounting of these unusual pilots as exists anywhere today. The names, statistics, and biographical data used in my text could not have been written without his collaboration.

I am indebted to Walter Boyne, former director of the National Air and Space Museum in Washington, D.C., and Robin Higham, former Royal Air Force flight sergeant and editor emeritus of the *Aerospace Historian,* for recognizing the potential story in earlier drafts of the manuscript and for encouraging its development. I am grateful to Dick Kohn, Chief, Office of Air Force History, for his advice to me on sensing my hesitation to undertake the writing of this book. "The only way to write a book," he said, "is to begin." Nor can I ignore the boost given my research efforts by the staff of the Air Force Museum's Research Division, especially its chief, Mr. Charles "Chuck" Worman, and his able assistant, Vivian White.

Gerald Hasselwander, formerly of the Air Force Historical Research Center, now retired, opened doors and turned on lights, illuminating much of the dormant material from which this history was constructed. Too, I am indebted to R. Cargill Hall, former Chief of the Research Division, USAF Historical Research Center, and now Chief of the Contract Histories Program of the U.S. Air Force Office of History, for critiquing my manuscript and suggesting many improvements for it. Ed Rice and George Haddaway of the History of Aviation Collection at the University of Texas, Dallas, are due my thanks for sharing pertinent information from that rich collection.

The late J. J. Smith provided especially valuable guidance during my search for enlisted pilots of the World War I period.

Colonel Jay Baker, former Commander, United States Air Force Instrument Training Center at Randolph Air Force Base, Texas, now retired, and Lt. Col. William Ercoline, formerly of that office and also now retired, are due the gratitude of every former sergeant pilot for conceiving and executing the plan to dedicate that center in honor of William C. Ocker, an early sergeant pilot and father of blind flight. I must also acknowledge the personal memories and insights into Ocker's most productive years, which were shared by the late Col. Carl Crane, collaborator with Ocker in the creation of the first book ever published on the subject, *Blind Flight in Theory and Practice*.

Charles C. Crain, Jr., former Chief, Office of History at Kelly Air Force Base, and staff members George W. Bradley III, Dr. Robert Giles, Ross Day, and Pete Skirbunt shared knowledge, time, and material with me despite heavy workloads and tight schedules. Ann K. Hussey, current chief of that office, and her staff, Dr. Robert Browning, S. Sgt. Thomas M. O'Donahue, and Lisa Manning, have continued that tradition, for which I remain grateful.

David W. Shircliffe, recently retired Chief of the Office of History, Air Training Command at Randolph Air Force Base, Tom Manning, his successor, and staff members Dick Bannon, master sergeants John Okonski and Jim Swinning are owed a grateful acknowledgment.

I am also grateful for the cooperation received from Fernando Cortez, curator of the Edward H. White II Museum (Hangar Nine) at Brooks Air Force Base, as well as Dr. Edward Alcott, Office of History at Brooks, and Senior M. Sgt. Robert C. Williford, of that office.

Sergeant Robert A. Beggs and M. Sgt. Albert L. Miller, 67th Tactical Reconnaissance Wing Historians at Bergstrom Air Force Base, Austin, have earned my heartfelt thanks for their support over the years.

Mrs. Marge Burge Waters, daughter of Vernon Burge, America's first enlisted pilot, has generously shared her father's personnel and personal records, photos, and documents with me. They are, in many cases, the only window through which I could peer back to his service during the earliest days of Army aviation, and to his service as an enlisted pilot. Mrs. Doris Ocker Osborn, daughter of William C. Ocker, has been similarly generous with her father's documents, as has Mrs. Jean Mackey Ertwine with those of both her fathers. A profound thanks is owed to each of them. The same thanks are due Mrs. Peggy Smith, widow of Carlton "C.P." Smith, Mrs. Evelyn Haynes, Louise Siebenaler, and Mrs. Emily Beigel, widows of sergeant pilots. They shared their husbands' memories, mementos, documents, and photos with me. The enlisted pilot history would have been incomplete without them.

Generals Carl McDaniel, "Gatty" Waldron, Maurice Beach, Noel Parrish, and colonels Paul Blair, Paul Jackson, Julius Kolb, Boyd Ertwine, Lloyd Sailor, Larry Brown, Loren Cornell, all from the "middle years" (1920–32), have shared their stories as enlisted pilots in that period, as well as photos, documents, and recollections.

My contemporaries, "former sergeant pilots," are also due much credit for their individual input into the project. Joe Casey spent much of his precious time interviewing former enlisted pilots of the twenties and thirties residing in California, thereby adding richness to the biographic material in this book. Bob Pace, Russell Shaw, Jack Hoover, Jack Hoye, and Herman Wood became linchpins in the sergeant pilot network. Their connections and contributions enabled me to add many diverse fragments of the picture to the whole.

Don Bergstrom, Richard Cooney, Larry Dye, John Rauth, Max Miller, Robert Lauducci, Joseph Vizi, Robert Van Ausdell, William Gatling, Lee Eddington, and Robert Bryant—all have furnished photos, anecdotes, and documents to illustrate the sergeant pilot story. Nathan J. Kingsley provided documents and photographs on those sergeant pilots who participated in the Guadalcanal campaign. Robert Haynes Murray's book about the Aleutian air war, *The Only Way Home,* sheds poignant light on his participation and that of his squadron mates in that campaign.

I am indebted to George Hicks, director of the Airmen Memorial Museum at Suitland, Maryland, for interrupting his hectic routine long enough to tighten my manuscript and write a foreword for it. Jan Williams, George Hicks's able assistant, has earned my gratitude for putting eleven chapters of the manuscript on wordprocessor disks. Len Morgan, contributing editor to *Flying* magazine, has also earned my gratitude for evaluating the manuscript in its earlier stages and urging me on with it.

I have never seen the face of the man who said "yes" to this manuscript: Felix Lowe, director of the Smithsonian Institution Press. Of course, we have corresponded and talked on the telephone, but I have to meet him one day, look him in the eye, and personally thank him for his faith in this book.

No author can claim sole credit for his or her creation. There is a standard to be maintained which is beyond the reach of more than a few of us. Fortunately, a guardian angel, sometimes called an editor, is assigned to guide an author in spite of his myopia and literary shortcomings to an achievement of that standard. During the editorial phase of this book, I have come to regard its editor, Therese D. Boyd, as my guardian angel.

Finally, I must acknowledge Chief M. Sgt. Wayne Fisk for his sustained advocacy of the nearly forgotten legacy, that of the enlisted pilots. While serving as the director of the USAF Enlisted Heritage Hall, an airmen's museum at Gunter Air Force Station (Base), Chief Fisk, a much decorated hero, found a place to honor the memory of the enlisted pilots. Because he represents the best of the current generation of Senior Air Forces NCOs, I have asked him to grace the early pages of this book with an introduction. The spirit that moved eight generations of American airmen to serve in the air resides in such men still.

PROLOGUE

IN FAIRNESS TO THE TERM *pilot*, the first enlisted pilot in the U.S. Army was probably Sgt. William Ivy, a former stunt balloonist. With Lt. Col. Joseph Maxfield aboard as observer, Sergeant Ivy piloted a much-patched-up balloon high enough on June 30, 1898, to see the Spanish fleet in the harbor of Santiago, Cuba, during the Spanish-American War.[1]

Five years later, Orville and Wilbur Wright demonstrated that powered flight was possible, generating an immediate and avid international following. Viewed at first as a novelty, the craft's potential as a weapon of war eventually became obvious to the U.S. Army.

In August 1907, the chief signal officer, Brig. Gen. James Allen made the sky the limit in a memo establishing an aeronautical division within the Signal Corps and charging it with "all matters pertaining to military ballooning, air machines, and kindred subjects."

That small unit went immediately to work with balloons. Thus was American military aviation born, not with the noisy clatter of smelly engines, but with the silent, stately ascension of balloons. Not until 1908, when the Army added a powered balloon to its inventory, did engines disturb the silence. The noise doubled in 1909 with the addition of the Wright aeroplane.

Among the first enlisted men assigned to that small aeronautical division was a youthful private, first class named Vernon L. Burge. In 1912, Burge, by then a corporal, became the first Army-enlisted aviator. Three thousand enlisted aviators followed in his wake during the next three decades.

The first enlisted pilot for the Navy is reputed to be Harold H. "Kiddy" Karr. Karr learned to fly in 1912 and was utilized by the Navy as an aviator, but was not officially designated as such until 1920. By 1982, five thousand Navy, Marine, and Coast Guard enlisted men had been designated as naval aviation pilots, or "Nappies," as they sometimes call themselves.

The first Marine enlisted pilot, according to one authority, was 1st Sgt.

Jacob Makohin, who was assigned to duty involving heavier-than-air machines in May 1915.[2] According to another authority, Marine W.O. Walter E. McCaughtry was the first.[3]

By the time America entered World War I, enlisted pilots were a fact of life, albeit a small one. A small number of Navy and Marine enlisted pilots was utilized in combat roles during World War I, but no record has been found indicating that Army enlisted pilots served in combat. However, by the time the Great War ended, sentiment was building to include them in combat organizations.[4]

That enlisted pilots were trained at all was, more often than not, because an insufficient number of officers was available. This was the case in the Army Signal Corps when Corporal Burge volunteered to become one of Lt. Frank P. Lahm's first students. So too for twenty-five Marines who became enlisted pilots in 1918 when they were accepted for flight training in order to bring the Corps up to its authorized pilot strength. Then such training was halted and did not resume until the 1920s.[5]

Among those Nappies who became famous, even legendary in their time, were such pilots as:

- Floyd Bennett, who flew with Adm. Richard Byrd on the 1925–26 Arctic expedition.
- The chief petty officers of Fighting Squadron Two who, with the exception of its commanding officer and key staff, were all enlisted pilots. They became a Navy legend.[6]
- Gunnery Sgt. M. T. Sheperd, Albert S. Munsch, and S. Sgt. Gordon W. Heritage, to mention just a few, were among those Marine pilots involved in the skirmishes in the late twenties and early thirties with the Sandinistas in Nicaragua.[7]
- Ken Walsh, a former Marine flying noncommissioned officer (NCO), became an officer and an ace in World War II, winning the Congressional Medal of Honor as well.[8]
- Wilbur B. "Spider" Webb, another Nappie, who also became an officer and an ace. Webb won a place in history for himself by downing six confirmed and two probable Japanese aircraft on a single mission over Guam during the "Marianas Turkey Shoot."[9]

From 1926 to 1932, the National Defense Act, as amended, required that 20 percent of the pilots assigned to tactical squadrons of the Air Corps be enlisted aviators. For the Navy, the requirement was 30 percent. In 1932, all of the services were standardized at 20 percent. While neither service ever came close to fulfilling that requirement, the Navy came closer than the Army. The Great Depression, however, had so reduced funding for the services that pilot training was cut back. For enlisted pilots it was completely eliminated. It was not resurrected in the Navy until the late thirties. In 1940, the Army Air Corps began considering a career NCO pilot plan, a plan that became law in mid-1941, only months before the Japanese attacked Pearl Harbor. The staff sergeant pilots produced by this program became a new breed for the USAAF units. For the first time in two world wars, they would take their place in the formations of many USAAF combat and operational groups in war theaters around the world.

In mid-1942, another kind of enlisted pilot began training when the rating of "liaison pilot" was created. Liaison pilots were trained primarily to support Army ground operations with light aircraft. Among the many frontline tasks performed by this valiant group of enlisted pilots were battlefield reconnaissance, artillery spotting, courier duty, and casualty evacuation. They wore wings similar to those worn by unlimited Army pilots, but with the letter L embossed on the shield.

Many civilian pilots were called directly into the service after Pearl Harbor and rated as "service pilots." Most were commissioned, but a few enlisted as NCOs and were later promoted to flight officer, and later still were commissioned. Their wings bore an embossed S on the shield. Lacking the specialized military training necessary to fly combat, they were normally limited to such noncombat assignments as freight and passenger hauling in nontactical situations or ferrying aircraft. However, many later flew transports over the Hump, certainly as hazardous as some combat duties.

A third category of enlisted pilot, unique to the Second World War, was the glider pilot. These were some of the bravest men this author ever knew. Every flight, whether training or combat, was one-way. Like the airplane sergeant pilots, they were promoted to the rank of flight officer and later commissioned. They became part of nearly every major airborne assault in the Mediterranean and European theaters. They became a legend in Burma and participated to a limited extent in the recapture of the Philippines. Overloaded with troops and explosives, their gliders were cut loose (sometimes by accident) at low altitudes, often at night, to glide into hostile territory where the penalty for a misjudged landing was gruesome.

Before America became involved in World War II, hundreds of adventurous young Americans went to Canada and enlisted in the Royal Canadian Air Force. Some became officers, other became sergeant pilots. After the Japanese attack on Pearl Harbor, many transferred to the U.S. Army Air Forces, at least 145 of them being sworn into Uncle Sam's Air Force as staff sergeants. They were the only sergeant pilots authorized to wear the wings of both nations.

During World War I, Great Britain, France, Germany, and Italy used a number of enlisted pilots in their air forces. Americans serving as pilots in the Lafayette Escadrille did so while holding some pretty lowly grades.

Britain, like the United States, trained only a limited number of enlisted pilots between wars, but during World War II maintained its enlisted pilot force at about one-third of the total. Among those who served as such in the Royal Air Force (RAF) during the war was Lord Cameron of Balhousie, who eventually became the chief of the British Defence Staff.[10]

In his book, *Airman's Odyssey,* Antoine de Saint-Exupery immortalized the French sergeant pilot "Hochede," describing his heroism in the air battles during the fall of France. The Soviet air force also used NCO pilots during World War II. Aleksandre N. Yefimove, one of them, rose through the ranks to become chief of the Soviet air force.[11]

There is a brotherhood among aviators. They know this even when they are fighting one another in the skies. All of them share a belief that they are unique. That brotherhood is made even closer when they share a unique event or status, as did the first aviators, or the airmail pilots of years ago, or those "few" RAF pilots to whom so much is owed by so many for their valor during the Battle of Britain. So it is with those who flew for their nation as enlisted pilots, for they too served in a unique status in a unique profession. The aim of this book is to preserve their names and accomplishments in the historical literature. By putting names and faces on those unusual men, their descendants will learn how they performed in an arena, and at a time when such duty was normally performed by officers only.

American enlisted pilots were a celebration of purpose . . . to fly! That they were also competent soldiers before becoming pilots, or that they continued to succeed in their post–sergeant pilot careers is "Lagniappe"— a little something extra. The important thing is that they flew, and flew with courage at a time in their nation's history when they were really needed. That little something extra is exactly what America got from its investment in them. They were only a small fraction of the force, but from 1912 when Burge became the first, until M. Sgt. George Holmes, the last, retired from the U.S. Air Force in 1957, that small fraction of the force paid a handsome return on their nation's investment in them.

AMERICA'S FIRST ENLISTED PILOT **1** 1907–1912

PROBABLY NO MAN IN THE ARMY WAS more qualified for flight training than Corporal Vernon Lee Burge. He was a bright, healthy young soldier, intimately familiar with the Wright aeroplane, and he was eager to fly. At this point in his career he had been privy to the experiences and mistakes of many of the outstanding aviators of his day. Qualified and eager as he might be, Burge was also aware that only officers were selected for flight training.

Burge looked younger than his twenty-four years. He was short, only five feet five, and looked out on the world through blue eyes set in a fresh and earnest face. He did not wear that defensive "chip" carried on the shoulders of so many short men. Moderately handsome, he was modest about it, a trait women found attractive. Straight blond hair fell to each side of a natural middle part on his head.

Born in Fisher, Illinois, on November 29, 1888, Burge attended public school in Ivesdale, Illinois. During his last year of school, he found part-time employment as a printer with the local newspaper, a job he held until April 16, 1907, when he enlisted in the U.S. Army Signal Corps.[1]

In 1911, Burge, by then an experienced aeroplane mechanician, was ordered to accompany a brand-new Wright aeroplane to the Philippines and to report to Lt. Frank P. Lahm, an officer under whom he had served previously as a balloon handler. His assigned task was to assemble and maintain the craft for Lieutenant Lahm, who intended to use it for his newly created Philippine aviation school at Fort William McKinley.[2]

Burge arrived in Manila on February 4, 1912. Lieutenant Lahm placed him in charge of a small detail of men who would assemble the aeroplane. The process was slowed somewhat by the lieutenant's frequent interventions, which Burge understood and tolerated. He sympathized with Lahm's concern for, having been absent from aviation since 1909, he had lost his

1

familiarity with the flying machine. Lahm was inquisitive about every aspect of the plane's assembly. Nevertheless, Burge managed to assemble most of the aeroplane between Lahm's visits to the hanger and had it ready for flight by March 19.[3]

On March 21, Burge watched with some anxiety as his lieutenant taxied the airplane up and down the field. After several trial runs, Lieutenant Lahm made a determined run down the field. Burge held his breath as Lahm lifted the plane off the ground and shot into the air at too steep an angle. Burge covered his eyes as Lahm, in apparent alarm, cut the engine and stalled the plane, which fell flatly back to earth. Burge spent the next two days repairing a broken right skid, two struts, and a skid brace.[4]

Two days later, Lieutenant Lahm and Corporal Burge trundled the freshly repaired aeroplane out of the hanger and again prepared it for flight. After nearly half an hour of taxiing the plane around the field, Lahm began a series of short hops a few feet high and several hundred feet long from which he continued to land rather awkwardly. As the days passed, and the hops became longer, Burge could see improvement in Lahm's handling of the machine, with the exception of his landings. The lieutenant had not yet learned to keep the nose down on the rollouts, a practice that resulted in bad landings.[5] After two weeks of practice, however, Lieutenant Lahm became proficient and confident enough to begin teaching others.

Although it was his intention to train officer volunteers, only one, Lt. Moss L. Love responded. Burge was aware that Lieutenant Lahm needed one more student and, viewing it as the opportunity of a lifetime, stepped forward. To Burge's surprise, Lieutenant Lahm consented.[6]

While retaining his position as mechanician for the aeroplane, Burge officially began his flying career on April 5, 1912. He made eight short flights with Lieutenant Lahm that day.

During the weeks that followed, few flights could be called routine. On April 9, for example, while Burge and Lahm were in the air, the plane's engine began losing power, causing the plane to drop in the turns and nearly crash into the trees. They recovered, but while gliding in for a landing, Lieutenant Lahm's hat blew off. When he released the controls to grab it, the craft landed heavily, breaking several struts. Burge reverted to his regular duties as mechanician and spent the balance of the day making repairs.[7]

On June 14, 1912, Burge satisfied the FAI (Federation Aeronautique Internationale) requirements for an aviator's certificate, whereupon Lieutenant Lahm dispatched a letter to the secretary of the Aero Club of America requesting that such a certificate be issued.[8] When Lieutenant Love qualified a short time later, Lieutenant Lahm proudly informed the chief signal officer of the Philippines that with three pilots on hand, that is, himself, Lieutenant Love, and Corporal Burge, they could now use additional aeroplanes. The chief signal officer included Lieutenant Lahm's request in his own report to the adjutant general in Washington.[9]

The reply stated that there would be a delay in the delivery of more planes, and it scolded Lahm for training an enlisted man as an aviator, declaring:

> It is not the policy of the War Department to train enlisted men in flying aeroplanes.
>
> Their military training is such that very few enlisted men are qualified to observe military operations and render accurate and intelligent reports of what they see from an aeroplane.
>
> Another objection is that very few enlisted men have sufficient knowledge of mechanics to appreciate the stresses to which an aeroplane is subjected during certain maneuvers.[10]

In spite of the rebuff, Lieutenant Lahm retained Corporal Burge as an aviator and mechanic. Flying continued until the arrival of the monsoon rains, which put an end to flying for the year.

Initially, the rains flooded only the lower portion of the airfield, but as they continued, the water rose steadily, threatening the hanger and its aeroplane. Burge had seen deluges before, but these Philippine rains were different. They arrived like a waterfall and did not abate until the season ended. As a result, water continued to rise, seeping into the hanger itself, making it necessary for Burge to place the aeroplane up on blocks.

The rains were still falling on August 1912 when Burge received an envelope containing his aviator's certificate from the FAI, bearing the number 154. Burge had become the first enlisted man in history to be trained as a pilot. A little later he received a promotion to the rank of sergeant.[11]

The hiatus from flying caused by the flooding gave Burge moments of idle time to reflect on the events that led to his selection for training as an aviator. In fact, he maintained a daily diary during his early career which, together with other personal notes, goes back to that day in late August of 1907 when he first volunteered for balloon duty.

Private Burge had just completed recruit training at Fort Omaha, Nebraska, when the sergeant called him out of ranks and ordered him to report to Capt. W. H. Oury, the company commander. Saluting stiffly as he reported, Burge focused his eyes a mile beyond his commander and held the salute. Captain Oury suppressed a smile, returned the salute, and placed Burge at ease. He explained that the Signal Corps was organizing a division that would specialize in balloon work, and that six recruits were to be selected from Fort Omaha. "This is a fine opportunity to become one of them," the captain declared.[12]

Hesitating for a moment, Burge recalled that the only balloon he had ever seen was at a carnival. He also wrestled with the wisdom of veteran soldiers who had advised him never to volunteer. But Burge, young, inexperienced, and intimidated by his commander's rank, took a deep breath and replied, "I'm willing to take a chance, sir!" With those words, he became one of a handful of men destined to launch the U.S. Army into a new phase of military aeronautics.[13]

The following day Burge was joined by five other volunteers, each of whom was promoted to private, first class, and paid before boarding the train for Jamestown, Virginia.

When the train pulled into the Jamestown station, the young soldiers found themselves in the midst of festivities marking the town's 300th anniversary. The first permanent English-speaking settlement in the New World had organized an exposition around the event, which was in full swing and well attended. Naval vessels from many nations were anchored at nearby Hampton Roads and dominated the exposition. By comparison, the aeronautical display was quite modest, intended only to acquaint the new men with balloons and create a public awareness of the Army's reawakened interest in aeronautics. It was to assist in this effort that Burge and his cohorts had been assigned.

The six volunteers were met at the station by Cpl. Edward A. Ward. Ward himself had been assigned to the newly created Aeronautical Division only days before, making him the first, a fact that commanded instant respect from the new arrivals. Ward marched his new charges to the exposition grounds where billet and messing facilities were provided for them by a detachment of the 23rd Infantry.

After stowing their meager duffel, the new soldiers were reassembled for a brief welcome by their new commanding officer, Capt. Charles de Forest Chandler, who explained that their training as balloon handlers would begin under a pair of professional balloonists; Israel Ludlow and J. C. "Bud" Mars.[14]

As well as training the new men, Ludlow was responsible for the building that housed the aeronautical display. In addition to balloons, the building contained a curious-looking bamboo glider that Ludlow had constructed. When time permitted, the new men assisted him in his attempts to launch the strange craft by towing it behind a boat. The effort failed, however.[15]

Mars taught the new men to carry passengers aloft in captive balloons. Throughout the first half of September 1907, Ludlow and Mars provided their charges with valuable hands-on experience with the balloons.[16]

On September 16, the detachment moved to Washington Barracks in the District of Columbia for additional balloon training under Leo Stevens, another prominent aeronaut and balloon manufacturer. The detachment traveled each day to the gas plant where Stevens taught them how to fold and inflate the balloons. Captain Chandler augmented the instruction with lectures on wind currents and weather.[17]

There was a ripple of excitement when the men learned that Lt. Frank P. Lahm, a lanky young West Point officer, would soon report for duty with the detachment. Lahm had soared to international fame a year earlier, in September 1906, when he and Maj. Henry B. Hersey were lofted 402 miles in their balloon, from Paris to the Yorkshire coast of England, in twenty-two hours to win the inaugural Gordon Bennett balloon race. Burge and his cohorts looked forward to this hero's arrival with pride and some awe.[18]

During the next few weeks, Captain Chandler, Leo Stevens, and another experienced civilian aeronaut, John C. McCoy, continued to sharpen the skills of the balloon detail until the young tyros became proficient. At this time the division was ordered to St. Louis to assist contestants in the 1907 Gordon Bennett International Balloon Races scheduled for October. Spirits soared when they learned of the assignment and of the opportunity to test their new skills.[19] Captain Chandler also shared the excitement, but for quite a different reason. Having just qualified for his FAI balloon pilot certificate, he was invited by McCoy, the pilot for the U.S. entry, to serve as his assistant for the race.[20]

When the detachment arrived in St. Louis, they were divided among the crews of the nine competing balloons from four nations. The United States fielded three: the *United States, St. Louis,* and *America.* Germany entered the *Pommern, Tschudl,* and *Dusseldorf.* The *Isle de France* and *Anjou* were entered by France, and the *Lotus II* was entered by England. Burge was assigned to the *Dusseldorf.* The men were happily occupied with chores that were important and visible enough to impress the pretty young ladies who watched attentively as they worked. It was an exciting and festive event, with pomp and pageantry enough to please the crowd estimated at 100,000.[21]

The race began on the afternoon of October 21 in fair weather with a light wind. The lead balloon, *Pommern,* rose from its launch site at exactly 4 P.M., followed at five-minute intervals, in designated order, by the remaining balloons.[22] The men did not learn the finishing order of the race until two days later. First place went to the German balloon *Pommern,* followed by the *Isle de France,* the *Dusseldorf,* and McCoy and Chandler in the *America.* The *St. Louis* took fifth place, the *Tschudl* came in sixth. *Anjou,* the *United States,* and the *Lotus* finished seventh, eighth, and last, respectively.[23]

The race and the fun ended on October 24, too soon to suit the men of the Aeronautical Division. Reluctantly, they boarded their train, waved goodbye to the belles of St. Louis, and returned to Washington. As winter set in, the balloons on which they had learned their skills were placed in storage, and the men moved to the Signal Corps School at Fort Wood, New York, for further training.

With the arrival of spring in 1908, the detachment moved to Fort Myer, Virginia. By summer, the men were busy with preparations for the flight trials of several experimental flying machines. One of these was a lighter-than-air dirigible, designed and constructed by Capt. Tom Baldwin, a prominent aeronaut. It was powered by a new, lightweight four-cylinder engine built by Glenn Curtiss. Two heavier-than-air flying machines were also to be demonstrated: one by Augustus M. Herring, the other by Orville and Wilbur Wright. The Wright Brothers' machine was considered the only serious contender. There were still skeptics, but they were not so much concerned with the machine's ability to fly; that had already been demonstrated. Instead, the skeptics wondered if the machine was yet sufficiently developed to carry out the military tasks envisioned for it.[24]

Glenn Curtiss and Capt. Tom Baldwin arrived at Fort Myer from Hammondsport, New York, in August 1908 with their dirigible. In describing the dirigible, Burge wrote:

> It looked like an overgrown cigar. Underneath was suspended a wooden frame-work which contained a Curtiss four-cylinder engine and its controls. Mr. Glenn Curtiss of aeroplane fame acted as engineer and rode in [the] forward compartment. Captain Baldwin rode in [the] rear and controlled [the] rudder surface, the elevator being controlled from the front compartment.[25]

The demonstration trial was successful, but just barely. The dirigible failed to attain the specified top speed by less than one mile per hour and, as agreed in the bid, the designers had to forfeit a percentage of the bid price.[26]

Although not yet officially accepted by the Signal Corps, the dirigible made its public debut at the St. Joseph, Missouri, Military Tournament. The detachment left Fort Myer for St. Joseph on August 17, 1908. Lieutenant Thomas Selfridge, one of the Aeronautical Division's up-and-coming young officers, stayed behind to observe the heavier-than-air trials. When the detachment returned from St. Joseph on September 20, they found the post in mourning. Lieutenant Selfridge, who had accompanied Orville Wright as an observer on a demonstration flight, perished when it crashed. Orville Wright had been seriously injured, and the future of heavier-than-air aeronautics at best seemed clouded. Burge was glad to be associated with the dirigible, now the only powered craft the Army possessed.

The dirigible was officially accepted on August 28, 1908, and became Signal Corps Dirigible No. 1. Its contract stipulated that Baldwin and Curtiss would train two pilots in its operation. In fact, they had trained three: lieutenants Frank Lahm, Benjamin Foulois, and Thomas Selfridge.[27] They also took particular pains to instruct the ground crew on the care and handling of the craft, and as a member of that crew, Burge paid careful attention to their admonitions.

With the coming of another winter, the division moved to Fort Wood, New York, for additional schooling, returning to Fort Myer in the spring of 1909. In May the dirigible and its crew were moved to Fort Omaha, Nebraska.[28]

Only days after arriving at Fort Omaha, the dirigible fliers discovered the prairie near Omaha, especially in the spring, was a risky place to fly. This became evident when capricious winds inflicted the craft's first serious indignity. On the evening of May 31, 1909, lieutenants Lahm and Foulois took the ship out for a five-minute flight in a brisk wind. Then Lt. John G. Winter, making his first flight, replaced Foulois. Under Lahm's guidance, Winter started well, but it soon became obvious to observers on the ground that the two officers were losing control of the craft. They circled the field once and headed back into the wind, but could make no headway. Lahm then threw out a drag line that was seized by three men on the ground. However, as Lieutenant Winter failed to shut off the engine, it was impossible to hold the ship. The line was then wrapped around a fencepost, which was promptly pulled out of the ground. The dirigible, leaving a pursuing crowd in its wake, continued to drift inexorably toward the telephone lines. Skimming at good speed about twenty feet above the ground, the dirigible struck one of the telephone poles head-on, tearing a great gash in the bag's nose.

The frame containing the motor, controls, and two frantic lieutenants came to rest on the wires. Escaping gas allowed the bag to collapse and settle heavily over the frame. The frame buckled in the center, forcing the whirling propeller into the telephone wires, cutting several and disrupting local phone service. Following that episode, the detachment conducted rope drills with captive balloons, maneuvering them around and over telephone lines, trees, and other obstructions.[29]

The wreck of the dirigible put the detachment in a bind, since it was scheduled to appear at the Toledo Military Tournament over the Fourth of July holiday one month hence.

Not only did the detachment have to rebuild the dirigible, itself an arduous task, but hydrogen gas had to be manufactured and then compressed into two hundred metal cylinders in order to refill the bag after arriving at Toledo. Several men of the division were sent to the supply warehouse at Fort Leavenworth, Kansas, to select a tent large enough to house the dirigible. The tent was located, unpacked, inspected, repacked, and loaded for rail shipment to Toledo.

Miraculously, the repairs were completed in just over two weeks, with testing and final adjustments taking another ten days. Weary from those labors, the small detachment finally loaded the dirigible and its support equipment onto cars of the N.W. & Wabash railroad. At nightfall, the men boarded the cars and fell asleep while the train carried them eastward through a steady rain.

Upon arrival at Toledo, the men were dismayed to find that only one company of infantry had arrived at the fairgrounds. Preparations that were supposed to have been made prior to the arrival of the dirigible crew remained undone. Consequently, one detail of the crew hastily unloaded and erected their camp tents, while a second erected the large dirigible tent, and a third unloaded the dirigible. In spite of hordes of mosquitoes and June bugs, the dirigible was eventually stowed safely inside the huge tent and made ready for inflation the following morning.

But when morning arrived, so did catastrophe. As the men inflated the dirigible, a strong wind blew through the tournament grounds, ripping apart the large tent and collapsing it onto the dirigible. The dirigible was damaged too severely to be repaired in time for the tournament. Disappointed and dispirited, the men, instead of starring in the tournament, now were captive spectators. They watched with envy as the infantry troops delighted the crowds with intricate drill routines on the parade ground. Much of each remaining day was spent sewing up the huge tears, more as an excuse to remain until the tournament was over than to effect real repairs. Some consolation came of the setback, however. Burge and his cohorts took advantage of an unexpected opportunity to mingle with the crowds and flirt with some of Toledo's prettier girls and, in the evenings, stroll with them through the park.

Such pleasant diversions ended all too soon as the detachment once again turned its attention to loading the damaged dirigible and its support equipment aboard the rail cars. While they labored, the rains returned, accompanied by horrendous lightning and thunder. The storm quickly turned lethal when a government teamster and his mules, assisting with the loading operation, were killed by a bolt of lightning. It continued to rain hard the following day as the men struck their tents and trooped aboard the rail cars for the return trip to Fort Omaha. They arrived at midnight two days later and unloaded the remains of their craft—still in the rain.

The next scheduled appearance for the dirigible and its detachment was the six-day Des Moines, Iowa, Tournament in mid-September 1909. The damage suffered by the dirigible at Toledo was repaired in three weeks, well before the Des Moines show. However, the rain that plagued the Toledo tournament reappeared, filling the men with new foreboding. The train carrying the dirigible and its detachment pulled into the Des Moines railyard in the rain. It continued to rain as the dirigible and its support equipment were unloaded. The men became soaked and disgusted. The disagreeable chores continued, as did the rain for more than two days. The men wallowed in mud as they struggled to erect the tent. With the arrival of an additional thousand troops on the tournament grounds, the wallow became a sea of mud.

In spite of such miserable conditions, the tournament commenced on schedule. On September 20, ten thousand people attended. There were no rains that day, but high winds prevented the dirigible from flying. Five thousand spectators showed up the next day, and while the high winds again prevented any flights, it was fortunate. The crew was unable get the engine running properly. That afternoon, the rains began again.

On the third day, another large crowd appeared. While the wind was not a problem this day, the engine again refused to run. The fourth day was scarcely any better. One short flight was made in the afternoon but, with a sputtering engine, it was a poor one.

On the fifth day, September 24, the weather was better, the crowd larger, and the dirigible made two fine flights in the morning and two in the evening. The sixth day began on a sour note when the engine again faltered as the flight began. Then the raising planes (elevators) refused to work and the crew had to make a forced landing a considerable distance from the tournament grounds. Adjustments were made on the spot and the crew succeeded in flying back to the tournament grounds to the sounds of a wildly cheering crowd. After securing the dirigible, the crew indulged in a little post-flight jubilation, then took up the task of deflating the bag and striking the tent hanger. Early in the morning of September 27, the men struck their own tents, broke camp, boarded the rail car for the return trip to Omaha, and fell asleep. The train arrived at midnight, but the weary men did not awaken until sunrise.

In September, the men were ordered to prepare the dirigible for another shipment. It was rumored that the dirigible and its crew would soon go east. Instead, they headed west to Los Angeles, to appear in the January 1910 air show. Burge did not accompany the ship this time as he was attending the Signal Corps School during the day and, seeking to broaden his education, attending night school in the evening,

In February 1910, Lieutenant Foulois was reassigned to Fort Sam Houston, Texas, to fly the Wright aeroplane purchased by the Army five months earlier. Foulois had previously received a few hours instruction from the Wrights, but had never soloed. Nevertheless, he was ordered to teach himself to fly it, then establish an aviation school at Fort Sam Houston.

That same month, Burge learned that he, too, was being transferred to Fort Sam Houston to serve under Lieutenant Foulois as a mechanician for the plane. It couldn't have been a happier assignment for Burge.

Arriving at the San Antonio rail station at dawn on March 5, 1910, scruffy from a jostled sleep, Burge found a barber shop, cleaned up, and took a streetcar to the fort. He was surprised to discover a very pretty post situated at the city's edge. He went immediately to the aeroplane shed and reported to Lieutenant Foulois who, with nine other men of the detachment, was repairing the aeroplane, which had been damaged on its last flight.[30]

An entire week passed before Burge had a chance to see the Signal Corps aeroplane fly. Foulois took it up three times in the morning and twice in the afternoon. He made four more flights during the following week, a period during which no repairs had been necessary. However, on the last flight of the day, Foulois landed in a small ditch and broke the skids. A series of minor crashes followed, each delaying further flying until the machine could be repaired. Other delays were caused not by repairs but by winds and weather.

Burge, fresh from the winter snows of Nebraska, found himself alternately shivering and sweating his way through the climatic caprices of the Texas spring season. Those Texas "northerners," as he called them, brought winds and rain that often made flying impossible. He watched his lieutenant, a scarcely trained aviator, braving "puffy" winds in the fragile flying machine. Early mornings and late afternoons soon became favored times for flying since the winds were usually lighter.

Burge and his cohorts watched apprehensively each time the machine rose from the parade ground and clattered about the sky with unsure jerkiness. Lieutenant Foulois was gamely trying to master the art of flying. They winced each time he slammed the craft back onto the parade ground and held their breath as it skidded to a dusty, graceless stop. They heaved a sigh of relief on seeing that the craft and its pilot had survived.

If adjustments to the engine were necessary, the chore usually fell to the mechanicians, who would start and run the engine to make the adjustments. If the iron harvester wheels, those cumbersome and heavy iron wheels used for ground handling, were attached, Burge would practice taxiing the plane a short distance. Later, when permanent wheels were affixed, he could taxi with ease.

More than a hands-on mechanician for Signal Corps Aeroplane No. 1, Burge was an avid "aeronautical buff." As a student of his trade, Burge eagerly followed every aviation event, attending every show that came to town. When other aeroplanes visited San Antonio, Burge was usually among the throngs that ogled and fingered the fragile craft. San Antonio, like all America, was taken by the novelty of flight and hosted every traveling air show in the country. He became familiar with the Curtiss machine and others such as "Captain" McMannis's modification of the Curtiss and Wright machines incorporating the novel, albeit frightening, feature of a swinging engine for altering the craft's center of gravity. He also examined the McCormick and Romme machines, the latter of which failed to get off the ground. Few of these machines ring a bell in anyone's memory today.[31] All of them reminded Burge of bridges—trussed, guyed, and braced as they were against the stresses imposed on them, it seemed that their designers had borrowed heavily from the art of bridge building.

Soon after his arrival in San Antonio, Burge learned through local newspapers that his former dirigible mentors, Glenn Curtiss and Capt. Tom Baldwin, were bringing an air show to San Antonio in mid-April 1910. Burge spent three days at the fairgrounds to witness the event and to visit with Curtiss and Baldwin. Accompanying the former was Charles Hamilton, a lean and laconic exhibition aviator. After seeing Curtiss and Hamilton entertain the crowd with breathtaking flights, Burge resolved to visit them between flights. Try as he might, the press of the crowd eager to do the same made it difficult. He eventually succeeded, and as they talked, Burge swelled with the pride of the privileged, basking in the reflected glory of their company.

Following the visit, Burge found Captain Baldwin hawking tickets for passenger rides in his tethered balloon. Happy to see the captain again, Burge volunteered to help him for the rest of the day. It was an offer Baldwin gratefully accepted.

In February 1911, Burge, now a corporal, visited the Bexar County fair-grounds for another air show. Once again the San Antonio newspapers trumpeted the arrival of a truly international program. Organized earlier by John and Alfred Moisant, the program promised wonderful aerial per-formances featuring "seven noted airmen" billed as "Monarchs of the Air." Charles Hamilton, now traveling with the Moisant team, was paired with Joseph Seymore, the only other American aviator in the group. Irishman John J. Frisbee, Swiss aviator Edmond Audemars, and French aviators Ren Simon, Rolland Garros, and Ren Barrier completed the team.

The reputation of these airmen had long preceded them and they did not disappoint their audience. Hamilton and Seymore put on a daring per-formance that made Burge proud to be an American. Then the "foreign" aviators put on a show matching that of Hamilton and Seymore. For the first time in his career, Burge realized the Americans did not have a monopoly on flying skills. Between acts, he picked the brains of these men while ex-amining their aeroplanes with more than idle curiosity, especially the fragile little Bleriot monoplane, an aeroplane he had not been near before.

The highlight of the meet was Military Day, Saturday, February 4, 1911. Spectator excitement ran high by showtime because the San Antonio papers had hyped the affair. For days the newspapers had speculated on which of the two adversaries would win the battle between the iron-throated monsters of war (horse drawn artillery) and the "Monarchs of the Air." According to the promotional copy, this was to be a "demonstration of the military value of the aeroplane under service conditions."

Burge was surprised how quickly the Frenchmen Simon, Garros, and Barrier located the hidden artillery with their flying machines. The artillery responded by firing blank charges at them, then chased the aeroplanes back to the fairgrounds where a noisy mock battle followed. The artillery con-tinued firing blank rounds at the circling planes, delighting the crowds.

The "Monarchs of the Air" gave their final performance on February 6, after which they packed up and headed west. Burge returned to his own routine at Fort Sam Houston, still riding on an emotional high.

Through an arrangement between the Army and Robert F. Collier, the Army leased the latter's Wright aeroplane. (Collier owned *Collier's*, a popular weekly magazine of the times.) Because it was a newer model, the Wright factory sent one of its exhibition pilots, Phillip O. Parmalee, to Fort Sam Houston to instruct Lieutenant Foulois in the particulars of its operation. Parmalee arrived at the fort on February 17, 1911; the plane arrived on the 21st. After Burge and his crew assembled the newer plane, old Signal Corps Aeroplane No. 1 was relegated to an adjacent tent and the new craft moved into the hanger.[32]

Parmalee took Burge for a short flight in the Collier aeroplane as a kind of reward for his work on the craft. It was a turning point for Burge, for from that moment on, he knew he would never be satisfied until he too became an aviator. There was absolutely nothing like it. When Parmalee left Fort Sam Houston on March 25, 1911, to return to the Wright factory, he left with Burge's eternal gratitude and respect.

Several days later, on April 4, 1911, Signal Corps Aeroplane No. 2, a new Curtiss machine, arrived and, over the next several weeks, was assembled by Burge and crew. On April 20, Parmalee's replacement, Frank Coffyn, arrived at Fort Sam Houston. So did Eugene Ely, the aviator for the Curtiss machine. Both aviators made flights with their respective planes that same day. Later, during a division review, Ely in his Curtiss and Coffyn in the Wright machine, carrying Lieutenant Foulois as a passenger, flew above the marching troops. Streaming proudly from the elevators of the Wright plane were two signal flags, and the Stars and Stripes.

Coffyn continued to instruct Lieutenant Foulois in landing the Wright machine, while lieutenants Paul Beck, G. E. M. Kelly, and John C. Walker, Jr., three recently arrived officers, began their instruction on the Curtiss machine under Ely. Burge and his men dutifully performed the maintenance and repairs on both machines.[33]

THE PHILIPPINE TOUR OF DUTY 2 1912–1914

VERNON BURGE WITNESSED A NEAR tragedy on May 2, 1911, when a student aviator, Lt. John C. Walker, Jr., took the Curtiss up for a flight in strong wind. While trying to make a righthand turn, Lt. Walker's machine pulled up sharply, stalled, then fell about fifty feet before miraculously righting itself. Then he almost flew into the tents but managed to regain altitude and circle the field. The shaken lieutenant seemed unable to control the machine as it darted about the field like a giant dragonfly. He then failed to shut off the engine as he attempted to land and bounced high into the air. While circling the field again, he narrowly missed the wireless antenna on the city watertower. The young officer eventually landed and dismounted, pale and shaken but obviously relieved. Burge wondered how the lieutenant ever got out of it alive—he supposed that Lieutenant Walker wondered, too.[1]

Eight days later, Burge witnessed a very real tragedy that he would remember vividly for the rest of his life. On May 10, Lt. G. E. M. Kelly brought out the Curtiss machine, which had just been repaired, and took it up without any preliminary ground inspection. He made several circuits of the field without incident, but when he tried to land, he descended at too steep an angle, struck the ground hard, and collapsed the front chassis. The machine then shot at least forty feet into the air. The pilot could be seen desperately trying to bring it down with controls that were obviously broken. The left wing dropped, then the nose, and the plane plummeted to the ground. Kelly was thrown fully ten feet in front of the machine. The young aviator never regained consciousness. The machine was a total wreck.[2]

Lieutenant Walker's close call and Lieutenant Kelly's death chilled the ardor for aviation that had prevailed at Fort Sam Houston for over a year. General W. H. Carter, the commander of Fort Sam Houston's maneuver division, ordered that no more flying be conducted.[3] Lieutenant Foulois, however, was able to make one final flight on July 12, 1911, shortly before

15

leaving for his new duties with the Militia Bureau of the War Department in Washington, D.C.

Burge remained at Fort Sam Houston with the Wright machine for a while as its caretaker, a chore that took little of his time since it now sat idly in its hanger.[4] To avoid boredom, Burge, a former printer's apprentice, volunteered part of his time in the post print shop. He also assisted with the installation of a new wireless station and clerked for the signal officer.

Just after Christmas 1911, Burge was ordered to Fort McKinley in the Philippines to join Lieutenant Lahm, already on duty there.[5] Burge was directed to accompany a newer Wright aeroplane to Fort McKinley and prepare it for use by Lahm. Lahm intended to establish an Army flying school in the Philippines and use the aeroplane for training new aviators.[6]

By this time, Burge had been a member of the Aeronautical Division for over four years. During that time he had become one of its most qualified airplane mechanics. Burge felt that such experience made him a natural for training as an aviator, yet he could hardly have hoped for so much as he prepared to leave Fort Sam Houston.

A fortnight later, Burge was aboard the U.S. Army transport *Sheridan* as it prepared to embark for the Philippines. After locating his berth and stowing his gear, Burge found a place along the rail from which to view the embarking ritual. He listened to the spirited marches played at dockside by the Army band. As the finale, the band played "Auld Lang Syne" while clusters of loved ones on the wharf waived tearful goodbyes to those on board the ship. Hawsers were loosed from their stanchions at the dock and tugboats eased the ship out of its slip.

As the *Sheridan* steamed out of San Francisco Bay on this fifth day of January 1912, the weather was perfect and the bay waters calm. But as the ship left sight of land, Burge became aware of a growing uneasiness in his stomach. There was no place to escape the pitch and roll induced by the ground swells. If he closed his eyes, it got worse. The sulfurous coal smoke belching from the ship's stacks followed him wherever he moved. Odors venting from the troop quarters, and especially those from the galley, aggravated his nausea. He gamely tried to place mind over matter, but that only made him more aware of the ship's pitching and rolling.

He was not alone. Faceless soldiers, pale and drawn, jostled him aside to find retching space along the ship's rail. Suddenly losing control of his own stomach, Burge joined the other miserable men draped over the railing.

It was two days before Burge was able to eat again, but from then on, he enjoyed the voyage. Having grown up in a small land-locked Midwestern town, he found the voyage an exciting novelty. He had heard others say that only wealthy people and soldiers could afford such voyages. Burge's only assigned duties were shifts of guard duty that took small and predictable parts of his days, allowing him ample free time. Alert and intelligent, Burge was not the type to become bored. The horizon, flat and unobstructed, invited his gaze and fueled his curiosity about what lay beyond. His attention was easily engaged by the rhythm and force of the waves through which the ship churned. The deep blue-green of the water gave him just a peek into its mysterious depths. Burge began to understand how men came to love the sea.

The *Sheridan* arrived in Honolulu on January 14, nine days after leaving San Francisco. She remained in port for two days while taking on coal for the next leg of the voyage. Because he was detailed to lend muscle to the coaling operation, Burge was able to visit Honolulu only briefly.

Underway again, the ship set course for Guam.[7] But several days out, the weather began to deteriorate and the sea became more disturbed. Again Burge wrestled with nausea, but this time it was not as severe. After several days of steadily worsening weather, Burge experienced his first real fear. To him the ship was out of control in the tormented sea. The deck was often awash, and the troops were forced to spend most of their time below in their bunks—a claustrophobic place in fair weather or foul.

The storm eventually passed. So too did the 180th meridian and the international date line with its traditional ceremonies. Early on the morning of January 28, the *Sheridan* steamed into Guam, exchanged cargo, and steamed out again, all in the same day. It was the last land the troops saw until February 3 when Samar, an island in the Philippine archipelago, appeared on the horizon. Soon afterward, the large island of Luzon appeared on the starboard side as the *Sheridan* steamed through the San Bernardino straits toward Manila.[8]

Burge arose the following morning to a whole new world. Sunrise tinted the roofs of port buildings as the ship moved ponderously through the small boat traffic toward its berth in Manila. From the railing, the soldiers exchanged exploratory glances with the native occupants of the small boats that crowded about the *Sheridan*. Manila was in the middle of a pre-Lenten celebration and Burge watched some of the festivities with interest. He never saw people so strange as these. They wore scarcely any clothes and the women smoked out in the open, in the streets, just like the men.

After disembarking from the ship, Burge hailed a carromata, a two-wheeled horse-drawn cart, to take him to the Signal Corps post. After going only a few blocks, the carromata was compelled to stop by a carnival parade. Resigning himself to the delay, he watched the parade from close range. Every sight, sound, and smell was new and exotic. The street din and festive babble nearly numbed his senses. Finally, the carromata began to make headway through the high-spirited crowds.

Burge noted that despite the chaos of the carnival, Manila was a lovely city. He was struck by the contrast between its massive modern governmental and institutional buildings, and the flimsy bamboo and palm frond huts on the outskirts of the city. Then, incredibly, he heard an aeroplane flying overhead. Looking up, he saw it, a circling exhibition aeroplane adding its own noise to the spectacle. It was a portent of his own future in this new land.[9]

As the carromata passed the polo grounds on Fort McKinley, Burge could see the unfinished shed in which the Wright aeroplane was to be housed, but until it could be completed, Burge would be assigned those duties that traditionally befall new arrivals: guard duty, charge of quarters, and supervision of certain "details." The hanger was finished on March 13, and the assembly of the aeroplane was completed six days later. Three weeks later, Burge began to fulfill an unlikely dream. Under the tutelage of Lieutenant Lahm, he was learning to fly.[10]

Among the spectators watching the flights at Fort McKinley was a tall, black-haired career soldier who was no stranger to the Philippines—a sergeant named William C. Ocker.[11] Having served there as a young artilleryman during the Spanish-American War and Philippine Insurrection, Ocker had survived skirmishes, an ambush, and capture. In fact, during negotiations for his release from captivity, Ocker refused to leave his captors until they returned his rifle. They obliged, but only with reluctance.[12]

Ocker returned to the United States and was serving at Fort Myer, Virginia, in 1909, when the Wright Brothers demonstrated their aeroplane for the army. While posted as a guard for their aeroplane, Ocker witnessed those flights and they fired his imagination. The desire to become an aviator took possession of his soul.[13]

Ocker was born in Philadelphia of German immigrant parents on June 18, 1880. Not a handsome man, Ocker, like Abraham Lincoln, transcended his homeliness with God-given abilities. He possessed an inquisitive mind that made him a tenacious student all his life.[14]

It was now, during his second tour of duty in the Philippines, that Ocker sat on a hillside at Fort McKinley and watched with envy as Lahm and his students took turns in the tropical sky.[15]

In March 1913, three additional student aviators reported to Lahm for training: lieutenants Carleton G. Chapman, Herbert A. Dargue, and C. Perry Rich.[16]

The new Wright C aeroplane, Signal Corps No. 13, requested earlier by Lieutenant Lahm, arrived from the United States in May. It was assembled by Burge and his crew, after which Lahm and Burge learned to operate its new duplicate controls. When Burge became familiar with both positions, Lahm utilized him as an assistant instructor.[17]

Throughout the summer months, Lahm and Burge perfected their skills in that machine. Then in September, pontoons were installed on the plane and Lieutenant Lahm attempted to test the new configuration in Manila Bay. However, Lahm was unable to get the aeroplane off the water. The following day, after making a few minor rigging adjustments, which he presumed would correct the problem, he tried again. Burge and Lieutenant Rich, attired in swimsuits, manned the oars of a skiff in case of any misfortune. Under their watchful eyes, Lahm positioned the machine for a takeoff and applied power. The plane accelerated slowly at first, and after a long run, reached about fifty miles per hour. At that time Lahm horsed it about ten feet off the water and remained airborne for only a moment. Then the plane pitched down sharply and struck the water with a frothy splash into which the plane, pontoons, and pilot disappeared.[18]

Burge and Rich rowed frantically toward the roiled water. Considering the force of the crash they feared the worst, but as they neared the wreckage, they found Lieutenant Lahm, buoyed by his kapok lifevest, trying vainly to resubmerge in order untangle his legs from the many wires and cables in which he was snared. Burge and Rich dove into the water and succeeded, with much splashing and sputtering, in freeing the pilot. More chagrined than hurt, Lahm was dragged into the skiff and rowed ashore.[19]

Shortly afterward, on October 18, 1913, Lieutenant Dargue and Sergeant Burge were reassigned to Fort Mills on the island of Corregidor. There they established facilities for the recently arrived but damaged Burgess-Wright hydroplane, Signal Corps No. 17. Except for a fabric-covered fuselage surrounding tandem cockpits, and pontoons rather than wheels, it was similar to other Wright aeroplanes. It was intended for aerial experiments in cooperation with the islands' coastal defenses, such as artillery spotting, airborne radio communications, and locating submerged mines.

During this assignment, Dargue, a West Point graduate, and Burge developed a solid relationship. From their association months earlier while flying together at Fort McKinley,[20] Burge came to trust Dargue's judgment, while Dargue valued Burge's competence with aeroplanes as both a mechanic and a pilot. They were the only aviators on Corregidor and shared the piloting duties on the island's only aeroplane. From November 6, 1913, until January 12, 1915, Dargue and Burge continued to milk credible flights out of the fragile hydroplane.[21]

While Burge frequently flew with Dargue, often piloting the plane himself, his primary role was as assistant pilot and crew chief for the hydroplane. Dargue was the creative force behind the experiments and as leader of the team flew most of the missions associated with them. He developed the ideas and adapted the Signal Corps and artillery equipment for use in the aeroplane. The most notable accomplishment of the team, however, was their ability to keep the aeroplane in productive service under demanding field conditions for fifteen months, even though it was obsolete and damaged when they received it.[22]

In 1914, lieutenants Lahm and Dargue encouraged Burge to apply for a commission in the Philippine Scouts. Burge secured laudatory letters from these officers and others under whom he had served, including Captain Chandler.[23] All recommended him, but in December 1914,[24] he was ordered to return to the United States for duty with the Signal Corps Aviation School at North Island near San Diego. Further pursuit of a commission in the Scouts became pointless.

On January 12, 1915, shortly after Burge departed the Philippines, Lieutenant Dargue, carrying Sgt. Wilburn C. Dodd as a passenger, wrecked the Burgess. With Fort Mills's only plane destroyed, Dargue was also ordered to the Aviation School at North Island, departing the Philippines on February 15, 1915.[25]

NORTH ISLAND 3 1915–1916

WHEN GLENN CURTISS ESTABLISHED AN aviation school at North Island in 1911, it soon became a mecca for aviation enthusiasts. Persons connected with, or who hoped to be connected with aviation, were drawn there: aviators, designers, engineers, and inventors anxious to apply their ideas to the new technology converged on the island. When the Army established its aviation station on the island in November 1912, the attraction was amplified.[1]

It was there Riley Scott demonstrated his system for aiming and releasing bombs from military aeroplanes,[2] while Lawrence Sperry experimented with his gyro-operated stabilizing device for aeroplanes.[3] Every exhibition flier in the nation seemed at one time or another to find reasons to visit North Island. Among them was Lincoln Beachey, the famous exhibition flier from whom all Army pilots, officers and enlisted alike, tried to seek advice.[4] Another was sports-pilot-turned-designer Glenn L. Martin, as well as Tiny Broadwick, the diminutive young lady who became the first person to make a parachute jump in the San Diego vicinity.[5] Anyone involved in American aviation before World War I eventually showed up at San Diego, the metropolitan beneficiary of the activity on North Island. It was the urban hub of the aviation set. Aviators were a new breed and provided ample copy for the press that tended to lionize them.

All this was new and heady wine for Burge, recently arrived from the Philippines and adjusting to his new duties. Flying was usually concluded by mid-morning each day when the winds picked up, and the officer aviators would return to the Coronado Hotel to resume pursuits interrupted by the morning's flying activities. Burge found the Strand, a promenade paralleling a stretch of nearby beach, a wonderful place to stroll and look the girls over, as were the beaches and the bathhouse at La Jolla, a short distance up the coast.[6]

Burge quickly became acquainted with other enlisted pilots at North Island. Corporal William A. Lamkey was one. Lamkey claimed the distinction of being the Army's second enlisted aviator. A product of the Moisant Aviation School, Lamkey was awarded FAI Certificate No. 183 in November 1912, just three months after Burge. Before they had a chance to become well acquainted, however, Lamkey purchased his discharge and headed for Mexico where, it was rumored, Pancho Villa was paying pretty good wages for aviators.[7]

Burge also met Sgt. William Ocker, that veteran soldier who had watched him fly at Fort McKinley in 1912. Since leaving the Philippines, Ocker had, by his own initiative, become the Army's third enlisted pilot. In September 1912, Ocker forfeited his rank as a sergeant, attained after fourteen years of service in the artillery and cavalry, when he chose to reenlist in the Signal Corps. Immediately after re-enlisting, he requested a transfer to the Aviation Section. The request was approved by his commanding officer, Capt. William "Billy" Mitchell, who confided to Ocker that he too was applying for reassignment to the Aviation Section.[8] At that time, no one in the Army could have guessed what a profound impact each would have on the future of aviation.

Ocker became an excellent mechanic whose services were frequently sought by visiting pilots. He began moonlighting as a mechanic in 1913 at the Curtiss Flying School, just a short walk up the beach, where for a time he worked on a Curtiss flying boat used to test an experimental stabilizing device. The device was a kind of early automatic pilot, the purpose of which was to reduce the tiring control forces that pilots had to endure on early aeroplanes, especially during long flights. These duties brought him together with the devices designer, Elmer Sperry, and his son, Lawrence. Ocker's association with the Sperrys was later to have a significant effect on aviation.[9]

In lieu of wages, Ocker took flying lessons in the Curtiss pusher from Theodore C. Macauley, one of the instructors with the Curtiss school. Since the pusher could carry only one person, Macauley would explain each step to his student, then seat himself in a chair at the edge of the field and cross his fingers.

Macauley would first explain how to taxi the airplane by requiring Ocker to follow a mile-long line of white lime. This was done until the desired proficiency was attained.

During this early phase, the foot throttle was restrained by a screw that allowed Ocker only enough power for taxiing, but not for takeoff. As the confidence of both teacher and student grew, the screw was adjusted to permit enough power to become airborne. Before receiving that privilege, however, Ocker was warned to fly no higher than four feet and no further than one hundred feet. In time, flights of fifty yards were permitted, then one hundred yards. Eventually, the permissible altitude was raised to ten feet. Each flight was accomplished along the same straight chalk line used for taxi practice. After each landing, Ocker dismounted from the plane, turned it around by hand, and flew the reverse track back to the starting point where Macauley sat in his chair.

As in most early flight training, it was necessary that there be little or no wind. Ideally, training was conducted in the still of the morning or early evening. Flying time was accumulated slowly while awaiting such conditions. In time, the height, distance, and power constraints were gradually removed until one magic day Ocker was instructed to try some simple maneuvers; to bank slightly left after getting aloft, leaving the course for a few seconds, then turning right to return to it. The process was then repeated to the right.

It wasn't long after these exercises that Ocker was permitted to complete a full circle to the left, and then to the right, returning each time to the line. Later, a full figure eight was permitted, then repeated with increasing skill. Finally, after detailed explanation, landings were attempted from various altitudes after shutting down the engine. When the full routine was understood, Ocker took a month-long furlough in order to practice for the FAI aviator test. When he was ready, Oscar Brindly, another Curtiss instructor, supervised the flight tests.[10]

A reporter for the *San Diego Union* covering the event filed the following account:

MECHANICIAN GIVES THRILLING NORTH ISLAND FLIGHT

To Private William C. Ocker, a mechanician attached to the First Aero Corps at North Island, falls the distinction of performing three of the most difficult and accomplished flights made on any aviation field in the United States or Europe, according to Francis Wildman, expert flying boat pilot and instructor at the Curtiss Aviation School.

Ocker performed his wonderful feats while taking tests for his Aero Club of America license. On his first flight the student birdman performed the required sets of figure eights and in the volplane [glide] he landed squarely on a section of the *San Diego Union* spread out to mark the landing place by Francis Wildman. In the cross-country flight test and with an adverse wind blowing, Ocker repeated the feat, bringing the machine down and landing within a fraction of an inch of the spot where the plane struck the paper before.

Ocker's last and by far the most spectacular test was made when he ascended to the height of 1200 feet, shut off the motor as required under the Aero Club rules, and then volplaned to the ground. The copy of the *Union* was held in place by a couple of stones and although the aviators present wagered that the young birdman could not repeat his two previous performances, Ocker astounded them by piloting the big Curtiss speed scout again squarely on the small section of newspaper.

"It was the most remarkable series of landings ever made by a student flying for a pilot's license," said Wildman. "Ocker's mastery of the machine was superb, and his feat of landing three times on a newspaper is one which few expert birdmen can duplicate."[11]

Ocker received FAI Certificate No. 293 in April 1914.[12]

While Burge had trained on the Wright machine, which permitted an instructor to accompany the student, Ocker had received his training on the Curtiss Speed Scout, which could carry only the student. Each aeroplane featured different flight control systems, which made it necessary to cross-train pilots on each system before they could become proficient on both. There were other technical differences, too. The Curtiss was fashioned chiefly of bamboo and some spruce, while the Wright was constructed mostly of spruce. The upper and lower surfaces of the wings and control surfaces of the Wright were covered with fabric, while only the top surfaces of the Curtiss were covered.[13]

With their limited power, the weight of the planes, as well as what they carried aloft, was critical. A few pounds made the difference between getting off the ground or staying on it. Ocker and his cohorts went to extraordinary lengths to reduce the weight. They sawed off the excess length of any bolts. They reduced the fuel load to only what they needed for the flight. In fact, in order to fly a little higher one day, Ocker removed his shoes and laid them on the ground at the takeoff point. On the landing rollout at the far end of the field, the engine died and balked at every attempt to restart it, forcing him to return barefooted through wide patches of sand burrs.[14]

As an institution, the Army had never been enthusiastic about training enlisted men as pilots. More often than not, it strongly disapproved. Had it not been for officers such as Frank Lahm, Billy Mitchell, and H. H. "Hap"

Arnold opening doors for them, few, if any, enlisted men would have become aviators.

Though limited in scope, the first authority to train enlisted pilots appeared in the Act of July 18, 1914, Section II (38 Stat. 514), and was published in War Department Bulletin 35, 1914. Later, at the insistence of Billy Mitchell,[15] the authority to train more enlisted "aviators" was included in the National Defense Act of June 3, 1916. Even so, when America entered World War I, fewer than two dozen could call themselves enlisted aviators.

That 1914 legislation[16] gave the commander of the Signal Corps Aviation School authority to train up to twelve enlisted men as pilots. To attain that number, the school commander, Capt. A. S. Cowan, persuaded several civilian aviators to enlist. One of those was William A. Lamkey. Another was Albert D. Smith, an exhibition aviator who began flying in the spring of 1913 when he and a partner pooled their meager resources and bought and rebuilt a wrecked Curtiss pusher aeroplane. Smith taught himself to fly, then flew it around eastern Washington, northern Idaho, and western Montana, making exhibition flights above the crowds at various state and county celebrations. But frequent crashes ate away their slender profits, so Smith left the partnership and headed south to San Francisco where, it was rumored, the Japanese were hiring aviators. The rumors proved to be true, and Smith soon had an offer in his pocket and a steamship ticket in his hand. However, when he learned that the ship taking him to Japan would not sail for another week, he made a quick trip to San Diego to observe the flying activities at North Island. While there, he visited the Signal Corps Aviation School and learned through conversations with two of the school's civilian instructors, Francis "Doc" Wildman and Oscar Brindly, that his talents as an aviator could be used right there if he cared to enlist. Smith mulled over this possibility for several days, confirmed the offer with Captain Cowan, then returned on March 10, 1915, and took the oath, becoming the sixth enlisted pilot.[17]

By that time, despite the objections of some of the early pilots, the Army had switched from pusher types, where the engine was located behind the pilot and pushed the plane through the air, to tractor types, where the engine was located in front and pulled the plane. Having flown only a pusher, Smith was retrained on the tractor types by Oscar Brindly, after which he joined sergeants Burge and Ocker as a member of a very unlikely band of enlisted aviators.[18] He was then assigned to Ocker's crew to help maintain the flying boat used by Doc Wildman. Later, Smith instructed student officers on the repair and overhaul of aircraft wings and fuselage sections. Later still, he taught some of them to fly.

A week later, two more enlisted pilots, Cpl. J. S. Krull and Sgt. Herbert Marcus joined that unique band. Krull received FAI Certificate No. 360.[19] However, Marcus, a fellow soldier from earlier days at Fort Sam Houston, was not so eager. "Detailed" to flight training at North Island, Marcus approached the assignment with a distinct lack of enthusiasm. He viewed flying as hazardous, rarely flew higher than seventy-five feet, and made as few turns as possible with the aeroplane. Marcus preferred to work on aeroplanes and leave the flying to others.[20]

During the months that followed, other enlisted men at North Island jockeyed for their chance to become aviators. Sergeant A. A. Adamson, corporals Ira O. Biffle, S. V. Coyle, Leo G. Flint, and Felix Steinle succeeded.[21]

The aviation school at North Island shared the facilities with the Army's 1st Aero Squadron. Initially organized at Texas City, Texas, in March 1913, the 1st Aero Squadron moved to North Island in November of that year. While the two outfits shared facilities, the aviation school was responsible for training aviators, and the 1st Aero Squadron was responsible for conducting field operations, tests, and experiments.[22]

In May and June 1915, the 1st Aero Squadron received new Curtiss JN-2s from the Curtiss factory at Buffalo, New York. Benjamin Foulois, recently promoted to captain and given command of the 1st Aero Squadron, recruited as many of his old mechanicians from their earlier days at Fort Sam Houston as he could lay his hands on. Among them were the reluctant aviator, Sergeant Marcus, and sergeants Steve Idzorek and Vernon L. Burge.

It was an ideal assignment for all of them, for it put them back in familiar company. They trusted Captain Foulois, and he in turn trusted them, and it was with high spirits and expectations that they awaited their new planes. Their skills would be put to good use assembling and testing the new Curtiss planes. But as they uncrated and inspected each one, defects were discovered. Some were serious enough to require overhaul or outright rejection. Their high spirits turned to disappointment, and disappointment turned to exasperation as extra time and effort was spent correcting the defects. By mid-July, with the more serious problems corrected, the planes were assembled, rigged, and test-flown. Their performance, however, fell short of expectations. The planes were overweight, underpowered, and could scarcely climb with two people aboard—a vexing situation indeed for the men who had expected much more.[23]

ARMY AVIATION GETS INVOLVED 4 1916–1917

WHILE THE MEN OF THE 1ST AERO SQUADRON were up to their elbows rebuilding the JN-2s, the squadron was ordered to Fort Sill, Oklahoma, to develop artillery-spotting methods in cooperation with the Field Artillery. Despite the many as-yet-uncorrected deficiencies, officers and enlisted men dismantled and repacked the planes for rail shipment to Oklahoma. They boarded the train on July 26, 1915, and accompanied their charges, still with high hopes.

Upon arrival, they discovered that no facilities existed for them, so, under a blistering summer sun they laid out a grid in the wide Oklahoma prairie. They then installed a water main and phone lines from Fort Sill to their encampment. Next they erected tents for themselves, for their mess, and tents to serve as plane hangers. Finally, tents went up to serve as a garage and as a storage shed.[1]

Turning their attention back to their planes, the squadron soon discovered that the difficulties imposed by the defective JNs were compounded by their poor aerial performance. Also, the demand for the squadron's services exceeded its capability. These limitations prevented the squadron from "cooperating" with the artillery to the degree expected. The planes were scarcely able to climb with two people aboard. This fact was brought home tragically when Lt. R. B. Sutton crashed soon after takeoff with Capt. G. H. Knox, an artillery observer, aboard. Sutton was injured and Knox was killed.[2]

To make matters worse, two crews were ordered to Brownsville, Texas, with their planes on August 14, 1915. Their mission was to work with the U.S. artillery batteries posted near the Mexican border[3] in an attempt to discourage the infiltration of bandits. In mid-November, just when all the aircraft were made flyable, the squadron was ordered to Fort Sam Houston.

The move was unprecedented. At the same time the planes were being flown to San Antonio—450 miles to the south—a motor convoy under the supervision of Sergeant Marcus moved some of the ground party. Others, under Burge—now the acting sergeant-major of the squadron—moved by rail. The motor convoy left Fort Sill on November 17; the rail contingent followed on the 18th, and the air echelon on the 19th. The entire squadron rendezvoused each evening, first at Wichita Falls, then Fort Worth, Waco, Austin, and finally San Antonio.

The squadron arrived at Fort Sam Houston on November 26, completing the first mass cross-country flight in aviation history.[4] This military migration, however, barely preceded the arrival of winter and the troops had to hustle to prepare their new field and building. As a result, little flying was done.

Just before Christmas 1915, Burge was ordered back to North Island to oversee the transfer of three old Burgess aeroplanes to Fort Sam Houston.[5] The trip gave him an opportunity to visit with Ocker, Smith, and Krull. He traded news of the Fort Sam Houston contingent for word about the North Island gang. Burge learned that Sergeant Ocker and Cpl. Albert D. Smith had received front-page coverage in the local papers. Ocker, it seems, had taken old No. 30—the Curtiss tractor—up for a flight and performed a series of fifteen loops. Shortly after landing, Smith, not to be outdone, climbed in, took off, and duplicated the feat.[6]

Scarcely two months after Burge returned to Fort Sam Houston, all hell broke loose seven hundred miles to the west. Pancho Villa and a band of followers crossed the U.S.-Mexico border on March 9, 1916, and raided the small railroad town of Columbus, New Mexico. The raiders killed a number of settlers and stung America's national pride, sparking outcries for retaliation. General Pershing's punitive expedition began pouring across the border and the 1st Aero Squadron was assigned to be its eyes and messenger. Four days later, the nation's total air might—consisting of eight JN-3s (the JN-2s, modified and redesignated)—was trainbound for Columbus.[7]

As soon as the train arrived at the siding, the planes were unloaded, uncrated, and assembled. The squadron's trucks were also made ready to transport the ground crews and equipment into Mexico.

But before preparations were complete, Captain Foulois received a message from General Pershing to proceed at once to Casas Grandes, over one hundred miles to the south. It was late in the afternoon of March 19, and the flight would take roughly two hours. Despite the low sun, Foulois led the departure. A little after 5 P.M., Burge watched the eight planes disappear over the southern horizon. He knew, as the sound of their engines faded, that it was unlikely they would make it by dark.

He was right. One pilot, Lt. Joseph E. Carberry, soon returned with engine trouble and remained until daybreak. Four others, Burge learned later, landed at dusk near Ascension, Mexico, and spent the night only halfway to their destination. As darkness fell, lieutenants Walter Kilner, Edgar S. Gorrell, and Robert H. Willis became separated from each other. Lost and alone, each flew on until they ran out of gas or fortitude. Each eventually landed in the darkened wilderness with varying results.

The next day, three of the four who had spent the night in Ascension arrived at Casas Grandes. The fourth plane was delayed but eventually appeared, circled the field, and, as it approached for landing, crashed. Its pilot, Lt. Thomas. S. Bowen, suffered a broken nose and a few bumps and bruises. Lieutenant Kilner, one of those who had landed in the wilderness after dark, appeared next. He was followed by Lieutenant Carberry arriving from Columbus, his engine now running smoothly. Lieutenant Willis arrived later, sharing the back of a horse with his Mexican host and the news that his aeroplane was down and damaged, but repairable.

The whereabouts of Lieutenant Gorrell, the last of the pilots to be accounted for, remained a mystery and a concern until he flew into Casas Grande a week later with a heavy growth of whiskers and an adventure to relate. It seemed that after he became separated in the dark, he developed a fuel leak and landed in the desert to avert further problems. Next morning, he was unable to locate the leak. Too low on fuel to proceed, he walked for four days before locating friendly forces. With their assistance he returned to his plane, made repairs, refueled, and flew to Casas Grandes.

While these events unfolded, Burge and his ground party rode into Mexico aboard their convoy of Jeffrey Quad trucks. One was fitted out as a mobile field shop, another as a kitchen, while others carried the squadron's personnel and duffel. The capabilities of the convoy were being tested in the high deserts of Mexico. Each evening, as a precaution against bandits, the trucks parked in a protective circle like the pioneers of a half-century earlier with their covered wagons. However, the bandits ambushed the convoy while it was in motion on the way to Casas Grande. After a short skirmish, a handful of bandits was subdued and taken prisoner.

Such misadventures set the tone for the remainder of the squadron's stay in Mexico. The underpowered planes were too fragile to withstand the rigors of spring in the mountains of northern Mexico. The cold, turbulent weather, the high, rugged terrain, and dry, dusty air took their toll. Even though Burge and his men labored mightily to keep the planes in the air, it became a losing battle.

After a month of diminishing operations, it became obvious that new and better planes were needed. The Curtiss N-8—in reality, a JN-4 simply re-designated as an N-8—was tested and also found wanting.[8] So were the new Curtiss R-2s which had been purchased for the squadron and sent to Columbus during the month of May 1916. The squadron returned to Columbus to re-equip itself with the newer models, which they made ready by July 21. Burge accompanied the planes into Mexico where he and his crews maintained them between flights to American frontier outposts, or courier flights between regimental command posts.

While the 1st Aero Squadron was busy on the border, the aviation school at North Island was busy training more aviators than ever. In addition to their regular flying and maintenance duties, the enlisted pilots were being increasingly utilized to assist officer instructors in the training of new fliers. To that end, a new enlisted pilot was added to their rolls. Joining Ocker, Smith, and Krull was Cpl. Ira O. Biffle, who had just qualified for his FAI Certificate at North Island in January 1916.[9]

It was during this time that Ocker became fascinated with the radio communication ideas being proposed by Capt. Clarence C. Culver, a radio specialist. Culver was experimenting with airborne radio, but was not a pilot at the time, so Ocker volunteered to take him aloft to test his ideas. The most noteworthy of these tests occurred when Ocker flew Culver from North Island to Santa Monica and back with a transmitter powerful enough to be heard at most receiving stations along the way. When near Santa Monica, Culver transmitted a message to North Island. The message was clearly heard and hailed as an astounding step forward. Other experiments involved transmissions from the ground to the plane, then two-way conversations between ground and plane, and finally, between aeroplanes. The 1st Aero Squadron in Mexico could have made good use of such technology had the equipment been available.[10]

While the 1st Aero Squadron was operating in Mexico, aeronautical planners in Washington were examining the manner in which the squadron was carrying out its mission. With the growing likelihood that the United States would ultimately become involved in the European war, they were especially interested in how aviation might relate to national policy. Out of that examination came a new act, creating a wider role for aviation, particularly military aviation. The act was of particular interest to enlisted men, as it removed several restrictions to their becoming enlisted pilots. While the Act of July 18, 1914, Section II (38 Stat. 514) may have legitimized the selection and training of enlisted pilots, it also restricted their numbers to just twelve men, of the aviation school commander's choosing. But Section 13 of the National Defense Act of June 3, 1916 (39 Stat. 175) elevated the authority for their selection to the secretary of war and removed the constraints on their numbers. Consequently, many enlisted men applied for such training. Few were accepted, however, and even fewer became pilots. Only seven of those who started training in the fall of 1916 successfully completed the course by the time America declared war on Germany and most of those were commissioned soon thereafter.[11]

In August 1916, Sergeant Ocker was sent east to the Hempstead Aviation Field near Mineola, Long Island, to demonstrate a flight stabilizer installed on the Martin TT. Some of his flights were interesting enough to attract the attention of the press. One reporter covering the event wrote:

> A trial of the Wilson stabilizer was made on the Hempstead Aviation Field yesterday. Many people prominent in the aviation world witnessed the tests. Among them were Lieutenant Richardson of the U.S. Navy; Lieutenant Carberry, U.S. Army; Henry Woodhouse, Secretary of the Aero Club, Allan Hawley, President of the Aero Club of America and Congressman Bleakley.
>
> Sergeant Ocker of the Aviation Corps of the U.S. Army was designated by the government to fly the plane in which the tests were made.
>
> On the first trial Lieutenant Richardson went up. The small box, about 15 inches square, was attached to the machine behind the driver's seat. The plane, a Martin with a 90-horsepower engine, was tipped at every angle and headed up and down. Within a second it would right itself with the aviator's hands off the wheel.
>
> Richardson tried in vain to upset the plane while the spectators gasped at his daredevil banking and turns. Several spectators went up for a flight.
>
> No one was allowed to see the new invention which was in a sealed box. John Wilson, the inventor, is a cousin of the president. The invention will probably be taken by the government. The stabilizer will be manufactured by the Macy Company.
>
> Lee Deforrest's wireless telephone was also tried out on the aeroplane. Despite the roar of the motor, the aviator was able to talk with those on

the ground. The current for the wireless is furnished by a small generator, operated by a windmill on top of the plane. Its maximum range is twenty-five miles.[12]

Representative-elect O. D. Bleakley, mentioned in the newsclip, was from Ocker's home state of Pennsylvania. The idea struck Bleakley to have native son Ocker fly him into the nation's capital from Franklin, Pennsylvania. He could, he surmised, arrive in Washington to take his seat in a most memorable fashion. However, Ocker felt that the distance and terrain from Franklin to Washington would be too formidable, suggesting instead that he be flown from Philadelphia. It was not a dull event. The press had been notified, of course, and the arrival was timed to coincide with the evening traffic rush. Ocker brought the Martin TT in low over the Potomac River and landed at Potomac Park, where he disembarked his passenger before the press. After a flourish of amenities, Ocker taxied a discrete distance from the crowd and took off again. He circled the Washington monument twice and headed for Fort Myer across the Potomac to spend the night.

Ocker remained available to Bleakley for the next few days and, at the latter's request, took one of the congressman's wealthy friends, Clarence W. King, president of the Washington Railway and Electric Company aloft. In a final magnanimous gesture, Congressman Bleakley offered the services of Sergeant Ocker and the aeroplane to President Wilson, should he desire to see Washington from above. Wilson, not yet convinced that aviation was here to stay, politely declined.[13]

While Ocker was in Washington, his former commanding officer, Billy Mitchell, now a major and assistant to the chief of the Aviation Section of the Signal Corps, used him for a variety of chores. One of these was to fly over several parcels of estuarian land on the banks of the Potomac River and judge their suitability for use as future airfields. In time, one of them would become Bolling Field.[14]

Ocker remained occupied with these and similar chores through the first weeks of January 1917. Then, he was at leisure for a short spell, spending time at home in Philadelphia while awaiting appointment as a commissioned officer. Finally, on January 27, 1917, he was discharged and commissioned in the Organized Reserves. Two weeks later, he was placed on active duty and assigned to Essington, Pennsylvania, to serve as the first commander of that flying field. When America entered the war on April 6, 1917, he was placed in charge of flying training at Essington.[15]

Burge, in the meantime, had returned to the 1st Aero Squadron base camp at Columbus, New Mexico, from his detachment in Mexico. In his pocket was a ninety-day furlough and an application for a commission in the Regular Army. Armed for the second time with recommendations from officers under whom he had served, Burge caught the train to Washington, D.C., and hand-carried his papers through channels. He then headed west to his home in Fisher, Illinois, and in March 1917 received word that he was soon to be commissioned.[16] But it was not until June 26, 1917—two and one-half months after America declared war on Germany—that Burge received his commission. He was then ordered to Fort Leavenworth, Kansas, for officer training. When finished, he was assigned to Kelly Field to assist with the establishment of a mechanics training department. Burge arrived at Kelly wearing his brand-new officer's tunic, riding breeches, polished cavalry boots, a riding crop and—thanks to two rapid promotions—a set of captain bars, none of which was yet three months old.

When Burge left San Antonio in the early spring of 1916 and headed west toward Columbus with the 1st Aero Squadron, Kelly Field did not exist. When he returned in the summer of 1917, Kelly Field was emerging out of the brush and mesquite plains southwest of San Antonio as a huge complex, still under construction and growing. Frantic efforts were underway to accommodate and train thousands of freshly inducted young men to meet the demands of a nation at war. Chaos and confusion reigned. It was into this situation that Burge reported for his first duty as a commissioned officer. He was immediately swallowed up in it.[17]

WORLD WAR I ENLISTED PILOTS 5 1917–1918

HAVING ENTERED THE GREAT WAR LATE, America possessed a pool of educated young men that had not been thinned by war's grim attrition. The Europeans, on the other hand, had suffered awful losses by then, and were having to conserve their manpower. Italy, Germany, and France relied increasingly upon enlisted pilots as the war wore on. Britain, though tardy, also began to man their squadrons with enlisted pilots.[1]

America was not prepared to fight when it went to war, its pool of educated manpower notwithstanding. The initial attempt at mobilization was characterized by chaos and confusion, and, in the frantic rush to arms, enlisted pilot training was simply trampled underfoot.

Burge's prewar enlisted pilot contemporaries—A. A. Adamson, Ira Biffle, S. V. Coyle, Leo G. Flint, and Felix Steinle—were commissioned shortly after America's declaration of war. Four other noncommissioned officers (NCOs) in training at Mineola, Long Island, New York, Sgt. A. E. Simonin, corporals R. K. Smith, H. D. McLean, and R. A. Willis, were commissioned after passing their Reserve Military Aviator (RMA) tests. Private, First Class Clarence B. Coombs and Cpl. K. L. Whitsett, also at Mineola, passed their RMA tests, but were not commissioned. Both, however, continued flying as sergeants throughout the war.[2]

In May of 1917, construction began at Kelly Field to house and teach aeronautical skills to the thousands of recruits then pouring into the field. By fall of that year an Air Service Mechanics Department was hastily organized to train mechanics. It was divided into two courses: an "airplane" course headed by Capt. D. J. Neumuller, and an "aero motors" course headed by Capt. Vernon Burge. It was Burge's first assignment as a commissioned officer.[3]

But there were problems at the outset. The nation's commitment to aviation had been far too tardy and meager to respond quickly to the sudden demands of a world war. The school was charged with the task of producing twenty-five-hundred trained mechanics a month, a figure it was unable to realize.

The Mechanics Department was located over a mile from the trainees' cantonment, which necessitated a long march. Also, a tug-of-war developed between unit commanders and school staff for the trainees' time. Unit commanders refused to let their charges attend classes until routine fatigue details were finished. Unfortunately, these details sometimes took days. Therefore, classroom attendance took a back seat, resulting in erratic attendance at best. Too, classes were conducted in tents with only one instructor, one engine, and little technical literature upon which to base organized instruction. Meagerly equipped and poorly supported, despite their best efforts, the staff was doomed to failure. The last straw occurred just before Christmas when a windstorm blew down the classroom tents. The training program for mechanics also collapsed. One historian observed, "This rather lofty aim . . . was another example of the grossly exaggerated and unreal objectives conjured up in the initial heat of wartime patriotic fervor."[4]

The school was given a fresh start following the disastrous windstorm, when Maj. George E. Stratemeyer was placed in charge of reorganizing the school. Properly staffed, equipped, and renamed, the Air Service Mechanics School reopened for business on March 18, 1918.[5] Burge somehow survived the shake-up and became active in this effort as well.

After the dust had settled, Burge was given command of a construction squadron and, in April 1918, ordered to Waco, Texas, to erect the buildings at a new field, which was being opened there.[6] The new facility was named Rich Field in honor of Lt. Perry Rich, an officer with whom he had served earlier in the Philippines. The field was equipped to provide primary flight training, an activity that began even before all its facilities were finished.

When the construction was completed, Burge was given command of the 280th Aero Squadron.[7] Until this time, Burge had been so occupied with his new duties as a commissioned officer that he had not flown a single hour. His current assignment now provided an opportunity for him to become current and to qualify for the wings of a "Military Aviator," wings he could not heretofore wear.[8] When Burge was awarded his FAI Aviator Certificate in 1912, no badge, military or civilian, had been devised. When the first Military Aviator badge was authorized by the War Department in 1914, a pilot had to be a commissioned officer of the Regular Army or Organized Militia to qualify, but Burge was a sergeant.[9] By the time the shoulder badge was authorized for enlisted pilots in August 1917, he was a commissioned officer and had not yet qualified under newer rules for the rating.[10]

Primary flight training was given in two types of planes at Rich Field in early 1918: the Standard SJ-1 and the Curtiss JN-4. Both were equipped with stick and rudder controls, a system Burge had not used before. Although he had already accumulated over five hundred hours before going to Rich Field,[11] those hours were in aeroplanes equipped with the Wright wing-warp system, or the Curtiss wheel-and-shoulder-yoke system. To qualify as a Military Aviator, Burge would have to learn the stick-and-rudder system.

Flying with lieutenants Martin T. Chamberlain and Maurice A. Sharp, Burge learned to use the stick and rudder controls. He soloed on June 7, 1918, passed his RMA test a little later, and rejoined the mainstream of Army aviation.[12] Ironically, when he received the rating, Burge became eligible for the first time in his career to wear the badge of a Military Aviator.

Among the first recruits to arrive at Kelly Field during its initial construction in 1917 were Orvil Haynes, a twenty-two-year-old Illinois lad who had enlisted only days after America entered the war, and Carlton P. "C.P." Smith, who had enlisted just three months before the war.

Haynes, a former auto mechanic, was assigned to the 37th Aero Squadron and, in August 1917, went with it to France.[13] Haynes and a large number of other mechanics were subsequently sent to the Nieuport and Gnome factories to train as mechanics on French airplanes. When he finished, Haynes and fifty-nine other graduates of that course were sent to the French flying school at Avord and taught to fly for the purpose of ferrying planes from the French factories to American squadrons at the front. During that time, Haynes rose through the ranks to master signal electrician, a rank he held until 1919. Later that year he was commissioned and continued to fly as an officer until he was separated in 1920 and took a job as a civilian aviator.[14]

To get an idea of how it must have been for Americans to learn to fly in a foreign land and under a foreign tongue, we must rely on the experience of Joe Cline, a sailor who became a U.S. Navy enlisted pilot under circumstances similar to Haynes:

> All of us were volunteers . . . utterly green and inexpressibly eager . . .
>
> Fifty landsmen for Quartermaster and 50 landsmen for Machinist Mate were selected. Quartermasters were to be trained as pilots and Machinist Mates were to be trained for maintenance and overhaul duty . . .
>
> We arrived at Tours, were loaded into trucks and driven to the Ecole d'Aviation Militaire de Tours and began flight training on June 22 [1917].

None of us had had any ground school instruction and few of us had any idea about the theory of flight. Our instructors did not speak English and we did not speak French. We were divided into small groups of eight or ten students, each group assigned to an instructor. One leather flying coat, one pair of goggles and one crash helmet were issued to each group and these were passed from one student to another as his turn came to fly.

The plane used for our primary instruction was the Caudron G-3, a French bi-plane with warping wings and a two place cockpit, powered by a 90-hp Anzani or Le rhone engine. The instructor sat in the rear cockpit. After take-off, he would turn the controls over to the student and instructions would begin. If the nose was too high, the instructor would push forward on your helmet. If it was low, he would pull back on the helmet. If the left wing was down, he'd tap on the right shoulder; right wing down, tap on the left shoulder. A flight lasted about 20 minutes.

After each flight, the instructor would pull out a pasteboard card with a line drawn down the center. One side was written in English and the other in French. The instructor would explain all the mistakes you had made while in flight. He gave you hell in French while pointing to the English translation. Perhaps it was just as well we did not understand his words.

The course at Tours included a cross-country flight to Vendôme, a British flight school about 80 miles distant and return, a spot landing from 4,000 feet with a dead stick on a small field we called the salad patch; and an altitude test to 8,000 feet where we were required to stay for one hour.

We were then sent to the Ecole d'Aviation Maritime de Hourtin on a small lake outside Bordeaux. This was a French Navy base where we were to receive our preliminary seaplane training. Our instructors were French non-commissioned officers, also not English speaking.

After a month at Hourtin, we were sent to Ecole d'Aviation de St. Raphael, in the south of France on the Mediterranean. This was the Pensacola of the French navy . . . Here we started right in flying all types of French seaplanes—F.B.A., Tellier, Salmsons, and Donet-Denhaut (DD)—completing the course in altitude tests, rough water landings, bombing and gunnery.

On October 17, 1917, I received my French Brevet, Number 346. My total flight time, including Tours, Hourtin and St. Raphael, was 31 hours and 52 minutes. I was ready for war, still a landsman for quartermaster; pay $17.60 a month.[15]

As American involvement in the war deepened, Orvil Haynes and his fellow enlisted Ferrier pilots became aware of the extensive use of enlisted pilots by the Europeans, a fact also noted by American aviation unit commanders. Their observations and ideas on the subject began to appear in reports and recommendations forwarded to higher command. Before the war's end, sentiment began building for their inclusion in future American combat squadrons. Major George E. A. Reinburg, for instance, as the commanding officer of the 2nd Day Bombardment Group, wrote in part:

> 1 . . . I am submitting herewith such tentative changes in the Air Service tables of organization (approved by G.H.Q., A.E.F., Sept. 8, 1918), as I believe to be desirable for the efficient functioning of a Day Bombardment Group . . .
>
> 6. With reference to officer personnel, I am of the opinion that the development of bombardment aviation in the army will render advisable the discontinuance of commissioning as officers, all pilots and observers. The British and French Air Services have adopted the plan of using non-commissioned officers, but I believe the most practical system for day bombardment in the United States Air Service, would be to commission as officers, flight leaders and leading observers and to create the grade of Pilot 1st Class, Pilot, Observer 1st Class, and Observer, with commensurate pay for the several grades. The presence of so many commissioned officers in a squadron, whose military training has been subordinated to flying training, is complicating and tends toward relaxation of military discipline. As this is a matter affecting policy I am not incorporating this in the table of proposed changes.[16]

Similar suggestions and proposals came from other sources as well, but the war ended before the idea could be fully developed. Nevertheless, enlisted men continued to be trained to fly, but only in limited numbers.[17]

While Orvil Haynes and his contemporaries were ferrying airplanes in France, an interesting experiment was taking place at Kelly Field. Seeking to give his ground school instructors a greater appreciation of the aviator's perspective, Major Stratemeyer, as commander of the Air Service Mechanics School, permitted them to receive limited flight instruction. The more adept were then designated "enlisted fliers." Oliver W. Thyfault, Merrill J. Tackley, Charles M. Duffy, and Sfc. Carlton P. Smith were among that group.[18]

Sergeant Carlton P. Smith, or C.P., as he came to be called, was a tall, lanky, easygoing young Oregonian from LaGrande with a smile always on the verge of laughter. When he reached his early teens, his family moved from LaGrande to Santa Monica, California, and then to Fargo, North

Dakota. Spending much of his adolescence in rural areas, he did not finish high school, but tinkering with the family's farm tractor and flivver gave him considerable mechanical savvy. He came to understand the internal combustion engine very well.

C.P. yielded to the blandishment of a recruiting sergeant in Fargo, North Dakota, and enlisted in the Aviation Section of the U.S. Army Signal Corps in January 1917. Though only in his late teens, C.P. was enamored with aviation and dreamed of becoming an aviator. The recruiting sergeant let him enlist with the naive assumption that he could easily become one.

But C.P.'s dream was put on hold. He was sent first to Fort Leavenworth for his recruit training, then on to Kelly Field, where he attended the mechanics school. He was then selected as a classroom instructor on the internal combustion engine. This was in October 1917, while Captain Burge was in charge of that department.[19] But it was not until September 1918, when Major Stratemeyer opened the door for his classroom instructors, that C.P. learned to fly, if only on a limited basis.

Others became enlisted pilots by a different route. "Sub-rosa" was the word James R. Bandy used to describe his training as a flier in 1918. Now a retired circuit judge residing in Mitchell, South Dakota, ex-sergeant pilot Bandy recalls those days:

> Unlike the more modern flying sergeants, I was just a crew chief who could fly airplanes. Actually I had no formal training at all. At Ft. Worth (Taliaferro Field, I think), we had a bunch of cadets in training. I could arrange for them to get a bit of extra time now and then and went along to "check" the aircraft. In that manner I picked up what they had learned. In those days a trainee went for his wings in about 25 hours and so none of us were particularly adept.
>
> It was not until much later that I was made an enlisted aviator. Lt. William T. Coates found out how it was done and sponsored me. In any event, I was so designated on Hazelhurst Field Special Order number 60 in 1918. I performed the usual duties of a crew chief and in addition [flight] checked repairs.

By the time he was discharged in 1919, Bandy had accumulated six hundred hours.[20]

Like Bandy, it was only natural that a few enlisted men would manage to slip into the cockpit by being in the right place at the right time. A number of enlisted men became pilots by this means, as in the case of M.S.E. Harry Thomas Wilson. Wilson, a private in the 193rd Aero Squadron at Taylor

Field near Montgomery, Alabama, learned to fly well enough in 1918 to be assigned as a pilot for Taylor Field's aerial ambulance, a converted JN-4.[21]

Eight sergeant pilots of the 4884th Air Service Mechanics School are shown standing in front of a DH-4 at Kelly Field in a December 1918 photograph. Also, five enlisted pilots are listed in the book *Kelly Field in the Great World War,* published by Kelly Field in 1919. They are Sgt. Maj. C. C. Biehl, Cpl. Howard H. Culmer, 1st Sgt. August Ball, Supply Sgt. B. B. Braley, and Mess Sgt. John Nessman.[22]

Other enlisted pilots are to be found only in reports of aircraft accidents from late in the war and immediately afterward.

- Corporal pilot M. E. Porter, on July 26, 1918, ran into trees while taxiing because he could not close the throttle of his JN-4D.
- Sergeant pilot Robert Bratch dug the wing of his JN-4D into the ground when he turned too steeply trying to avoid a hanger during a takeoff from Hazelhurst Field on September 8, 1918.
- Master Signal Electrician pilot R. T. Davidson of Rockwell Field lost control of his JN-4D on December 10, 1918, when an "air pocket" overturned his plane while landing.
- Master Signal Electrician pilot John C. Stoll of Mitchell Field made a forced landing in the street on Christmas Day, 1918, and nosed the plane over to avoid going through a house.[23]

Toward the end of the war, four NCOs at Rich Field became competent enough to be assigned to the stable of flying instructors. They were M.S.E. Douglas S. Christie, sergeants, first class Leroy B. Gregg, Rufus C. Lillard, and William F. "Pinky" Cottrell.[24]

As the tempo of flying slowed after the Armistice, these NCO pilots joined the officer pilots of Rich Field, Captain Burge among them, in flights to rural Texas communities to recruit young men for the Air Service. Airplanes were an exciting sight in the small central Texas towns and attracted crowds of curious spectators. Local newspaper reporters wrote gushing accounts of these appearances. One reporter, after a flight with Sergeant Christie during such a visit to Brownwood in the summer of 1919, wrote:

> The ace of all aces who attained a fame that will live in my memory for the rest of my natural born days is he who this morning brought down

one lonely American plane and brought it down in an orderly manner. Sergeant Douglas S. Christie has no medals on his breast and is not known in the ranks of the doughty fliers who busted the Kaiser's flying squadrons, but if it were left up to my choosing, he would have medals all over him, and the D.S.C. that he bears as initials would have a more tangible significance.

There is another thing that impressed me during my first airplane ride. That was that the higher one goes from Brownwood, the better it looks, even when it is hidden beneath the floating cloud banks. At the beginning, one's ambition is to go up, and up and up; after climbing about 3500 feet the order is reversed, and one wishes to come down, down, down until again within hailing distance of terra firma. Going up, one wonders whether there is a weak place in the machine; coming down, one prays that there be no weak place in the man in the front seat with his hand on the control levers.[25]

Immediately after the Armistice, M.S.E. Douglas Christie took his discharge and moved to Montana. He never flew again.

Sergeants Leroy Gregg and Rufus Lillard ended their service to Uncle Sam and vanished into the same opaque mists from which they had appeared, without fanfare or forwarding address. As the last cadets were transferred to Love Field at Dallas to complete their training, airplanes and ground equipment were prepared for storage. With no further need to train pilots, personnel strength at Rich Field fell to eleven officers and two hundred enlisted men—a mere housekeeping force.

Of the four NCO flying instructors, only William "Pinky" Cottrell was retained at Rich Field.[26]

The question of enlisted pilots had always posed a dilemma for the U.S. Army. Some critics question whether enlisted pilots existed at all during World War I. As late as 1921, for instance, the Army-Navy Register declared that "no ratings as 'Enlisted Aviator' have ever been given by the Air Service."

When Corporal Burge became the Army's first in 1912, the War Department disapproved. Even after training of enlisted pilots was authorized by the National Defense Acts of July 18, 1914, and June 3, 1916, traditionalists continued to disapprove of the idea of enlisted pilots. Those trained by the French during World War I, for example, found their role limited to non-combat duties.

The status of Air Service enlisted pilots remained vague throughout the war. It was not resolved until January 22, 1919, several months after the Armistice, when the commanding officer of the Air Service Mechanics School at Kelly Field, with good intent, sent a memo dated December 20, 1918, to the Office of Military Aeronautics. In it, he requested an interpretation of the terms "enlisted aviator" and "aerial fliers," as it had a bearing on which of them would be permitted to wear the enlisted aviator insignia on the upper right shoulder of their tunic.

The Office of Military Aeronautics pondered the question within the context of the aforementioned acts of 1914 and 1916, then on January 31, 1919, responded with three paragraphs, the key one declaring:

> In regard to the matter raised by the commanding officer of the Air Service Mechanic School in his letter of December 20th [1918], you are advised that although Uniform Regulations and Specifications provide for the insignia to be worn by "enlisted aviators" the grade itself has never been created and consequently there is no one in the service entitled to wear the insignia provided for such grade.[27]

It was not the reply that the mechanics school commander or his enlisted pilots expected. While the decision may have stripped them of the badge, it did not stop them from flying, for at this very time, enlisted pilots were being recruited[28] and selection procedures publicized on squadron bulletin boards and in base newspapers.[29] Embarrassing evidence of this appears in an Air Service report of nonfatal accidents for 1919, where:

> On March 4, 1919, Sergeant pilot Chester D. Willard, while practicing banks in a JN-4D at Kelly Field, fell into a tailspin and crashed. He lost an eye as a result.
>
> Engine trouble forced Sergeant H. G. Phillips into the trees lining the small field into which he tried to land his JN-6H on October 24, 1919.[30]

Although they were not authorized to wear the Military Aviator badge after the aforementioned ruling, enlisted pilots indeed flew Uncle Sam's airplanes and did so with the apparent blessing of their superiors. Nevertheless, it must have been an absurd moment in their careers when they were instructed to remove their wings and informed that as "enlisted aviators" they did not exist.

That 1921 Army-Navy Register cited earlier declaring "no ratings as 'enlisted aviator' have ever been given by the Air Service" can be better understood when one considers their limited numbers, low profile, and the cessation of war just as they were becoming reestablished. It is small wonder that enlisted pilots of that era were little known or remembered.

AFTER THE GREAT WAR 6 1919–1923

THE MODEST RESURGENCE OF FLYING training for enlisted men continued into mid-1919, serving as a seedbed for several successful aviation careers, namely those of William Beigel and Walter Beech.

On January 30, 1919, the Director of Military Aeronautics issued new instructions concerning the training of enlisted pilots.[1] Post Sergeant-Major William E. Beigel of Rich Field was in a perfect position to take advantage of that opportunity, since such instructions passed over his desk. Beigel applied at once.

Beigel was an Illinois lad, born on November 17, 1888, in Gibson, Illinois. He grew up in Iowa and Nebraska, where he completed two years of business college. He then served as the city clerk of Onawa, Iowa, until enlisting in October 1917 at Omaha, Nebraska. Ordered to Kelly Field, Beigel was assigned to the 150th Aero Squadron, which then moved to Waco, Texas, in November 1917 to establish the flying school at Rich Field. Beigel's first duties were in the motor shop, but it didn't take his superiors long to recognize his clerical value, for he quickly became the assistant squadron sergeant-major. Next he was detailed to the Engineers Office as chief clerk. He then became the First Sergeant of the 150th Aero Squadron. When the squadron was broken up in December 1918, Beigel became the Sergeant-Major of the Cadet Detachment and, finally, of the entire field. It was while serving in the latter capacity that he applied for training as an enlisted pilot.[2]

Together with 152 other applicants, Beigel took the flying physical and mental examinations. He and nine others of the group passed and, in June 1919, began their primary flight training under Sgt. "Pinky" Cottrell.[3] Six finished the course, Beigel among them, and were certified by 2nd Lt. Edgar E. Glenn on October 27, 1919.[4] Sergeant Beigel explained their new status in a letter to his former cohorts:

Practically every one of the old bunch that stayed here can fly and fly good, but the only ones that finished the course were Sergeant 1st Class Homer H. Sheffield, Jr., Chauf Cleason E. Shealer, Sergeant 1st Class Walter H. Beech, Chauf Wick Chamlee, Sergeant 1st Class Harold S. Dale and myself. Of course you may know that we are all decorated with our wings, but as to what we really are, we have no idea. We call ourselves Enlisted Military Aviators.[5]

Enlisted pilots were also trained at March Field during the same period, but their names are now lost to posterity.[6]

With the end of the war most of the Rich Field personnel were discharged and sent home. Of the enlisted pilots, Sergeant Dale took his discharge, but Sgt. Pinky Cottrell and five of his former students re-enlisted for an additional year in order to continue flying. Remaining at Rich Field with Pinky Cottrell to assist closing the field were Sergeant-Major Beigel, Chamlee, Shealer, Shaffer, and Beech.[7]

Walter Beech was born on January 30, 1891, on a farm near Pulaski, Tennessee. When educated and old enough, he left the farm and found employment as a mechanic for an American truck firm. He acquired some flying experience in 1914 when he and a friend bought a wrecked Curtiss pusher, restored it, and taught themselves to fly. Beech later represented the truck firm in Europe, returning to the United States just before America became involved in the Great War. He enlisted on August 6, 1917, and was sent to Kelly Field, where his innovative flair as an airplane mechanic was quickly recognized. He was placed on a project to convert a JN-4 for use as a flying ambulance.[8] Later, he was transferred to Rich Field where he developed a reputation for solving problems unique to aircraft. One was a method for preventing the accumulation of ice on wings and fuselage.[9]

The third pilot of the six was Wick Chamlee, a handsome young lad from Gatesville, Texas. Chamlee earned himself the nickname "Tailspin Chamlee" the hard way when his JN-4 spun into the ground from three hundred feet and he walked away unhurt.

Little is recorded concerning Cleason E. Shealer, the fourth enlisted pilot of the group, except that he was from Detroit and held the grade of Chauffeur.

Homer H. Sheffield, Jr., a Berkeley, California, boy, was the flamboyant and reckless one of the group. He was twice forced to bring his plane down unexpectedly. On July 31, 1919, when his JN-4 developed engine trouble, he was forced to land in a very small field bordered by trees, some of which he hit. He emerged unscathed from that incident. The second occurred on

August 27, 1919, when a broken connecting rod forced him down again. The episode was reported a little melodramatically by the *Times-Herald,* a local newspaper, which read:

SERGEANT SHEFFIELD HAD NARROW ESCAPE AT MARLIN

Marlin, Tex., Aug. 28.— Sergeant (pilot) H. H. Sheffield, Jr. of Rich Field near Waco, probably faced death and felt he was closer to his finish than ever before yesterday, when he discovered his plane was ablaze while about 5000 feet in the air. Taking a nose dive of 4000 feet, this fanned the flames out, but it is thought quite a narrow escape from death again missed him when he drove the plane head first into the ground. When he leveled out, about 1000 feet up he saw that the blaze was extinguished except for some smoke still rising so this was gotten after with the assistance of a hand extinguisher, which act was followed by the forced landing.

It is agreed that the escape of the pilot is quite remarkable, but a little headway of the flames would have reached his gasoline tank and the machine could have been consumed and the pilot burned while in the air.

Sergeant Sheffield boarded a freight train and came to Marlin, telephoned Rich Field for assistance and calmly awaited further developments. The plane suffered damage to such an extent that a wrecking crew and truck was sent out from Rich Field to take the plane in. Sergeant Sheffield, it is learned, suffered an accident just recently by coming in contact with a chicken house while visiting an aunt near Hillsboro.[10]

Sergeant Pinky Cottrell did not go unscathed either. Flying very low over the countryside one afternoon near Georgetown, Texas, just north of Austin, Cottrell misjudged the height above the telephone wires over which he was hurdling. The wires snatched the plane out of the sky and flung it ungracefully into a weedy pasture. Aside from a few bumps, bruises, and injured pride, Pinky was unhurt, but the plane had to be disassembled and trucked back to Rich Field.[11]

Pinky's low flying and fast speed were not confined to airplanes alone. During the waning months of the war, he and Sergeant Beigel assembled a racing vehicle of some merit from sundry automobile parts and raced it at various events in the Waco area. When the racer was not so engaged, or down for maintenance, the "belles of Waco" were invited to hop in with them and "take a spin" in the racer.[12]

After Rich Field was deactivated, the sextet of enlisted pilots and seven officers flew Rich Field's surplus airplanes to Love Field for further disposition. The event, a kind of swan song for Rich Field, was hailed in a Waco newspaper article:

> Rich Field commissioned and enlisted pilots have just completed a last flight from Rich Field to Love Field, Dallas, Texas, flying seven ships representing the last shipment of 124 ships and 89 motors which have been transferred from Rich Field to Love Field within fifty days. This feat was done in addition to the other routine duties of the field and 127 ships were flown via air. A remarkable feature of the transfer of ships is that not a single accident occurred within the fifty days. A large number of these ships were flown by enlisted men who received all of their flying instruction at Rich Field, and who were recently designated as fliers in the air service. All of these ships were pronounced in excellent condition upon their being received at Love Field, which is evidence of the excellent engineering supervision, the credit for which is due to Captain Charles R. Forrest and his able enlisted mechanics of this department.
>
> Following are the names of the pilots that flew the 127 machines to Dallas; Major H. H. C. Richards, Lieutenants James B. Kelsey, Edgar E. Glenn, Deway Miller, Edward E. Hildreth, Richard H. Magee and Alfred R. Coningsby; Sergeants Cottrell, Sheffield, Beigel, Beech, Shealer and Chauffeur Wick Chamlee.[13]

After their discharge in 1920, all but two of the former enlisted pilots continued to pursue their interest in flying. Sergeants Pinky Cottrell and Sheffield received their discharges and faded into obscurity. Chamlee attended flying school as a cadet but was killed at Brooks Field, near San Antonio, in 1923 when struck by a propeller. Bill Beigel and Cleason Shealer remained in the Waco area, demonstrating and selling surplus army planes, giving prospective buyers rudimentary flying instructions if it would help seal the deal.[14]

Beech barnstormed the country for a time after his discharge, then found employment with the Swallow Airplane Company. He called his old friend Beigel to help him demonstrate and sell airplanes for the company. By 1924, Beech had become the company's general manager.[15]

One and one-half years after the Armistice, the National Defense Act of 1916 was amended by the Army Reorganization Bill of June 4, 1920 (41 Stat. 768).[16] The provision that had provided for the training of enlisted men, in grade, as pilots was omitted and replaced by a requirement that subsequent flying school students be entered as cadets. Meager as the training of enlisted pilots had been in the past, it now ceased altogether.

Much had ceased for the Air Service as well, for by the fall of 1920 it had been reduced to a fraction of its wartime strength. From a force of over 150,000 officers and enlisted men in 1918, it had dwindled to 1,000 officers and 10,000 enlisted men. Funding fell from nearly 1 billion dollars to 28 million.[17] Support for military aviation waned as the public returned its attention to domestic affairs. The community of airmen once again became small and fraternal.

The early twenties was a period of great adjustment for the Air Service. In the two years following the Armistice, the situation changed from one in which there were too few airplanes to one in which there were too many. Hundreds were sold as surplus. Many others were simply destroyed. The exodus of trained pilots increased the workload on those remaining in the Air Service, including the small number of enlisted pilots who continued to fly but only on a tentative basis. The only primary flying schools remaining active by 1920 were Carlstrom Field in Florida and March Field in California, each having produced at least ten enlisted pilots since the Armistice.

One of the first to be trained as a "cadet" under the reorganization bill of 1920 was Chester F. Colby. Thanks to his meticulous recordkeeping, it is possible to follow Colby through his entire training process.[18]

Born in Gardiner, Maine, in 1895, Colby attended Mechanical Arts High School in Boston, graduating as a statistical clerk. He worked at that trade until enlisting in the Air Service on November 11, 1917. He was sent to Kelly Field in mid-December and assigned to the 187th Aero Squadron for training as a mechanic. From there he was sent to England, then to France where he was wounded but recovered and continued to serve as a mechanic in his squadron.

Colby was a sergeant when he returned to the United States after the Armistice. He was sent to Mitchell Field, Long Island, New York, where he applied and was selected for local enlisted pilot training similar to that being given at Rich Field, Kelly Field, and other locations. By the time the reorganization bill came into effect, Colby had acquired nearly thirty hours of flying time, two-thirds of which was solo in JN-4s and JN-6s. On November 16, Colby was ordered to Carlstrom Field to began his flight training as a cadet. His official training began on January 1, 1920.

Completing the primary phase in June 1920, Colby was then sent to Post Field, Fort Sill, Oklahoma, for observation training. After finishing at the top of his cadet class on February 7, 1921, he was commissioned in the Officers Reserve Corps, discharged, and immediately re-enlisted as a private.

He was retained at the school as a flight instructor. By March 17, 1921, Colby had been promoted to the grade of staff sergeant. Coincidentally, while he was an instructor at the observation school, Captain Burge took the observation course there.[19]

Cadet Carl B. McDaniel, a former private, was a classmate of Colby's at Carlstrom, but opted for advanced training in DH-4s at Kelly Field. Following graduation, McDaniel and his entire bombardment class was discharged. Most returned to civilian life, but a few who, like McDaniel and Colby, had come from the ranks were given the option of accepting their discharge or reverting to their former rank and remaining in the Army. Not wanting to give up flying, McDaniel opted for the latter and re-enlisted in his old rank—a "Buck-ass Private, the lowest ranking private in the entire air service"—but this time with wings.[20]

McDaniel didn't remain a private very long. In fact, he was promoted to corporal before noon of his first day of duty. By evening he was a sergeant. By noon of the following day, while waiting to be promoted to staff sergeant, word was received that promotions were now frozen. He remained a sergeant for the next three years.[21]

A third enlisted man who became a cadet under the new legislation was Peter Biesiot. A contemporary—though not a classmate—of Chet Colby and Carl McDaniel, Biesiot began his primary flight training at Carlstrom Field in 1920 under the instruction of M. Sgt. Billy Winston.

Biesiot was having difficulty with his landings, so Winston loaded him into a Curtiss "Jenny" one Sunday morning and flew to a satellite field for some practice landings. After several satisfactory dual landings Biesiot was sent aloft to practice a few solo landings. The first few appeared satisfactory to Winston, watching from midfield, but on the last one Biesiot landed hard and began a series of bounces that ended only after the Jenny flipped over onto its back. As Winston ran toward the plane, he saw Biesiot's head and shoulders dangle from the cockpit, then suddenly retract. When Winston arrived at the site, he saw the reason. Directly beneath Biesiot's head, coiled malevolently in the grass, was a large, angry rattlesnake![22]

Biesiot won his wings in 1921 and, like Colby and McDaniel, opted to remain in the Air Service as an enlisted pilot. But Biesiot's landings, at times thereafter, appeared to be "snake-bit." In August of 1922, for example, and again in November of that year, he nearly destroyed his DH-4B while attempting to land. His landings, no two of which were alike, made Biesiot a legend among his peers who made bets as to where the plane would touch down. Nobody ever won.[23]

Obviously, Biesiot was not the first—nor would he be the last—enlisted pilot to ding an airplane. Some were fatal: Sgt. Charles D. Allen of the 147th Aero Squadron at Kelly Field crashed into the brewery at New Braunfels, Texas, after his engine quit. He perished in the fire that followed.[24] Sergeant Strong B. McDann, an experienced test pilot, lost his life at McCook Field, Dayton, Ohio, on October 4, 1920, when the engine of his Sopwith Camel quit. Sergeant Wayman Haney perished in the crash of his DH-4 while on forest patrol operations in northern California in July 1920.[25]

Staff Sergeant pilot Tracy Johnson, one of those cadets who re-enlisted after graduation rather than accept a discharge, was assigned to the 94th Pursuit Squadron of the 1st Pursuit Group at Kelly Field. Johnson moved with the group when it was reassigned to Selfridge Field, Mt. Clemens, Michigan. On September 9, 1922, while taking off from Saginaw in a JN-6H Johnson was killed when his engine quit and the airplane crashed.

Sergeant Samuel Davis was more fortunate. His DH-4 engine quit while he was flying over the hills of Maryland, and he had to land on the only spot available—a small clearing on the steep slope of a hill near Ellicott City. He made it, but lost the landing gear in the process.[26]

Due to limited education, some of the students accepted for flying training in 1920 should not have been. Rated as pilots upon graduation, they were denied commissions, which drew the following comment in the Kelly Field newsletter:

> The progress of the cadets is very satisfactory as far as their flying is concerned. It is very unfortunate that some of them have not had enough previous education to enable them to be recommended for reserve commissions. It is not their fault but rather their misfortune. The fault lies with the officers who permitted these cadets to start their training. It is a clear waste of government time and money to permit any man to start his training unless he is mentally equipped to pass the examinations. Notification has recently been sent out from the office of the Chief of Air Service that more care is to be taken in the future in regard to the selection of men for this training and it is to be hoped that hereafter the classes will have a smaller percentage of men to whom we cannot offer reserve commissions.[27]

In the meantime, Sergeant McDaniel, on duty at Kelly Field, and the mechanic assigned to his airplane were given the chore of retrieving airplanes that had crashed or made forced landings elsewhere. Mechanic Sgt. Bernard Wallace—who would himself become an enlisted pilot in 1927—and Mc-

Daniel would fly to the site of the forced landing, look the plane over, and decide if it could be flown out. If it could, they flew it back to Kelly. If not, they made appropriate repairs before doing so. If neither was possible, the plane was disassembled and trucked back to the field.

Most of the planes they retrieved were DeHavilland-4s from Kelly, the same type assigned to McDaniel. He became very competent with it and developed a routine wherein he would buzz a selected landing site downwind, then pull up sharply and climb to the edge of a stall, rudder it into a wingover and land out of the recovery. It was a showy maneuver.[28]

Sergeant Jerome C. Ainis, a fellow pilot and friend, wanted to learn McDaniel's trick and persuaded him to demonstrate it. McDaniel agreed, but since his own airplane was in the hanger for maintenance, they used Ainis's. On March 14, 1921, the pair flew out to a remote little pasture, which McDaniel buzzed, then pulled up into a wingover. But just before reaching the top, the airplane stalled and entered a spin. McDaniel recovered just in time to avoid a serious crash. While the fuselage cleared the ground, the wheels did not. The impact fractured the landing gear and popped the ground wires loose from their moorings but spared the propeller. Stunned, the two sergeants were surprised to find themselves still airborne. Assessing the damage, they noted a few wires and tatters trailing in the slipstream, but the flying wires appeared taut, the engine still ran, the prop still turned, and the plane was still controllable. They looked at each other, shrugged, and headed back to Kelly. The airplane held together just fine during the return flight, but when they landed, the wings lost lift and began to sag. The plane's full weight then settled onto the fractured landing gear, which veered the plane into a dusty ground loop. It was a most subdued pair of pilots who stood watching in silence as the drooping DeHavilland was towed slowly to the repair hanger.[29]

Three weeks later, on April 5, Sergeant Ainis was at the controls of another DH-4 with McDaniel as a passenger. Ainis took off from a short field obstructed at the far end by a row of trees. The field was soft and overgrown with weeds, which slowed the takeoff. As the plane left the ground, it became frightfully obvious to McDaniel that they were not going to clear the trees. Ainis, however, did not share McDaniel's apprehension. The top branches snagged the landing gear and flung the plane to the ground on the other side, where it burst into flames. Dazed, McDaniel was slow to realize that his arm was caught in some of the twisted wreckage. As his senses returned, he tried—with great difficulty—to extract his arm. Then he saw and smelled the fire. In panic now, he jerked his arm free, leaving patches of skin and flesh behind as he scrambled out of the burning wreck. Meanwhile, farmers rushed to the scene to pull Ainis from the burning wreck. One of them turned and shouted to McDaniel, now nursing his injuries, "Your ass is on fire, boy!" McDaniel promptly plopped down and snuffed out the fire. Both were lucky—they each recovered after considerable time in the hospital but bore the scars of the crash for the rest of their lives.[30]

When McDaniel had time to spare at Kelly Field, he volunteered to fly anything available, including the ungainly and unbearably loud GA-X attack plane. The GA-X (Ground Attack-Experimental) was a two-engined, tri-plane with an armor-plated fuselage. Few other pilots seemed eager to fly the heavy beast. In fact, one commander disciplined his wayward officers by threatening to schedule them to fly it.

Two 442-horsepower Liberty engines powered the plane. Mounted on the rear of each engine was a large four-bladed propeller that pushed rather than pulled the plane through the air. The propeller tips cleared the armor-plated cockpit by only an inch and made a sound similar to that of a 50-caliber machine gun. The sound could be heard for miles. Pilots were cuffed nearly deaf by the noise, but McDaniel considered the GA-X a challenge and accumulated approximately one hundred hours of hard-to-get and valuable multi-engine time in it. He made it a practice to take the flight mechanics up in the GA-X to qualify for their monthly flight pay, thus assuring himself a well-maintained airplane.[31]

Occasionally, McDaniel and his mechanic Sgt. Bernard Wallace joined other flight crews to put on special demonstrations for the public or visiting brass. A favored way to entertain them was to drop parachutists. Flying in formation, the pilots would carry their charges aloft. When high overhead, the jumpers would climb out on the wing and jump or hurl themselves over the cockpit combing, pull the ripcord, and float to earth.

McDaniel and Wallace had performed this act many times and knew the routine well. But one day a parachute specialist visited Kelly to tout a new method that prescribed holding on to the wing strut nearest the fuselage, and when ready, pull the ripcord. The prop wash was supposed to deploy the chute more efficiently and pull the jumper free.

Sergeants McDaniel and Wallace were the guinea pigs for trying this new method and it nearly ended in tragedy. After reaching the jump altitude, Sergeant Wallace dutifully climbed out onto the wing and held on to the inboard strut as instructed. When over the jump site, he pulled the ripcord, then froze in horror as his chute streamed out and snagged on the horizontal stabilizer. It was only a momentary snag; as McDaniel, reading the panic in Wallace's eyes, looked back, the canopy pulled free and blossomed, jerking Wallace rudely from the wing. Wallace struck the horizontal stabilizer as he went by. Feeling the jolt and fearing for Wallace's safety, McDaniel began a tight descending spiral in order to keep his friend, hanging limply beneath the oscillating canopy, in sight. McDaniel continued the spiral until Wallace hit the ground, then landed nearby and rushed to his mechanic's side. As it turned out, Sergeant Wallace, bruised and shaken, had no broken bones or serious bleeding. However, as the pair walked toward the airplane, they could see that the horizontal stabilizer would need repairs.[32]

McDaniel spent three years at Kelly Field, during which time he courted and married his sweetheart, Ruth Morris. Ruth attended college, became a teacher, then a mother, and in her spare time tutored McDaniel on the examinations for a Regular Army commission. He passed in 1923 and became a second lieutenant in the Regular Army, after which he was reassigned to Brooks Field for duty as a flying instructor.[33]

When McDaniel reported to Brooks, enlisted pilots were still a small but normal part of its community. Eight of them were stationed there at the time. Sergeant Chet Colby, McDaniel's classmate, was one, having come to Brooks in a round-about fashion. Colby had been transferred on June 30, 1922, from Post Field at Fort Sill, Oklahoma, to the 13th Air Park (later to become the 68th Service Squadron) at Kelly Field, where he served as a test pilot and instructor at the advanced training school.[34] On September 14, 1923, together with staff sergeants R. C. Ashley, Byron K. Newcomb,[35] and Roy L. Mitchell,[36] Colby was placed on temporary duty as a primary flying instructor at Brooks Field.[37] Also assigned were sergeants Billy Winston,[38] Robert "Gloomy Gus" DeWald, John Waugh, and Fred Kelly,[39] the latter two on duty as test pilots.

Two months later, in November 1923, sergeants Newcomb, Mitchell, and Kelly found an opportunity to show their skills by volunteering to take part in an air carnival hosted by Kelly Field to raise funds for the Army Relief Drive. Their act, flying a tight V formation while their planes were tied together with cords, was only part of a larger show in which Army balloons, a dirigible, a bombing demonstration by three Martin bombers, an aerial balloon-busting contest, parachute jumps, and skywriting gave record crowds their money's worth.

In the meantime, Sgt. C.P. Smith continued through the years to do the thing he loved best—to fly. In the spring of 1919 C.P. was transferred from Kelly

Field to Langley Field, Virginia, but found little opportunity there to fly. Therefore, when he re-enlisted in 1920, he requested duty at Carlstrom Field in the hope of finding a better opportunity. Alas, things were no better at Carlstrom. Although C.P. was now a technical sergeant, he still saw little of the sky, so he bought a surplus JN-4D and became a recreational pilot of sorts. Barnstorming the Florida countryside during his offduty time, he accumulated several hundred hours in this manner.[40]

Finally, in March 1924, C.P. was sent to Brooks Field for primary flying training. It was his first formal flight training. Upon completion, he was awarded the rating of Junior Airplane Pilot, or "JAP," a peculiar rating instituted in 1922, awarded to those completing primary flight training.[41] In October 1924, C.P. was sent to Kelly Field for advanced training, after which he was assigned to the 3rd Attack Group stationed there. When the 3rd Attack Group moved to Fort Crockett, Galveston, Texas, in July 1926, C.P. moved with it.

A quintessential tinkerer, C.P. became fascinated with airborne radio, wondering why aircraft were not equipped, like ships at sea, with a loop antenna for direction finding. He installed various radios in a JNS and made many flights to determine the most suitable antenna design and position for it on the aircraft. In 1926 he installed the equipment in a JN-6H and perfected his creation. In 1928, C.P. flew from Fort Crockett to San Diego, with the equipment installed in an O-6, a Thomas-Morse rework of the old Douglas O-2. On arriving, he located the airfield, descended through an overcast sky, and landed, using the antenna to "home in" on the field's radio transmitter. In 1930, C.P. again flew from Fort Crockett to the West Coast and returned, this time accompanied by a radio operator, Sgt. Frank Bobulski. They tested a procedure for communicating with home base while in flight by sending messages to the nearest land stations along their route. In turn, these would then be relayed to the appropriate message center.[42]

Captain Burge, in the meantime, with the closing of Rich Field, was ordered to the pursuit school at North Island in January 1919. Since his last visit there in 1915–16, the flying field had been renamed in honor of Lt. Louis C. Rockwell, killed in an airplane crash in 1912.

Between January and August 1919, Burge accumulated seventy-eight hours in Spads, Thomas-Morse Scouts, SE-5s, and Fokker D-7s. After completing the pursuit course in early August, he was assigned to Ellington Field, near Houston. There he assumed command of the 166th Aero Squadron, a subordinate unit of the 1st Day Bombardment Group. In mid-

September 1919, he moved with the group to Kelly Field.

There, on November 11, 1919, Burge suffered the first crash of his career, when a student under his instruction froze at the controls during a bad landing. In the ensuing confusion, the plane, a JN-4, stalled and crashed. While the student was only slightly hurt, Burge was hospitalized for three weeks and convalesced for an additional four. When fully recovered, he was ordered to March Field, remaining there until December 1920. He was then ordered to Post Field for communications training. In July 1922 he completed the training and was reassigned once more to Kelly Field. One year later, he was sent to the Philippines for a second tour.

Arriving at Kindley Field, located at Fort Mills on Corregidor Island, in July 1923, Burge assumed command of the 2nd Observation Squadron, which was equipped with Curtiss HS2L aircraft. The HS2L was a large bi-winged seaplane with the hull attached to the lower wing and a four-hundred-plus horsepower Liberty engine—mightily braced—mounted just under the top wing. Once again he was flying seaplanes in cooperation with the Corregidor defenses from the very place he had flown just a decade earlier. The 2nd Observation Squadron, in addition to its training mission, performed a multimission role of reconnaissance flights, coast artillery spotting, Navy aerial observations, VIP flight support, and, at times, escorted mainland-based DeHavilland-4s on overwater flights between the islands of the archipelago.

Kindley Field was not an airfield in the normal sense of the word. It was a facility for handling only such water-based aircraft as Curtiss HS2Ls.[43] But shortly after Burge arrived, the 2nd Observation Squadron received two Loening S-1 "Air Yachts." The craft, a monoplane with the wing mounted atop the cabin and its single pusher Liberty engine mounted atop the wing was a small but true flying boat. Outrigger pontoons stabilized the craft on the water, and twin rudders were supposed to stabilize it in the air.

However, on checking it out in flight, Burge found it to be anything but stable. He and a young lieutenant discovered that when they made a shallow left turn at about five hundred feet, it was more boat than airplane. The nose turned but the plane continued to track straight ahead—sideways—losing speed, altitude, and aileron effectiveness. Burge shoved the nose down, which did nothing to aid in the ship's recovery. The plane continued skidding toward the water, but just when impact seemed imminent it straightened itself out, and the crew returned to Kindley by the most direct route. Landing with a new respect for the skittish "Air Yacht," Burge's only comment was "tricky to control."[44]

THE SERGEANTS
RETURN TO FLYING SCHOOL 7 1924–1933

WHILE VERNON BURGE WAS SERVING IN the Philippines, the Air Service began to realize it had lost an effective motivational tool when its authority to train qualified and deserving enlisted men to fly, under Section 13 of the National Defense Act of 1916, was revoked. The Chief of Air Service felt the authority should be restored and said so in a letter to the adjutant general dated May 31, 1923. In it, he proposed that noncommissioned officers (NCOs) of the first three grades, between twenty-two and thirty years of age, and holding a commission in the Officers Reserve Corps, be detailed in their enlisted grade to flying school if physically qualified for flying.[1]

Despite reservations held by the Judge Advocate General concerning the legal aspects of the proposal, the letter moved through the bureaucratic maze and was approved by the chief of staff in June 1923. In September of that year, the first four NCOs entered primary flying school at Brooks Field, Texas. Only two, T. Sgt. Ezra Nendell and M. Sgt. Stewart Smink, won their wings in August 1924.[2] Sergeant Nendell was assigned to a detachment of the 12th Observation Squadron stationed at Fort Sam Houston, while Sergeant Smink was assigned to Phillips Field, Maryland. Smink's duties involved flight testing of air ordnance at nearby Aberdeen Proving Grounds where he was frequently teamed with T. Sgt. Sam Nero, a fabled enlisted bombardier.[3]

These enlisted pilots, like their prewar predecessors, were already proven airplane mechanics when they reported for flight training. Many had accumulated considerable flying experience, courtesy of pilots for whom they worked and, after winning their wings, often returned to their former positions as flight chiefs, line chiefs, or maintenance inspectors in addition to their flying duties. All of them routinely performed test flights.

Two NCO mechanics—who would later become enlisted pilots—were at this time engaged in earnest competition for a position as flight mechanic on the first flight around the world. They were sergeants Alva Harvey and Paul Jackson.[4] Harvey was from Bono, Texas, a small cluster of farmhouses near Fort Worth, while Jackson was from Albany, Georgia. They shared a common background. Both were reared in a rural environment. They were familiar with hard work and hard play. Lovers of the outdoors, each was a good horseman, a crack shot, and could fish with the best of them. These talents, combined with insatiable curiosity and a thirst for adventure, made the Air Service a strong attraction for both men.

For Harvey, it was the handsomely uniformed pilots of an Army plane that landed in a pasture near the family home that fired his desire to enlist. It was the first time he had seen a plane and its pilots close-up, and he knew then he wanted to be one of them.[5]

For Jackson, it was Lincoln Beachey's flying exhibition in Albany that fired his aeronautical aspirations.[6] Beachey was a flamboyant exhibition flier in those days who toured the country with his aeroplane.

Harvey enlisted in Dallas, and Jackson at Souther Field near Americus, Georgia, shortly after the Great War ended. They became acquainted after each was ordered to the Air Service Mechanics School at Kelly Field. The pair was so enthralled by the novelty of airplanes that they talked their engineering officer, a Lieutenant Carter, into letting them to set up quarters in one of the hangers to keep an eye on the airplanes. Harvey recalled how "we watched over those planes like a mother hen over her chicks."[7]

When the mechanics school moved to Chanute Field, near Rantoul, Illinois, in January 1921, Harvey and Jackson went with it. Then, as their experience grew, so did their rank and responsibilities. They took every advantage of opportunities to fly with the most sympathetic pilots, that is, those willing to impart flying instructions.

Always eager for action, Harvey and Jackson volunteered to parachute at air shows and other events, such as cities where new airports were being dedicated.[8] Carried aloft on the wingtops of DH-4s or Martin NBS-1s, they were flown high over the grounds, where they jumped with breathtaking effect toward the gawking crowds below. Jackson remembers:

> My first jump was from the top wings of a DH-4. It was necessary to use two chutists in order to maintain the airplane's balance. Each would lay prone on a little duck board attached to the top of the upper wing near the tips. You hung onto a rope fastened to a strut and pulled over the wing top. Knots were tied into it by which you could maintain a grip. The prevailing idea in those days, once sufficient altitude was reached, was to

pull the ripcord and let the chute pull you off. If the parachute didn't open, supposedly you didn't have to go. They always opened though, believe me! When you pulled that ripcord, you went! In those days, opening a parachute at 70 miles per hour gave you one hell of a jolt. It took all the wind out of you.

A rumor persisted in those days that one lost consciousness and stopped breathing if one stepped from the plane and fell free. Despite those horror stories, it didn't take many teeth jarring pull-offs to persuade me there was a better way. Soon I was jumping straight. That is; leaving the plane before pulling the ripcord.[9]

One newsclip of the day describes it this way:

> The crowd, with the memory of Mrs. Garver's recent fatal accident still in their minds, was horrified when Sergeant Jackson leaped from a plane at 1,500 feet, holding a parachute in one hand. As soon as the thing opened he lost his grip and started falling through space. He fell 300 feet when he pulled the string which released a second parachute, and floated gently to earth.[10]

Jackson continued jumping until receiving his pilot wings in 1927.[11]

The days of the air shows, heady and exciting, gave Harvey and Jackson the chance to rub elbows with many of the most famous aviators of the day: Jimmy Doolittle, Frank Hawks, Wiley Post, Al Williams, Roscoe Turner, Hal Halverson, and Howard Hughes.

By 1923, they had become NCOs at Chanute Field. Each, along with other contenders, was being considered for the duty of flight mechanic on an around-the-world flight being planned by the Air Service in the spring of 1924. The adventure was to be led by Maj. Fred Martin, the commanding officer at Chanute. Major Martin was a pilot who had often flown with both Harvey and Jackson and who knew them very well.[12]

The airplanes for the flight were specially built by Douglas and named in honor of four cities: *Boston, Chicago, New Orleans* and *Seattle.* In time, Sergeants Harvey and Jackson emerged as semifinalists for the project. In the end, Harvey won the coveted position. While Harvey was jubilant and Jackson understandably disappointed, subsequent events proved both reactions premature.

The second contingent of NCOs selected for flight training—a group of seven—reported to Brooks Field in March 1924, just five months after former

"Buck-ass Private" Carl McDaniel, now a second lieutenant and flight instructor. One of the group, S. Sgt. Boyd Ertwine, was assigned to McDaniel as a student. Five of the group: T. Sgt. C. P. Smith, staff sergeants Jimmy Craine, Irven Mackey, Leslie L. Wells, and Boyd Ertwine eventually won their wings,[13] but Ertwine had a shaky start.[14]

According to McDaniel, Sergeant Ertwine handled the airplane well enough in the air, but had a problem with his landings as he neared the time to solo or be eliminated. Aware of the crisis, Ertwine became increasingly anxious, which further affected his landings. To convince Ertwine that he really could land the plane by himself, McDaniel climbed out of his cockpit and onto the wing beside Ertwine while the plane was on its final approach. Clinging to the cockpit combing with one hand, and cupping his other near Ertwine's ear, McDaniel shouted, "Go ahead and land her, then slow her down so I can jump off. When I'm clear, take her around until I wave you in." A stunned Ertwine, realizing that no guiding hand would be on the controls with him this time around, just nodded. McDaniel jumped free, Ertwine opened the throttle and lifted the Jenny from the turf. Although he was alone now, McDaniel's "voice" seemed to coach him through all the proper moves. Half a dozen landings later, McDaniel waved him in. Ertwine was not sure if he was taxiing toward good news or bad until he was within sight of his instructor's grin.

This was the only time Ertwine's flying career was ever in jeopardy. "I was so surprised that I forgot to be nervous," he recalled. McDaniel contended that "Ertwine was really a very good student. He just didn't know it, and needed a little boost in his confidence."[15] Ertwine, on the other hand jokingly contended McDaniel was temporarily insane.

While Ertwine was celebrating his first solo flight at Brooks Field, four pontoon-equipped Douglas World Cruisers lifted off from Lake Washington near Seattle and headed northwest on the first leg of the flight around the world. Major Fred Martin and his flight mechanic, Sgt. Alva Harvey, led the formation in the flagship *Seattle.* Forming loosely on the *Seattle* were the *Chicago,* flown by Capt. Lowell Smith and Lt. Leslie Arnold, the *New Orleans* with lieutenants Eric Nelson and Jack Harding, and the *Boston* flown by Lt. Leigh Wade and flight mechanic Sgt. Henry Ogden. Although neither Sergeant Harvey nor Sergeant Ogden was a rated pilot at the time, both could fly. That skill had been one of the criterion for their selection.

Although Harvey had considered himself lucky to be chosen for this flight, he began to have doubts during the Seward-to-Chignik, Alaska, leg when oil began streaming from the engine. At the same time the oil pressure gauge showed an alarming drop, a situation demanding quick action. Major Martin decided to make an emergency landing in the waters of Portage Bay, where they discovered the *Seattle*'s oil sump plug had worked loose. They also determined that the engine would have to be changed. A launch from the U.S. Navy destroyer *Hull* towed the *Seattle* into a cove near the small village of Kanatak, and a replacement engine was brought in from Dutch Harbor.

With the help of two locals, Sergeant Harvey worked throughout the night, changing the engine under the most primitive conditions. First, he drained the oil from the crankcase into buckets and instructed the locals to keep it warm over their stoves. After removing the old engine and mounting the new one, he was still faced with the task of starting a cold engine.

At this point an exhausted Harvey felt that the odds were stacked against getting it started. Someone located a bottle of acetylene, apparently left behind by a welding crew in a lean-to next to a village shack. Gingerly and at great risk, as the local help pulled the propeller through several times, Harvey valved the volatile acetylene into the carburetor. He fully expected to be "blown to hell." But these were desperate circumstances requiring desperate measures. After several attempts, the engine caught—much to his relief—and while it idled, he quickly poured the heated oil back into its tank. Harvey left the engine running throughout the remainder of the night while he made the necessary settings and adjustments. By morning the engine was broken in, tuned up, and ticking smoothly. Harvey and the major climbed into their cockpits, secured themselves, waved goodbye to those who had been so helpful, and took off. As the cove receded, Harvey wondered if he could have ever started that new engine without the acetylene.[16] Perhaps it would have been better had he not. In retrospect, neither man could have been blamed for wondering if the oil plug misfortune was an omen, for as Harvey wrote later:

Radio messages received on the morning of April 30 reported Dutch Harbor weather as being clear. Other reports from ships along the route were less favorable, but sufficient to warrant our departure. We departed Chignik at 10 A.M., our flight plan was to cross the portage below Chignik, pick up the coastline, then proceed on course. After being airborne for an hour we observed a formation ahead resembling a clear body of water to the west. Consequently, Major Martin turned in that direction expecting to pick up the coastline, but to our surprise, this formation turned out to be a heavy fog bank. We continued on course and soon were enveloped in a dense fog. Visibility zero. At this time Major Martin started to climb but the heavily loaded plane climbed slowly. We later learned that the

westerly course we followed took us north of the highest mountain range
to a hilly area on the Bering Sea side of the Alaskan peninsula. The top
of the fog bank was never reached and the dense fog lying on snow-covered
ground made it impossible to see anything ahead. We crashed into the
mountain side at 11:30 A.M. Major Martin came out with a pretty good
"shiner," but aside from shock, I was unhurt. After scrambling out of the
wreckage, we walked back to inspect the position of initial impact. We
found the airplane had struck on a slope of a rather steep hillside, the
pontoons and right wing striking first. The airplane had continued to skid
up the slope for some two hundred yards, tearing itself to pieces as it went.
As we recovered from the shock of the crash, we realized that the next
item on the agenda was an estimation of our situation. Prior to our
departure from Chignik, Mrs. Osborne had prepared two sandwiches for
each of us, along with a quart thermos of coffee which was destroyed in
the crash. We ate the sandwiches with relish, for they were to be our last
solid food for several days.[17]

After a ten-day trek out of the Alaskan wilderness, Major Martin returned
to Washington, D.C., and Harvey to Chanute Field, where he secured a
furlough and went home to Bono, Texas, for a rest. His attention, however,
remained fixed on the progress of his fellow airmen as they winged their
way westward around the world.

The months of June and July found me on furlough, visiting my family
and others, just loafing. August brought the dawn of a new era. I received
orders to report to Brooks Field to enter pilot training school. Glory be![18]

At the time Harvey was celebrating his good news, Sgt. Boyd Ertwine
continued to advance through successive phases of flying school. During that
time, he also developed a friendship with classmate Sgt. Irven Mackey.[19]
Mackey, like most enlisted pilots, had been an airplane mechanic—a prece-
dent set in the very beginning by men like Burge, Ocker, Albert D. Smith,
and others, all enlisted pilots who had been mechanics. Most of them viewed
flying as a natural extension of their skills as mechanics. Sergeant Mackey
was a product of that tradition. Before he went to flying school he was a
highly regarded engine instructor at the mechanics school at Chanute Field.

On the eve of his graduation from advanced flying school, Mackey and
his wife "Buddy," expecting their first child, invited Ertwine to their quarters
to celebrate Mackey's graduation. Several days later, on March 16, 1925,
Mackey drew his first flying assignment: take photographers aloft in a

Martin NBS-1 to record maneuvers of the 3rd Attack Group. Tragically, while jockeying into a suitable position, the bomber stalled and spun into the ground only two and one-half miles from Kelly Field.[20] All perished in the crash.[21]

Five hundred miles west of Kelly Field, planes of the 12th Observation Squadron maintained a border patrol between the United States and Mexico as late as 1925. The 12th Observation Squadron was based at Biggs Field, El Paso, Texas, and worked with infantry units at Fort Bliss, Texas, and cavalry units at Fort Huachuka, Arizona. The cavalry was still being used in those days to stabilize the Southwest, and the planes of the 12th were utilized as its extension, and also as

> a means of investigating rumors—immediately. By the time cavalry or other troops could march to the scenes of such reports the emergency would cease to exist. The Air Service therefore relieves all ground troops of much fruitless marching, such as was experienced prior to placing the Air Service at Fort Bliss.[22]

Patrols were staged from airfields at Dryden and Marfa in Texas and from Douglas, Nogales, and Tucson in Arizona. They covered the U.S.-Mexico border between Fort Quitman, Texas, and Columbus, New Mexico, whenever bandit activity was reported or suspected.

In addition, crews flew reconnaissance, photo, and artillery adjustment missions, not to mention courier, passenger, and test flights. They also filled training squares by practicing formation, aerial gunnery, and bombing flights. Moreover, two planes were routinely dispatched round-trip each month to San Diego to gather data on flying conditions along the route of a proposed airway. The route roughly paralleled the Southern Pacific Railroad between Texas and California, and was used as a navigation aid by pilots.

If one drew a line on a map from San Antonio to San Diego through El Paso, it would pass through the three regional deserts over which the pilots of the 12th Observation Squadron flew: the Chihuahuan, Sonoran, and Mojave. Nowhere within their entire flying range were these pilots ever out of these deserts. El Paso itself was nearly dead center of the Chihuahuan Desert, but it was home for two-thirds of the squadron. The other third operated out of Fort Sam Houston.

The crews were literally outdoorsmen. Open cockpits exposed them to every harsh feature of the desert, including unmerciful heat in summer and bone-chilling cold in the winter. Jarring turbulence from thermal drafts and mountain winds was unending. Sand and dust were constant enemies of pilots and their machines.

Anyone who has flown over the deserts of the Southwest, especially at the lower altitudes common to the planes in the twenties, can appreciate the toughness and durability of such pilots. Forced landings were frequent, and it was often a long, hot walk to water. The historian of the 12th Observation Squadron noted with some pride that "an indication of the expertness of the pilots is the fact that no planes were washed out and only eight forced landings were had."[23] Pilots and observers routinely carried food and water for that eventuality since a forced landing could never be ruled out.

Aircrews also worried about getting lost and drifting into Mexico where they could fall into the hands of bandits. Their worry was not without cause for more than one crew came to grief in that fashion, as in the case of lieutenants Connelly and Waterhouse of Rockwell Field. In August 1919, they became lost while flying near the border and were forced down in Mexico where they were subsequently murdered. Two months later, on October 14, lieutenants Sweeley, Duke, and McCarn, also flying out of Rockwell, became lost and landed south of the border. Fortunately, they were returned, but not without considerable hardship.[24]

In August 1919, lieutenants H. G. Peterson and P. H. Davis were forced to land on the Mexican side of the big bend of the Rio Grande. There they were captured and held for a $15,000 ransom, a sum quickly raised by ranchers on the Texas side of the Rio Grande. The bandits planned to murder the downed pair after the ransom was delivered, but their plan was foiled and nearly half the ransom recovered when the fliers were rescued by intrepid Army Capt. Leonard F. Matlack, whose exploits would have made wonderful script material for the 1980s action movie hero Indiana Jones.[25]

Lieutenant Alexander Pearson, one of the 12th Squadron's own, went down in Mexico while attempting a coast-to-coast flight in February 1921. Bandits were not a problem during his lonely ordeal, but the hostile environment was. In reality, it was the desert—not the bandits for whom they patrolled—that posed the greater threat for pilots of the 12th Observation Squadron.[26]

When given the opportunity, pilots combined pleasure with "official business," as when flying passengers to San Antonio or San Diego, or representing the squadron at gunnery and bombing meets at Langley Field or the air races at Mitchell Field.

Two sergeant pilots, staff sergeants Fred O. Tyler and Fred I. Pierce, flew with the Biggs Field contingent, while T. Sgt. Ezra Nendell flew with the contingent based at Fort Sam Houston. Sergeants Tyler and Pierce created their own brand of recreation by flying to Vermejo Park in the spectacular Sangre de Christo mountains of northern New Mexico to hunt for deer. If the hunt was successful, they returned triumphantly with the deer lashed atop the lower wings.[27]

Recreation on a grander scale was offered to the squadron in November 1925, when crews were invited to fly in the dedication of a new airport at Tucson. Lieutenants Charles Douglas and Lloyd E. Hunting, together with sergeants Tyler and Pierce, formed a team to represent the 12th Observation Squadron at the ceremonies. Kelly Field, Brooks Field, and the Navy at San Diego sent flying teams as well.[28]

It was a festive occasion, with bunting, balloons, and many flying events. The dedication began with a roar as planes took off for the first leg of a relay race from Tucson to Cochise, Arizona. Waiting to fly the next leg to Douglas were teams from Biggs, Kelly, and a combined Army-Navy team. A third set of planes and pilots flew the final leg back to Tucson, closing a 225-mile triangle over formidable terrain in two hours, five minutes, and forty-one seconds. Lieutenants Douglas and Hunting, and Staff Sergeant Pierce, the team representing the 12th Observation Squadron, won the race. Each was awarded a wristwatch; a silver cup was awarded to the squadron. The Kelly team finished second and the Army-Navy team third. Army Private Donnelly of Biggs Field won the parachute jumping event that followed.[29]

Fascinated crowds also watched as a short-field landing contest took place. Contestants had to plop their planes down as quickly as possible after passing a cloth hurdle. Lieutenant Hunting won first place; Lt. O. P. Weyland, a pilot of the Fort Sam Houston contingent, took second place; and Lieutenant Wallace, a Marine Corps pilot, took third.

Other events followed. By dropping a message that fell nearest a flag marker located in front of the crowd, Lieutenant Douglas won the aerial message-dropping contest for the 12th Squadron. Lieutenant Hunting and Staff Sergeant Tyler won the troubleshooting event, in which the competitors took off, circled the field, and landed, then shut their engines down. They then removed and replaced all twelve sparkplugs and took off again. The shortest time between engine shutdown and subsequent takeoff determined the winning team.

The most spectacular event of the dedication was aerial acrobatics. Each competitor tore up the sky with reckless abandon. When it was over, Sergeant Tyler had won his second watch and put the 12th Observation Squadron on top against some pretty tough competition.

The men of the 12th Squadron were a hardworking bunch. By the end of 1925, the El Paso contingent had accumulated just under 3,000 hours— an annual average of about 426 hours for each pilot.[30] It was truly a "hot" outfit. Sergeant Tyler's service with the 12th Squadron ended in 1926 with his transfer to the Philippines. Tyler replaced S. Sgt. pilot George Wiggs in the 3rd Pursuit Squadron at Camp Nichols in the Philippines and Wiggs rotated to the United States as a replacement for Tyler.[31]

During that same mid-twenties period, Orvil Haynes—that former World War I enlisted Ferrier pilot—re-enlisted. In March 1925, after five years as a civilian aviator, Haynes enlisted at Fort Crook, Omaha, as a staff sergeant pilot for duty with the 16th Observation Squadron.[32] He was one of the few pilots of that era who made no claim to being a barnstormer. One of the tasks assigned to the 16th at that time was to fly the mail to President Calvin Coolidge at his vacation retreat.[33] Haynes performed that task during the summer of 1926, flying between Chicago and Superior, Wisconsin, when the president vacationed at Brule. Again during the summer of 1927 he flew between North Platte, Nebraska, and Rapid City, South Dakota, while the president vacationed in the Black Hills. The mail notwithstanding, most of Haynes's flying chores were of a routine nature in the DH-4, but there were exceptions, as noted in a brief local newspaper clipping:

FORT CROOK AVIATOR FORCED DOWN IN IOWA

Sergeant O. W. Haynes, enlisted Air Service pilot stationed at Fort Crook, was compelled to make a forced landing forty miles from Iowa City Monday, while flying from Omaha to Fairfield, Ohio.

Engine trouble or some mechanical defect compelled Haynes to land in a field, and he tore one wing of his plane loose in a collision with two fences.

Pilot Haynes got in communication with the air mail field at Iowa City, and a plane was sent out with emergency repair parts. He was able to fly his plane to Iowa City Tuesday morning, and after additional repairs were made by mechanics at the air mail hangers, he proceeded to Fairfield, arriving there Wednesday.[34]

While Sergeant Haynes was serving in the Midwest during the mid-twenties, sergeants Cecil Guile, Tom Fowler, and Paul Woodruff were serving at

Crissy Field, a landing strip serving the Presidio at San Francisco. The field was located just above the high-tide mark on the south shore of the bay near the present site of the south abutment of the Golden Gate Bridge.

Sergeant Guile became the center of a little drama in June 1925, while flying a DH-4 to Rockwell Field. As he passed over Newport Beach, California, smoke suddenly burst from under the engine cowling. He shut the engine down, turned off the ignition, and established an approach for an emergency landing on the beach. At five hundred feet, pieces flew from the engine and it caught fire. Guile put the plane down on the shore, but as it slowed, the steep slope of the beach pulled the burning plane into the surf where it overturned, nearly drowning and incinerating him at the same time. The flames were soon extinguished by the surf, and Guile was rescued by onlookers. Investigation showed that his engine had thrown a piston and connecting rod through the crankcase and oil tank.[35]

After the Armistice that ended World War I, America celebrated the event by declaring November 11 Armistice Day. Each year on the anniversary of that day, pilots of Crissy Field were in great demand in communities all over California, invited by civic groups and city leaders to join in their celebrations. They were also reminded to bring their airplanes and "put on a show." On that day in 1925 Col. Frank Lahm responded by leading a flight of seven airplanes to Clover Field near Santa Monica to provide thrills for a group of Hollywood celebrities. Sergeant pilot Tom Fowler was part of that flight.

Lieutenant Caleb V. Haynes led another flight of Jennys to Modesto, California, to participate in the Armistice celebrations there, while S. Sgt. pilot Cecil B. Guile, in company with Lt. W. R. Taylor, flew up to Sebastapol, in the heart of California's wine country, to join with the American Legion in their celebration.[36]

George Washington's birthday, February 22, was another patriotic holiday often celebrated in style by pilots of the Air Service in cooperation with city leaders. In 1926, seventy-five Army, Navy, Marine, and civilian pilots were invited to participate in an air meet hosted by the Bakersfield city leaders and the local chapter of the National Aeronautical Association. Fifteen thousand citizens attended the event. Sergeants Guile, Fowler, and Woodruff—three of the seven pilots—from Crissy Field, arrived ready and eager to perform. So did the Navy and Marines, who promptly posted the required bond. The Army, for some reason, failed to do so and was therefore barred from performing. Sadly, the Army aviators, standing with the rest of the crowd, watched while the Navy and Marine pilots, unchallenged, put on a spectacular flying show.[37]

As noted earlier, Sgt. Al Harvey entered primary flying school in September 1924, but because he was compelled to attend so many celebrations honoring the round-the-world fliers, his training was frequently interrupted, sapping time from his training schedule that he could ill afford. He discussed the problem with his instructor, S. Sgt. Roy Mitchell,[38] who suggested that he request permission from his superiors to complete the course the following year. Harvey's request was granted, and he was held over until March 1925, graduating in February 1926.[39]

A little over a year after Harvey won his wings, his friend of long-standing, Sgt. Paul Jackson, entered flying school with the class beginning March 1927. After completing primary, he too was held over and graduated with the next class in June 1928.[40]

Following graduation, Jackson returned to Chanute Field with the intention of picking up his old job as flight chief, but the job was taken. However, there was still plenty for him to do: testing flying aircraft coming out of overhaul or repair; drop-testing parachutes; carrying parachute school students aloft for their graduation jump; and flying freight or passengers to distant destinations. In time, Jackson got his old job as flight chief back. In the interim, he had developed an aerial acrobatic routine that he put on at air shows around the country. By the early thirties he had established a reputation for himself. A Chicago newspaper declared:

> Sergeant Paul Jackson, another acrobatic pilot of note, is perfecting his own creation, "the octagonal loop." In this trick he pauses eight times while making a loop to give the octagonal effect.[41]

Another newsclip:

> One of the most daring of the army aces was Sergeant Jackson who did everything but fall to earth with his plane. Particularly thrilling was the full power dive made by Sergeant Jackson from a height of 2000 feet. After attaining the desired altitude the engine of the craft was thrown into full power and the plane made an almost vertical dive to earth, swooping upward again at 100 feet to throw a tremendous roar from the exhaust and propeller into the throngs. For Sergeant Jackson it seemed just as easy to fly his plane upside down as right side up and once he piloted the craft for fully a half mile up-side-down.[42]

Later, Jackson was transferred to the 68th Service Squadron at Kelly Field where so many of the sergeant pilots before and after him had served. The 68th was responsible for overhauling, repairing, and testing airplanes. Jackson's job was to test-fly them after repairs were made.

Sergeant Jackson was a finicky pilot, having seen Murphy's law loosed upon the unwary too many times to be otherwise. But on one particular day, while conducting his preflight ritual before test-hopping a freshly over-hauled PT-3, Jackson was distracted for a reason now forgotten. Upon resuming the preflight, he overlooked an important step, that is, verifying that the control surfaces responded correctly to the movement of the controls in the cockpit. Jackson taxied out onto the field, opened the throttle, and, as the plane came off the ground, realized the ailerons were operating in reverse. He cut the throttle and switches and plopped the trainer back on the field, throwing a lot of gravel and dust in the process. The plane was only slightly damaged, but it was the last time he took anything for granted.[43]

One of the many airplanes Jackson flew at Kelly was the Douglas C-1, a single-engine bi-winged transport that could carry six passengers, a load of freight, or a combination of both. While flying the C-1 near Seadrift, Texas, one day, the oil plug worked loose, forcing him down in a remote area of gentle sand dunes. He got the plane down, but not before the engine expired. He walked for miles before locating a phone from which to report his predicament. Staff Sergeant pilot Jerome McCauley flew a replacement engine down to him, and together with their mechanics, they replaced it.[44]

Jackson has never forgotten one particular flight in a C-1 that had been modified to serve as an ambulance plane. He was stationed at Kelly Field at the time and was sent to Fort Ringold near Rio Grande City on the border with Mexico. There he was to pick up a soldier who had shot himself in the head and fly him to Dodd Field for hospitalization at nearby Fort Sam Houston.[45]

It was a particularly hot and dry summer day and he had to put up with a stiff headwind. Sitting in the open cockpit behind a hot Liberty engine made Jackson terribly thirsty. Jiggling the controls, he summoned the medic from his seat in the cabin and asked him to fetch the thermos of ice water normally placed on the plane. When the medic appeared, he had to inform a parched pilot that the thermos jugs had been left behind.

Arriving at Fort Ringold after what seemed an eternity, Jackson hastened to find a drink of water while the patient and fuel were being placed aboard his airplane. When Jackson returned, the doctor pulled him aside and told him that the patient had very little chance of surviving the trip, but that it was better than remaining at the fort. Jackson recalled:

Those two distractions were a mistake, for while preoccupied with water and the doctor, the airplane was serviced with a full load of fuel. Ordinarily, it would have been all right, but not on a day as hot as this. I didn't realize my mistake until takeoff, which was long and labored and only cleared a cemetery fence at the end of the parade ground by a whisker.

Right away, I noticed the engine water temperature was up past boiling, and I was getting a spray of water through the overflow pipe onto the windshield, some of which was being blown into the cockpit. The moment I retarded the throttle, the airplane wanted to stop flying. The air was so hot that it had little substance to it. I wanted to get back around and land, 'cause I didn't know if I was going to be able to stay aloft or not. I couldn't climb, nor did I dare turn, so I kept heading south into the wind, toward the Rio Grande. I could see the river ahead in the distance, sort of downhill from me. I finally made the river and made a shallow turn to head downstream and stay just above the water in the hope of cooling the engine down. No such luck. Flying 50 or 100 feet above the river, I tried to find the happy compromise between spark control, cooling shutters, throttle and mixture control to reduce the heating and still maintain flying speed. It didn't take long to find out that I couldn't do it. I wasn't going to make it back to Fort Ringold. I debated landing in the mesquite and decided that was no good because I would probably flip over. Then I thought I might put it down in the river, then ruled that out because I didn't want to drown the patient. So I just continued cruising down the river, trying to think of something to do, when I spotted a large cumulus cloud about five miles down the river. I thought, if I can just get under that cloud, I might make it. I finally did, but that last mile was a long one.

Under a cloud of that type, there is usually a convection current and a little shade, too. The atmosphere is a couple of degrees cooler than in the clear. I knew that if I could catch that convection current, I might get up high enough to cool the engine and make it back to San Antonio.

I was lucky! I hit the convection current the moment I flew into the shade of that great cloud. I felt the old plane rise a little bit each time I circled. I climbed up through two, four, and finally leveled off at six thousand feet where the engine slowly cooled off enough to where I was losing no more water. Only then did I set course for San Antonio. It didn't take nearly as long to return to San Antonio as it did to get to Fort Ringold. Not only did we have a tail wind on the return leg of the flight, but I kept as much throttle on as wisdom would allow, wanting to hurry the patient to the hospital. After a while though, Cass, the medic came forward and said, "Well, you can slow down a little bit if you want to—he's gone."[46]

Another airplane Jackson flew frequently was the Fokker C-14 transport, a high-winged, high-lift monoplane. Because it formerly bore the designation YIC-14 while undergoing operational suitability tests for the Air Corps, pilots often derisively called it the "Yic-14." The pilot sat in an open cockpit midway between the engine and the vertical stabilizer. An enclosed cabin occupied the space between the cockpit and the engine. Of it, Jackson says:

> It had a short control stick mounted on top of a pedestal protruding between the pilot's knees. It gave the pilot a strange sensation he was flying a large airplane, but with little leverage. I liked the plane. It offered good visibility, and was a nice airplane to fly, but it didn't have much acceleration.

That deficiency nearly got Jackson into trouble on a flight to the Big Bend country of southwest Texas one day. He and a mechanic named Mitchell flew a replacement engine out to an old Keystone bomber that had been forced down because of engine failure. They ran into some rough weather near Dryden and detoured to the south near the beginning of the Big Bend country. The rough air bounced the plane around so badly that Jackson could feel the engine in the cabin working loose from its lashings. In the cabin, Mitchell's hands were full trying to keep the engine from punching holes in the fuselage.

> After passing the front, we found the bomber in a hell of a big pasture near the highway and railroad about six miles east of Marathon, Texas. We had plenty of room to get down. No trees. No obstacles of any kind, and flat too, although the mountains began south of there.
>
> I started circling the bomber to the left at reduced speed, taking the measure of where best to land. Suddenly the nose dropped. I had flown into a "whirly-gig," "dust devil" or whatever you call those small circular winds that are so much a part of the desert southwest and it nearly threw me into the ground. I jammed the throttle full forward, but having little reserve of speed or altitude I was just barely able to recover from a very bad situation.

After landing, Jackson and Mitchell set up camp and began changing the engine on the grounded bomber.

It took a little longer than we anticipated and we began to run short of food and water. However we were able to swim, bathe and cool off each day in a windmill-fed livestock tank.

After a few days the ranch foreman rode over to us and reined his horse to a stop. He sat there a moment looking around and finally said, "How're you boys makin' out?" We told him we were making out fairly well, and he said, "What are you gettin' to eat?" We told him, "Not much." There were a few cans lying around on the ground. He looked at those and finally, he said, "It don't look to me like you boys are doin' too good." He said he would see what he could do about it and rode off.

Mitchell and I didn't expect to see him anymore, but that afternoon a cowhand rode up with a couple of gunny sacks and a sheet of galvanized tin. He got off his horse and, paying no attention to us, began fooling around with the corrugated tin and the grub. He had brought some wood and started a little fire with it. He still didn't want to make conversation. He was an Indian or a Mexican, I guess. Never did say anything to us, but he cooked a good meal; biscuits, meat, that sort of thing. When he got through, he gathered up his stuff and rode off. He came back each day after that until we finished the job.[47]

During the airmail days of January to May of 1934, Jackson shuttled crews and equipment in and out of Chicago in the tri-motored Ford C-9. When the mail episode was over, he was transferred to France Field in the Panama Canal Zone to relieve Sgt. pilot Julian Joplin, due for rotation to the United States.

One of the many flying chores Jackson inherited was to fly an old Keystone bomber for the searchlight batteries to practice on. He would take the bomber, at night, to ten thousand feet, then crisscross the area. All the while, antiaircraft listening devices attempted to locate the plane and direct searchlights to it. If the lights caught him, their intensity would nearly blind him, making it very difficult to read his instruments.

You could fool them if you wanted to, but you always wound up foolin' yourself, 'cause the more difficult you made it for them, the longer you had to stay up. When you approached the target and the lights were coming pretty close, you could throttle back a little. That indicated to the people on the ground that you had passed over and were getting away, so the search lights would move out ahead of the plane. It was self-defeating though, so we didn't do it very often.[48]

Another chore Jackson liked even less was that of towing antiaircraft targets across the Panamanian sky. The targets were towed on a fifteen-hundred-foot cable behind an old Thomas-Morse O-19. It was not much fun because it took all the power of the engine just to stay aloft, and the gunners had proven themselves in the past to be fallible.[49]

Sergeant Jackson, like Sergeant Harvey, would have been quite comfortable in the company of today's multiskilled soldier or airman. He was a first-class adventurer, for as long as he could remember he had been curious about what lay beyond the horizon. As he grew, so did his curiosity and his thirst for travel and adventure.

Early in his career, Jackson had met Sgt. Ralph Bottriell, one of the Army's pioneer parachutists. At the time, Bottriell had just tested a manually operated backpack parachute of his own design and was trying to get it accepted as standard equipment for all fliers. Bottriell's zeal was contagious and Jackson, always ready for a challenge, made his first jump under Bottriell's supervision.[50]

While in Panama, another challenge attracted him—prospecting for gold. Taking a furlough in August 1936, he and a few of his cohorts followed likely streams deep into the Panamanian jungle and panned for the yellow stuff. They found it, too, but in such limited quantity and in areas so difficult to get to that supplies had to be air-dropped. In time, they decided the prize was not worth the price.[51]

As he had done at Chanute and Kelly fields, Jackson test-hopped aircraft coming out of Aero Repair. In fact, it was on just such a flight with a Boeing P-12 that he experienced a humiliating crash.

> The plane belonged to Maj. Lewis Brereton, the commanding officer, and had just come out of the shops after receiving a major overhaul, including a complete recovering and a dazzling new paint job. The plane had just been rigged and rolled out of the hanger for me to test hop. But it was lunch time and I was tying it down in order to go to lunch when Major Brereton drove up and said he wanted it ready as soon as he came back from lunch, so Cpl. C. D. Smith helped me untie it. I climbed in and, with Smith's help, started it and took off for a short test hop.
>
> The weather wasn't too good, so I climbed to altitude through breaks in the clouds and weaved between intermittent rain storms. When high enough, I stuck the plane into a dive, then jerked the stick back hard! We used to do that to "set" the rigging, that is, to stress the flying wires enough to reveal any latent slack. That was the way you handled a newly rigged

airplane; then you adjusted the rigging after the flight. Anyway, as I stuck the nose down, the carburetor float became stuck, I think, 'cause the engine began to flood and I couldn't get any power out of it.

I didn't know exactly where the runway was, although I knew I was pretty close to France Field. They were all coral runways in those days—no pavement—and you had to put it down *on* the runway. If you got down off the end of it, you got in the mud. It was always wet; a lot of rain in that country. Naturally, I was getting a little power and was hanging onto what I had, although it wasn't enough. Well, I didn't get *on* the runway. I hit short. Ka-Bam! My wheels went first one way and then the other and the carburetor float came unstuck! Since I hadn't closed the throttle, and I hadn't cut the switch, and I hadn't busted the propeller, I was back in the air with the engine wide open and a busted landing gear. I was still headed down the runway, sort of in control, so I decided to get it over with, and put the plane back on the ground. It slid, skidded, and finally flipped up-side-down. I got a little cut up, and some teeth were loosened, but my pride, and the C.O.'s freshly overhauled airplane was a mess.[52]

Two years earlier, on July 21, 1934, six Boeing P-12Es based at Albrook Field on the opposite end of the Panama Canal Zone fired up and took off. Puerto Armuelles, on the southwest coast of Panama—250 miles to the west—had just been hit by an earthquake and the fate of a number of Americans living on plantations there was not known. Lieutenant Colonel W. C. McChord, concerned for their safety, organized the flight to investigate and lend assistance if necessary. Colonel McChord led the first element. Flying on his wing were Capt. Ennis C. Whitehead and 2nd Lt. Bill Sindo, a Reserve officer. Captain Frank O'D. Hunter led the second element. Second Lieutenant Charles Lesesne, also of the Reserves, flew on one wing. Master Sergeant pilot Julius Kolb, the assistant line chief of the 74th Pursuit Squadron, flew on Hunter's other wing.[53]

From his position in the formation, Kolb contemplated the sight as the feisty little pursuit planes climbed through breaks in the morning cumulus. Once on top, they banked west toward Puerto Armuelles, paralleling the Panamanian shore line. The clouds over which they flew soon thinned, then disappeared, revealing a colorful vista. Kolb gazed at the other planes, yellow sun-washed wings standing out brightly against the blue-green gulf. Emerald foliage cascaded from the mist-shrouded shoulders of the coastal hills and tumbled to the shore line.

Three planes still wore olive drab on their fuselages while three others, including Kolb's, had been repainted with the new light blue. The sight reminded him again—as these rare moments did—just how rich the rewards of flying could be. Leveling off, the formation spread out, allowing Kolb's attention to drift back in time to the events that brought him to this place.

His military career had begun in 1921, when he enlisted in the Air Service at Camp Jackson, Columbia, South Carolina. He was subsequently sent to Kelly Field as a mechanic with the 95th Pursuit Squadron of the 1st Pursuit Group, the only pursuit group in the Army. He moved with it to Ellington Field, Houston, then to Selfridge Field, Michigan, during which time he got to know the enlisted pilots of the group quite well. Among them were sergeants Byron Newcomb, Lee Wasser, Charles Wisely, Leroy Manning, and George Pomroy. In fact, it was Pomroy who had given Kolb many hours of bootlegged instruction in JN-4s while at Selfridge.[54]

Reflecting on those events today Sergeant Kolb says:

> One memory which stands out in my mind is that of 1925 when my squadron engineering officer, Lieutenant "Cy" Bettis was to fly the Army Air Service entry in the Pulitzer Race against Lt. "Al" Williams of the Navy at Mitchell Field, N.Y., in specially built Curtiss R3C-1 aircraft. Having been crew-chief to Lieutenant Bettis, he took me with him to work with the Curtiss crew to look out for his and the Army Air Service interests.
>
> History records the fact that Lieutenant Bettis won the Pulitzer race, and the Curtiss Company built four of these airplanes—the last of specially built racing planes for the military (one for static tests, one for the Army, and two for the Navy).

After the Pulitzer race, Sergeant Kolb accompanied the Curtiss racing crew to Bay Shore, Baltimore, Maryland, to fit the racer with pontoons for the Schneider Cup races. This configuration was designated the R3C-2. Kolb remained with the Curtiss crew until Lt. Jimmy Doolittle flew the racer to victory against entries from the U.S. Navy, Britain, and Italy.[55]

In November 1931, Kolb was given the opportunity to attend flying school and, together with classmate sergeants Arthur Hanson, Ancil Lovvorn, Raymond Stockwell and Charles Cunningham, won his wings in October 1932. He was subsequently assigned to the 8th Pursuit Group at Langley Field, Virginia. From there he volunteered for duty in the Panama Canal Zone, a move that had brought him to this point in his career.

Approaching Puerto Armuelles, Captain Hunter signaled his wingmen in tight. Kolb snugged his little P-12 in close and, reading Hunter's nod of approval, felt a wave of pure joy sweep through him. Master Sergeant pilot Julius Kolb was a happy pilot.

The NCOs of the twenties and thirties—like Harvey, Jackson, and Kolb—were very good at their chosen specialties. Most were mechanics who had often flown with the pilots they served. By the time they reported to flying school they had become veterans in the air. All had been bitten by the "flying bug" early in their lives and were in the Air Service for that reason. It was a given in those days that when the mechanic went along on a flight, the pilot—when convenient—offered him the stick and a little coaching. By this means, they had developed considerable flying skill and absorbed a significant degree of aerial savvy. In fact, to avoid being branded as "know-it-alls" or "smartasses" while at flying school, most pretended to know little about the skill.[56] After graduation, NCO pilots were assigned where needed, but their mechanical expertise was normally utilized by assigning them additional duties in line with their former specialty.

In 1926, legislation (the Act of July 2, 1926 [44 Stat. 781]) was enacted that would seem to establish enlisted pilots more firmly in unit tables of organization. One of its provisions stated, in effect, that after July 1929, in peace time, no less than 20 percent of a tactical unit's pilots be enlisted.[57]

That same year, on March 4, 1926, sergeants Smink and Nero and radio operator Sergeant Willard were returning to Phillips Field after dropping two two-thousand-pound experimental bombs on the test range at the Aberdeen Proving Grounds in Maryland. A connecting rod on the right engine of the bomber came loose, forcing Smink to shut the engine down and take a shortcut that carried them unwittingly over an active antiaircraft range. Fortunately, the range officer saw the bomber in time to stop the firing, thus allowing it to pass safely through the range.[58]

Two years later, in September 1928, that same crew exemplified a proposal submitted to the War Department by Brig. Gen. Benjamin Foulois, the acting chief of staff of the Air Corps. Before the provision of the Act of July 2, 1926, was to take effect, Foulois wrote a letter to the adjutant general suggesting that each tactical unit be authorized a quota of enlisted pilots, enlisted bombers (bombardiers), and enlisted gunners on its tables of organization, with distinct grades created for each.[59] By November Foulois had his authority.[60]

That authority should have settled the matter of how enlisted air crews would be utilized in the squadrons, but divergent interpretations concerning their status compounded confusion. Authorizing enlisted aircrews for combat units was one thing; finding the welcome mat for them was quite another. So few were added to the rolls—far less than the required 20 percent—that Foulois's authority became pointless.[61]

Sadly, by 1933, the flying training program for NCOs had became a casualty of the Great Depression. With the graduation of T. Sgt. Frank J. Siebenaler and M. Sgt. C.P Smith in June 1933, the peacetime sergeant pilot program had come to an end. Between 1923 and 1933, however, the program had accepted seventy-eight NCO candidates for flight training and graduated thirty-three of them, after which it simply ran out of funds.[62] In the process, C.P. Smith became unique among Army pilots. He was the only pilot known to have graduated from three flying training programs at Kelly Field in each decade of his career: first, as an "enlisted aviator," from Maj. George Stratemeyer's "limited" program in 1918; second, as a "junior airplane pilot" in 1925; and third, from advanced flying school as a full-fledged "military pilot" in 1933. By this time in his career C.P. Smith had logged nearly sixteen-hundred hours and fifteen years of military service.[63]

A DIFFERENT BREED OF CAT 8 1931–1935

AFTER THE STOCK MARKET CRASH OF 1929, the Air Corps—as after the Armistice—was faced with a reduction of funds. America could not afford the cost of maintaining a "large" military establishment. While one consequence was the termination of flight training for noncommissioned officers (NCOs), another was the influx of flying privates. Many reserve officer aviators were released from active duty and forced into a job market already glutted with pilots. In order to continue flying, scores of pilots re-entered the army as privates.

If the sergeant pilots were an unusual presence among Army pilots, the flying privates were absolutely unique. As one of their own put it, "We were a different breed of cat."[1] A paragraph appearing in a 1931 Air Corps Newsletter noted that trend:

> A slight increase occurred in the number of enlisted pilots as compared to losses in prior years. This situation is no doubt due to the fact that no vacancies in the grade of second lieutenant were available in the Regular Army for graduates of the Advanced School, and also the existing business depression and lack of demand for pilots in civil life. At the present time there are a total of thirty-one enlisted pilots on duty at the various Air Corps activities. It is expected that this number will further increase in the fiscal year 1932.[2]

Indeed, their numbers did increase. By 1934 such enlistments raised the number to sixty-two.[3] Among those former officers who found a niche were Lawrence ("Larry") O. Brown, John D. Kryssler, Harold Kreider, Noel Parrish, Jimmy Treweek, Vernon Byrne, Loren Cornell, Tracy Dorsett, William C. McDonald, John H. "Luke" Williamson, Russell "Gatty" Waldron, and Lloyd Sailor.

Although the pay was meager, it seemed the best of the options available to them. Food, lodging, and clothing were provided, as were duties by which they could maintain their flying skills. Their pay while serving as young second lieutenants had been scant enough for the lifestyle they were expected to maintain, but learning to cope on the pay of a private took some doing, even with flying pay thrown in. Most of them were able to increase their pay after qualifying in an additional specialty such as aircraft mechanic, engine mechanic, parachute rigger, or administrative specialist.

Larry Brown, for example, enlisted as a flying private at Patterson Field, Ohio, in the fall of 1933. His base pay was $21.00 per month, plus 50 percent for flight pay, which amounted to a total of $31.50. After passing an examination for air mechanic, first class he was awarded the rating for that specialty, which increased his pay to $84.00. To that was added $5.00 per diem for every day he was away on flights. Since he was unmarried, he managed well enough. In fact, he was able to put his monthly pay into a bank and live on the per diem alone.

Brown recalled the time when the base pay was cut 15 percent for all ranks. In the case of a flying private, 15 percent of $21.00 reduced his base pay to $17.85, a pittance when compared to the amounts cut from officer and senior NCO pay.[4]

The position Brown found for himself at Patterson Field was made possible through action taken two years earlier by Hugh Knerr, then chief of the Air Corps's Field Service. Knerr aimed to improve the existing air transport system. In his book, *A Few Great Captains,* DeWitt S. Copp recounts the event.

> When he had become Chief of the Field Service, in June 1931, following graduation from the Army War College, Knerr's plan of action was to establish better means of contact with the principal operational bases by better means of transportation. Rail delivery was slow and, to the Air Corps, costly. Knerr's previous duty as CO of the 2nd Bomb Group had convinced him that there was a special need for air transport. His proposal to organize such a group was approved even though there were no cargo aircraft available. By slowly commandeering a flock of worn-out bombers, a couple of tri-motors, C-27 Bellancas and anything else that looked as if it might carry a load, he formed the 1st Transport Group. It consisted of four squadrons of refurbished and modified aircraft purely for cargo operations—a meager forerunner of the Air Transport Command.[5]

On reporting for duty at Patterson Field, Private Brown found himself in company with M. Sgt. pilot Cecil B. Guile and two other flying privates,

Jimmy Treweek and Noel Parrish. The unit had no commissioned pilots.[6] Their primary flying duties involved flying freight and passengers in the Bellanca C-27 "Air Bus."

While their planes had radio receivers on board, their frequency range was limited. Too, those few stations that did broadcast weather reports were never within that range. The only broadcast in the Dayton area was located at Cincinnati, sixty miles south of Patterson Field. Therefore, when returning, pilots would tune in the Cincinnati station and, if the weather was favorable, proceed. If not, they would land somewhere along the way and wait until the weather cleared.[7]

During the first few months of 1934, several flying privates, such as Pvt. John D. Kryssler, at times flew the mail or performed other flying chores associated therewith. Kryssler and his crew chief, Sgt. Harry Hines, normally flew freight from Rockwell Field near San Diego, to Oakland, California. But shortly after the Air Corps began airmail operations in the spring of 1934, the pair was dispatched to Oakland in a freshly overhauled Keystone bomber modified to carry freight. From Oakland they were ordered to Washington, D.C., with 1,200 pounds of mail aboard. The first leg took them over the Sierra Mountains at Donner Pass to Reno, Nevada. There they took on fuel and put up for the night.

Long before sun-up the next morning, they headed east over the deserts of Nevada and Utah. After lumbering over the Rockies, they landed for fuel at Denver. Pressing on, they watched the plains of Nebraska, the checkerboard farms of Kansas, and the green vistas of Missouri pass under their yellow wings before landing at St. Louis for more fuel. The last leg of the day took them on to Louisville, Kentucky, where they remained overnight. Again they rose early the next morning and continued to Bolling Field in Washington, D.C. Upon their arrival, a brief ceremony by the Army Air Corps and postal officials acknowledged the transcontinental delivery of mail but failed to acknowledge that the crew was an all-enlisted one.

The return flight was uneventful until they landed at Reno, where Kryssler was informed that a captain would ride with them to Oakland, their final destination. Private Kryssler told the officer on duty that he was under orders to depart an hour before daylight and that the passenger should be so informed. At boarding time no passenger appeared, nor did one appear before they took off. When they arrived in Oakland, a flagman waved them to a parking place before a gathering of dignitaries and gentlemen of the press. Almost before they could shut down the engines, an unhappy officer climbed onto the lower wing and shouted into the cockpit that the captain they were

to pick up in Reno was still there. Enlisted men, it seemed, were not authorized to fly the mails, so the captain had been sent to fly the plane from Reno
"to avoid embarrassing publicity."[8]

Harry Hines experienced an eerie episode while flying with another flying
private. It remains indelible in his memory. On this particular flight, Hines
was the crew chief for flying private O. K. Harris.

> After landing at Salt Lake City following a flight from the West Coast,
> Pvt. O. K. Harris borrowed my GI overcoat to wear into town for a hot
> date that night. He caught a taxi which, on the way into town, collided
> with a train at the railroad crossing. Harris died in the collision, but the
> authorities, finding my name on the coat he was wearing, notified my
> superiors that I was dead. It came as great shock to me that they could
> mistake me for Harris . . . until I remembered the coat![9]

Enlisted pilots flew a wide variety of planes and missions during those years.
In addition to the routine training flights, they performed the test flights
following scheduled maintenance. And there were the *weather* flights.

Between July 1934 and mid-February 1936, the Air Corps and U.S.
Weather Bureau collaborated on a project to collect atmospheric data in
specially instrumented airplanes. Pilots were briefed to fly a precise profile
to relatively high altitudes and return. Their planes carried an instrument
with the jaw-breaking name "Aerometeorograph," which was suspended
between the wings to record time, barometric pressure, temperature, and
relative humidity. Pilots of all grades, including the flying privates, were
assigned to weather flights, which sometimes led to unanticipated adventures.

At Maxwell Field in Alabama, sergeants Luke Williamson and Billy
McDonald, and Pvt. Gatty Waldron took turns flying the weather flight.
They flew the Thomas-Morse O-19, a two-seat observation biplane with
yellow wings and tail and olive-drab corrugated metal fuselage. The flights
normally took off at 2 o'clock in the morning and climbed to 18,000 feet,
leveling off every 3,000 feet and flying for three minutes, then resuming the
climb. The flights had their moments of excitement because very little
weather information was available and there was no radio contact with the
base.

Gatty Waldron remembers one such flight. After climbing to 15,000 feet,
he noticed that he was no longer climbing at the expected rate. He applied

more power but still could climb no higher. Playing his flashlight beam along the leading edge of his wings, Waldron saw they were covered with ice, a very real but little understood threat to flying in those days. He began to ease the airplane down on a southerly heading, away from the hills to the north. When he tried to level off at the altitude prescribed in the flight profile, he could not maintain it. Only after descending to 3,000 feet was Waldron able to hold his altitude. He flew around with that heavy load of ice until dawn, at which time he descended through a deck of clouds and broke out at 2,000 feet. Ice still covered the wings and, of course, he was lost and low on fuel. He found an auxiliary field and landed with almost full power because of the ice load. After shutting his engine down, Waldron climbed out of the cockpit and examined the ice remaining on the wings. It was still three-quarters of an inch thick.[10]

During a similar weather flight out of Scott Field, near Belleville, Illinois, Pvt. Arnold T. Johnson established a record altitude of 21,000 feet for this type of mission in the O-19.[11]

Maintenance test flights, considered by many pilots to be rather tedious and boring, were another way enlisted pilots built up flying time. Lloyd Sailor, who served as a flying private and private, first class for nearly six years at March Field recalled, "There were two full groups at March Field then, plus some miscellaneous stuff, all of it needing periodic flight testing. I flew more hours during 1933, '34 and '35 than any other pilot, officers included."[12]

In 1933, when Pvt. Larry Brown reported to Patterson Field for his new duties with the First Provisional Transport Squadron, similar squadrons were also being created at the three other depots. The Second Provisional Transport Squadron was formed at Middletown Army Air Depot, located near Harrisburg, Pennsylvania, the Third at San Antonio Army Air Depot near San Antonio, and the Fourth at Rockwell Army Air Depot on North Island. Each was responsible for moving air freight and passengers within and between the areas it served. The workhorse of the squadrons was the Bellanca C-27 "Air Bus." Its lower W-shaped wing braces were, in reality, another wing. Pilots who flew the plane maintained that the wing braces would, during the landing flare-out, continue flying after the top wing had stalled.

Three enlisted pilots had the thrill of their lives while flying the Bellanca. In the spring of 1934, Larry Brown was on the initial approach to Middletown Air Depot when he heard something go "whirrr" inside the engine. While the RPM increased alarmingly, the propeller ceased to pull and the throttle had no effect. With no time to ponder choices, Brown made an immediate 360-degree overhead approach and landed. He remembered the event well:

> With the river on one side of the field, mountains on the other, and shops at the far end, it had to be an accurate approach and a good landing. Also, in order to keep flying speed, I had to drop the nose sharply . . . almost straight down . . . and then pull out. My past life flashed in front of me on the way down, and when I pulled out, the plane just squatted on the edge of the field. I just sat there in the cockpit as staff cars and emergency vehicles raced out to the plane. They offered to take me back to operations, but I just said to them, "Thanks, but you're going to have to wait until I get my strength back!"[13]

Not until after he regained his composure did Brown learn the reason for the engine failure. The reduction gearing in the engine had failed, severing engine power to the propeller. Without its connection to the engine, the propeller simply ran wild. Despite that scare, Brown liked the Bellanca. He considered it a stout load carrier. The entire airplane was an airfoil, including the fuselage, landing gear, and wing struts. He remembered how its wide landing gear made it possible to fly out of short fields with heavy loads by accelerating to forty miles per hour at 90 degrees to the wind, then turning into the wind for takeoff.

Staff Sergeant Loren Cornell, another enlisted pilot, was forced down in the Bellanca C-27 near Eastman, Pennsylvania, in 1935. After running one fuel tank dry, the engine sputtered before he could switch to the full tank, and it failed to catch. As the plane headed downward, Cornell tried everything he knew to restart it. Still nothing. The terrain below was not at all suitable for forced landings and the only likely spot he could find was a small field divided by a rock fence with a gap in the center. He made a nice approach, aiming for the gap as he flared for a dead-stick landing. The gap appeared wide enough to steer the plane through, but this was not Cornell's day. Stretched across the gap was a wire fence which snared the landing gear as plane rolled through, tripping it up onto its nose. The damage, though slight, made it impossible to fly the plane out. It had to be disassembled and trucked away.[14]

That same year, 1935, Pfc. Noel Parrish became the third enlisted pilot forced down while flying the C-27. Taking off from Patterson Field in the spring of 1935, Parrish realized he was in trouble the moment the heavy cargo plane became airborne. He felt a sinister tug on the controls unlike anything he had experienced before. As he tried to gain altitude, it became obvious that control of the airplane was being steadily pried away from him. As he turned the craft back toward the field, the Bellanca became progressively more difficult to control. While still in the turn and over a golf course, the plane entered a slip that he could scarcely override so he aimed for a fairway. Nearing the ground, Parrish cut the power and switches. The plane hit the turf and bounced once, slid a short distance, tipped onto its nose, and settled back on its haunches. The impact drove the wheels up through the lower wing struts, bent two of the three propeller blades back, and crumpled the lower half of the ring cowling.

The reason for the Bellanca's abnormal behavior became obvious after Parrish scrambled, weak-kneed and shaking, from the cockpit. Examining the plane he discovered a fuselage longeron near the tail section had buckled, perhaps as a result of the takeoff with the heavy load over rough terrain. That buckling had altered the angle of attack of the right horizontal stabilizer more than trim and muscle could offset. In fact, had Parrish not put the plane back on the ground when he did, it is likely that he would have lost all control, with grim consequences.[15]

Private, First Class Harold Kreider suffered a different kind of trauma in connection with a flight to Mitchell Field, Long Island, in a Bellanca C-27. Kreider, accompanied by his crew chief, was carrying a planeload of West Point cadets returning from summer camp at Langley Field. The crew chief was an old sergeant named Haws who "tacked" his stripes on lightly, " 'cause he went up and down in rank like a yo-yo," recalls Kreider. On this particular flight, Haws wore buck sergeant strips tacked onto his coveralls, over which he wore a leather flight jacket given to him by some major. If one looked closely, one could make out the faded gold leaves still painted on the epaulets. Sergeant Haws had never bothered to remove them.

Upon landing at Mitchell Field, the airplane was led by the alert crew to a parking spot in front of Base Operations. As Kreider got out of the airplane, the Officer of the Day, a young second lieutenant, discovered that Kreider was only a private and bellowed, "What the hell are you doing parked here? You should have parked way over there!," pointing as he spoke. Kreider replied that this was the spot the crew had led him to. About this time Haws got out of the back of the airplane and, wearing the leather jacket with the faded gold leaves, said, "LOOTENANT!" Motioning the O.D. toward him, he said, "You got anything to say to my pilot, say it to me!" Intimidated by Haws's apparent rank and gravely bark, the lieutenant gave him a snappy salute and responded, "Yes sir!"

"Now where's our transportation?" Haws continued.

"Right here," said the O.D., waving the staff car up to the plane. As they boarded the car, the O.D. told the driver to take them to the Officer's Club. Unruffled, Sergeant Haws asked the driver what squadron he was from. The driver told him. Then Haws said, "How's the food there?" "Wonderful— best on the base," replied the driver, steering toward the Officer's Club.

By now Private Kreider was pretty shook, " 'cause I was just a private and Haws was just a sergeant acting like a major—a pretty high rank in those days—and impersonating an officer was a pretty heavy offense under the existing Articles of War."

Kreider feared for both of them as Haws continued to play out his role. "If it's that good, why don't you take us to your mess?" said Haws, and the driver complied. As they entered the mess hall, the mess sergeant, a huge man, was riding herd on his K.P.s following the noon meal. Although the mess hall was closed, Haws, wearing his jacket, addressed the mess sergeant. "SAWDINT! This driver here tells me you got the best chow on the base. Do you think you could whip us up some scrambled eggs and maybe some ham, toast, and coffee for my pilot and me?"

"I'd be happy to," replied the mess sergeant.

Haws pressed on. "Now I want you to sit down and have a cup of coffee with us. I want to ask you about the mess." As Haws continued to flatter the mess sergeant, the kitchen help muttered darkly as they "whipped up" a tardy breakfast. Sergeant Haws continued his flattering patter as he and Private Kreider leisurely worked their way through the huge breakfast and dawdled through two more cups of coffee. When finished, Haws asked the mess sergeant if he would let him inspect his kitchen. Following behind the mess sergeant, Haws, with Kreider in trail, looked the mess hall over as though he had all the time in the world. He asked Kreider to make a note of this or that, or get this man's name or that man's name, "for the fine job your boys are doin'." By the time Sergeant Haws and Private Kreider boarded the staff car and headed back to Base Operations, the mess sergeant was eating out of Haws's hand.

"I filed the flight plan for the return flight to Langley, scared to death that someone would call Sergeant Haws's bluff and throw us both in the stockade before we could take off," concluded Kreider. "I was never so happy to get out of a place in my life as I was that day!"[16]

Of course, hauling freight, passengers, and—at times—the mail were not the only missions these flying privates performed. Like their higher-ranking sergeant counterparts, they also made test flights to determine the operational suitability of certain aircraft for use by the Air Corps. Privates Larry Brown and Noel Parrish were teamed up in November 1934 to test the Curtiss YC-30 Condor, a twin-engine, bi-winged transport plane, to determine its suitability for freight and passenger operations. While they flew it under trying conditions for many hours, the YC-30, except for the initial purchase of two models, was not adopted by the Air Corps.[17]

Not all their flights were as challenging as operational testing, however. Among the more mundane flying chores was the drop testing of parachutes, which were tested periodically by attaching weighted dummies to them and dropping them from an airplane. A static line connected the ripcord to the plane and opened the chutes seconds after being pushed overboard. The airplane most often used for this task was a Fokker C-14 transport.

This was the plane that Pvt. Jimmy Treweek flew out of Patterson Field in the fall of 1934 on a terribly dusty day. He headed for the Midwest to pick up a load of freight, but as evening approached, visibility became worse. Treweek first missed one checkpoint on his map and then another. As the sun set, he realized he was lost and began circling to locate any familiar landmark. With mounting anxiety, Treweek continued circling until the sky darkened around him. As night set in, so did his sense of doom. He ran out of gas while circling. Treweek abhorred the idea of using a parachute, so he steadied his course, lowered the seat, and, using his instruments, established a glide. Not daring to look out, he committed himself to a crash landing while uttering an urgent prayer. Treweek prepared himself to die. After an eternity, he felt an easy bounce and knew he was on the ground, alive, intact, and in shock.

Still in shock. Treweek saw automobile headlights bouncing out of the darkness toward him. They belonged to the farmer on whose wheat field he had landed. The farmer, hurrying to see what remained of the plane, seemed a little disappointed when he saw that both plane and pilot were intact. Nevertheless, he invited the frightened private to phone in his predicament from the farmhouse, and to await rescue there. Treweek accepted the hospitality and thanked the farmer. However, as they headed toward the house the adrenaline from the ordeal started to affect Treweek, who began to babble with scarcely an interruption or a complete thought, reason enough for the farmer keep a wary eye on him all the way to the farmhouse.

Early next morning, Treweek was up and out of the house, looking over the landscape. The dust had settled overnight, leaving the air clear. The land was flat as a pool table and his airplane easily visible in the distance. His plane and the nearby farmhouse were the only prominences on the entire horizon. Even the boundary fences of the field lay on the limits of his vision. Treweek turned his gaze toward the bright rising sun and sent a prayer of thanks skyward. He had been very lucky.[18]

In 1935, a limited number of slots for commissions in the Regular Army were created, for which hundreds of aspirants competed, including most of the enlisted pilots. That they were already enlisted men in the Regular Army placed them in a privileged position. To achieve the same parity, a number of reserve officer pilots enlisted from civilian life as privates. This caused the number of enlisted pilots to soar, by April 1935, to an all-time high of 117. Ironically, it was the nearest the Air Corps ever came to satisfying the 20 percent enlisted pilot quota.

Understandably, the enlistment of reserve officers during this period raised a degree of anxiety among the Regular Army enlisted men. As Lloyd Sailor put it, "There was some resentment among the enlisted men of the outfits we were assigned to because promotions were at a standstill and they were afraid that we, as possibly a select few might grab off any non-commissioned grade which occurred, depriving some worthy mechanic of long service his rightful turn."[19]

The fact was, it was rather difficult for those reserve officers to enlist. The normal procedure required that a Table of Organization vacancy exist for the particular grade and specialty and that special approval be secured to fill it. Even for the enlisted pilots, that was not always easy. Larry Brown had to visit a friend in the War Department office in Washington to secure such permission. Lloyd Sailor had to get special permission from the Air Corps Chief of Personnel, which came only after his old commanding officer sent a personal letter to Gen. "Benny" Foulois, chief of the Air Corps.[20]

The resentment expressed by the enlisted men who felt threatened by the flying privates must have been heard by the top echelons of the Air Corps because on December 2, 1936, a letter from the adjutant general ended further enlistments of reserve officers. However, by that time, forty-eight of them had already received commissions in the Regular Army and the number of enlisted pilots on the rolls fell to fifty.[21]

The 20 percent quota, while never attained, did serve a useful purpose: it enabled the U.S. Army to retain a number of pilots who continued to accumulate valuable military flying experience before World War II in a comparatively inexpensive way. Further, it gave temporary berths to many pilots who might otherwise have become discouraged and taken up other careers in the civilian sector.

Those few officers who enlisted served the Air Corps loyally through some pretty austere times. In the long run, that loyalty paid off, for after being called back to active duty at the onset of World War II, they rose in rank on a par with most of their Regular Army contemporaries and, at the end of their careers, were serving in grades ranging from lieutenant colonel to general.

No account of these unique airmen would be complete without mentioning the phenomenal aerial stunt team put together by Claire Chennault at Maxwell Field in the mid-thirties. Dubbed "Three Men on a Flying Trapeze," they thrilled crowds at the Miami and Cleveland Air Races, or wherever they performed with their sassy little P-12s. The team was originally composed of Chennault, Lt. Haywood S. ("Possum") Hansell, Jr., and Sgt. Luke Williamson. Sergeant Billy McDonald replaced Lieutenant Hansell when the latter was reassigned. Staff Sergeant pilot Ray Clifton flew as solo stunt and backup pilot for the team.[22] Private Gatty Waldron was just starting to train as a backup pilot when he received his Regular Army commission and was reassigned.[23]

While sergeants McDonald and Williamson both took the examinations for Regular Army commissions, neither was appointed. Consequently, they resolved to accept offers from China to instruct student pilots in the Chinese air force. When their enlistments expired they did just that.[24] Chennault, after retiring from the service, joined McDonald and Williamson in China, where he subsequently became Madame Chiang Kai-Shek's aviation advisor. Out of that relationship emerged the suggestion to train some of China's pilots in the United States, as well as the creation of the fabled "Flying Tigers," a fighting force made of American volunteer pilots. Their story is familiar history.

Over one hundred—and probably more—Army pilots who received their flight training as cadets served as enlisted pilots at one time or another between 1923 and 1933. They enlisted primarily as a means to continue flying, and their dedication to the profession was tested beyond doubt. Summarizing his six years as an enlisted pilot, Lloyd Sailor wrote: "We worked like hell to maintain a reputation for skill and reliability. We were a proud bunch." Extraordinary men, they were indeed a "different breed of cat."[25]

IN SEARCH OF A NICHE 9 1935–1940

IN THE EARLY DECADES OF MILITARY aviation, transport aircraft were "whatever was available." While the Fokker T-2 was the designated transport by the early twenties, few were on hand. More often available was the Curtiss JN-4 "Jenny," DeHavilland-4, Martin NBS-1, or Curtiss NBS-4. These became the transports of necessity.

Such was the case in July 1925 when the 1st Pursuit Group sent a flight of six Curtiss P-1s from Selfridge Field, Michigan, to San Francisco. They flew to San Francisco during daylight hours, but the last leg of the return flight—Cheyenne, Wyoming, to Chicago—was flown at night over the newly installed lighted airmail route. But since the P-1s had neither batteries or lights, a Curtiss XNBS-4 bomber was loaded with the necessary personnel and equipment and dispatched to Cheyenne to install them. Staff Sergeant Julius Kolb—later to become an enlisted pilot himself—went along as one of the mechanics; staff sergeants Charles Wisely and Lee Q. Wasser piloted the bomber.[1]

By 1927, the Douglas C-1, based on the design of the famous "Round-the-World Cruiser" of 1923–24, was in widespread use by the Air Corps as a standard cargo and passenger carrier. Appearing in the inventory in the mid-twenties, C-1s were at first assigned to and controlled by tactical units such as the 1st Pursuit Group. They rendered yeoman service moving support personnel and equipment where needed.

As today, some missions were difficult, often exposing men and machines to cruel and primitive conditions while offering scant reward. In January 1927, for example, Sergeant Kolb and five other mechanics comprised an all-enlisted crew that escorted the 1st Pursuit Group into Canada on winter maneuvers in a Douglas C-1 flown by S. Sgt. pilot Byron Newcomb. The difficulties and ironies encountered on this mission were not uncommon, but as described by Kolb, it had an ironic postscript.

We accompanied our 12 P-1s (all on skis) with the first stop at the RCAF station at Lake Simco, Ontario, for lunch, thence to Ottawa for the first night. Landing on a frozen area of the Ottawa River, then on to Montreal the next day. It was around 20 degrees below zero when we reached Montreal and it hovered around 25 below for the next two days while we serviced up. It then "warmed up" to around zero the third day, the day of our departure.

The P-1s had landed at the Montreal airport near Cartierville and [Sergeant] Newcomb landed the C-1 on a nearby frozen area of a bay near the airport, so we put up at a nearby hostelry while the P-1 pilots put up in a Montreal hotel in the city. This being "pre-Prestone" days, we were using a 50 percent water-alcohol mix which had frozen to mush and would not drain out. We obtained a small steam-boiler sled (horse-drawn) from the railroad which they used for thawing "switch frogs" in railroad yards. We played live steam on the radiators and engine blocks to remove the water-alcohol mixture, then placed the hose in the expansion tanks running steam through the engine blocks so we could turn the propellers and start up with steam until the proper oil pressure was obtained, then fill with another 50-percent mix. As each three-ship element was readied, they took off for Alexander Bay, New York.

We followed them to Alexander Bay in the C-1 and serviced them for the return flight to Selfridge Field. Flying to Selfridge the next day, we realized that the snow was disappearing so we landed at Gananoque, Ontario, and wired Selfridge for wheels, which incidentally, arrived a few days later—"collect!" We installed the wheels, and with an overnight stop at Toronto, Ontario, arrived safely back at Selfridge.

The real payoff was after each enlisted man had received about $75.00 in per-diem in March, the following December, each had about $35.00 deducted from his pay because the comptroller had ruled: there being more than twelve men on the order, it was considered a "troop movement" therefore the $8.00 per-diem did not apply.[2]

Several transport aircraft were added to the Air Corps inventory during the late twenties, including the Fokker C-2 tri-motor and the Ford tri-motor series, C-3, C-4, and C-9. Somewhat later, the single-engine Fokker C-14 was added. In 1932, the distinctively styled Bellanca C-27 "Air Bus" appeared and was used until 1939. The Douglas C-32, a military version of the Douglas DC-2 appeared in the Air Corps's livery in 1936, and the DC-3 (C-39) was acquired in 1938 and, with later improvements, became the venerable C-47.

The antecedents of today's medical evacuation services can be traced back to World War I when a few aircraft of that era were specially modified to carry patients. Curtiss JN-4s were modified for the task at most flying training fields. In 1919, M.S.E. Harry T. Wilson flew the Jenny version of the ambulance plane at Taylor Field near Montgomery, Alabama.

Between wars, a succession of planes, such as the Douglas C-1 and Fokker C-14, were modified to serve as ambulance planes. The first Army plane designed specifically for ambulance service was the Cox-Klemin A-1. One of these was stationed at Kelly Field, Texas, throughout the mid-twenties and used for recovering crash victims in the San Antonio area. Sergeants Ezra Nendell, Frank Siebenaler, and Bernard Wallace flew this plane. Later, sergeants Peter Biesiot and Paul Jackson joined Bernard Wallace in flying not only the Cox-Klemin A-1, but also ambulance versions of the Douglas C-1 and Fokker C-15. In fact, enlisted pilots flew the full range of ambulance planes, from the Jenny to the C-47.

Pilots flying ambulance airplanes gained a unique kind of experience not found in pursuit, attack, observation, or bombardment flying. They often had to land on unprepared ground near crash sites, often in spite of miserable winds and weather conditions. As a result, they acquired an inordinate amount of experience in transport operations. Such experience was to become extremely valuable as the force matured with the approach of World War II.

Sergeant Paul Jackson was typical of this breed, having flown each style of ambulance aircraft during his career. His first assignment after winning his wings and returning to Chanute Field at Rantoul, Illinois, was to carry the students graduating from parachute school aloft for their final examination, a jump with the built-in incentive of using a parachute they had packed themselves.[3]

In August 1929, when the Ford C-3 tri-motor transport arrived at Chanute Field, it proved roomy enough for the jumpmaster to stand behind his students as they faced the open doorway and "encourage" them to take that first long step. If they balked at the door, he could simply boot them out. Watching these students leap from his plane reminded Jackson of his own jumps years earlier under the guidance of friend and mentor M. Sgt. Ralph Bottriell. Bottriell was already a famous parachutist when he and Jackson first became acquainted at McCook Field in Dayton in 1920. It was shortly after that meeting that Jackson made his first jump under Bottriell's supervision.[4]

Bottriell's own career began in 1910 when, at age 16, he began jumping from balloons at county fairs and exhibitions. By 1918, he had made over 700 jumps and designed a number of improvements in his parachutes. Among his designs was the "D" ring and attached "ripcord," a feature that allowed the jumper to deploy the 'chute at will after leaving, rather than depend on a lanyard attached to the plane. He tested the chute at McCook Field on May 19, 1919, and became the first Army man to jump with the device.[5]

The following year, on June 28, Bottriell nearly perished while conducting a test jump from 20,600 feet. As he prepared to go over the side of the cockpit, the parachute "D" ring snagged on a protrusion and deployed. It dragged him out of the airplane and through the tail assembly, both severely cutting and breaking his left arm. His chute was also damaged. The pilot, M. Sgt. Strong B. McDann, shaken but unhurt, knew something dreadful had happened to Bottriell, not to mention the airplane. The rudder was gone and the vertical stabilizer was badly damaged but remained in place. Having no parachute himself, McDann had his hands full getting the plane safely back on the ground.

Bottriell, meanwhile, descended slowly to earth, unconscious and bleeding badly. At 15,000 feet he regained consciousness and, aware that he could not move his left arm, used his right to lift the injured arm over his head and secure it in the parachute harness. Weakened by the loss of blood, he could do little else during his twenty-two-minute descent until, near the ground, he was able to open his spare chute to slow his final descent. Farmers in fields below followed him and, upon his landing, rushed to his aid. Medics quickly on the scene rushed Bottriell to the hospital at McCook where he eventually recovered.[6]

Sadly, just four months later, Master Sergeant McDann lost his life at McCook Field on October 4, 1920, while testing a Sopwith Camel.[7]

Sergeant Paul Jackson counted another parachute expert among his friends: M. Sgt. Erwin H. Nichols, NCO in charge of the parachute school at Chanute Field. Sergeant Nichols, like Bottriell, had coached Jackson in parachute jumping several years earlier.

While Jackson personally considered Nichols the custodian of the concept of airborne warfare, the idea can be traced back at least to World War I.[8] However, much of Nichols's time and energy was devoted to the development of special equipment for the delivery of troops and supplies by air. His basic notion was to drop machine guns and ammunition from one plane

and troops from another. Nichols designed, fabricated, and tested specialized parachutes to carry out his ideas.

An intelligent man who could clearly communicate his ideas, Nichols
wrote letters and papers on the subject, stimulating enough interest among
War Department officials to prompt a visit from them to witness a demonstration. Pathe Newsreel cameramen were also present to film the demonstration. They were to film from Jackson's NBS-1 bomber, which would
also drop guns and ammunition while the troops jumped from a Ford
C-3 tri-motor flying in formation with Jackson.

It was a hot day as Sergeant Nichols drew Jackson into the shade of the
bomber's wing for a final briefing. While speaking, Sergeant Nichols pitched
forward and fell face down at Jackson's feet, hitting the ground with a
"terrible whallop!" Distraught, Jackson hailed a passing car and sped his
friend to the hospital, where doctors worked futilely to revive him. Jackson
did not realize it at the time, but Nichols was dead of a heart attack before
he hit the ground. Despite Nichols's death, the demonstration was carried
out as he had planned, but now as a sad requiem for a parachute pioneer
and cherished friend.[9]

Meanwhile, fifteen hundred miles to the west, high above March Field
in southern California, M. Sgt. Boyd Ertwine viewed the world from a very
lofty perch. At 32,000 feet one early morning in 1933, the view from the
cockpit of his Boeing P-12 was literally breathtaking. Clad in fleece-lined
flying togs, gloved and masked against the awful cold of the stratosphere,
Ertwine inhaled oxygen from a wooden nipple at the end of a thin rubber
hose while surveying the world beneath him. Circling high over Riverside,
California, in the cloudless sky, he could see Los Angeles to the west, San
Diego to the south, and Yuma, Arizona, to the southeast.

It had taken him nearly an hour to coax his P-12 to such a great height.
The engine was operating earnestly enough, but the diminutive little fighter
felt slippery in the thin air of this altitude. Ertwine likened the feeling to
that of treading water. His plane seemed suspended in a sky of such deep
blue that an occasional star winked faintly at him. The earth beneath his
wings was sun-washed bright and crisp.

Ertwine was aloft that morning because scientists from the California
Institute of Technology, in order to better understand the nature of cosmic
rays, had installed an instrumented lead shell eighteen inches in diameter
in his P-12. His task was to fly the sphere as high above the screening effect
of the earth's atmosphere as the plane would take it.

As the flight progressed, Ertwine chewed on the wooden nipple of the oxygen hose. This caused an uncomfortable accumulation of saliva. While trying to clear the nipple, Ertwine lost consciousness, and the P-12 fell into a spin from which it did not recover until he regained consciousness some two miles below.[10]

At the time of the tests, Ertwine was near the mid-point in his thirty-year career, having spent fourteen years in Army aviation, eight of them as a pilot.[11] Enlisting as a private in 1919, he became a staff sergeant in 1924, the same year he was selected to attend flying school. Graduating in 1925, he first flew with the 3rd Attack Group at Kelly Field, Texas, for over a year. This was followed by a tour of duty with the 23rd Bombardment Squadron at Luke Field, Hawaii. There he flew the Martin NBS-1, the DH-4, and the Douglas C-1. A number of his missions were flown in co-operation with entomologists from the University of California who were surveying the island's vegetation and insect life. While Ertwine was in Hawaii, his former instructor, Carl McDaniel, now a captain, reported for duty with the 23rd Bombardment Squadron. Upon learning that Ertwine was an assigned pilot, Captain McDaniel requested that his former student be permitted to check him out on the Martin NBS-1. The squadron commander balked at the idea, but McDaniel assured him that he had taught Ertwine to fly well enough to handle the job.[12]

During his tour of duty in Hawaii Ertwine experienced only one forced landing. The engine of his DH-4 quit shortly after takeoff from an auxiliary field, forcing him to put the airplane down on a nearby beach. Just as the airplane slowed on the landing roll and he was congratulating himself for a very good dead-stick landing, the wheels mired in a soggy spot and flipped the plane onto its back.

Ertwine returned to the United States in 1929 and re-enlisted at March Field near Riverside, California, one of two primary flying training fields in use at the time. But in 1930, primary training at March and Brooks fields was moved to Randolph Field, the newly constructed "West Point of the Air" near San Antonio. March Field then became the home of the 17th Pursuit Group. Wanting to remain at March Field, Ertwine transferred to the 17th, and subsequently became the line chief of the 73rd Pursuit Squadron.

Early in 1934, when the Air Corps was ordered to take over certain airmail routes, Sergeant Ertwine was sent with a Ford C-4A tri-motor transport to Salt Lake City to fly freight and personnel wherever needed. His plane was to also serve as an ambulance airplane, should the need arise. There he found himself again in the company of his former primary instructor and friend, Captain McDaniel. McDaniel had been assigned a Martin B1-12 to fly the mail between Salt Lake City and Cheyenne, Wyoming.

While engaged in these operations, Ertwine made frequent flights to Cheyenne. Several times, the Cheyenne postmaster—apparently unaware that Ertwine was a noncommissioned officer, therefore not authorized to carry the mails—placed it aboard Ertwine's plane with the admonishment to "get it to Salt Lake City, and don't bring it back here or entrain it [put it on the train] along the way." It was an admonition that Ertwine, more than once, found impossible to honor. Twice on the return from Cheyenne, the winds were so strong out of the west that Ertwine was forced to return to Cheyenne or risk running out of gas before arriving at Salt Lake City.[13] By the time the airmail chores were finished in June 1934, Ertwine had become quite happy with flying transports and continued to fly them at every opportunity when he returned to March Field.

In July 1936, Ertwine transferred to the 4th Transport Squadron at Rockwell Air Depot situated at Rockwell Field on North Island near San Diego. Rockwell was one of the air depots to which the new Douglas C-33 transport was assigned, as were an increasing number of enlisted pilots to fly them.

Sergeant Paul Jackson was assigned to the airmail operations in early 1934. He was ordered from Chanute Field to Randolph Field to pick up a Fokker C-14 and fly it to Galveston, Texas. There he took on a load of mechanics and flew them to their new airmail duty station at Chicago. There, Jackson— like Ertwine in Salt Lake City—was assigned a Ford C-4 tri-motor for use as a passenger and freight hauler and, if necessary, as an air ambulance. Jackson remembers it as one of the best airplanes he ever flew, saying:

> It was one of the toughest airplanes ever made. It had three reliable engines, and could get along pretty well on two, or could stretch a glide on one. I always felt that it should have been developed as a bomber in its earlier days because it could carry more weight than any of the bombers in the inventory at that time. Best of all, it had an enclosed cockpit in which you could stay warm, and in that winter of 1933–34, that was a real factor. Many of the pilots flying the mail that winter did so in open cockpits in what seemed to me the worst winter I ever experienced. We lost a few fellows that winter. I considered myself fortunate to fly the Ford that winter. It was quite an experience.[14]

The airmail experience made it clear enough that to become an effective force, the Air Corps must be capable of operating in all kinds of climate and weather. Jackson continues:

> With the coming of spring [1934], came the dust storms. That dust, combined with Chicago smoke, made landing hazardous—sometimes impossible. Some days you couldn't see across the street. On those kind of days, no one flew, not even the airlines.
>
> It took the airmail experience to make us recognize the fact that we needed money, planes, and training to operate properly. After that, things began to pick up for us, otherwise we would have got an even later start for World War II than we did.[15]

Prior to 1934, the Air Corps had stoutly defended its preference for "seat-of-the-pants" flying as the most appropriate for its purposes.[16] This, in spite of a blind flying system developed by two of its own officers, former sergeant—now major—William C. Ocker, and his young colleague, Lt. Carl Crane. Together in 1932 they published their ideas and observations in a book entitled *Blind Flight in Theory and Practice.*[17]

Pan American Airways, aware of the work being done by these two officers, invited them to train its pilots operating in Mexico and Central America where weather caused frequent cancellations. After the pilots became proficient in the technique, cancellation rates fell dramatically. Of course, other airlines quickly recognized the value of the system and adopted it as well. The Air Corps tentatively taught the system at Kelly Field as early as 1930, but the effort became serious only after the airmail experience of 1934.[18]

Following the airmail operations, enlisted pilots were assigned to transport squadrons in growing numbers. Staff Sergeant Maurice M. Beach was one of them. Beach enlisted in the U.S. Army Air Service in January 1923 as a private. By 1925 he was a sergeant and when he qualified for in-grade flight training in 1929, he was a staff sergeant. Beach entered flying school in July of that year and graduated in June 1930. He was the only NCO pilot to be called to extended active duty in his reserve rank of second lieutenant. He was assigned to the 3rd Attack Group at Fort Crockett, Galveston, Texas.

During the Great Depression Beach found himself among those reserve officers who were relieved from active duty late in 1932. However, instead of re-enlisting as a private, he was permitted to revert to his previous grade of staff sergeant and remain on flying status. He was transferred to Hawaii that same year and served with the 19th Pursuit Squadron of the 18th Pursuit Group at Wheeler Field near the center of the main island of Oahu in the Hawaiian Islands. Completing his tour in 1935, Beach transferred to Brooks Field near San Antonio for duty with the 12th Observation Squadron. He flew with that unit until late in 1935 when it was directed to transfer its enlisted pilots to the transport squadrons based at the various Air Corps supply depots. Beach requested Middletown Air Depot at Harrisburg, Pennsylvania, but was transferred instead to Rockwell Field in California.[19]

Technical Sergeant pilot Paul Blair, serving with the 1st Photo Section at Brooks Field, was transferred to the 3rd Transport Squadron at nearby Duncan Field on November 20, 1936.

Born September 4, 1907, in Sparta, Illinois, Blair enlisted on May 3, 1927. He then attended the Army Photographic School at Chanute Field. Following graduation he was assigned to the 1st Photographic Section, then stationed at Dodd Field, San Antonio. His assigned duties included the operation of aerial cameras and the laboratory work connected therewith. At the time the 1st Photo Section was photomapping the entire U.S.-Mexico border between the Pacific Coast and the Gulf of Mexico for the International Boundary Commission. Later the unit photomapped the Colorado River canyons in Arizona and Nevada for use by planners in determining where to place a huge hydroelectric dam. The dam, when completed, became known as both the Hoover and Boulder Dam. While operating the camera during this time, Blair also accumulated considerable experience and flying instruction from generous pilots with whom he flew. By the time he reported for flight training in March 1932, Blair had already learned to fly well.

After graduating in February 1933, he was once again assigned to the 1st Photo Section. This time he flew as both pilot and photographer, photomapping the Rio Grande River from El Paso to Brownsville for the International Water Commission. The work was finished in November 1936 and Blair was transferred to the 3rd Transport Squadron at Duncan Field.[20]

Master sergeants Stewart Smink, Raymond Stockwell, and Bernard Wallace were exceptions to the enlisted pilot drift toward transports. Smink, for example, continued to test air ordnance out of Phillips Field, Maryland,

and—except for a tour of duty in the Philippines during the mid-thirties—remained in that highly specialized work.

Sergeant Raymond Stockwell, the second exception to the drift toward transports, was a large and kind man. Stockwell covered his sensitivity with the skin of a grizzly bear and a voice to match. His eyes pierced right through the cockiness and bravado of new second lieutenants, warning them that, until proven otherwise, he—the sergeant—outranked them all. Addicted to chewing tobacco, his habit of spitting from the open cockpit earned him the nickname "Uncle Chew." Anyone could spot the plane he had just flown by the brown streaks of tobacco juice trailing back along the fuselage toward the tail. It took a "special" kind of courage to ride in the rear cockpit when Uncle Chew was at the controls! However, unlike most of the enlisted pilots, whose specialty was aircraft maintenance, Stockwell's was in aerial photography. An accomplished photographer whose work appeared in the *National Geographic* magazine, it was only logical that he should remain in that specialty after earning his wings.[21] His work was diverse and far-reaching, extending to the remote western regions of North America where he mapped terrain over which the proposed Alaskan-Canadian (ALCAN) highway was one day to pass.

Stockwell always took particular pride in his mustache, boasting that it was "virgin hair" and had never been shaved. In fact, his mustache had been allowed to merge with a growth of beard while on detached service in Alaska. Stockwell was joined in that venture by other pilots of the detachment, including the squadron commander, as it seemed in character with their role as "arctic explorers." The commander of the site from which these pilots were operating confronted the group one day and wanted to know what that was on their faces. "That's hair, sir," Stockwell replied, speaking for the group. "It grows there." Not happy with that response, the commander ordered his adjutant to review the regulation on beards, which he did, reporting back in a few minutes with the disappointing word that they were perfectly legal if kept neatly trimmed. They were.

An army colonel—a nonflier—once asked the commander of the small Alaskan fort to make his most experienced pilot available for a flight. Sergeant Stockwell was summoned to meet the colonel. When Stockwell reported, the colonel said, "A sergeant?" On hearing this, Stockwell turned to the fort commander and said, "Sir, I don't want to take this gentleman." He then dismissed himself, saluted, and walked out.[22]

Naturally skilled, forceful, and charismatic personalities such as "Uncle Chew" do not fade into history; they live on as legends in the minds of those who knew them. Retired colonel Charles W. Johnstone, a brand-new second lieutenant fresh out of flying school at the time, remembers "Uncle Chew" with fondness: "We kids, we Second Lieutenants just loved Uncle Chew. He was our idol. No Second Lieutenant was too small for Uncle Chew to reach down, pick up and help out. We all adored him and followed him around like little puppies."[23]

Johnstone also remembered when Uncle Chew gave him the "chewing out" of his life. Both were based at Fort Lewis, Washington, and on a particular morning had taken off for separate flights to McClellan Field at Sacramento, California. Uncle Chew departed early while Johnstone followed later in an O-46. It was Johnstone's first long, unsupervised, cross-country flight. On board was a West Point officer as a passenger.

Lieutenant Johnstone had no trouble getting to Medford, Oregon, where he refueled, checked the weather—which seemed to present no problems—and took off for McClellan.

> Shortly after climb-out, I found myself on the gauges, so continued climbing. At 20,000 feet, I was all through climbing and still on the gauges. After about thirty minutes of this, I broke into the clear from what seemed a solid wall of clouds and, amazingly, I was still on course. After landing at McClellan, I pulled up in front of operations and was waved to a parking spot by Sgt. Emmett Wheaton who saluted as I shut down and hollered, "Hi Lieutenant, you better not let Uncle Chew see you!" "What's the matter?" I asked. "He's really mad," Wheaton replied. I repeated the question, "What's he angry about?" "Here he comes now, you'll find out!" warned Wheaton.
>
> Sure enough, here came Uncle Chew stomping across the flight-line with a cheek full of tobacco and his mustache just quivering. You could hear his big bull voice booming clear across the ramp, "You goddamned stupid little bastard! What do you think you're doing getting into weather like that with this plane?"
>
> Well, here I am, a second lieutenant still sitting in the cockpit and that master sergeant is down there on the ramp waving his arms and pointing at me, cussing me out and my West Point passenger is sitting wide-eyed in the back seat.
>
> When the tirade was over, the West Pointer and I climbed down from our seats and I introduced Uncle Chew to him. The West Pointer was a small, prim engineer-type and Uncle Chew was a very large walrus of a man. I could see that the West Pointer had no way of understanding what he had just witnessed. While I recognized Uncle Chew's tirade for what it was—an expression of concern for my safety—and was accustomed to

his gruff manner, the West Pointer, not wise to the relationship which existed among pilots in those days, was simply speechless.[24]

Retired colonel Frank N. Graves, then a second lieutenant, also served with Stockwell in 1940–41, and came to know him well.

> Uncle Chew was afraid of no man. He was the best pilot we ever had, but he did not like to fly instruments. In talking with senior officers, he could be insolent—but not enough to make a point of it. To the younger officers, he had a way of saying " 'tenant" which sounded both disdainful and intimidating. When I finally gained his acceptance, I felt like I had really accomplished something. He was promoted to warrant officer in the summer of 1941, and two months later he became a first lieutenant. Stockwell now outranked me and I was calling him " 'tenant."[25]

Master Sergeant Bernard Wallace was the third sergeant pilot to remain unaffected by the drift to transports. He was born in 1901 in Bellefontain, Ohio, and moved to China, Texas, in 1903. Wallace enlisted at Kelly Field in 1919 and became an airplane mechanic at Kelly, where he served with Sgt. Carl B. McDaniel on an aircraft retrieval team until 1923. Wallace spent the next two years in Panama, then in 1926 was selected for flying school, winning his wings in 1927.

Wallace was assigned the task of flying the Cox-Klemin ambulance airplane at Kelly Field until 1930, at which time he was transferred to Hawaii where he flew the "Duck," an amphibian used for sea rescue and ambulance duties. After returning to the United States in 1933, he was assigned to Randolph Field and became a line chief and test pilot, remaining there until the approach of World War II, at which time he was called to active duty as a commissioned officer.[26]

As part of a modest modernization of the Air Corps in 1933, enlisted pilots found themselves being transferred in growing numbers to four regional depots to fly transports. Among those assigned to the 1st Provisional Transport Squadron at Patterson Field were master sergeants Cecil Guile and Sam Davis, S. Sgt. Tom Rafferty, and T. Sgt. Doug Swisher. Others serving at one time or another in the 2nd Provisional Transport Squadron at Middletown Air Depot were S. Sgt. Loren Cornell, T. Sgt. Frank Siebenaler, Pvt. Hamish McLelland, and sergeants Gilbert Layman, Julian M. Joplin, and Harry Coursey. Serving with the 3rd Provisional Transport Squadron at

Duncan Field, Texas, were staff sergeants Tracy Dorsett, Opal Henderson, and John H. Price, M. Sgt. C.P. Smith, and privates John Gebelin, Jr., and L. P. Kleinoeder. Staff sergeants Chet Colby, Paul Blair, Fred O. Tyler, and T. Sgt. Paul Jackson served a little later. It is probable that privates Marvin F. Stalder, Dolf E. Muehleson, and Mell M. Stephenson, Jr., flew as transport pilots with the 4th Provisional Transport Squadron out of Rockwell Field, since they were assigned there from 1933 until commissioned in the Regular Army in July 1935. In 1936, M. Sgt. Boyd Ertwine joined the others at Rockwell Air Depot, as did sergeants Maurice Beach, Art Hanson, Jerome B. McCauley, and John Waugh.[27]

In June and July 1935, the four provisional transport squadrons were redesignated simply "transport squadrons" and remained under the 1st Transport Group. They continued to be manned primarily by enlisted pilots. In May 1937, the 1st Transport Group consolidated with the 10th Observation Group and became the 10th Transport Group. The four squadrons retained their numeric designations and locations; however, the 1st Transport Squadron was divided into two flights, one stationed at Wright Field, Dayton, Ohio, and the other at Patterson Field, Fairfield (now Fairborn), Ohio.[28]

Between the mid- and late thirties, transport operations expanded from intraregional to interregional. When the new twin-engine Douglas C-33 (DC-2) joined the inventory in the late summer of 1936, aerial supply flights took on the character of an international airline with flights to Panama and Alaska. With the activation of the 10th Transport Group, the migration of enlisted pilots accelerated.[29] At the same time, the system grew and its operations became more sophisticated. A few of the enlisted pilots were called to active duty as officers in their reserve grade. Sergeant Paul Blair, serving with the 3rd Transport Squadron at Duncan Field, was called to active duty as a second lieutenant and retained in the same unit. He recalled:

> Among the 20 reserve officers assigned to transport operations at that time were 5 former enlisted pilots, all of whom had been stationed at the air depots prior to going on extended active duty and all of whom were among the first of the enlisted pilots to engage in this activity: Tracy Dorsett, Maurice Beach, Lloyd Sailor, Arthur Hanson, and myself. . . .
>
> We pioneered the transport of air freight both within the continental limits of the U.S. and from the U.S. to Panama at a time when small sodden fields, navigational aids and weather information were of such limited nature as to make our long distance flight operations hazardous.[30]

Blair and Paul Jackson were frequently teamed together on some of those early flights to Panama. Blair recalled that sometimes the entire crew was made up of enlisted men.

> The route was used by Pan American Airways and the only navigational aids available were locator beacons at Vera Cruz, Guatemala City, Managua and San Jose. You'd fly over the beacon, "box" the station tightly to get down through the clouds and into the valley, hoping to avoid the surrounding hills.[31]

Commenting on his flights with Blair, Jackson said:

> Blair was one of my good friends. We flew together on many long flights and I was always very comfortable with his flying. I always knew what he was going to do, and I think he knew pretty much what I was going to do. Paul was a good instrument pilot, navigator, and weatherman. He also had a rare sense of humor.
>
>   Those flights were made in the days when we had a pretty good idea we were eventually going to get into the war in Europe, and young officer pilots were being assigned to us for training in multi-engine and cross-country flying. We all got along well together. The sergeant pilots were pretty knowledgeable, and reasonable. We had the experience, and they needed it. They flew as copilots and took it pretty well. We would train them on repeated flights around the country and to Panama, then turn them loose. I expect that most of those young pilots we trained in transport operations went on to become leaders in the Troop Carrier and Air Transport Commands which were created several years later.[32]

Summarizing those years of expanding transport operations, Blair wrote:

> The monthly flying time of these personnel averaged far above those of other pilots of the Air Corps during that period. Flight operations were conducted in the old Keystone bomber, Bellanca single-engine transport and the first of the Army two-engine Douglas planes. The tonnage carried indicated that these aircraft were operated at near maximum performance.[33]

The late summer of 1937 marked the first full year of operations with the Douglas C-33 aircraft and the eight pilots of the 3rd Transport Squadron had produced some impressive statistics with it. They had flown 5,511 hours during the year, averaging 688 hours per pilot. Sergeant Jackson was "high man" with 785 hours. They had moved over one and one-half million pounds of freight and passengers without so much as a minor accident, despite one forced landing at Austin when a fully loaded plane lost an engine. In fact, not a single life was lost on these operations between 1935 and 1940. This was a highly experienced group of pilots whose individual total flying time by then averaged 3,070 hours.[34]

Almost every flight using the Douglas C-33 transports established a new record of some kind. In January 1938, for instance, S. Sgt. Fred O. Tyler and copilot Lt. J. Will Campbell of the 3rd Transport Squadron set a distance record flying their C-33 over the Denver-to-Fairfield, Ohio, leg of their route, a distance of 1,090 miles.[35]

During that same period, on a similar flight along the same route, Blair and Jackson flew into a situation that could have easily become a tragic newspaper headline. In Jackson's words:

> At the time we were coming out of Denver and there was a gale coming out of the west which was picking up a lot of heavy dust. We were in it and I didn't like that one bit.
>
> We kept climbing until we were on top of it 'cause we didn't want to grind up our engines. We cruised along above the dust for a while, then realized that we were overtaking the dust. Far ahead we could see this well-developed front extending across our course from north to south. While trying to decide which way to go to get around it—go above or below it—the sky began to take on an odd color that is hard to describe and hard to forget.
>
> Then we were confronted by a cloud deck and decided to try climbing over it. It wasn't long before we realized that the deck was coming up faster than we could climb, and we were going be in it momentarily. The nose of the plane had no sooner hit that cloud, when—Bam! The damned airplane had set off a lightnin' bolt which made the cloud appear to blow up. It had also hit the plane just in front of the windshield.
>
> Suddenly it was dark and while we were fumbling around in the cockpit trying to turn the lights on, we could smell the awful odor of burning electrical wiring. Then we hit hail and it sounded like a wagonload of gravel had been dumped on us. It didn't last over three minutes and then we were out of it and in the clear.
>
> Our radios were gone and so were some of our instruments. The noise of the strike had partially deafened us, and as I could not hear the engines, I thought the lightning had burned out our ignition as well, but a check of the tachometers put my mind at ease on that score.
>
> That was a storm I couldn't help turning around and looking back at.

Three hours later, when we got to Dayton, it turned out that the lightning had hit the pitot head [i.e., head of the pitot tube] and burned it like a blow torch. There were holes burned in the wing. Metal was fused at many points in the wings. Holes were burned through spots where fabric covered the movable control surfaces. The radios were ruined and the antennas were burned off.[36]

Blair's version of the same incident:

After leaving Denver for Dayton we climbed to 11,000 feet to top the dust storms blowing in eastern Colorado and western Kansas. Well before getting into the Kansas City vicinity, we began to thread our way between and through the lighter part of numerous thunderstorms. When it got dark, we could no longer see the light spots even though considerable lightning was flickering all around us.

The left side of the windshield was leaking the rain so badly that I spread my leather jacket across my lap and fashioned a little trench to divert the stream of water to the floor. With all the lightning flashing around and knowing water was a good conductor of electricity, I was a little apprehensive I might get a lapfull if we were hit by lightning for that stream of water was about finger-size.

We had just passed over Kansas City and were flying the east leg of that beam outbound when simultaneous with a loud crash in the ear phones, a four- or five-foot tumbleweed red-hot barbed-wire-like lightning bolt appeared on the nose of the airplane only two or three feet ahead of the windshield.

Temporarily blinded, I soon regained my sight and realized we were proceeding okay with about the same amount of turbulence as before, although our radio was now dead. Looking around, I saw Jackson put down his 'chute, pull on his leather jacket, then again grab his 'chute. Then realizing we were okay, he resumed his seat. When I asked what he had planned to do, he answered, "Dammit, it's raining out there!" Apparently if he had to bail out, he was going to protect himself from the elements as best he could.

After a few minutes of heavy hail and more rain, we broke out of the clouds into good weather and made the balance of the flight navigating by pilotage, being particularly observant for other traffic as we could no longer communicate with anyone.

Shortly after the bolt hit us Jackson sniffed a couple of times and asked, "Do you smell that peculiar odor?" I answered, "I think it's burnt wiring and ozone." He said, "It's not all ozone." Then after a short while he asked, "Do you know what I'm going to do as soon as we get in?" I suggested that we both get us a good stiff drink and some late dinner. He said, "That's next, first I'm going to take a shower."

After circling Patterson Field and getting a green light, we landed and found the pitot under the cockpit looked like someone had put a blow torch to it and it had started to melt and drop off. Then we found about four or five inches inboard of the left wing tip a hole in the dural [duralumin, an alloy used in aircraft construction] on the underside of the wing where the lightning had left the plane. I now knew that metal skin provided an easier path for the lightning than that finger-sized stream of water.[37]

Latecomers to transport operations were S. Sgt. Jerome B. McCauley and M. Sgt. Julius Kolb.

McCauley enlisted in the Army in June 1923 at Dallas and was sent to Fort Meade, Maryland. He entered primary flying school at Brooks Field in March 1931 and graduated from advanced flying in February 1932. Stationed at Kelly for the next two years, McCauley flew test hops on aircraft coming out of aero repair. Late in 1934, he was transferred to the 18th Pursuit Group, and assigned to the 75th Service Squadron at Wheeler Field, Hawaii. There he continued to test fly the Group's airplanes—such as Boeing P-12s, Curtiss A3s, and A12s—after periodic inspections or repairs. In addition, he acquired considerable time in the amphibious twin-engine Douglas OA-3, and its more recent, larger counterpart, the Sikorsky Y10A-8.[38] To maintain currency in his combat specialty, which was "attack," McCauley flew with the 26th Attack Squadron, at the time equipped with the Curtiss A-3B.

Master Sergeant Julius Kolb, meanwhile, was performing similar duties at Wheeler Field with the 19th Pursuit Squadron, another squadron assigned to the 18th Pursuit Group.[39] Nearly all of Kolb's military career was centered around pursuit aircraft, both as a mechanic and pilot.

Following his graduation from advanced flying at Kelly in October 1932, Kolb was assigned to the 8th Pursuit Group at Langley Field, Virginia. This was followed by a tour with the 74th Pursuit Squadron in the Panama Canal Zone where he flew P-12s. He was then transferred to Selfridge Field, where he had previously served as a mechanic. While there, he flew the Boeing P-26 "Peashooter" and the Consolidated PB-2 with the 1st Pursuit Group.

In August 1937, Kolb was transferred to the 18th Pursuit Group in Hawaii, where he found himself back in his beloved P-12. Kolb and McCauley occasionally flew together in the amphibians during special air/sea rescue or on transport missions.[40] On one such mission, on February 4, 1938, they took off in the Sikorsky Y10A-8 with twelve mechanics aboard. When airborne, they discovered that only one of the main landing gears would retract. While circling the field, they lowered the retracted gear, but this time the tail wheel failed to extend. They determined that the hydraulic pressure line to the tail wheel had ruptured, leaving no fluid in the system, thus no pressure to keep the gear locked down for landing. There was no spare fluid on board and instructions from huddled heads in the control tower advised them to bail out. Postponing that advice, McCauley and Kolb huddled with the mechanics and decided to crimp off the line to the tail wheel. Then, "passing the bucket," so to speak, they collected enough urine from those aboard to refill the hydraulic tank and build up enough pressure to raise the main gear. The plan worked and they made a safe water landing.[41]

In March 1938, McCauley was transferred to the 4th Transport Squadron at Rockwell Air Depot at San Diego, leaving Kolb as one of the last sergeant pilots remaining in a tactical outfit. Kolb realized that most all other enlisted pilots were now flying with transport outfits and, while he was loathe to leave pursuits, he knew the greater number of his contemporaries seemed quite satisfied with their assignments. In time, Kolb, too, decided to join them and requested a transfer to the 1st Transport Squadron at Fairfield Air Depot near Dayton. The transfer was approved in August 1939.[42]

As it had historically, the presence of enlisted pilots in an organization distorted the command lines for a number of reasons. First, unit commanders were forced to choose between the obvious advantage of placing an experienced enlisted pilot in the left seat of the cockpit, only to have him outranked by even the newest second lieutenant. Second, commanders felt that reserve officers, because of the temporary nature of their assignments, were uneconomical to train for air depot engineering or supply duties. Even as transport pilots, their retention was limited. Enlisted pilots, on the other hand— because of legal constraints—were not vested with sufficient authority to fill those positions. They had usually been promoted as far as they could go, and yet they were performing duties and responsibilities in the air far beyond those normally granted their rank. Commanders felt vulnerable when valuable cargo, lives, and expensive airplanes were flown by enlisted pilots. It was a problem begging for solution.

Confronting the situation, Brig. Gen. George H. Brett ordered a study to be made of a special rating system for transport pilots. On May 12, 1939, the study was forwarded to the chief of the Air Corps, recommending that a grade of Flight Warrant Officer be established and 156 positions for them be allocated among the four squadrons, anticipating the assignment of thirteen planes per squadron. Additionally, such flight warrant officers should become further trained in the various depot functions, in order to use them on a part-time basis when not engaged in transport flight operations. If or when they became disqualified for further flying duties, they would continue in those depot jobs.[43]

General Brett's study came to naught in the fall of 1939, however, when war erupted in Europe and the remaining enlisted pilots were called to active duty as commissioned officers.

It was the right time for the nation to call to active duty those enlisted pilots who had for so long endured the austerity imposed by the Depression. Their knowledge and experience in the area of transport operations were becoming useful in building a transport force that would soon become global—a force that would dwarf anything the world had ever known.

In December 1940, the 10th Transport Group spawned its first generation of five new groups; the 60th, 61st, 62nd, 63rd, and 64th.[44] By that time, most of those who had served as enlisted pilots in the 10th Group were officers and had been assigned to command and staff positions in the expanding transport system. Several individuals would later return and command the parent group.

THE APPROACHING WAR **10** 1939–1941

BY THE TIME GERMANY MARCHED INTO Poland in the fall of 1939 and ignited World War II, most of the enlisted pilots in the U.S. Army Air Corps had been called to active duty in their reserve officer rank. This was one of many responses by the Air Corps to the developing crisis in Europe. Because the Army had trained no new enlisted pilots since 1933, the number remaining in enlisted status continued to decline.

Those numbers had never been large—only thirty were on the rolls in 1930. The number nearly doubled in 1934, and again in 1935 when many former officers joined the enlisted ranks to compete for Regular Army commissions. Nearly fifty of them were commissioned in the Regular Army in the summer of 1935, which dropped the number of enlisted pilots to sixty-three by September of that year. In 1937 it fell to forty-four when sergeants Paul Blair, Tracy Dorsett, Maurice M. Beach, Lloyd Sailor, and Arthur Hanson, to list a few, were ordered to active duty as officers.[1]

Between the world wars the sergeant pilots, like their officer counterparts, seemed to be locked into the same grade forever. The decade between 1929 and 1939 was a particularly spartan one. It was not at all unusual for officers and noncommissioned officers to remain stalled in one grade for a decade or more.

However, as the thirties came to an end, so did the severe austerity under which the Air Corps had been operating. As the need to prepare for war became more obvious, appropriations began to flow; promotions occurred more frequently and some of the enlisted pilots were ordered to extended active duty as reserve officers.

Staff Sergeant Jerome B. McCauley, for instance, was promoted to technical sergeant in December 1939, then to master sergeant in November 1940. He enjoyed his rank as a master sergeant for only one month before he was called to active duty in his reserve grade as a captain and transferred

111

to the 5th Transport Squadron at Patterson Field near Dayton, Ohio.

Master Sergeant C.P. Smith was promoted to warrant officer in March 1940. In January 1941 he was a first lieutenant, and by November, a captain. Master Sergeant Julius Kolb was ordered to active duty as a captain in 1940 and given command of the 4th Transport Squadron at McClellan Field, Sacramento.[2]

Staff Sergeant Maurice Beach was ordered to active duty in 1938 as a first lieutenant and assigned to the Air Force Procurement and Supply Section at Wright Field, Dayton, to take over operations for the growing air transport system. In April 1941 he was given command of the 10th Transport Group, which at that time had fifteen transport aircraft. After the attack on Pearl Harbor, things became hectic for Beach and the 10th Group. General Henry H. "Hap" Arnold ordered one hundred commercial airline pilots holding reserve commissions to active duty and directed them to report to Beach, now a major, at Patterson Field. "The first I knew of this," recalls Beach, "was when they came to my headquarters with telegram orders in their hand asking what was going on."[3]

There followed a quick series of expansions and moves for Beach and his 10th Group. Orders were received to move to Milwaukee, where they utilized the airline pilots in training new crews. Airline DC-3s, including sleeper versions, were commandeered from the airlines, being considered more important for war training duty than airline use. By this time Beach had been promoted to lieutenant colonel; the 10th group had doubled in size, and had become "busier than hell." In August 1942 Beach was given command of the newly activated 53rd Troop Carrier Wing.[4]

As the first generation of early enlisted aviators faded from the scene, the second generation, those from the twenties and thirties, began to move into command and staff positions in the newly created units.[5] Shortly after Pearl Harbor, Julius Kolb, still a captain but now serving as group operations officer for the 62nd Troop Carrier Group, ran into his old flying school classmate and friend, Raymond "Uncle Chew" Stockwell, in Base Operations at McClellan Field. They enjoyed a short visit before each was to take off in different directions.

During their conversation, Captain Kolb learned that Stockwell had been promoted, first to warrant officer, then ordered to active duty as a second lieutenant. A promotion to first lieutenant followed shortly afterward. Stockwell commented to Kolb that he had flown through nasty icing conditions on his flight to McClellan Field, adding, "Never again!" These were prophetic words, for only days later while flying a Beechcraft F-2 on a photomapping mission from Fort Lewis to McClellan Field, Stockwell disappeared in adverse weather. Several months elapsed before the wreckage containing his body was located in the southern Cascade Mountains.[6]

Only twenty-seven enlisted pilots remained on the rolls by early 1939. In September, war erupted in Europe and, as that year ended, so did the era of the second generation of Army enlisted pilots. A handful remained, but that small number was rapidly approaching zero.[7]

Boyd Ertwine was one in that handful. After fourteen years as a master sergeant, he was promoted to warrant officer in February 1942. Two months later, he was called to active duty as a captain. By April 1942, Ertwine was a major, and in July 1942, he became a lieutenant colonel.[8]

Vernon Burge, in the meantime, continued his long career. Just before the stock market crash of 1929, he had returned to the Philippines for a third and final tour of duty. Still a captain, he was assigned to the 4th Composite Group at Nichols Field where he took part in flights to the far reaches of the sprawling group of islands that comprise the Philippines. He also took part in and, in some cases, led aerial surveys of previously uncharted sections of the archipelago. Other flights were designed to establish airway routes.[9]

Upon his return to the United States in September 1932, Burge was assigned to the 7th Bomb Group at March Field. When a detachment of the 7th was later posted to Crissy Field at San Francisco, Burge went with it, remaining there until December 1933. From Crissy Field, he was sent to Maxwell Field, Alabama, to attend the Air Corps Tactical School and, upon graduation, was assigned to Mitchell Field on Long Island.

In September 1936, Burge was ordered to France Field in the Panama Canal Zone and given command of the Panama Air Depot. For flying purposes, he was attached to the 7th Squadron of the 6th Composite Group. In February 1937, he was assigned for flying only to the 25th Bombardment Squadron and later to the 7th Reconnaissance Squadron, 6th Bomb Group. Finally, in October 1937 he was given command of the 16th Air Base Squadron at France Field where he remained until September 1939. He was then ordered to Selfridge Field, Michigan, followed by an assignment to Boston as the Air Officer for the Fourth Army Corps Area.[10]

At this point in Burge's career, few of his old enlisted pilot comrades were still in the service. He knew of only two others from the pre–World War I period: Col. Bill Ocker and Lt. Col. Albert D. Smith. Interestingly, Ocker was approaching retirement in 1940, but he "discovered" an old family Bible in which his "true" birthday was entered. It seems his actual year of birth occurred four years later than the one he had enlisted with forty-one years earlier. Ocker presented this new evidence to Gen. Malin Craig, who directed his adjutant general to accept the document and correct the record. Thus Ocker parlayed his timely discovery into a four-year delay of his retirement.[11]

A. D. Smith, on the other hand, commissioned during the Great War, remained in the Army as an experimental aircraft test pilot until injured in a crash at McCook Field at Dayton in October 1918. He sustained injuries that led to a medical retirement in 1923. In 1930, Smith went to work for the airlines and remained with them until 1940 when the Air Corps called him out of medical retirement to help establish its air transport facilities.[12]

Of the officer pilots whom Burge had been associated with in those early years, Charles de Forest Chandler was now retired, as was his old friend and mentor Frank Lahm. Benjamin Foulois, whom Burge had so faithfully served, was also retired. Burge's flying companion at Corregidor in 1913–14, Herbert Dargue, was now a major general and the only officer pilot of those earlier years still active.

Reflecting on the exodus of his friends and contemporaries, Burge felt a little like "an old shoe," especially in the company of the younger generation of pilots. Believing that his usefulness was waning, Burge requested retirement. It was approved and orders were issued to become effective on January 31, 1942.[13] That pioneer aviator who first flew in April 1912 made his last flight in October 1941, a four-hour, forty-five-minute cross-country flight in an AT-6. Upon landing, he closed his flight log on a career that spanned the first thirty-five years of military aviation—thirty as a pilot—during which 4,667 hours and 55 minutes had been logged.[14]

As Burge awaited his retirement, the Japanese attacked Pearl Harbor. Five days later, Maj. Gen. Herbert Dargue perished in the crash of a transport while enroute to the West Coast with important war plans.[15]

With wars on two continents and the second generation of enlisted pilots being rapidly absorbed into the expanding officer corps, the subject of continuing the enlisted pilot program was resurrected. A detailed study prepared by Capt. A. L. Moore in February 1940 for the chief of the Air Corps recommended that "the present policy based upon existing law pertaining to enlisted pilots be continued in effect." However, the "existing law" contained two seemingly incompatible provisions. First, all aviation students must be flying cadets. Second, in time of peace, not less than 20 percent of the total number of pilots assigned to tactical units would be enlisted men. This meant in effect that the only way to become an enlisted pilot was to complete flying school as a cadet, then enlist in the ranks after graduation, or after release from active duty. Indeed, a number had become enlisted pilots in this manner. Captain Moore's study concluded that this system should continue unchanged, rendering future flight training for enlisted men in grade effectively a dead issue.[16]

The question was re-examined, however, after the Nazis invaded the Netherlands, Belgium, and France in the late spring of 1940. The collapse of those governments and the subsequent German aerial assault on the British Isles gave new urgency to American plans to expedite the creation of a huge air force. In light of this far more ambitious vision, it now appeared that college graduates—or even those with two years of college—would not provide enough candidates to meet these goals. Since the Army and Navy were also competing for these men, tapping the most qualified of its young Regular Army enlisted men began to make increasing sense to Air Corps planners.

While the Air Corps was pondering this proposition, many young, impatient, non-college-educated American men took their aspirations north to Canada, already at war in Europe, and offered themselves to the Royal Canadian Air Force (RCAF). Canada accepted and by the time of the Japanese attack at Pearl Harbor, many were wearing the wings of RCAF pilots, some with commissions, but more as sergeant pilots.

George W. Brandt began his military flying career with the RCAF and recalled how they were treated and trained by the Canadians, and how they fared after transferring to the USAAF. While attending junior college in California in early 1940, Brandt took advantage of a Civilian Pilot Training course and by fall of that year had accumulated forty-one hours in a J-3 Cub, earned a private pilot rating, and became hooked on flying.

Brandt contacted the U.S. Army and Navy about getting into their flying training program, but as the United States was not yet at war, they were not interested. His next recourse was the Clayton Knight Committee from England, which was looking for young Americans with some flying experience to join the Royal Air Force (RAF). Brandt rushed to San Diego where he was interviewed and accepted, pending his parents' approval as he was not yet twenty-one. His parents agreed—in a parental ploy to dampen his zeal—to give their consent if he instead went to Canada and joined the RCAF.

In December 1940, Brandt and two of his buddies went to Vancouver, British Columbia, and found an RCAF recruiting office where they were welcomed with open arms. Just prior to signing the final paper, however, they were informed they must relinquish their U.S. citizenship. They declined, but returned and signed up sixty days later when informed by wire that the rules had changed, allowing them to retain their U.S. citizenship. Brandt and his friends were sent to the RCAF Manning Depot at Brandon, Manitoba, where they joined young men from Canada, New Zealand, Australia, and South Africa.

In Brandon, they found themselves in plain old basic military training similar to that given in the United States, including guard duty, K.P., drill, spit and polish, more drill, and a preponderance of rules and regulations on how to wear the uniform and conduct one's self. It didn't take them long to realize the corporals and warrant officers ran the RCAF.

The discipline and training were excellent, as was the cultural exchange with the fellows from other parts of the world. But as they neared the end of their basic training, the trio began to sweat out their next assignment: the Initial Training School, or ITS. Here they would begin their ground school, which would last for nearly two months. Before leaving basic training, they were promoted to Leading Aircraftsman and had earned the right to wear a white "flasher" in their flight caps, indicating that they had been selected for flight crew training.

Sent to Regina, Saskatchewan, for ITS, Brandt recalled a beautiful city with wonderful friendly people, but with a cold climate, even in May and June. There they found good quarters and an exacting academic layout. "It was there that we received one of our first shockers," Brandt said, recalling a notice on the bulletin board he still remembers:

> As for you Americans who have seen fit to join us as comrades in arms, we really appreciate what you are doing. However, because we want to be sure that you will be able to keep up with the rest of us academically, you will not only attend all the regular day time courses, but also courses each evening from six to nine P.M.

"Much as we resented the extra hours," Brandt admitted in retrospect, they were right. "We Americans needed them to keep up with the rest of the class because our schools were at least two years behind the Canadian schools." Competition was keen and all worked hard in order to be selected for pilot training. Other aircrew positions were fine, these Americans felt, but they had come to Canada to be pilots.

The social life for the Americans was outstanding in the beginning, as they wore their uniform with the USA and the white flasher in their flight cap. But as time passed, treatment by the local girls cooled considerably. "Seems the fellows holding the ground jobs had passed the word that those wearing the white flasher were forced to do so to signify VD," says Brandt. "Mark one down for the ground types."

The longer the class was together the closer their relationships became.

> The older ones looked out for we younger ones. A case in point: Many of we younger ones were not used to the large bottles of strong Canadian beer. So in trying to keep up with the older guys we sometimes passed out at the table. In Canada the Military Police were out there to *help* the military personnel. The older troops would just pin a card on the victim containing his name, rank and serial number, and where he was quartered, then call the M.P.s who would see that he ended up in his bunk back at the base.
>
> One thing that caused us all problems were the Aussies who would not salute a British officer no matter how we tried to convince him [them] that our liberty was at stake.

As the end of Initial Training School neared, the students were all in a cold sweat as to who would be selected for pilot training. Fortunately, the three who left California four months earlier were selected for that training and ordered to Sea Island, near Vancouver, for basic flight training. It was a dream location, and they enjoyed every minute of it. The ground school was intensive, as was the flying, for after all Canada was at war. The Americans no longer needed to put in extra hours studying. However, recognizing the competition among all the trainees, they didn't allow themselves the luxury of idle time.

While flying Canada's Tiger Moth trainer was a new and exciting experience for them, the loss of a third of the class to "washouts" and crashes was an upsetting part of the training. On the up side, however, the social life in Vancouver was enjoyable. In addition, being close to the United States gave them the opportunity to keep tabs on the gals south of the border.

After graduation from basic flight training, Brandt was selected for twin-engine advanced training at Claresholm, Alberta. Advanced training was much different because of the strictly military environment. There was no wasted motion. Most of the instructors had already flown combat overseas. Instruction stressed flying under adverse weather and wartime conditions. For example: "We did lots of night flying, landing with only hooded runway lights which became visible only when on the correct glide slope. We did not have two-way radios," Brandt recalls, "but communicated with the Aldis lamp and CW [continuous wave] radio on which we could receive range stations. For radio nav equipment, we had an ADF [automatic direction finder] indicator."

While they were in advanced training, a group of about thirty British students was put into their class and into their barracks. This immediately led to many fights, as the English kept referring to the Americans, South Africans, Australians, New Zealanders, and Canadians as "colonials." "In turn," said Brandt, "we 'colonials' let them know how we felt about them. It finally got so bad and so bloody that the commandant put the British back a class and moved them to other quarters."

Advanced students were checked out in the Avro Anson aircraft without the benefit of a copilot. Although designed for two, there were not enough pilots to permit two for each aircraft. "It was lonesome flying around by oneself over western Canada," lamented Brandt.

Until early October 1941, little thought had been given to the rank and assignment they would receive upon graduation. As the Americans understood the British system, one-third of the class would be commissioned as pilot officers, and the remainder would be given three stripes and the grade of flying sergeant. They did not know the selection criteria and frankly didn't worry about it. However, about two weeks before graduation, they began taking more interest in their class standing, speculating on who would become officers and go to tea each afternoon, and who would be become the red-hot flying sergeants and win the war.

As it turned out, of the seventeen selected to be pilot officers, only six were in the top 20 percent of the class. In fact, two were next to last and the spot above. It wasn't until the selections were announced that they became aware of *the* overriding factor in the British selection system, and that, of course, was the social position of one's parents. While none of them got too upset about this turn of events, Brandt remembers some of the class asking the sergeant major if they would have to salute these jokers after graduation. His reply was, "You will give a very fine 'Highball,' and under your breath and behind a big smile will say, 'You S.O.B.'"

Brandt recalls with some pride that "the Duke of Windsor and his wife 'Wallie' Simpson presented our wings and stripes at the graduation ceremony which took place at Claresholm on the 7th of November 1941. It was a thrill to be the recipient of a presentation by a former King of England," he adds. (It should be noted that in the British system only pilots were awarded the full wing. All other flying positions wore a half wing.)

Brandt's orders after graduation were a disappointment to him. He had expected to go to war. Instead, he was sent to the flying instructors' school at Trenton, Ontario. But before reporting, he took a furlough to California and married his high school sweetheart.

Although instructing wasn't what he really wanted, Brandt did learn a great deal and enjoyed his new status as a sergeant pilot in the RCAF. While there were enlisted troops of all ranks and grades in the RCAF, the flying sergeants were a different breed and were treated with considerable respect.

Brandt flew both the Avro Anson and the Harvard aircraft, but enjoyed the Harvard most because it was single-engined, and he still had hopes of ending up in fighters. He completed school in January 1942 and was ordered to the Conversion Training Squadron at Rockcliffe Air Station, Ottawa, Ontario. This squadron provided indoctrination and aircraft familiarization training to civilian pilots coming directly into the service. He flew the Harvard primarily, but also got to fly the Fairy Battle and Bolingbrook, recalling:

> As an instructor I was given the same courtesy and respect as the commissioned instructors no matter who my students were. I was provided with quarters and a Bat Man, a personal valet responsible for my welfare and attire; shoes shined, uniform pressed, brass polished, that sort of thing.
>
> Each afternoon at three-thirty, all pilots—officer and sergeant pilots alike—would land and proceed to our quarters, exchange our flying gear for our dress uniform and retire to the club for afternoon tea and discussion.

In May 1942, representatives of the U.S. Army, Navy, and Marines came to Canada with the authority to negotiate transfers for those who were willing. Brandt talked with each of them and opted for the Army Air Forces, whose representative said they needed him as an instructor but could only offer the grade of staff sergeant until he had a total of five hundred hours, after which they promised a commission and an assignment to fighters. He took the Army at its word and agreed to join them.

Soon Brandt was on his way to Maxwell Field, Montgomery, Alabama, where he confronted the biggest mess one could possibly imagine. "Masses of personnel were arriving at Maxwell from all over the country and nobody knew what to do with them. This was a rude awakening after being in such an effective organization as the RCAF. However, I viewed the situation as 'growing pains.'"

Brandt was ordered next to Eglin Field, Florida, for duty as a tow target pilot where he met recently graduated sergeant pilots of Army Air Force flying schools performing the same job. Their morale was at rock bottom, and he soon discovered why:

> The only apparent difference between a staff sergeant pilot and a private was pay. Although we were NCOs, it seemed so in theory only, for in reality we were just another GI. This was another rude awakening.
>
>   We had all been promised some type of promotion and reassignment after we put in a few months as tow target pilots, unfortunately these promises went unfulfilled. Consequently, some of the Sergeant Pilots refused to fly and were reduced to private by the squadron commander. This of course created quite a stir, the upshot of which was that, having been created by Congress, Sergeant Pilots could only be reduced by Congress.

Their rank was restored and once again they flew, but this time with the knowledge that someone was looking into their situation.

> While this was going on a few of us decided to take in a dance at the local Legion hall. While dancing with a young lady, a first lieutenant M.P.-type came over and asked me what I was doing wearing pilot wings. I responded that I was a military pilot and authorized to wear them. He informed me that there was no such thing and had me escorted to the local brig where I spent the night. Two weeks later at a full squadron parade and review that lieutenant was directed to apologize for his ignorance; another example of the Sergeant Pilot situation in 1942.

At the end of 1942, with well over five hundred hours, the sergeant pilots were finally told that they were all to be promoted. Instead of a commission as a second lieutenant, however, they were, according to Brandt, "appointed to some abortion called a Flight Officer, a grade that was neither beast nor fowl, and signified by a little gold bar with a blue mark on it."

They were also advised that because of the hassle they had been through, they could now have their choice of overseas assignments. Brandt opted for the fighter outfit at Harding Field at Baton Rouge, Louisiana. He knew they had P-40s and were slated to receive P-51s.

Even though nobody seemed to know what a flight officer was, the training was excellent. In early 1943, Brandt received orders to the Fighter Replacement Training Center in Casablanca, North Africa, and entered combat training in P-40s. Still, no one seemed to know what a flight officer was.

Just prior to completing fighter training, Brandt was called in by the operations officer and asked about his RCAF multi-engine time. Two days later, he was on his way to the Bomber Training Center at Rabat-Salé, Morocco. There he flew B-17s as copilot until ordered to the 99th Bomb Group at Navarin, North Africa, and assigned to the 384th Bomb Squadron. "The C.O. there asked me what the hell type of insignia I was wearing," recalls Brandt. "I informed him that I was a Flight Officer, and he said, 'Get yourself a gold bar and start wearing it. We'll make it official as soon as possible.'"

Brandt enjoyed his tour with the 99th because he found dedicated people there, doing an exacting job in actual combat. As much as he missed fighters, he was pleased to be with these people. "I started flying combat as a flight officer/co-pilot, drawing 20% rather than 10% overseas pay. This always made for a point of confusion and laughter."

Finally, after twenty-five missions as a copilot, primarily because they were unable to get him promoted any other way, Brandt was given a battlefield promotion to second lieutenant. With rank in hand, he took over as pilot-in-command and flew twenty-five more missions in the B-17, completing his fiftieth on January 29, 1944.[17]

Ironically, at the same time Brandt was enlisting in the RCAF in the winter of 1940–41, the Army Air Corps's enlisted pilot proposal began to pick up momentum. A revised and condensed version was prepared by the office of the chief of the Air Corps and circulated among its various staff agencies.[18] The staff judge advocate suggested that if existing legislation was modified to make an exception of the rule that all flying students must be cadets, the authority to train enlisted men in grade would be created.[19]

On January 25, 1941, the personnel division of the War Department General Staff also circulated a memorandum on the subject with an eye toward creating an additional pilot group within the Air Corps, with career advantages for individuals lacking the educational qualifications required for appointment as flying cadets, in essence, officer candidates. The memorandum recommended that candidates be enlisted men of the Army of the United States already in federal service; unmarried male citizens of the United States between the ages of 18 and 26 years inclusive; high school graduates or equivalent; and of excellent character, sound physique, and excellent health. It carried a final recommendation that the chief of the Air Corps take the necessary steps to begin the training of enlisted men in grade as aviation students on or after July 1, 1941, provided Congress remove the present restriction to this class of training.[20] The maximum age was subsequently lowered to twenty-two, and the high school equivalency option was dropped and replaced by a requirement that candidates be graduates of the top half of their high school class, with at least one and one-half credits in mathematics.[21]

Correspondence moved between Air Corps staff and subordinate commands as preparations were made to accommodate this new "creature." On February 26, 1941, Col. George E. Stratemeyer informed Gen. George Brett that the sergeant pilot study had been approved and was now in the office of the assistant chief of staff, G-1, where legislation was being prepared for its enactment. General Hap Arnold, however, stated the legislation should not be submitted at the moment, as it might jeopardize the cadet pilot legislation that was before Congress. As soon as that legislation was passed, G-1 should promptly submit the sergeant pilot legislation.[22]

On April 5, 1941, the Executive of Plans was informed that General Arnold now desired the proposed legislation authorizing the training of enlisted pilots be submitted to Congress without delay. The Executive of Plans replied that the proposed legislation had been forwarded to the Bureau of the Budget on March 7, 1941, for clearance by that agency, and that action would be taken immediately in accordance with General Arnold's desires.[23]

The legislation, Public Law 99, was passed on June 3, 1941. It contained the requested authority and gave enlisted flying students the title of "Aviation Students." It also contained a provision for life insurance coverage in the amount of ten thousand dollars for each student undergoing training by the U.S. government.[24]

The door was now open. A news statement was released by the War Department Bureau of Public Relations on June 4, designed to notify potential candidates of the new law.[25] An advanced copy of the regulation governing their selection, training, and employment was publicized with such urgency that candidates were applying before the regulation itself was actually received in the field. When the regulation finally did arrive at the various bases, it contained several surprise stipulations to which candidates were required to agree. One was that each graduate be awarded the rating of pilot and warranted as a staff sergeant, regardless of his current grade. Another forbade marriage for three years following graduation.[26] The former called for real sacrifices by those who were already technical or master sergeants, and there were a number of them. The latter forced some to put anticipated wedding plans "on hold."

Qualified enlisted men scrambled to apply and, by August 21, 1941, the first class of 122 Aviation Students reported to the Spartan School of Aeronautics at Muskogee, Oklahoma, for primary flying training. Brayton Flying School at Cuero, Texas, received a like number, and each month thereafter a growing number of aviation students entered primary flying schools at Stamford, Texas; King City, Santa Maria, and Hemet, California; Bush Field and Decatur, Alabama; Bennetsville and Camden, South Carolina, to list just a few.

For ease of administration, cadets and aviation students were usually billeted and messed separately, but their flight and academic training was identical. The airplane in which primary training was conducted varied from school to school. Some were furnished the beautiful bi-winged Boeing (Stearman) PT-13 and PT-17; others used the more sedate Fairchild PT-19 or the sporty little Ryan PT-22.

Cadets and aviation students alike shared the spectrum of emotions generated by such intense training: the excitement of learning to fly; the dread of failure; the intoxication of their first flight with an instructor; the anguish for those who were eliminated, while praying at the same time that they would not be next. They shared the jubilation after landing from their first solo flight and, as they progressed, the apprehension of twenty- and forty-hour check rides. All suffered the tyranny of their upperclassmen. All strove mightily to succeed.

Though younger on average than the cadets, aviation students were, by virtue of their time in service, more familiar with military airplanes. Many were former aircrew members, and of these a number had acquired considerable time actually flying the plane under the tutelage of their pilots. Too, they were not as easily intimidated by rank. In fact, while in primary flying school, higher rank was sometimes intimidated by them, as there were generally enough NCOs of the top three grades in each class of aviation students to "interpret" Army regulations or school policy to suit their own purposes. There were also enough "guard house lawyers" among them to coax the flying school staff back into line if they felt the staff was exceeding its authority. Also by virtue of their prior experience, aviation students performed their military drill with seasoned sureness. The cadets, on the other hand—fresh from civilian life—were as ragged as any recruits, at first.

After completion of primary flying training, cadets and aviation students alike were sent to basic flying schools in Alabama, California, Georgia, Oklahoma, and Texas. There they learned additional flying skills such as formation and instrument flying, cross-country navigation, and night flying in the Vultee BT-13, a larger, more complex airplane than their previous trainers.

Upon completion of basic flying training, the young students were sent to advanced flying schools where they were introduced to the combat aspects of flying: gunnery and bombing, tactical maneuvers, high-altitude flying, cross-country and more advanced instrument flying. Some schools specialized in single-engine training, using the North American AT-6, or its predecessor, the BC-1. Schools specializing in twin-engine training used such aircraft as the Beechcraft AT-7 and AT-11, the Cessna AT-8 and Curtiss AT-9. Years later, former students who flew the AT-9 would still hyperventilate when they talked about that plane because of its steep descent when the engine power was cut—or failed.

What was it like to be an aviation student, an enlisted man in training to become a sergeant pilot? For one thing, there was an almost uncontainable sense of joy. The odds against being there at all were staggering. For every one selected for primary flight training, three had been rejected. By the time the primary phase was completed, nearly half had been eliminated. Those lucky enough to go on to the basic and advanced phases were acutely aware of their great good fortune.

Inevitably, throughout each phase of training, some among the school staff seemed hostile to the idea of training enlisted men to become pilots and took few pains to hide their feelings. Most, however, made the aviation students feel quite welcome. Most heartwarming of all was the way the ground crews championed and pampered the aviation students—embarrassingly so at times—yet the aviation students loved it. An unspoken "conspiracy" existed between aviation students and ground crews, the latter forming a kind of "cheering section," who showed their support by thoughtful little gestures.

For example, seat and back cushions used to pad student pilots comfortably in their cockpits seemed always to be in short supply. However, the ground crew never failed to pull these cushions out of thin air for aviation students, especially for the shorter ones. Crew chiefs, mechanics, radio specialists, and armorers always gathered in clusters to watch and gave a "thumbs up" when aviation students taxied out for takeoff. When returning to the parking ramp after a flight, especially on very hot days, students found a member of the ground crew was usually waiting with a frosty bottle of Coca-Cola. With a calloused hand—knuckles barked and bloody—he would offer it up to the sweat-soaked enlisted student pilot. Aviation students returned these kindnesses by trying not to abuse or break their planes. Ground crews knew enlisted men could fly and were determined to help them prove it to the rest of the world. The aviation students were determined not to let them down.

Even as their flight training began, however, confusion persisted concerning the future use of this new generation of sergeant pilots.[27] To forestall more uncertainty, the Office of the Chief of the Air Corps in Washington, D.C., sent a teletype message dated August 6 to its division chief directing that plans for their utilization be prepared and submitted. On August 27, 1941, General Stratemeyer, Chief of the Army Air Corps Training and Operations Division, in turn, asked for recommendations from various subordinate commanders.[28]

Lieutenant Colonel F. S. Borum, commander of the newly activated 50th Transport Wing responded, declaring he could use 351 sergeant pilots in his wing. If he could get a sufficient number to fly all the transport trips, this would allow him to make thirty officers available for transfer to other tactical organizations.[29]

But Col. Robert Olds, commanding officer of the Air Corps Ferrying Command (ACFC), responded differently and on September 8 protested that enlisted pilots would not fit into his organization now operating successfully under the control of the ACFC. Olds believed that the training received by combat pilots while on duty in the ACFC fitted them into any combat organization designated for overseas service without further training. Enlisted pilots, on the other hand, "cannot be used successfully on long- or medium-range airplanes as airplane commander (First Pilots), therefore, such training as they might receive in this organization would be at the expense of the type of pilots needed for this class of work." Olds added, "It is urgently recommended, in view of the mandatory requirement that the Air Corps use enlisted pilots against the judgment of practically every experienced pilot in the Air Corps, that plans for the employment of enlisted pilots be confined exclusively to pursuit squadrons of the various interceptor commands where their operations as wing men under immediate supervision of officer pilots can be scrupulously supervised." His reply ended with a parting shot, "It is re-iterated there is no place in this organization for enlisted pilots."[30]

General Stratemeyer countered immediately stating that the Training and Operations Division did not concur with the views expressed by Colonel Olds. Scolding Olds somewhat, and listing counterarguments, General Stratemeyer "recommended" the Ferry Command be required to accept enlisted pilots up to at least 50 percent of its total pilot strength.[31]

General Muir S. Fairchild, executive in the Office of the Chief of the Air Corps, intervened, adding his own comments to the routing and record sheet before it was returned to Colonel Olds. Taking a reasoned approach, General Fairchild pointed out how enlisted pilots might be effectively utilized in the

Ferry Command, suggesting a number of tasks they could perform, including ferrying single-engine planes. He then asked Colonel Olds to indicate what percentage of enlisted pilots he might employ in his organization under the conditions likely to prevail at the time of their graduation from flying school.[32]

Responding on September 27, Colonel Olds's reply was short and to the point:

> 1. From the existing production schedule of aircraft, both domestic and foreign, it has been found that of the airplanes to be manufactured from October 1, 1941 to July 1, 1942, that approximately 31% of the pilots to be used will be used on single engine combat and trainer-type airplanes.[33]

Final word on the matter came from the Office of General Stratemeyer. Dated October 1, 1941, it said:

> The ACFC estimates that 500 enlisted pilots can be utilized by that organization beginning early in 1942 with the possibility of an increase after December, 1942 depending upon the scope of the duties assigned.[34]

By this means, the Army had finally tapped into a pool of fresh and eager pilots. While they were younger and less formally educated than their cadet counterparts, they proved to be rapid learners. Their prior military experience, coupled with a strong desire to fly, offset any educational limitations. Three classes were in flight training by December, 1, 1941. A fourth was preparing to enter when the Japanese struck at Pearl Harbor, making it a whole new ballgame.

At that time, most of the second-generation sergeant pilots, those of the twenties and thirties, were assuming the mantle of leadership in the ever-expanding Air Transport System. In fact, four of them subsequently returned to command the 10th Transport Group, the organization in which each had flown as an enlisted pilot: Maurice Beach, a captain at the time, commanded from April 1 through August 1, 1942; Maj. Loren Cornell from August 1 to 30, 1942; Maj. Douglas M. Swisher from August 30 to October 25, 1942; and Lt. Col. Boyd Ertwine from October 25, 1942, until January 28, 1943.

In February and March 1942, a second generation of transport groups was created when the 89th, 313th, 314th, 315th, 316th, and 317th Transport Groups were activated. All transport groups were redesignated as troop carriers in July 1942.[35]

Former private, first class Hamish McLelland, by then a captain, assumed command of the 315th. Former staff sergeant Jerome B. McCauley, also a captain, took command of the 316th.[36] These and the other former enlisted pilots—products of the period between the wars—had met every challenge of the Great Depression. They had grown with each new responsibility. Now they faced the greatest challenge of all: to lead a new generation of pilots, including new sergeant pilots, into a war of unprecedented magnitude.

THE SERGEANT
PILOTS JOIN THE BATTLES

11

"Those are the youngest pilots I've ever seen," observed the personnel clerk as he processed the new pilots into the field. "They don't look old enough to be officers."
    "They're not," volunteered another. "They're sergeants."
    "That's even worse," concluded the first.

So went the barbs in mid-March 1942 as fifty-four new sergeant pilots from Kelly Field and thirty-nine from Ellington Field, Houston, reported to Dale Mabry Field near Tallahassee, Florida, for transition training in P-39s. They were the youngest ever trained by the Army and wore their new wings and stripes with obvious pride. But the cool reception from the personnel of Mabry Field on their arrival simply intensified an already desperate situation.[1]

The current crop of pilots being checked out in the P-39 was a class of Chinese pilots nearing the end of their training in the United States. Unfortunately, they were wrecking the planes faster than Mabry Field could repair or replace them. Mabry's mission was in serious jeopardy.[2] Consequently, training for the sergeant pilots was put on hold. Visiting brass—some say Gen. Henry "Hap" Arnold—learned of the sergeants' plight and directed they be transferred immediately to a unit that could utilize them. Orders were issued assigning all of the sergeant pilots to the 82nd Pursuit Group at Harding Field, Baton Rouge, Louisiana.

Upon their arrival at Harding Field in late April 1942, the sergeant pilots discovered that the 82nd had moved to a remote location in the desert of southern California.[3] A few days later, they located the elusive group settling in at Muroc Dry Lake in the Mojave Desert. After reporting, the sergeants were promptly divided among the three squadrons of the Group—the 95th, 96th, and 97th. After being given the P-38 technical order manual to study, they were required to take a cockpit blindfold test. They were then shown how to start the engines, before being turned loose over the California desert to get acquainted with the hot new fighter.[4]

Colonel Robert E. Kirtley, then a captain and commander of the 95th, recalled:

> We knew they were coming, and we knew they would be different. We were happy to discover, when they arrived, that these guys took up flying to get into action, not to get out of it. Many were NCOs before going to flying school. Some had even agreed to a reduction from a higher NCO grade upon graduation to qualify for the program. They were there for the love of flying. Their crew chiefs and ground crew came to worship the ground they walked on.[5]

According to Jess Yaryan, one of the sergeant pilots of that class, things happened quickly after the transition to P-38s began:

> Staff sergeant [Lawrence] Larry Liebers experienced an overheated engine while flying over the Mojave Desert one night. He shut it down, feathered the propeller, and continued flying. Then the other engine overheated, so he feathered that one, too, and glided down through the dark night to a dead-stick, wheels-up landing in the desert. Liebers was located the next morning and a crew was sent with a vehicle to retrieve him. When the crew arrived, they found Larry writing a note with his finger in the dust which had settled on top of the wing. The note read, "This airplane is no damned good."

Yaryan continued:

> Staff Sergeant Arthur Knack lost an engine after takeoff, just as the wheels were coming up. He put the P-38 right back on the ground where it skidded to a stop on its belly, leaving a wake of dust. When the plane came to rest, it was on fire. Knack bolted out of the cockpit, leaped off the nose and ran like hell . . . straight ahead. It was the only clear route out of the inferno. He did not realize his mistake until 50-caliber ammo began ricocheting all around him as it cooked off. He wasn't hit, but he was upset. When rescue arrived, he shouted, "That's the last time I fly one of those sons o' bitches. It tried to kill me in the air and it tried to kill me on the ground!"[6]

While there was some humor attached to those incidents, others were tragic. Staff Sergeant Rudolph C. Dear perished on May 6, 1942, when he tried to bail out of his P-38 during a high-speed dive from which he was unable to pull out.

Staff Sergeants Bill Rath and Victor Thacker died when they collided during a formation flight over Santa Ana, California. Staff Sergeant Wayne Winks was killed while attempting a single-engine landing at Glendale, California, and S. Sgt. Eugene W. Babb disappeared without a trace from a flight of four P-38s that were patrolling for enemy submarines off the California coast. In his book *The Only Way Home,* Robert Murray, then a staff sergeant pilot leading the flight, described the event:

> After sighting what appeared to be a surface vessel, I signaled the flight to "echelon right" and looked back to see all aircraft in position. I started a routine descent to make certain that the merchantman below was indeed what he appeared to be.
>
> Immediately after passing the vessel and receiving the proper identification signal I looked aft of my right wing to count my "birds." One was missing. Believing him to be simply out of formation I called for him to "tuck it in." No answer. I called again and again; still no answer. I disbursed the remainder of the flight to look for the missing P-38.
>
> We saw nothing.
>
> I called for an "in the clear" frequency to communicate with the ship, which informed me that all four aircraft were in plain sight when we started our descent. Suddenly there were only three. We looked for splash marks on the ocean. Nothing. The freighter after searching reported sighting nothing. I called my base to send out a flight of search aircraft. They arrived on the scene within 25 minutes and after searching found nothing. We looked everywhere. No sign. No signal. Nothing.
>
> Eugene W. Babb, age 22, of Columbia, South Carolina, and his P-38 had vanished without a trace from the face of the earth forever, in full view of his fellow pilots and the deck crew of the ship at sea.
>
> And no one saw him disappear. We only saw that he was not there.[7]

On March 21, 1942, just days after that first class of sergeant pilots had graduated, Brig. Gen. Muir S. Fairchild, Director of Military Requirements, routed a note to Col. Hoyt S. Vandenberg, Assistant Chief Air Staff for Training, stating:

> 1. It is the understanding that enlisted pilots will make up practically the entire pilot strength of the units to which they are to be assigned. The graduates of the present class, March 16th from the Advanced Flying School, have all been assigned to the 79th Pursuit Group, Talla-

hassee, Florida . . . As of February 25, 1942 there were 2,299 enlisted
men undergoing pilot training.

2. It is requested that a determination be made of the units to be filled
with enlisted pilots exclusively in order that the proper proportion of
enlisted pilots goes to each type of Advanced Flying School.[8]

Vandenberg, probably aware of pending legislation designed to convert all
sergeant pilots to flight officers, responded on March 28, 1942:

1. This Division has no knowledge of the proposal to assign entire pilot
strength of a unit as enlisted pilots. It was our understanding that General
Arnold had directed that no additional enlisted men be trained as pilots,
navigators, or bombardiers.

2. Request the latest decisions on the status of enlisted pilots.[9]

A telephone conversation intervened during which the sergeant pilot program
and its effect on the various commands was explained. Vandenberg's final
response on April 6, 1942, stated:

1. Pending final action on the Pilot Training Program which deals with
the number of enlisted pilots to be graduated each class, this Division
is of the opinion that enlisted pilots should be assigned to the following units:
     1. Pursuit Groups
     2. Light Bomb Groups
     3. Transport Groups
     4. Depot Groups[10]

P-38 transition training was finished on May 22, 1942, and the 82nd Pursuit
Group was redesignated the 82nd Fighter Group. Its three squadrons moved
to airports in the Los Angeles area. Mines Field (now Los Angeles International Airport) became the new home of the 95th Fighter Squadron. The
96th Squadron moved to Glendale and the 97th went to Long Beach.[11] From
those fields, the pilots took over the aerial defense of Los Angeles while
continuing to sharpen their combat skills.[12]

In retrospect, the Group's mission to defend Los Angeles may seem an
overreaction, but it must be remembered that this was only five months after

the Japanese attack on Pearl Harbor. Wake Island had been lost on Christmas Day 1941. The Philippines had fallen only two weeks before the 82nd moved to Los Angeles. Further, the battle of the Coral Sea had just been fought to a draw. Closer to home, a Japanese submarine had lobbed shells ashore in suburban Santa Barbara. Invasion jitters ran high and paranoia prevailed on the Pacific coast. The only good news was Doolittle's April 18 raid on Japan.

Despite the fatalities suffered by the Group, these were halcyon days for its pilots. Their pilot wings were still shiny; their airplanes were hot—and all of Los Angeles was their playground. Remembered Yaryan, "You couldn't pay for a drink in Los Angeles."[13]

By September 1942, the 82nd Fighter Group had finished its combat training and was alerted for movement overseas. The Group was then split up; about half of the pilots departed with the group while the other half remained behind to cadre new units and train their new pilots in the P-38. At the same time nearly all of them were promoted to second lieutenant. Yaryan later went to Europe with the 20th Fighter Group, while Robert Haynes Murray would later join classmate Marshall Hyde flying P-38s with the 54th Fighter Squadron in the Aleutians campaign. Reflecting on his sergeant pilots at that time, Colonel Kirtley says, "Seventy-five percent of them were good enough to take to war. Of those, twenty-five percent were outstanding!"[14]

Just how outstanding? Of the seventeen former sergeant pilots who became aces during World War II, ten came from this first class of Kelly and Ellington Field graduates. William J. Sloan, the top-scoring ace in the Mediterranean theater was credited with twelve; Claude Kinsey, Lawrence Liebers, and Sam Wicker with seven; Bill Schildt, Herman Visscher, and Charles Zubarik with six; Claude Ford, Wayne Jorda, and Gerald Rounds with five. That's better than one ace in every ten graduates! During World War II, 130 enemy airplanes were destroyed by former sergeant pilot graduates of that first class.[15]

Just before the 82nd Fighter Group was alerted for movement overseas, it was directed to send eight of its P-38 pilots, crew chiefs, and armorers to Hamilton Field for transportation by air to New Caledonia in the South Pacific. Staff sergeants Wilbert L. Arthur, Ray W. Bezner, William P. Irwin, Nathan J. Kingsley, James E. Obermiller, Theodore C. Pippin, Jr., Grant L. Reagh, and Eugene D. Woods were selected for that assignment.[16] When they arrived at Hamilton Field, one of the sergeant pilots, James Obermiller, had received a promotion to second lieutenant. The remaining seven, for some unknown reason, had not.

The pilots and their crews were flown by C-87 (the cargo version of the Consolidated B-24) to Tontouta Air Base, New Caledonia. There, six of them—Bezner, Kingsley, Obermiller, Irwin, Reagh, and Woods—were assigned to the 67th Fighter Squadron of the 347th Fighter Group. While awaiting the arrival of their P-38s via cargo ship, they checked out in Bell P-39s and P-400s, an export version of the P-39. Obermiller describes the checkout:

> We were first assigned to the 67th Fighter Squadron and checked out in P-39s and P-400. The 67th, of course, was already active in Guadalcanal and the P-39 had been relegated to the category of a dive-bombing/strafing machine, thus we were to be replacement dive-bomber pilots. This was the situation when Bill Irwin was killed. [Irwin spun out of a turn toward the ground target on a gunnery training exercise.] This was a little "sticky" when you were doing the 37mm-cannon thing. First you reached down under the seat, grabbed the "T"-handle charging cable, extended it out in front and over your shoulder. If you were unfortunate enough to let the handle slip, it flailed about the cockpit, while returning to its nest. Then it was fun! Press the firing button and the cockpit was covered with hydraulic fluid. Now you're maybe one hundred yards from the target and trying for the pull-out. It is a wonder that we lived to see the P-38s uncrated at Noumea.[17]

When the ship carrying the crated P-38s finally arrived, the anxious pilots, crew chiefs, and armorers went to work. They unloaded, uncrated, reassembled, and flew the fighters off the nine-hundred-foot strip at Noumea to Tontouta Air Base where both men and aircraft were prepared for combat. When the task was finished, they checked out ten veteran pilots of the 67th Squadron who had been involved in earlier fighting at Guadalcanal.

One was Capt. Dale D. ("D.D." or "Doc") Brannon. It was Doc Brannon who was to lead the P-38s to Henderson Field on Guadalcanal where the battle for that island was still raging. Staff Sergeant Nathan J. Kingsley remembered:

> We were flying behind Captain Brannon in a two-stage flight to Guadalcanal. A B-25 with a navigator aboard was acting as "mother hen" but chose an altitude with a lot of clouds. I recall nervously trying to decide

whether to throttle back, throttle ahead, slide-in, slide out, up or down each time we encountered the clouds.

As we neared Guadalcanal, the B-25 radioed us: "Sorry, fellows. I'm going to have to turn back. Guadalcanal is under attack and I don't dare risk this aircraft against the Japs." So, leaving us, he said, "Keep straight on, men. You're right on track."

I can recall how tense a moment it was when we spotted Guadalcanal. Our own ships were in the harbor, and they briefly fired at us. Captain Brannon circled "Tojo's Ice House"—a Japanese pagoda on a small rise north of the runway which was being used for Henderson Field operations—to see which flag was flying. Spotting the American flag, he knew it was safe to land. He cautioned us, however, that as we crossed the river on the final approach, there was a Japanese gunner with a machine gun. He suggested that we slip the aircraft so the gunner would lead us at the wrong angle. All of us landed safely.[18]

Obermiller remembered landing at "Fighter One Strip," just south-southeast of Henderson Field.

Landing there was something to remember. That "mudhole" had to be the shortest strip I ever saw. I missed the first approach, made the second one, and taxied off. When I got out of the airplane there were four or five marines waiting with tears in their eyes—absolutely confident that the daily bomber attacks would now cease. The bombers did not come back the next day![19]

The new sergeant pilots quickly discovered that there were more pilots on Guadalcanal than there were planes. Kingsley recalled:

From then on we had our choice. Every time the coast watchers warned us that Jap Zeroes were coming down from Bougainville, we had our choice of Navy F-4Fs, Army P-39s or P-38s. As I recall, it seemed to me that the first man to an airplane was the guy that got to fly it.[20]

The first mission in which the sergeant pilots took part was on November 18, 1942, when the squadron escorted B-17s for a raid on Kahili Field on the island of Bougainville. Sergeant Grant Reagh destroyed a Japanese bi-winged float plane over Tonalei Harbor, Lt. James Obermiller shot down another over Kahili, but Sgt. Eugene Woods was lost in action.

Meanwhile, back in Florida, Dale Mabry Field began receiving sergeant pilots from later classes for transition into fighters. By this time, airplanes and instructors were readily available and training commenced at once. Some of the airfields to which they flew during the cross-country phase of their training had apparently never heard of sergeant pilots. Craig Field, near Selma, Alabama, had its first experience with them in September 1942 when three P-39s appeared overhead, peeled off smartly, and landed in trail. They followed the alert vehicle to the parking ramp and shut down their engines. There was nothing unusual about that; transient aircraft routinely landed here for fuel and service. However, the three became the focus of inordinate attention when they dismounted from their planes and headed for operations. Onlookers discovered that they were all staff sergeants. On filing their return flight plan, the base operations officer, alerted to this strange trio of pilots, studied their flight plan warily. With some hesitation, he approved it. Doubts must have lingered, however, for as they taxied toward the runway the airdrome officer intercepted them in his jeep. Waving wildly, he motioned them to a stop. Climbing onto the leader's wing, he shouted into the open side window with all the authority he could muster: "Enlisted men are not authorized to taxi aircraft on this field!"

"Well, then, Lieutenant," responded the flight leader, "you better get three officers out here right away to taxi them for us 'cause our commander gets ugly with people who make us late, and in exactly two minutes we are taking off for Mabry Field."

As the absurdity of the situation dawned on the airdrome officer he shrugged his shoulders, jumped from the wing, and waved them on.

By the fall of 1942, twenty-five-hundred sergeant pilots from eight classes—42-C through 42-J—had been produced. They were, as Colonel Vandenberg suggested, assigned to pursuit, bomber, and transport groups, and many subsequently fought in combat theaters around the globe. Personnel from old units were divided into cadres and became the nucleus for new groups, which were then manned with officer and sergeant pilots from those classes. While all of Class 42-C went to fighters, most of Class 42-D was retained by the Air Training Command to fly student bombardiers, navigators, and aerial gunners aloft for combat training. A few of that class later found a way to transfer into fighter units.

Nearly all of classes 42-E and 42-F, and one hundred new sergeant pilots of Class 42-G, were used to bring various transport groups up to full strength. Another hundred from Class 42-G were assigned to tactical reconnaissance and photomapping units being formed at Peterson Field, Colorado Springs, Colorado. Some of these were subsequently reassigned to medium bomb groups bound for combat theaters. One hundred and forty-seven others were assigned to the Air Transport Command. Thirteen were assigned to tow target duties at Langley and Hunter fields and sixteen were assigned to the 334th Bomb Group at Greenville, South Carolina.[21]

Classes 42-H, 42-I, and 42-J were assigned to fighter, bomber, troop carrier, and anti-sub units where needed. Five sergeant pilots of Class 42-H, and one who transferred from the Royal Canadian Air Force, became basic flying instructors at Minter Field, near Bakersfield, California.

The sergeant pilot program contained several ironies, one of which required all graduates to be warranted as staff sergeants. While this was a promotion for those of lower rank, it changed nothing for those who already held the rank. However, for those who already held the grade of technical or master sergeant, it meant a reduction. This inequity persisted until midway through the program, when, on June 26, 1942, Col. John H. McCormick—acting Assistant Chief of Air Staff, A-1—wrote a memo to G-1 on the subject. Paragraph 5 of the memo stated the crux of the dilemma:

> 5. . . . It is possible for a technical sergeant or a master sergeant to train in grade, but impossible for him to hold such a grade after he has been rated airplane pilot and has thus enhanced his potential value to the Army. As already noted, glider pilots retain the grades held during training. This latter provision was made in order to encourage enlisted men to apply for glider pilot training. It would appear wise to offer similar encouragement to enlisted men of the first two grades to qualify as airplane pilots, at least it would appear unwise to discourage them.[22]

The memo contained a recommendation to correct the problem and must have had the desired effect since subsequent technical and master sergeant graduates retained their rank.

Another irony was the confusion created when sergeant pilots reported to their initially assigned bases following graduation. Traditionally, pilots had always been officers and had followed an established protocol when reporting. In pre–World War II days, officers and noncommissioned officers knew and understood their "place" in the scheme of things. Customs of the service and the rules of rank and precedence governed their relationship. But when staff sergeant pilots began reporting to units— especially if they constituted the majority of pilots—it created some pretty bizarre situations.

Such was the case when S. Sgt. Bob Van Ausdell and his classmates, fresh out of advanced flying school, reported to Albuquerque Army Air Base for their first operational assignment. The military police picked them up for wearing pilot wings and charged them with impersonating officers. They were held until the provost marshall was convinced their orders were legitimate. Upon release, the provost marshall remarked, "You mean to tell me you fly airplanes just like a second lieutenant?" "No sir!" replied Van Ausdell. "We fly them better."[23]

It took a while for the traditional customs of the service to adjust to the novelty of so many sergeants flying airplanes. The first sergeant of many units saw their arrival as a windfall for the duty roster. They would be a big help in supervising squadron details. But squadron commanders could not afford the inevitable conflict between the roster and the flying schedule.

First sergeants quickly learned the sole duty of sergeant pilots was to fly and sergeant pilots quickly took advantage of the situation. Sergeant William Cather recalled:

> We lived in barracks with the other members of the combat crew but our salvation was that "pair of silver wings." When any detail except flying came up, we could always renege by saying, "I can't—I'm a pilot." Any officer duties were handled just the reverse with: "I can't—I'm an enlisted man."[24]

Likewise, commanders had to wrestle with the question of on what basis first pilot assignments should be made: rank or skill? Remembering his earlier days as a sergeant pilot, retired colonel Luther W. "Wes" Feagin said:

> In September 1942, about ten of us reported to Page Field, Ft. Myers, Florida. We were greeted with the expected, "What's an enlisted man doing wearing pilots wings?" and then placed on the usual rosters: guard duty, latrine orderly and K.P. After about a week of the "idiot" treatment we were called into a meeting with Lt. Col. Joshua T. Winstead, our group commander and two West Point Majors. They informed us that since we had received the same training as the cadets, we would, except for use of the Officer's Club, have the same privileges as the newly assigned officers, including the opportunity to qualify as First Pilot in the B-26.[25]

Bill Cather, remembering his own thoughts at the time, added:

> We never doubted our ability to fly as good as—or better than Air Cadets, but to be given the opportunity to prove it was a stroke of luck.[26]

Though proud of their status, sergeant pilots remained at a disadvantage in comparison with their officer counterparts when selections were made for

1. Private Vernon L. Burge at the time he, together with a half-dozen other recruits, volunteered for "balloon duty" with the newly created Signal Corps Aeronautical Division in August 1907. (Courtesy of Marjorie Burge Waters)

2. Joining Cpl. Edward Ward, the first enlisted man to serve with the Aeronautical Division, are *(back row, left to right)* Pfc. Vernon L. Burge, Pfc. Charles De Kim, Pvt. Eldred O. Eldred; *(middle row)* Pvt. Stewart K. Rosenberger, Ward, Pvt. Cecil Coile, Pvt. William E. McConnell. Sitting on edge of the gondola are Pvt. John Crotty *(left)* and Pvt. Benjamin Schmidt. The mascot remains unidentified. (Courtesy of Marjorie Burge Waters)

3. Novice balloon handlers of the Aeronautical Division prepare one of their charges for ascension. (Courtesy of Marjorie Burge Waters)

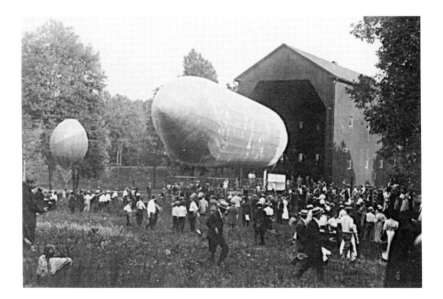

4. The first powered aeronautical machine purchased by the U.S. Army was not the Wright Brothers aeroplane, but the balloon dirigible pictured here emerging from its shed at Ft. Myer, Virginia. Burge became a "mechanician" for the Glenn Curtiss engine that powered the craft. (USAF photo)

5. Because no funds had been appropriated for the purchase of replacement aeroplanes, Robert F. Collier of magazine fame loaned his own Type B Wright plane to the U.S. Army. Corporal Burge *(center foreground)* and other ground crew members move the plane into takeoff position. (Courtesy of Marjorie Burge Waters)

6. Vernon Burge sits in the driver's seat of the Wright Aeroplane that he accompanied to the Philippines and assembled at Fort McKinley in February 1912. (Courtesy of Marjorie Burge Waters)

7. Lieutenant Herbert Dargue and Sergeant Burge flew this Burgess-Wright Hydroaeroplane (Signal Corps No. 17) for nearly two years from its base on Corregidor in the Philippines. (Courtesy of Robert Casari)

8. Sergeant William Ocker *(fourth from left),* standing with other student aviators in front of the Curtiss pusher belonging to the Curtiss Flying School at North Island, San Diego. By moonlighting his trade as an airplane mechanic, Ocker earned flying lessons with the Curtiss School. (USAF Museum photo)

FÉDÉRATION AÉRONAUTIQUE
INTERNATIONALE
—
AERO CLUB OF AMERICA
—
No. 293

The above-named Club, recognized
by the Fédération Aéronautique
Internationale, as the governing
authority for the United States of
America, certifies that

William Charles Ocker

born 18th day of *June* 1880
has fulfilled all the conditions required
by the Fédération Aéronautique
Internationale, for an aviator pilot,
and is brevetted as such.

Dated *April 29th* 1914

Alan R. Hawley
President.

O. C. Gage
Acting Secretary.

Signature of pilot:

William C. Ocker

9. Federation Aeronautique Internationale Aviator Certificate No. 293, awarded to Sgt. William C. Ocker. (USAF Museum photo)

10. Corporal Ira O. Biffle standing in front of the Martin T.T. in which he logged many hours while at the Signal Corps Aviation School at North Island. (USAF Museum photo)

11. Lined up for inspection are five enlisted pilots serving with the Signal Corps Aviation School at North Island, San Diego, in 1916. *Left to right,* sergeants William C. Ocker, Felix Steinle, Albert Smith, James Krull, and Cpl. Ira O. Biffle. (USAF Museum photo)

12. With the entry of the United States into World War I in April 1917, ten years after his first enlistment, Burge is commissioned in the Regular Army. (Courtesy of Marjorie Burge Waters)

13. That American enlisted pilots served in Europe during World War I has been difficult to document, but photos such as this reinforce the notion. Shown here on a postcard mailed from Europe immediately after the Armistice are a group of American officer aviators *(standing),* and at least two enlisted aviators *(kneeling first and third from right),* as indicated by the enlisted aviator badge worn on the upper-right shoulder of their tunics. (USAF Museum photo)

14. The names of seventeen enlisted pilots have been found in articles published in World War I issues of the *Kelly Field Eagle,* the field's newspaper. Eight of them, as yet unidentified, are shown in this December 1918 photo. (Kelly AFB photo)

15. Four Rich Field NCOs became enlisted flying instructors toward the end of World War I. *Left to right:* M.S.E. Douglas Christie, Sgt. Leroy B. Gregg, Sgt. William F. "Pinky" Cottrell, and Sgt. Rufus C. Lillard. (From *Rich Field Flyer,* February 6, 1919)

16. Sergeant Cottrell flanked by five of his newly fledged enlisted pilots. *Left to right:* Homer Sheffield, Walter H. Beech, Cleason E. Shealer, Cottrell, Wick Chamlee, and William E. Beigel. (USAF Museum photo)

17. Preparing for a flight out of Luke Field, Territory of Hawaii, M. Sgt. pilot Chester Colby takes the back seat of the O-19, behind Lt. Col. Gerald C. Brant, commanding officer of the 18th Composite Wing Headquarters. (USAF Museum photo)

18. Sergeant Bernard Wallace, airplane mechanic, and his pilot, Sgt. Carl McDaniel, used the DH-4 to fly to forced landing cites where downed aircraft could then be repaired and flown back to Kelly Field. At other times, they demonstrated parachute jumping. Here Sergeant Wallace is "chuted-up" for a jump as Sergeant pilot McDaniel eases himself into the cockpit. (Courtesy of Elfin Wallace)

19. Ground Attack-Experimental airplane (GA-X) was one of several types flown at Kelly Field by Sgt. pilot Carl McDaniel in the early twenties. This airplane wears the emblem of the 13th Attack Squadron of the 3rd Attack Group. (Kelly Field photo)

20. Master Sergeant pilot Carlton P. "C.P." Smith *(left)* stands with an unidentified companion in front of the Curtiss A-3, a type in which he accumulated nearly 500 hours while flying with the 3rd Attack Group at Fort Crockett, Galveston, Texas. (Courtesy of Peg Smith)

21. Staff Sergeant pilot Byron Newcomb leans jauntily on the wheel of the Douglas C-1 transport that he often flew while serving with the 1st Pursuit Group at Selfridge Field, Michigan, during the mid-twenties. (Courtesy of Medora Kolb)

22. Staff Sergeant pilot Orvil Haynes of the 16th Observation Squadron dressed for a mid-twenties flight in the biting winter wind of the Midwest. (Courtesy of Evelyn Haynes)

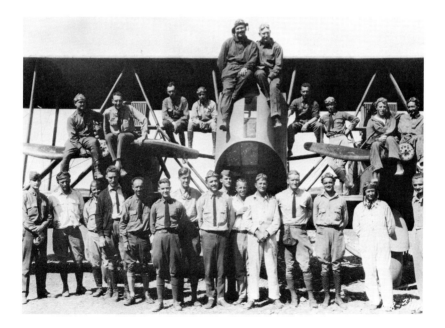

23. Among the many Army pilots who flew for the movie *Wings* were sergeant pilots Silas A. Moorehouse *(left)* and Ezra Nendell (sitting on the propeller of the no. 1 engine of this Martin NBS-1). (Kelly AFB photo)

24. After service as an airplane mechanic in France during World War I, Sgt. Irven Mackey became an engine instructor at the Air Service Mechanics School at Chanute Field. In 1924 he was selected to attend flying school. Sadly, he was killed several days after graduation while flying a Martin NBS-1 bomber on a photo mission. (Courtesy of Jean Mackey Ertwine)

25. Staff Sergeant Irven Mackey *(second from right)* stands with several of his cadet classmates beneath a Martin NBS-1 bomber at Kelly Field. (Courtesy of Jean Mackey Ertwine)

26. Between 1924 and 1927, Army flying students received their primary training in the Curtiss JN aircraft. Between 1928 and the early thirties they were trained in progressive models of the Consolidated primary trainer; PT-1 through PT-3. Pictured here is the PT-3. (Courtesy of Jane Byrne)

27. Over the same time period, basic flight training was given in various versions of the DeHavilland-4. (Courtesy of Jane Byrne)

28. Master Sergeant pilot Boyd Ertwine *(right)* stands with Lt. C. H. Dowman in front of the Douglas C-1 transport they occasionally flew while at March Field. (Courtesy of Jean Mackey Ertwine)

29. Sergeant Paul Jackson *(left),* a mechanic and parachute jumper before becoming a sergeant pilot, stands beside his parachuting mentor M. Sgt. Erwin Nichols. Nichols was the NCO in charge of the parachute school at Kelly Field and Chanute Field where he also became an important contributor to the concept of airborne warfare. (Courtesy of Paul Jackson)

30. In the early twenties sergeants Paul Jackson and Alva Harvey made numerous parachute jumps from the wing tops of any airplane that could carry them aloft. (USAF photo)

31. Sergeant Ralph W. Bottriell, standing beside a DH-4, displays the parachute "D" ring he designed. The "D" ring enabled the jumper to open the parachute at his own discretion. In 1933, Bottriell was awarded the Distinguished Flying Cross in recognition of his part in the development and testing of parachutes. Bottriell was another who inspired Jackson and others to take up the art of parachuting. (USAF Museum photo)

32. Technical Sergeant pilot Paul Jackson test-hopping a Curtiss P-1B out of Fairfield Air Depot near Dayton, Ohio, in 1928–29. (Courtesy of Paul Jackson)

33. Five sergeant pilot graduates of Kelly Field, Class of October 1932. *Left to right:* S. Sgt. Ancel L. Lovvorn, M. Sgt. Julius A. Kolb, T. Sgt. Raymond Stockwell, S. Sgt. Arthur Hanson, and Sgt. Charles G. Cunningham. (Kelly AFB photo)

34. Noncommissioned officers entering flying school in March and July 1932 were the last to be trained "in grade" as pilots. Five who graduated in March 1933 are *(left to right)* staff sergeants Tom Rafferty, Paul Blair, Gil Layman, Cpl. Fred "Duke" Tyler, and Sgt. Fred Wilson. (Courtesy of Paul Blair)

35. Wearing a white helmet, M. Sgt. pilot Julius Kolb prepares to climb into his pursuit plane at Selfridge Field, Michigan, sometime in the mid-thirties. Kolb fashioned the helmet out of white linen while attending parachute school at Chanute Field and wore it while flying as a mechanic for a number of years before becoming a pilot. It became his personal trademark. (Courtesy of Medora Kolb)

36. On a cold winter day at Selfridge Field, Michigan, T. Sgt. pilot Frank Siebenaler pauses reluctantly for a photograph before climbing into his Boeing P-26 "Pea-shooter." In addition to flying, NCO pilots served as line chiefs, flight chiefs, or as technical inspectors in their organizations. (Courtesy of Louise Siebenaler)

37. Movie actor Wallace Beery *(right)* on location at Randolph Field in 1934 to play the part of a seasoned old master sergeant pilot in the movie, *West Point of the Air.* Beery gets some firsthand pointers from the real article: M. Sgt. pilot Carlton P. "C.P." Smith. (Courtesy of Peg Smith)

38. Between the world wars, service outside the United States was limited to U.S. territorial possessions such as Panama, Hawaii, the Philippines, and later to Alaska. Six sergeant pilots stationed in Hawaii during the mid-thirties are pictured here *(left to right):* master sergeants Samuel J. Davis, John L. Waugh, Bernard Wallace, Chester Colby, Arvin E. Miller (a "lighter-than-air" pilot), and S. Sgt. Maurice M. Beach. (USAF photo)

39. Mission preparation is just about the same today as it was in the early thirties. Flying Cadet Vernon Byrne, equipped with a box lunch, a jug of water, and a map prepares for a cross-country training flight over West Texas. (Courtesy of Jane Byrne)

40. Prominent among those enlisted pilots of the thirties were sergeants John "Luke" Williamson *(right)* and William McDonald *(left),* who flew wing on Capt. Claire Chennault's *(center)* aerial acrobatic team billed as "Three Men on a Flying Trapeze."

41. Vernon Byrne *(third from left, front row)* and classmate Hamish McLelland *(sixth from left, front row)*, 1930 graduates of the Advanced (Bombardment) phase at Kelly Field. (Courtesy of Jane Byrne)

43. Contemporary enlisted pilots flew most planes in the Army inventory between 1907 and 1957, including trainer, pursuit, and bomber aircraft, as well as observation and transport types. Examples follow, beginning with the Martin XT-1 or GMP, an adaptation of the first Martin Bomber. Both the bomber and transport version of this aircraft were used to transport cargo and personnel. (USAF Museum photo)

42. "Three Men on a Flying Trapeze" take center stage at the 1935 Miami Air Show. (USAF photo)

44. A workhorse of the early twenties, the Fokker T-2 became famous following its history-making nonstop, coast-to-coast flight in 1923, the first in history. (Courtesy of Marjorie Burge Waters)

45. The Douglas C-1 was the first plane put into widespread use as an Army transport aircraft. (Courtesy of Jane Byrne)

46. At least one Douglas C-1 was converted to an ambulance plane and used at Kelly Field in the mid-twenties. (Brooks AFB photo)

47. Built specifically as an ambulance plane, this Cox-Klemin XA-1 was flown by sergeant pilots Ezra "Pop" Nendell and Bernard Wallace while stationed at Kelly Field during the mid-twenties. (USAF photo)

48. The pilot behind the windshield was not always an officer. Here M. Sgt. pilot Boyd Ertwine and his crew chief Sgt. Ralph Dean prepare to start up the Ford C-4 Tri-motor transport for a flight from Kelly Field Texas to March Field, California. (Courtesy of Jean Mackey Ertwine)

49. The Bellanca C-27 "Air Bus" did yoeman service carrying cargo and passengers between the air depots and the Air Corps stations they serviced. They were also used to shuttle crews and equipment during the 1934 airmail episode. (USAF photo)

51. Former RCAF and USAAF Sgt. pilot Richard W. Oxley, after his promotion to flight officer, flew eighty-five missions with the 83rd Fighter Squadron of the 78th Fighter Group in the European theater during World War II. He is credited with the destruction of one enemy aircraft and two damaged. (Courtesy of Richard Oxley)

50. Master Sergeant pilot Bernard Wallace, line chief and test pilot at Randolph Field in the late thirties, holds a post-test discussion with the maintenance supervisor. (Courtesy of Elfin Wallace)

52. Four of the Americans who became sergeant pilots in the RCAF and later transferred to the USAAF in their equivalent grade are shown here. Shortly after their arrival at Maxwell Field in May 1942, they were sworn in as staff sergeant pilots in the USAAF. *Left to right:* Charles "Hong Kong" Wilson, Bert S. Saunders, Dowaine C. Daniels, and Arthur Raymond Eno. (Courtesy of Charles Wilson)

53. Undergoing primary flight training at King City, California, aviation student Richard Cooney checks the Form-1 of the Ryan PT-22 before climbing into the cockpit. (Courtesy of Dick Cooney)

54. Another primary trainer was the Consolidated PT-13, here in use at the Hancock College of Aeronautics at Santa Maria, California. (Courtesy of Dick Cooney)

55. Basic flying training was given in the BT-13 and 15, or the "Vultee Vibrator," as it was dubbed. (Courtesy of Dick Cooney)

56. After successful completion of basic flying training, students were assigned either to single-engined advanced training as illustrated by this North American AT-6 from Stockton Field, California . . . (Courtesy of James Streitwieser)

57. . . . or to multi-engine training in aircraft such as this Beechcraft AT-10 photographed over Arizona in the summer of 1942. . . . (Courtesy of J. H. MacWilliam)

58. . . . or in this Curtiss AT-9. (Courtesy of J. H. MacWilliam)

59. Ten staff sergeant pilots of the 95th Fighter Squadron, 82nd Fighter Group, on duty at Mines Field, Los Angeles, during the summer of 1942. All were graduates of flying school Class 42-C from Kelly and Ellington fields. *Left to right, back row:* Marshall E. Hyde, Archie Mallette, and Virgil S. White; *middle row, sitting:* William W. Conner, Jr., Claude E. Ford, and William J. Schildt; *front row, standing:* Harold G. Manning, Alex K. Hamric, Charles R. Langdon, and Samuel P. Bradshaw. (Courtesy of Col. Robert Kirtley)

60. Sergeant pilots of the 82nd Fighter Group are briefed on their part in a practice exercise to defend Los Angeles during the summer of 1942. *Left to right, front row:* William W. Conner, Jr., John S. Litchfield, and Vern M. Yahne; *back row:* Ray Bezner, C. D. Powell, Jesse G. Oliver, Graham E. Jones, Ralph C. Embrey, and Grant Reagh. (Courtesy of Ralph Embrey)

61. In 1942, hundreds of staff sergeant pilots were assigned to the rapidly expanding number of transport/troop carrier groups. The 316th was a case in point. Approximately eighty sergeant pilots, over half of the pilots assigned, made up the advanced echelon of the 316th Troop Carrier Group as it flew from Austin, Texas, to the Middle East in November 1942. The group went immediately to work supporting Allied forces during their drive to oust Axis forces from Africa. Photographed just prior to their departure are the sergeant pilots of the 36th Troop Carrier Squadron, 316th Group. *Front row, left to right:* Ed Christman, Edward Bosarge, Elmer Jackson, Ernest Bourne, James Leach, Dick Welter, and Myron Miller. Gerald Johnson is standing in front of command car grill. Sitting atop hood are Jay Fischel, Lee Call, Bob Pace, and LaVoi Davis. Standing to the right are Don Riggs, Lucien Mobley, George Quisenberry, Jim Wilkins, and Bob Hawley. Atop the command car are an unidentified sergeant pilot and Lee Arbon *(right)*. Jim Loffredo and Wendell Courier, on running board, round out the group. (From author's files)

62. Seven sergeant pilots of the 37th Troop Carrier Squadron of the 316th Group take a "smile" break for the camera. Kneeling *(left to right)* are Dick Crawford and Rex Medcalf. Standing are Guy T. Humphreys, Gene Giles, Robert Burchard, William Andrews, and Billy M. Smith. (Courtesy of Col. Rex Medcalf)

63. The confusing variety of uniform styles worn by sergeant pilots in the Middle East piqued the curiosity of many, including a *Yank* magazine photographer. (Courtesy of *Yank* magazine)

64. The 374th Troop Carrier Group was organized from the battered survivors of the initial Japanese offensive in Southeast Asia, the Philippines, and New Guinea. Reinforcements from the United States began to arrive in the fall of 1942 and spring of 1943. Many of them were sergeant pilots. *Left to right:* staff sergeant pilots John M. Meeks and George W. Beaver; Edward O. Harvey, an Australian pilot officer assigned as a third or relief pilot for some of the long overwater missions in the southwest Pacific area; crew chief T. Sgt. Paul Shireman; and radio operator Sgt. Curtis Mills. (U.S. Army photo)

65. Sergeant pilots Bill Morrison *(left)* and Ed Lehhardt *(second from left),* of the 374th Troop Carrier Group, face the camera with their flight engineer, Sgt. A. Kelly, and mechanic Sergeant Trock during a break in operations in New Guinea, January 1943. (U.S. Army photo)

66. These staff sergeant pilots of the 13th Troop Carrier Squadron, together with their crews and airplanes, were commandeered by Maj. Gen. Millard F. Harmon as they landed at New Caledonia en route to New Guinea. General Harmon, commanding the U.S. Army Forces in the South Pacific Area at the time, immediately pressed them into service supplying the goods of war for the battle of Guadalcanal. *Back row, left to right:* staff sergeant pilots Gilbert Zieman, Charles Cruncelton, Jack Bell, Alva Adams, and Jack Alexander; *front row:* Roy Farmer, John Blankenship, Roger Bernard, Don Bergstrom, and Gordon Baldry. (Courtesy of Don Bergstrom)

67. Having just been promoted from staff sergeant pilot to flight officer, Robert Bryant, flying with the 27th Fighter-Bomber Group in North Africa, grins broadly beside his North American A-36, a dive-bomber version of the early P-51. (Courtesy of Col. Robert Bryant)

68 and 69. The view from the cockpit during operations in New Guinea could, at times, be dramatic, as when these P-40s of the Royal Australian Air Force escorted troop carrier C-47s of the 317th Troop Carrier Group on a mission. (Courtesy of Max Miller)

70 and 71. For every urgent load brought into the forward zone, there was one to be taken out. (Courtesy of Max Miller)

72. Although most sergeant pilots were promoted to flight officer or second lieutenant by May 1943, orders had not yet caught up with some of them. Consequently, a few were still flying as sergeant pilots when they perished in operations. Staff Sergeant pilot Dick Engle was one of these. Engle died in the crash of his transport plane while flying the "Hump" in April 1943. (Courtesy of Bobbie Engle Schenck)

73. On the eve of his retirement in 1941, Colonel Burge, who began his flying career in 1912 as America's first enlisted pilot, poses for a final "official" photo. (Courtesy of Marjorie Burge Waters)

74. The trio of pioneers in the science of blind flying pauses for a photo session at Brooks Field in the early thirties. Standing is Capt. William Ocker, creator of the "Ocker blind flying system." Seated in the "Barney chair" beside the plane is Maj. David A. Myers, the flight surgeon who contributed to an understanding of the physiological and psychological aspects of blind flight. Seated in the cockpit of the Douglas O2-K is Lt. Carl Crane, a collaborator with Ocker, and coauthor of the first book ever published on the subject. Like Ocker, Crane devoted his energy to refining and promoting the system of instrument ("blind") flying. Strangely, the "Ocker method," as it was called, was more cordially received in the airline industry and in the air forces of foreign nations than in the Army Air Corps, which maintained that its pilots must be able to fly "by the seat of their pants." (USAF photo)

75. Warrant Officer Chester Colby *(center)* is flanked by master sergeants George Holmes *(left)* and Tom Rafferty *(right),* as they discuss old times as their flights crossed at Kelly Field Base Operations. Each served as an enlisted pilot before World War II, rising into the officer ranks during the war, and re-enlisting after hostilities ended. (USAF Museum photo)

leadership positions within the units. Their youthfulness—averaging some two years younger than their officer peers—created the perception that they were less mature. Further, sergeant pilots could not legally be given certain responsibilities, nor held accountable to the same degree as the commissioned officers. The sergeants were therefore less constrained by caution, and flew with greater abandon (some say immaturity).

This concerned some of their commanders, who were at first skeptical that sergeant pilots had been trained to the same level of competence as their officer pilots. For some, their misgivings were analogous to those of a father whose newly licensed teenaged son has just asked him for permission to take his date to the prom in the brand-new family car. Wes Feagin recalls:

> In October 1942, I had an all enlisted crew and cross-countryed from Fort Myers, Florida, up to Mobile, Alabama. At that time the "Fartin' Martin" [Martin B-26 "Marauder"] was still new enough to draw quite a crowd at most air patches. When we were ready to return to Ft. Myers I filled out the clearance and handed it to a Major behind the counter in Base Operations. The Major said: "Where's the pilot?" I told him that I was the pilot and proudly pointed to my shiny new wings. The Major said: "No, no who's flying the B-26?" I told him that I was. The Major became quite angry and snapped, "Where is the officer-in-charge of your crew?" I said that I didn't have an officer-in-charge of my crew, but that my radioman was a Tech Sergeant if he would like to talk to him. The Major went into an adjacent office and came back with a rather ancient Bird Colonel. I thought that the old fellow was wearing ribbons from the Spanish-American War, but perhaps they were from WW I. In any case, he put his arm over my shoulder and said: "Well you brought the B-26 in here and there is nothing that I can do to keep you from taking it out. But son, I don't think that you should be flying that airplane."
>
> After takeoff, I called the tower and said I wasn't sure that my landing gear had retracted properly and would it be possible to fly by for a gear check? The tower operator said O.K., and needless to say, we made a pass down the parking ramp at what some might consider to be a rather low altitude, like about two feet. I never did hear anything about the slight buzz job at Mobile. If any complaints came in, they must have been fielded by the front office. Actually, I wasn't too worried because Colonel Winstead, our mentor, had said that we would be flying at minimum altitude in combat, and that he wanted us to know how before we got there.[27]

Relationships between the sergeant pilots and officer pilots within a given organization were usually excellent. There were exceptions, however. Staff

Sergeant Roger N. Salmonson had one flight with a second lieutenant copilot who, during takeoff, refused to raise the landing gear because he wouldn't take orders from an enlisted man.

While most other relationships were more positive, the question of where sergeant pilots should be billeted was never answered to everyone's complete satisfaction. Even after the novelty of their status wore off and sergeant pilots became an accepted feature of their units, problems often arose when they flew to other bases. Staff Sergeant Harold C. Thompson, assigned at the time to the 46th Squadron of the 317th Troop Carrier Group, recalled:

> On November 4, 1942, we flew two C-47s to Wright Patterson from Laurinburg-Maxton Field in North Carolina, to pick up over-water emergency gear and deliver it to Brookley Field, Mobile, Alabama. Two Second Licutenants flew one of the planes; the other was flown by myself and another Staff Sergeant Pilot.
>
> By the time the cargo was loaded, we had put in a long day and decided to remain over night. Patterson Field, like many older established bases, had sleeping accommodations in the base operations hanger. When we attempted to sign up for rooms, we were advised that they were for officers only. Our two Lieutenants vigorously supported our case, but without success. The operations personnel were adamant; there was "no room at the inn" for enlisted pilots.
>
> The Lieutenants decided that if the sergeant pilots were not welcome here, we would all go somewhere else. Tired as we were, we flew to Nashville, Tennessee, checked into a hotel where we were more welcome and, since the weather went sour, spent the next two days going broke on good food, good liquor and whatever. I shall always remember the two lieutenants. It was probably no more than three months later those two were again flying together over the Coral Sea and never came back.[28]

"They won't send us into combat until they commission us" was the speculation often voiced by staff sergeant pilots in mid-1942. Such speculation was based on the notion that fliers would be much better treated as officers if captured. The belief was reinforced when the staff sergeant pilots of the 82nd Fighter Group were promoted to second lieutenant on the eve of their shipment to Europe in September 1942.

So prevalent was the belief among subsequent graduates that they purchased officer uniforms, a practice that was not discouraged, provided the sleeve braid was removed and only the enlisted insignia worn. Consequently, many sergeant pilots reported to their new units wearing stripes on the sleeves of officers' uniforms.

In November 1942, after considerable restudy of the sergeant pilot program, the U.S. Army Air Forces again realized serious inequities existed, especially the requirement that dealt with civilian educational attainment. Therefore, the USAAF concluded that, upon graduation, aviation students should be appointed to the rank of flight officer, a new rank equivalent to warrant officer. The following paragraph from "AAF Training History" succinctly summarized the process:

> Removal of educational obstacles for aviation cadet appointment in January 1942, making the sole mental requirement a passing score on the qualifying examination, was instrumental in bringing about a third important congressional act, the creation of the grade of flight officer in 1942. Abandonment of the prerequisite of two years of college and removal of age differences between cadets and students wiped out the essential distinctions between the two groups and necessitated greater parity of treatment, especially in the matter of rating or commissioning upon graduation. The AAF was still unwilling to compromise on the requisites of a good second lieutenant. But it could not in justice commission some pilots and make others equally qualified only staff sergeants. Now the anomalous status of warrant officer (though here called flight officer) was reproduced among flying personnel. *In the future there were to be no more sergeant pilots; cadets and students were to be made either second lieutenants or flight officers,* depending upon the capacities for leadership they evidenced during the training period.[29]

Early in 1943, the Army Air Forces instructed its subordinate commanders to promote all of their sergeant pilots serving in the field to that new rank. It took time for the word to get out to all the units, many already heavily engaged in campaigns all over the world. While most of those in the continental United States were promoted promptly, those serving overseas experienced delays. It was not uncommon to find a mix of sergeant pilots, flight officer pilots, and officer pilots serving in the same outfit, or on the same crew.[30] Sixty-seven, still serving as sergeant pilots after their arrival in England, created a whimsical organization that they called "The 67 Sad Sacks." Among them were a number who had been plucked from the sea after the ship bringing them to England was torpedoed.

After they became flight officers, the former sergeant pilots facetiously dubbed themselves "third lieutenants." Although essentially an enlisted rank, it had an advantage: since enlisted personnel were paid an additional 20 percent of their base pay while serving overseas—and officers paid only 10 percent of theirs—a flight officer would make more than a second lieutenant.

When the Allied invasion of North Africa took place on November 9, 1942, many of the aircraft taking part were flown by sergeant pilots. Nearly half of the troop carrier C-47s that were flown from England to North Africa and took part in the campaign that followed were manned by sergeant pilots. They were also at the controls of a number of P-39s, P-40s, and Spitfires involved in the campaign. George E. Myers and Jack H. McFarland flew their first eleven combat missions as staff sergeant pilots in P-39s of the 154th Reconnaissance Squadron. Staff Sergeant James Butler flew a Spitfire with the 52nd Fighter Group and had downed four enemy aircraft over Tunisia before he was lost in action on April 20, 1943.[31]

Some of the A-20s, A-36 fighter-bombers, B-25s, and B-26s were also flown by pilots whose stripes had only recently been replaced by flight officer bars. Many of the P-38 pilots who flew from England early in 1943 to join the battles in North Africa had also been sergeants only months before.

When the 325th Fighter Group joined the fight, it did so in a most unusual way. Its pilots flew their P-40s from the deck of the aircraft carrier *Ranger* in mid-January 1943, and landed at Casablanca. More than two dozen of its pilots were promoted from staff sergeants to flight officers just before boarding the carrier.[32]

Nine of the pilots assigned to the 27th Fighter Group in the Mediterranean theater had recently been staff sergeant pilots.[33] Robert C. Allen, Robert L. Bryant, Roy T. Carter, Lawrence W. Dye, Leeirby Libby, Eloy Trujillo, Glen F. Van Vliet Jr., Joseph C. Vizi and William H. Willis replaced their chevrons with the new rank of flight officer before going into action in the summer of 1942. Ted W. Ripley, another former sergeant pilot, joined the 27th Fighter Group after winning a transfer out of the 60th Troop Carrier Group.

Few combat groups in the Mediterranean theater during the winter of 1942–43 were without their share of sergeant pilots or former sergeant pilots. All of the belligerents in that theater, Allied and Axis alike, had their share of enlisted pilots taking part in the swirling air battles throughout that theater.[34]

Of the five troop carrier groups operating in the Mediterranean during the winter of 1942–43, all were commanded by former enlisted pilots and nearly half of their pilot strengths were staff sergeants. Four of the Troop

Carrier Groups operated out of Morocco, Algeria, and Tunisia in support of Allied operations in Northwest Africa: the 60th, commanded by Lt. Col. Julius Kolb; the 62nd, commanded by Lt. Col. Samuel Davis; the 64th, under Col. Tracy Dorsett; and the 315th, led by Col. Hamish McLelland.

Over one thousand miles to the east, the 316th Troop Carrier Group operated under Lt. Col. Jerome B. McCauley. Flying out of Egypt and Libya, the Group supported the British Eighth Army, as well as American and British air force units operating in that theater.[35]

The 316th was only one example of the new logistic capabilities being introduced by troop carrier units around the world in the late fall and winter of 1942–43. The 316th arrived in Egypt in late November 1942, one month after the British Eighth Army launched its final offensive against the Axis forces at El Alamein. By the end of the first week of November, the Germans were in retreat and the Eighth Army was in hot pursuit. Several U.S. Army Air Forces combat groups were already on hand in the Middle East theater before the battle began and, in concert with the Royal Air Force, launched assaults against Axis troop concentrations and facilities. The B-24s of the 98th Bomb Group, B-25s of the 12th Bomb Group, and P-40s of the 57th Fighter Group quickly became battle-wise. Out of this mixture the "Desert Air Force" soon developed a very effective system and doctrine of cooperation between the air and ground forces.

The 316th Troop Carrier Group arrived in Egypt just in time to sustain the Eighth Army's pressure on the retreating Axis forces. Its personnel went to work at once flying critical supplies to air and ground units racing ever further from their source of supply.[36]

The aircraft were bound for El Adam, just south of Tobruk in Libya and nearer the front. Because the damaged Libyan port facilities—through which the rapidly advancing Eighth Army would eventually be supplied—could not be repaired quickly enough, the 316th Troop Carrier Group, operating as an airborne caravan, became crucial. From El Adam, its planes flew fuel, bombs, and ammunition to British and American fighter units near Benghazi and El Agheila. On the return flights, they evacuated battle casualties to Benghazi, or in some cases to Alexandria and Cairo. Then they returned to El Adam to begin the process all over again the following morning.[37] As many trips as daylight permitted were made.

To veterans of the British Eighth Army, the American transport airplanes were a new and welcome sight. Under the umbrella of hard-won air superiority, ground troops of the Empire could now ride atop convoy vehicles in relative safety. Formations of C-47s scooted westward with them, flying so low that at times, like porpoise cavorting among sea swells, they were obscured from view by the undulations of the terrain. From their vantage overhead, transport crews could view British motorized columns on the move trailing a wake of dust behind them as far as the eye could see.

Staff Sergeant Bob Pace, later to retire as a colonel, recalled his first Christmas Eve in combat.

> The landing ground at Marble Arch on the Libyan coast had just been taken from the Germans. We were flying in with gasoline in fifty-five-gallon drums and flying out with wounded. Mine clearing operations were still going on at the field as we landed. Directly ahead of us, as I rolled to a stop, was a British truck with about eleven men standing in the bed. The truck drove over a buried mine, a "daisy cutter," which popped out of the ground and exploded, wounding all eleven men.
>
> We coasted right up to the riddled truck and began throwing off the drums of gasoline. While we were doing this, a British officer rushed up to the open cargo door and asked us if we would take the eleven wounded men to Benghazi, where the nearest large hospital was located. We agreed, since it was pretty much on the way back to El Adam, so they threw them on. No medic was with them, and some were very badly wounded, or even dead.
>
> We took off and headed for Benghazi full bore. The crew chief, radio operator, and myself went back to the cabin and tried to do what we could, but we didn't know what we were doing. We bandaged them as best we could with the little first aid pack which were carried aboard the plane, but they were dying like flies.
>
> By the time we got to Benghazi, which wasn't very far, only three or four were alive. One of the wounded to whom I had been talking during the flight, one that I didn't think had been hurt very badly, died just before we got to Benghazi. As we were lifting him out of the plane, his jacket hung on one of the seat belts. In order to get him out, I had to remove his jacket. When I did, one arm came off with the jacket. That was my first look at someone who was badly hurt, and I didn't care for it at all.
>
> We had been promised a big steak dinner back at El Adam, including beer and real bread. Well, by the time we got the dead and surviving wounded transferred to ambulances, it was dark. You simply didn't fly in that desert after dark, so we sat out Christmas Eve and the big dinner at Benghazi. Not all was lost however, for we had our C-rations on board.[38]

Early in the desert operation, the 316th Troop Carrier Group suffered its first battle casualties when a three-ship element of C-47s bound for the front became lost. The flight leader turned the formation north toward the Mediterranean coast, flying low over a motorized column that was presumed to be British. Instead, it was a retreating German column, which fired on the three planes. Staff Sergeant Howard Robeson, flying on the wing of the leader, was killed instantly and his plane burst into flame. The copilot, S. Sgt. Marshall Wells, crashlanded the plane beside the road, and, together with the surviving crew members, was taken prisoner. The German troops buried Robeson on the site.[39]

Two more fatalities occurred shortly afterward when staff sergeants Harry C. Rowe and Robert F. Burchard, while examining a German mortar shell found on the airdrome at El Adam, were killed when it exploded in their faces.

Casualties of a lighter sort occurred when several pilots of the 316th flew too low over the desert dunes. During the early phases of the campaign in Egypt and Libya, flights between the Nile Delta and the battle zone were briefed to fly no higher than fifty feet in order to avoid German radar located on the island of Crete. For the pilots of the 316th, it was a license to "buzz," and most of them flew below fifty feet. Inevitably, some misjudged their height and dinged a propeller, which in most cases resulted in an engine change. If the offender was a sergeant pilot, he was usually reduced to the grade of private, fined, and assigned to convoy duty driving a truck from Egypt to Libya. Officers, under like circumstances, were usually grounded for a week or two before being returned to flight duty.

Staff Sergeant John P. Williams was a case in point. On December 15, 1942, Williams was part of a three-ship formation flying personnel from Kabrit, a British base on the Suez Canal, to the front near El Agheila, Libya. As usual, the flight leader was staying low. Flying a bit lower, Williams clipped the top of a sand dune with the right propeller. Oddly, no vibration resulted, but Williams decided to feather the propeller and make a precautionary landing at Gambut on the Egyptian/Libyan border.

Upon assessing the damage, a decision was made to remain with the plane until a new propeller could be flown up to them, after which the plane was flown back to base. The entire crew was punished for this incident. Sergeant Williams became Private Williams and found himself driving a personnel carrier from Cairo to Benghazi. Lieutenant Helmuth, his copilot, was grounded for two weeks.[40]

Williams was later promoted to flight officer and reassigned to the U.S.-Middle East headquarters at Cairo. There was a certain "status" attached to this assignment as it often involved flying the senior brass around. There were other times, though, when the mission led to genuine adventure, as occurred on the night of October 21, 1943, when Williams and his crew flew into Nazi-occupied Greece to supply clandestine intelligence personnel operating with local guerrillas and to rescue surviving American bomber crew members.

Since flights of this nature were always conducted at night, they carried an RAF navigator who knew his way in and out of the place. Once the plane arrived over the designated landing place, guerrillas lit the field briefly and dimly to facilitate a rapid landing. Cargo was quickly off-loaded and passengers on-loaded without shutting down the engines. While taxiing back to the takeoff position, the plane became bogged down in marshy ground. Unable to proceed, the wheels began to settle deeper, so Williams cut the engines before the propellers could slice into the soggy turf. Digging and flying the plane out before sun-up was out of the question, so the guerrillas hid the plane from the German occupation forces with freshly cut saplings. They spent the next three days in cold rain digging inclined trenches by which the plane could be towed free. Finally, with house-lifting jacks stolen from the Germans, the plane was lifted enough to place heavy planks under its wheels. It was then manhandled up the trench slopes and out of the bog.

Early in the morning of October 24, taking advantage of the fog and clouds in the valley, Williams took off and spiralled upward until he broke out on top at 6,000 feet. This was enough to clear the mountains surrounding the valley, but a German fighter was spotted just after clearing them, so Williams dove back into the clouds again where he remained until out of danger. The flight earned Williams the Distinguished Flying Cross.[41]

Staff Sergeant Ed Wenglar, also of the 316th, was another who was "busted" for "intemperance." Wenglar was reduced to a private, and placed on K.P. for two weeks. His rank was reinstated on Christmas Day, but without back pay and allowances. Later a retired brigadier general, Wenglar claims to be the only general who started from the rank of private—twice.[42]

The practice of punishing sergeant pilots in this manner ended in the early spring of 1943 when Maj. William H. Matthews, commanding the 37th Squadron of the 316th Troop Carrier Group, refused to go along, reportedly saying, "I am not going to bust my sergeant pilots unless I can bust my officer pilots for the same offense." Needless to say, he became a hero to his sergeant pilots, and while none were similarly punished thereafter, Major Matthews was eventually reassigned. His stand was vindicated later when the correspondence relating to all such previous reductions was returned by higher headquarters directing that those affected be reinstated in their former grades, with back pay and allowances.

The year 1942 had not been a good one for the Allies in the Pacific. Only after the Battle of Midway in June were they in a position to take the initiative. While Allied offensives were underway in the Mediterranean theater, those in the Pacific were beginning to make their first moves against Japanese forces in New Guinea and Guadalcanal.

Transport aircraft by which the goods of war were distributed throughout the vast Pacific region became as crucial to combat operations as did combat aircraft themselves. To that end, transport planes—or those which could serve as such—were scrounged wherever they could be found. Crews to fly them were "scrounged" as well and assigned to an air transport system operated by war-weary Dutch and Australian pilots. American C-33s and B-18s, flown by airmen who had escaped from the Philippines, also joined the tired and ragged system. From this desperate hodgepodge, the 374th Troop Carrier Group, one of the rare American groups organized outside the United States during World War II, was formed in November 1942.

The 374th Group was brought up to strength in the fall of that year when some staff sergeant pilots were rushed to New Guinea. A number of them perished in the operations that followed: Sgt. Glen E. Webb, flying with the 6th Troop Carrier Squadron, was killed on October 16 while dropping supplies near Efogi, New Guinea; classmates and staff sergeants Ray Van Hensman and Robert C. Dillman were shot down by Japanese ground fire on November 8, as they took off from Henderson Field, Guadalcanal; sergeants Marvin L. Brandt and Quentin C. Ruecker perished when their C-47 was shot down by Japanese fighters on November 26, 1942, near Dobodura, New Guinea.

In October 1942, the U.S. Army Air Forces sent two troop carrier squadrons to the southwest Pacific to join what was to become the 374th Group. The 6th Troop Carrier Squadron was detached from the 63th Troop Carrier Group, while the 13th was detached from the 61st Troop Carrier Group for that purpose. While the 6th Squadron arrived in New Guinea on October 13, and was operating in November, the 13th Squadron, which included eleven staff sergeant pilots, never quite made it, having been commandeered on arriving at New Caledonia to fly fuel, bombs, and ammunition to Guadalcanal.[43] When that task was finished, the 13th Squadron became a part of the legendary South Pacific Combat Air Transport Command, affectionately known as SCAT. In February 1943, its eleven staff sergeant pilots—

Floyd H. Abernathy, Jr., Alva T. Adams, Jack D. Alexander, Gordon L. Baldry, Jack B. Bell, Don J. Bergstrom, Roger Bernard, John J. Blankenship, Charles E. Cruncleton, Jr., Roy C. Farmer, and Gilbert W. Zieman—were commissioned. By that time the 13th had earned a Presidential Unit Citation for its part in the battle for Guadalcanal.

Although most sergeant pilots had been promoted to flight officer or commissioned by early 1943, a number at the far ends of the communication lines did not receive theirs until May or June. One of these was S. Sgt. Forrest Bruce, who arrived in Australia by ship and was assigned to the 33rd Squadron of the 374th. Later, while flying casualties out of Dobodura, Bruce noticed that one of the waiting walking-wounded, an American infantry sergeant, was watching him with more than casual interest.

> The bloody and battle-weary sergeant watched me and my copilot, who happened to be a second lieutenant, for a minute or two, then preparing to board, he paused and asked, "Are you the pilot of this plane?"
>
> "Yes," I answered.
>
> "Are you the boss?" he asked skeptically.
>
> "Yes," I repeated.
>
> Glancing toward my copilot again he asked, "Do you tell him what to do?"
>
> "I sure do," I assured him.
>
> A smile slowly broke on his face and continued to widen. Shaking his head, he boarded the plane for his trip out of hell.
>
> Boarding the plane myself, I ambled up to the crew compartment and took the left seat. Looking back into the cabin I could see by the still-present grin on his face I had made his day.[44]

In January 1943, the 374th was joined by elements of the 317th Troop Carrier Group, which had flown across the Pacific Ocean from the States. By this time, all of the staff sergeant pilots in the 317th Group had been promoted to flight officers. Thus, in one of the countless quirks of war, the new group arrived flying new airplanes and wearing shiny new flight officer bars, while the veteran staff sergeant pilots of the 374th still flew the war-weary aircraft. The two groups joined forces to move Allied troops and equipment over the Owen Stanley Mountains in an effort to stem the Japanese tide at Buna and Sanananda on the Papuan peninsula of New Guinea. Then, a reverse irony at the end of the Papuan campaign: the 317th Group was ordered to relinquish its newer planes to the 374th, and to take possession of the latter's worn-out assortment.

Sergeant pilot losses, like those among the officer pilots, continued to mount in the 374th Troop Carrier Group during the Papuan campaign. Staff Sergeant Elmer Crowley, serving with the 22nd Squadron, perished on March 11, 1943, when his plane crashed during an air-drop mission over Skindawai, New Guinea,[45] and S. Sgt. Lorenzo R. Gower failed to return from a combat mission to the vicinity of Oro Bay, New Guinea, on May 12, 1943.[46]

Air cover for the transport operations in New Guinea was provided by fighters of the 35th and 49th Fighter Groups, the latter of which included two staff sergeant pilots, Sammy Pierce and Merrill Wolfe. Pierce began a string of seven confirmed victories in New Guinea while flying as a staff sergeant pilot.

Four others who had recently been promoted to flight officer were also assigned to the 49th: Warren Z. Coleman, Louis C. Martin, James M. Menger, and Arthur Lee Talmage. All were fresh from the indoctrination school in northern Australia, and reported as replacement pilots to the 49th operating out of Port Moresby and Dobodura, New Guinea, in January 1943.[47]

By late summer of 1943, the focus for air transport operations moved to airstrips near Lae, Salamaua, Nadzab, and Wau, all located on or near the Huan Gulf coast of northeast New Guinea. In one operation, Allied airborne troops were dropped on the coastal plains near Lae. The Japanese fought hard for these fields but, then, so did the Allies.[48]

Nearly five thousand miles to the west-northwest, planes and crews arrived in India in increasing numbers to begin a historic air operation: an airlift of the goods of war to China. The Japanese had expanded their occupation of Southeast Asia into Burma, effectively cutting off the Burma Road over which such materials were heretofore transported. In his book *Over the Hump,* Lt. Gen. William H. Tunner describes the scope of the China-Burma-India (CBI) operation.

> There was now no other way to get supplies into China except by airplane from the Assam Valley itself all the way to Kunming, over the mountains and jungles of northern Burma. . . .
>
> Remember that once the airlift got underway, every drop of fuel, every weapon, and every round of ammunition, and 100 percent of such other diverse supplies as carbon paper and C-rations, every such item used by American forces in China was flown in by airlift. Never in the history of

transportation had any community been supplied such a large proportion of its needs by air, even in the heart of civilization over friendly terrain. Yet this was achieved in the Himalayan Airlift, undertaken with no previous experience and under the most difficult conditions.[49]

On December 1, 1942, the Air Transport Command was given that mission and among the hundreds of aircrew ordered to India that month to take up the task were thirty staff sergeant pilots: Robert W. Adams, Truman R. Ashbrook, Thomas C. Blackshear, James L. Browning, Stanley J. Budris, Cyrus F. Carter, Jr., Joseph F. Crane, Gilbert G. Fincher, Eugene F. Giles, Kenneth E. Grill, James R. Holder, Joseph C. Howell, William E. James, Franklin O. Johnson, Edwin L. Leonard, Charles M. Linden, Paul F. McGinley, Jr., Lloyd L. Marlaire, Charles W. Martin, Robert C. Martin, Jr., Frank K. Mattson, Howard L. Peterson, Monzell J. Phipps, James C. Plummer, James P. Pool, Lee V. Ruffin, Donald E. Sanders, Marvin H. Sellers, James H. Short, and Max E. Wilbur. Flights over the "Hump" began almost immediately with an assortment of C-47s and C-53s.[50]

Eight additional pilots and four airplanes were sent to India the following month from the 316th Troop Carrier Group operating in Libya. Only two of the pilots were officers; lieutenants Guy W. Hoagland and William R. McCauley. Six were enlisted pilots: Richard W. Plummer, Elmer Eberhardt, Richard J. "Dick" Engle, Robert M. Lay, Ernest M. Wilcox, and Richard L. Wilson.[51]

The pilots of each airplane took turns leading a leg of the long flight to India. The leg into Karachi was led by Pvt. Richard W. Plummer (who had been reduced to private for the same "intemperance" in Ismalia, Egypt, as Ed Wenglar). As the formation approached Karachi, pilots pulled in tight, wanting to make a good "first impression." The operations officer at Karachi was obviously impressed, for it was the only four-ship formation he had seen since his arrival. He reasoned someone important was on board. After landing, Plummer's plane was led to the parking area and spotted by the major who then boarded and worked his way through the maze of boxes and baggage lashed to the cabin floor. The major stuck his head into the cockpit and extended his hand. "Welcome to Karachi! I'm Major So-and-So." "Thank you, Major, I'm Private Plummer!" was the response to a thoroughly baffled major.[52]

By March 1943, all but two staff sergeant pilots had been promoted to flight officer and subsequently commissioned as second lieutenants. Dick

Engle and Robert M. Lay declined the promotion, choosing instead to remain staff sergeants.

In April 1943, pilots flying the Hump reported sighting a thick column of black smoke rising through the layer of clouds over which they were flying, clouds that obscured the high mountain peaks astride the route. The C-47 flown by S. Sgt. Dick Engle and F.O. Ernest Wilcox over the route that day never arrived at its destination. It is presumed the smoke rising from that remote site marked their funeral pyre.[53]

Before operations in the CBI theater were concluded, many former sergeant pilots had served there. Twenty-four are known to have perished, fourteen of them while flying the "Hump."[54]

Staff Sergeant Lay accepted a promotion to technical sergeant before finishing his CBI tour, but remained a sergeant pilot well into his second overseas tour, this one in Europe with Troop Carrier Command Headquarters in England. Lay, together with another reluctant sergeant pilot, Arthur M. "Mike" Gray, was commissioned in late May 1944, but they did not receive notification of this until they returned from the Normandy airborne mission on June 6, 1944.[55]

In November 1942, Public Law 99, the law that authorized the training of staff sergeant pilots, was replaced by the Flight Officer Act of July 8, 1942—Public Law 658.[56] With rare exceptions, those sergeant pilots produced by the program were promoted to flight officers.

The history of enlisted pilots, which began with Corporal Vernon Burge in 1912, now came to an end. Literally on the wing, their unique identity was relegated to the annals of history. Commissioned soon thereafter as second lieutenants, they became indistinguishable from the thousands of other new second lieutenants being produced. Therein lay the final irony. These veteran combat pilots now wore the same shiny gold bars as did the new, unblooded second lieutenants coming into their units as replacements. Not wanting to be identified as "new" officers, the former sergeant pilots scoured their new gold bars in the sand until only the silver base remained, making them appear as seasoned first-lieutenant bars. With such acts they took their place in the military pecking order as "officers and gentlemen," then blended into that great anonymous sea of commissioned pilots—their exploits and unique distinction as sergeant pilots only echoes in the halls of heaven.

EPILOGUE

ALTHOUGH THEIR CAREERS AS SERGEANT pilots were now over, their careers as fliers continued uninterrupted by their new status. They had by this time become widely distributed among the many Air Force units stationed around the globe and were making significant contributions to the war against the Axis.

Was the sergeant pilot program a good idea? Did it work? According to the record, sergeant pilots acquitted themselves very well. Seventeen became aces.[1] Eddie Russell became a personal pilot for Field Marshal Bernard Montgomery, Charles I. Bennett for General Eisenhower. Louis H. Carrington and his crew were awarded the Mackay Trophy in 1952 for making the first nonstop transpacific flight of an RB-45 multiengine jet bomber, with two air refuelings. At least 760 retired as field grade officers (major through colonel), many having been commissioned in the Regular Army or Air Force. Eleven became generals.[2]

Those choosing to return to civilian life after the war became as productive as they had been while serving as sergeant pilots. Many took jobs as airline pilots, becoming captains of their ships. Still others returned to the classroom and later entered professions, became businessmen, or returned to the farm. Carroll Shelby, for instance, became a famous race car driver and designer. Bob Hoover became a world-famous test pilot and later a world-class aerial demonstration pilot.

In a report on the enlisted pilot program for the Air Command and Staff College, Maj. Harry O. Mamaux III concludes that the program was successful for a number of reasons. He writes:

> The program's success was not a result of actions by the U.S. Army. The success lay with the motivation and spirit of the enlisted men it trained. These men made the program. They had been given an opportunity of a

lifetime, to fly. They wanted to fulfill their dreams and be a success. They wouldn't—and didn't—fail.[3]

What motivated them so much? They were younger, more impressionable, and highly grateful for the legislative miracle that enabled them to become pilots. They were also aware that the "system" accepted them with reluctance. Finding themselves cast in the role of underdog, it was only natural that they tried harder to prove themselves.

Although the sergeant pilot program ended in November 1942, the subject has never quite been put to rest. The notion is resurrected from time to time in magazine articles and professional periodicals and in letters to the editors of such publications. Lieutenant Colonel Carl M. Putnam, for example, put forth his own ideas on the subject in an August 1973 article written for *Armor* magazine, stating in part:

> The noncommissioned officer is the cornerstone of every good Army organization. Why then should Army aviation units be the exception? Only in aviation is the commissioned officer used as the operator of a combat vehicle. With aviation unit employment becoming the rule rather than the exception, it is time for a reevaluation of aviation and a decision to utilize the flying sergeant in an organizational structure similar to the other combat and combat support organizations. This means a rated commissioned platoon leader, commanding a platoon of noncommissioned aviators and other members of the aircraft's crew.[4]

When World War II ended, two old-time sergeant pilots, George Holmes and Tom Rafferty, then still serving as officers, opted for separation. Each immediately re-enlisted in his permanent grade as master sergeant and each retained his aeronautical rating. In 1947, when the Air Force became a separate service, the two sergeants elected to "suit up" in the new Air Force blue uniform, thus becoming the first, last, and only sergeant pilots to serve in the U.S. Air Force.

Sadly, late in 1949, Rafferty lost his life in the crash of a C-47 near Donner Pass on the California-Nevada border. This left George Holmes as the sole member of the breed. His retirement in 1957 ended the enlisted pilot era for the Air Force.

From time to time in their development, the institutions of man pause, look back, and reconsider what they have discarded on the march to bigger and better things. Sometimes an old idea is returned, rethought, and reintroduced with a brand-new advantage. Each time the national economy wanes, the idea of enlisted pilots re-emerges and begs for attention.

Today, all Air Force pilots are officers, a testimony to the importance of the position. That some enlisted men also once occupied the cockpit is a testimony to their uniqueness. That group of pilots literally defied the law of gravity. Those still living today are retired now and, as their numbers decline, look back on their youthful days believing they were the best investment Uncle Sam ever made.

LIST OF APPENDIXES

ACT OF JULY 18, 1914 A APPENDIX

July 18, 1914.
[H. R. 5304.]

[Public, No. 143.]

CHAP. 186.—An Act To increase the efficiency of the aviation service of the Army, and for other purposes.

Be it enacted by the Senate and House of Representatives of the United States of America in Congress assembled, That there shall hereafter be, and there is hereby created, an aviation section, which shall be a part of the Signal Corps of the Army, and which shall be, and is hereby, charged with the duty of operating or supervising the operation of all military air craft, including balloons and aeroplanes, all appliances pertaining to said craft, and signaling apparatus of any kind when installed on said craft; also with the duty of training officers and enlisted men in matters pertaining to military aviation.

Army.
Aviation section of Signal Corps created. Duties, etc.

Sec. 2. That, in addition to such officers and enlisted men as shall be assigned from the Signal Corps at large to executive, administrative, scientific, or other duty in or for the aviation section, there shall be in said section aviation officers not to exceed sixty in number, and two hundred and sixty aviation enlisted men of all grades; and said aviation officers and aviation enlisted men, all of whom shall be engaged on duties pertaining to said aviation section, shall be additional to the officers and enlisted men now allotted by law to the Signal Corps, the commissioned and enlisted strengths of which are hereby increased accordingly.

Officers and enlisted men provided for.

Additional to regular Corps allotment.

The aviation officers provided for in this section shall, except as hereinafter prescribed specifically to the contrary, be selected from among officers holding commissions in the line of the Army with rank below that of captain, and shall be detailed to serve as such aviation officers for periods of four years, unless sooner relieved, and the provisions of section twenty-seven of the Act of Congress approved February second, nineteen hundred and one (Thirty-first Statutes, page seven hundred and fifty-five) are hereby extended so as to apply to said aviation officers and to the vacancies created in the line of the Army by the detail of said officers therefrom, but nothing in said Act or in any other law now in force shall be held to prevent the detail or redetail at any time to fill a vacancy among the aviation officers authorized by this Act, of any officer holding a commission in the line of the Army with rank below that of captain, and who, during prior service as an aviation officer in the aviation section, shall have become especially proficient in military aviation.

Details from line officers.

Tour of service.

Vol. 31, p. 755.

Redetail of proficient aviators.

There shall also be constantly attached to the aviation section a sufficient number of aviation students to make, with the aviation officers actually detailed in said section under the provisions of this Act, a total number of sixty aviation officers and aviation students constantly under assignment to, or detail in, said section. Said aviation students, all of whom shall be selected on the recommendation of the chief signal officer from among unmarried lieutenants of the line of

Aviation students.

Selection, tour of service, etc.

the Army not over thirty years of age, shall remain attached to the aviation section for a sufficient time, but in no case to exceed one year, to determine their fitness or unfitness for detail as aviation officers in said section, and their detachment from their respective arms of service which under assignment to said section shall not be held to create in said arms vacancies that may be filled by promotions or original appointments: *Provided:* That no person, except in time of war, shall be assigned or detailed against his will to duty as an aviation student or an aviation officer: *Provided further,* That whenever, under such regulations as the Secretary of War shall prescribe and publish to the Army, an officer assigned or detailed to duty of any kind in or with the aviation section shall have been found to be inattentive to his duties, inefficient, or incapacitated from any cause whatever for the full and efficient discharge of all duties that might properly be imposed upon him if he should be continued on duty in or with said section, said officer shall be returned forthwith to the branch of the service in which he shall hold a commission.

SEC. 3. That the aviation officers hereinbefore provided for shall be rated in two classes, to wit, as junior military aviators and as military aviators. Within sixty days after this Act shall take effect the Secretary of War may, upon the recommendation of the Chief Signal Officer, rate as junior military aviators any officers with rank below that of captain, who are now on aviation duty and who have, or shall have before the date of rating so authorized, shown by practical tests, including aerial flights, that they are especially well qualified for military aviation service; and after said rating shall have been made the rating of junior military aviator shall not be conferred upon any person except as hereinafter provided.

Each aviation student authorized by this Act shall, while on duty that requires him to participate regularly and frequently in aerial flights, receive an increase of 25 per centum in the pay of his grade and length of service under his line commission. Each duly qualified junior military aviator shall, while so serving, have the rank, pay, and allowances of one grade higher than that held by him under his line commission, provided that his rank under said commission be not higher than that of first lieutenant, and, while on duty, requiring him to participate regularly and frequently in aerial flights, he shall receive in addition an increase of 50 per centum in the pay of his grade and length of service under his line commission. The rating of military aviator shall not be hereafter conferred upon or held by any person except as hereinafter provided, and the number of officers with that rating shall at no time exceed fifteen. Each military aviator who shall hereafter have duly qualified as such under the provisions of this Act shall, while so serving, have the rank, pay, and allowances of one grade higher than that held by him under his line commission, provided that his rank under said commission be not higher than that of first lieutenant, and, while on duty requiring him to participate regularly and frequently in aerial flights, he shall receive in addition an increase of 75 per centum of the pay of his grade and length of service under his line commission.

The aviation enlisted men hereinbefore provided for shall consist of twelve master signal electricians, twelve first-class sergeants, twenty-four sergeants, seventy-eight corporals, eight cooks, eighty-two first-class privates, and forty-four privates. Not to exceed forty of said enlisted men shall at any one time have the rating of aviation mechanician, which rating is hereby established, and said rating shall not be conferred upon any person except as hereinafter provided: *Provided,* That twelve enlisted men at a time shall, in the discretion of the officer in command of the aviation section, be instructed in the art of flying, and no enlisted man shall be assigned to duty as an aerial flyer against his will except in time of war. Each aviation enlisted man, while on duty that requires him to participate regularly and frequently in aerial flights, or while holding the rating of aviation mechanician, shall receive an increase of fifty per centum in his pay: *Provided further,* That, except as hereinafter

---

Marginal notes:

No vacancies created by detachment.

Provisos. Details not compulsory. Assignment to cease if officer inefficient, etc.

Aviation officers rated. Junior military aviators. Qualifications of present officers for.

Subsequent ratings.

Aviation students. Increased pay.

Junior military aviators. Increased grade and pay.

Military aviators. Rating limited.

Increased grade and pay.

Personnel of enlisted men.

Rating of aviation mechanician.

Provisos. Instruction in art of flying.

Increase of pay.

Qualification certificates required.

provided in the cases of officers now on aviation duty, no person shall be detailed as an aviation officer, or rated as a junior military aviator, or as a military aviator, or as an aviation mechanician, until there shall have been issued to him a certificate to the effect that he is qualified for the detail or rating, or for both the detail and **Examination.** the rating, sought or proposed in his case, and no such certificate shall be issued to any person until an aviation examining board, which shall be composed of three officers of experience in the aviation service and two medical officers, shall have examined him, under general regulations to be prescribed by the Secretary of War and published to the Army by the War Department, and shall have reported him to be qualified for the detail or rating, or for both the **Issue of certificates.** detail and the rating, sought or proposed in his case: *Provided further*, That the Secretary of War shall cause appropriate certificates of qualification to be issued by the Adjutant General of the Army to all officers and enlisted men who shall have been found and reported by aviation examining boards in accordance with the terms of this **Service as aviation** Act, to be qualified for the details and ratings for which said officers **student prior to detail.** and enlisted men shall have been examined: *Provided further*, That except as hereinbefore provided in the cases of officers who are now on aviation duty and who shall be rated as junior military aviators as hereinbefore authorized, no person shall be detailed for service as an aviation officer in the aviation section until he shall have **Military aviators.** served creditably as an aviation student for a period to be fixed by **Rating require-** the Secretary of War; and no person shall receive the rating of **ments.** military aviator until he shall have served creditably for at least **Payments in case of** three years as an aviation officer with the rating of junior military **death from accident.** aviator: *Provided further*, That there shall be paid to the widow of any officer or enlisted man who shall die as the result of an aviation accident, not the result of his own misconduct, or to any other person designated by him in writing, an amount equal to one year's pay at the rate to which such officer or enlisted man was entitled at the **In lieu of other al-** time of the accident resulting in his death, but any payment made **lowance for death in** **service.** in accordance with the terms of this proviso on account of the death **Vol. 35, pp. 108, 735.** of any officer or enlisted man shall be in lieu of and a bar to any payment under the Acts of Congress approved May eleventh, nineteen hundred and eight, and March third, nineteen hundred and nine (Thirty-fifth Statutes, pages one hundred and eight and seven hundred and fifty-five), on account of death of said officer or enlisted man.

Approved, July 18, 1914.

ACT OF JUNE 3, 1916 B APPENDIX

Signal Corps. Constitution of.

SEC. 13. THE SIGNAL CORPS.—The Signal Corps shall consist of one Chief Signal Officer, with the rank of brigadier general; three colonels; eight lieutenant colonels; ten majors; thirty captains;

Aviation section. Vol. 38, p. 514.

seventy-five first lieutenants; and the aviation section, which shall consist of one colonel; one lieutenant colonel; eight majors; twenty-four captains; and one hundred and fourteen first lieutenants, who shall be selected from among officers of the Army at large of corresponding grades or from among officers of the grade below, exclusive of those serving by detail in staff corps or departments, who are qualified as military aviators, and shall be detailed to serve as aviation

Details, etc. Vol. 31, p. 755.

officers for periods of four years unless sooner relieved; and the provisions of section twenty-seven of the Act of Congress approved February second, nineteen hundred and one, are hereby extended to apply to said aviation officers and to vacancies created in any arm, corps, or department of the Army by the detail of said officers

Redetails of proficient aviators.

therefrom; but nothing in said Act or in any other law now in force shall be held to prevent the detail or redetail at any time, to fill a vacancy among the aviation officers authorized by this Act, of any officer who, during prior service as an aviation officer of the aviation

Ratings of aviation officers.

section, shall have become proficient in military aviation.

Aviation officers may, when qualified therefor, be rated as junior

Certificates of examinations, etc.

military aviators or as military aviators, but no person shall be so rated until there shall have been issued to him a certificate to the effect that he is qualified for the rating, and no certificate shall be issued to any person until an aviation examining board, which shall be composed of three officers of experience in the aviation service and two medical officers, shall have examined him, under general regulations to be prescribed by the Secretary of War and published to the Army by the War Department, and shall have reported him to be

Service required.

qualified for the rating. No person shall receive the rating of military aviator until he shall have served creditably for three years as an aviation officer with the rating of a junior military aviator.

Aviation officers.

Each aviation officer authorized by this Act shall, while on duty that requires him to participate regularly and frequently in aerial

Increase of pay.

flights, receive an increase of twenty-five per centum in the pay of

Junior military aviators.

his grade and length of service under his commission. Each duly

Increase in grade, pay, etc.

qualified junior military aviator shall, while so serving, have the rank, pay, and allowances of one grade higher than that held by him under his commission if his rank under said commission be not higher than that of captain, and while on duty requiring him to participate regularly and frequently in aerial flights he shall receive in addition an

Military aviators. Increase in grade, pay, etc.

increase of fifty per centum in the pay of his grade and length of service under his commission. Each military aviator shall, while so serving, have the rank, pay, and allowances of one grade higher than that held by him under his commission if his rank under said

162

commission be not higher than that of captain, and while on duty requiring him to participate regularly and frequently in aerial flights he shall receive in addition an increase of seventy-five per centum of the pay of his grade and length of service under his commission: *Provided further*, That the provisions of the Act of March second, nineteen hundred and thirteen, allowing increase of pay and allowances to officers detailed by the Secretary of War on aviation duty, are hereby repealed: *Provided further*, That hereafter married officers of the line of the Army shall be eligible equally with unmarried officers, and subject to the same conditions, for detail to aviation duty; and the Secretary of War shall have authority to cause as many enlisted men of the aviation section to be instructed in the art of flying as he may deem necessary: *Provided further*, That hereafter the age of officers shall not be a bar to their first detail in the aviation section of the Signal Corps, and neither their age nor their rank shall be a bar to their subsequent details in said section: *Provided further*, That, when it shall be impracticable to obtain from the Army officers suitable for the aviation section of the Signal Corps in the number allowed by law the difference between that number and the number of suitable officers actually available for duty in said section may be made up by appointments in the grade of aviator, Signal Corps, and that grade is hereby created. The personnel for said grade shall be obtained from especially qualified civilians who shall be appointed and commissioned in said grade: *Provided further*, That whenever any aviator shall have become unsatisfactory he shall be discharged from the Army as such aviator. The base pay of an aviator, Signal Corps, shall be $150 per month, and he shall have the allowances of a master signal electrician and the same percentage of increase in pay for length of service as is allowed to a master signal electrician.

The total enlisted strength of the Signal Corps shall be limited and fixed from time to time by the President in accordance with the needs of the Army, and shall consist of master signal electricians; sergeants, first class; sergeants; corporals; cooks; horseshoers; private, first class; and privates; the number in each grade being fixed from time to time by the President. The numbers in the various grades shall not exceed the following percentages of the total authorized enlisted strength of the Signal Corps, namely: Master signal electricians, two per centum; sergeants, first class, seven per centum; sergeants, ten per centum; corporals, twenty per centum. The number of privates, first class, shall not exceed twenty-five per centum of the number of privates. Authority is hereby given the President to organize, in his discretion, such part of the commissioned and enlisted personnel of the Signal Corps into such number of companies, battalions, and aero squadrons as the necessities of the service may demand.

Marginal notes:
- *Provisos.*
- Former provisions repealed.
- Vol. 37, p. 705.
- Married officers eligible.
- Enlisted men.
- Age limit removed.
- Appointment of aviators from civil life.
- Grade created.
- Discharge.
- Pay, etc.
- Enlisted men, Signal Corps.
- Grades established.
- Percentages of grades.
- Privates.
- Unit organizations authorized.

STANDARD OPERATING PROCEDURE FOR ENLISTED FLYING INSTRUCTION

ORGANIZATION OF AIR SERVICE FLYING SCHOOL

FLYING TRAINING OF ENLISTED MEN

Stencil T-138 issued by the Director of Military Aeronautics, January 30, 1919, states in detail the method of handling the training of enlisted men authorized to take flying instruction.

This training of enlisted men should be so arranged as not to interfere in any way with the training of Cadets or Officers as outlined elsewhere. The procedure that an enlisted man follows in making application for flying training is:

(1) He writes a letter to the Commanding Officer of his Field requesting that he be ordered before a Board of Officers for the purpose of determining his qualifications for training as a pilot.

(2) At the discretion of the Commanding Officer the applicant will be ordered to appear before the Board by a Post Special Order.

(3) Board Proceedings in the case of each applicant will be forwarded to the Director of Air Service, which will give the name of the applicant, his mental and physical qualifications, (stated as satisfactory or not satisfactory), and then the recommended classification. The enlisted man will be classified in the Board Proceedings as follows:

A.—Suitable material for training and commission, if the emergency for commission should arise.

B.—Suitable for training as pilot but not having enough education and other qualifications for commission. If classified as A or B the applicant for training will be given a physical examination.

This report will be signed by all members of the Board and the report of physical examination enclosed with same. In the event that applicant is not a member of the Regular Army, it will be necessary to forward a certificate containing his sworn statement that he is about to become a member of the Regular Army. It is not intended that any but enlisted men in the Regular Army shall receive this flying training.

The Board Proceedings are submitted to the Commanding Officer who will forward same to the Director of Air Service with an indorsement recommending approval.

The course of flying training will be the same as that given Cadets and Non-flying Officers, as described in Stencil T-84. The Academic instruction is covered in detail in Chapter VIII.

As soon as the enlisted man has completed his training, the Commanding Officer will forward to the Director of Air Service a certificate in the form of a military letter, stating that he has finished his course.

A weekly report will be rendered the Director of Air Service as of Thursday night each week, showing:

(a) Number of enlisted men (this does not include Cadets) under dual training.

(b) Number of enlisted men (this does not include Cadets) under solo training.

If applicant does not pass a satisfactory physical and mental examination, he will be notified by the Commanding Officer and record of his examination will be filed in the Flying Office, and not forwarded to the Director of Air Service.

D
ACT OF JULY 11, 1919 — APPENDIX

SIXTY-SIXTH CONGRESS. Sess. I. Ch. 8. 1919.

AIR SERVICE.

Air Service.

Expenses of flying schools, aviation stations, etc.

Appropriations, Air Service: Creating, maintaining, and operating at established flying schools, courses of instruction for aviation students and enlisted men, including cost of equipment, and supplies necessary for instruction and subsistence of students, purchase of tools, equipment, materials, machines, textbooks, books of reference, scientific and professional papers, and instruments and material for theoretical and practical instruction at aviation schools; purchase of supplies for securing, developing, printing, and reproducing photographs made by aerial observers; to maintain and replace the equipment of organizations already in service; improvement, equipment, maintenance, lease, and operation of aviation stations, balloon schools, plants for testing and experimental work, including the acquisition of land, or any interest in land by purchase, lease, or condemnation, where necessary to procure helium gas; procuring and introducing water, electric light and power, telephones, telegraphs, and sewerage, including maintenance, operation, and repair of such utilities; salaries and wages of civilian employees in the District of Columbia or elsewhere as may be necessary, and payment of their traveling and other necessary expenses as authorized by existing law; experimental investigation and purchase and development of new types of aircraft, accessories thereto, including helium gas rights, and aviation engines, including patents and other rights thereto, and plans, drawings, and

Purchases, manufacture of aerial machines, etc.

specifications thereof; purchase, manufacture, construction, maintenance, repair, storage, and operation of airships, war balloons, and other aerial machines, including instruments, gas plants, hangars, and repair shops, and appliances of every sort and description necessary for the operation, construction, or equipment of all types of aircraft, and all necessary spare parts and equipment connected therewith, and also for the purchase or manufacture and the issue of special clothing, wearing apparel, and similar equipment for aviation purposes; for all necessary expenses connected with the sale or disposal of surplus or obsolete aeronautical equipment, including the hire of civilian employees, and the rental of buildings, and other facilities for the handling or storage of such equipment; for the services of such consulting

Consulting engineers.

engineers at experimental stations of the Air Service as the Secretary of War may deem necessary, including necessary traveling expenses:

Provisos.
Limit.
Special apparatus, etc.

Provided, That the entire expenditures for the services of consulting engineers for the fiscal year 1920 shall not exceed $100,000; purchase of special apparatus and appliances, repairs, and replacements of same used in connection with special scientific medical research in the Air

Aviation stations in the Philippines.

Service; for the establishment of aviation stations in the Philippine Islands, including the lease of land or any interest in land for landing fields only and the preparation of land now owned by the Government

165

necessary to make the same suitable for the purpose intended, buildings, heating, lighting, plumbing, water, sewer, roads, and walks, at a
total cost not to exceed $350,000; in all, $25,000,000: *Provided*, That
claims not exceeding $250 in amount for damages to persons and
private property resulting from the operation of aircraft at home and
abroad, may be settled out of the funds appropriated hereunder, when
each claim is substantiated by a survey report of a board of officers
appointed by the commanding officer of the nearest aviation post, and
approved by the Director of Air Service: *Provided further*, That claims
so settled and paid from the sum hereby appropriated shall not exceed
in the aggregate the sum of $150,000: *Provided further*, That here-
after actual and necessary expenses only, not to exceed $8 per day,
shall be paid to officers of the Army and contract surgeons when
traveling by air on duty without troops, under competent orders:
And provided further, That section 3648, Revised Statutes, shall not
apply to subscriptions for foreign and professional newspapers and
periodicals to be paid for from this appropriation.

The Secretary of War is hereby authorized and directed to establish
and maintain at one or more established flying schools courses of
instruction for aviation students.

Aviation students shall be enlisted in or appointed to the grade of
flying cadet, Air Service, which grade is hereby established: *Provided*,
That the total number of flying cadets shall not at any time exceed
one thousand three hundred.   The base pay of a flying cadet shall be
$75 per month, including extra pay for flying risk as provided by law.
The ration allowance of a flying cadet shall not exceed $1 per day, and
his other allowances shall be those of a private, first class, Air Service.

Upon completion of a course prescribed for flying cadets, each flying
cadet, if he so desire, may be discharged and commissioned as a
second lieutenant in the Officers' Reserve Corps: *Provided*, That the
Secretary of War is authorized to discharge at any time any flying
cadet whose discharge shall have been recommended by a board of
not less than three officers.

Marginal notes:

Damages to private property, etc.

Amount for settlement, limited.

Allowance for traveling by air on duty without troops.

Periodicals.
R. S., sec. 3648, p. 718.

Schools for aviation students.

Flying cadet grade established.
Proviso.
Limited number.
Pay, etc.

Commissions in Officers' Reserve Corps.

Proviso.
Discharges.

SIXTY-NINTH CONGRESS. Sess. I. Chs. 717, 718, 721. 1926.

July 2, 1926.
[H. R. 10827.]
[Public, No. 446.]

CHAP. 721.—An Act To provide more effectively for the national defense by increasing the efficiency of the Air Corps of the Army of the United States, and for other purposes.

Be it enacted by the Senate and House of Representatives of the United States of America in Congress assembled, That the Act entitled "An Act for making further and more effectual provision for the national defense, and for other purposes," approved June 3, 1916, as amended, be, and the same is hereby, amended so that the Air Service referred to in that Act and in all subsequent Acts of Congress shall be known as the Air Corps.

Air Corps, Army.
Air Service to be known as.
Vol. 39, p. 166.

SEC. 2. COMPOSITION OF THE AIR CORPS.—That section 13a of the Act entitled "An Act for making further and more effectual provision for the national defense, and for other purposes," approved June 3, 1916, as amended, be, and the same is hereby, amended by striking out the same and inserting the following in lieu thereof:

Composition.
Vol. 41, p. 768, amended.

" SEC. 13a. AIR CORPS.—There is hereby created an Air Corps. The Air Corps shall consist of one Chief of the Air Corps, with the rank of major general; three assistants, with the rank of brigadier general; one thousand five hundred and fourteen officers in grades from colonel to second lieutenant, inclusive; and sixteen thousand enlisted men, including not to exceed two thousand five hundred flying cadets, such part of whom as the President may direct being formed into tactical units or bands, organized as he may prescribe: *Provided,* That the Chief of the Air Corps, at least two brigadier generals, and at least 90 per centum of the officers in each grade below that of brigadier general shall be flying officers: *Provided further,* That in time of war 10 per centum of the total number of officers that may be authorized for the Air Corps for such war may be immediately commissioned as nonflying officers: *Provided further,* That as soon as a sufficient number can be trained, at least 90 per centum of the total number of officers authorized for the Air Corps for such war shall be flying officers: *Provided further,* That hereafter in time of peace in order to insure that the commissioned officers of the Air Corps shall be properly qualified flying officers and, for the purpose of giving officers of the Army an opportunity to so qualify, the Secretary of War is hereby authorized to detail to the Air Corps officers of all grades and such officers shall start flying training immediately upon being so detailed, but hereafter such officers shall not remain detailed to the Air Corps for a period in excess of one year or be permanently commissioned therein unless they qualify as flying officers: *Provided further,* That any officer who is specifically recommended by the Secretary of War because of special qualifications other than as a flyer may be detailed to the Air Corps for a period longer than one year, or may be permanently

Air Corps.
Creation and composition of.

Flying cadets.

Proviso.
Percentage of flying officers.

Nonflying, in time of war.

Training for flying officers, in time of war.

Details for flying instruction in time of peace.

Period limited.

Longer details because of special qualifications.

167

Not included as flying officers.

commissioned in the Air Corps, but such officers, together with those flying officers who shall have become disqualified for flying, shall not be included among the 90 per centum of flying officers: *And provided further*, That nothing in this Act shall be construed to limit the number of officers in each grade that may be detailed to the Air Corps for training as flying officers except that the total number of officers allotted to the Air Corps shall not be exceeded. Flying units shall in all cases be commanded by flying officers. Wherever used in this Act a flying officer in time of peace is defined as one who has received an aeronautical rating as a pilot of service types of aircraft: *Provided*, That all officers of the Air Corps now holding any rating as a pilot shall be considered as flying officers within the meaning of this Act: *Provided further*, That hereafter in order to receive a rating as a pilot in time of peace an officer or an enlisted man must fly in heavier-than-air craft at least two hundred hours while acting as a pilot, seventy-five of which must be alone, and must successfully complete the course prescribed by competent authority: *And provided further*, That in time of war a flying officer may include any officer who has received an aeronautical rating as a pilot of service types of air craft and also in time of war may include any officer who has received an aeronautical rating as observer. Officers and enlisted men of the Army shall receive an increase of 50 per centum of their pay when by orders of competent authority they are required to participate regularly and frequently in aerial flights, and when in consequence of such orders they do participate in regular and frequent aerial flights as defined by such Executive orders as have heretofore been, or may hereafter be, promulgated by the President: *Provided*, That nothing in this Act shall be construed as amending existing provisions of law relating to flying cadets. On and after July 1, 1929, and in time of peace, not less than 20 per centum of the total number of pilots employed in tactical units of the Air Corps shall be enlisted men, except when the Secretary of War shall determine that it is impractical to secure that number of enlisted pilots.

Training details not limited.

Command of flying units.

Flying officer defined.

Pilots considered flying officers.

Pilot rating qualifications in time of peace.

In time of war.

Pay increase for participating in aerial flights.

Flying cadets. Vol. 42, p. 724. Percentage of enlisted pilots after July 1, 1929.

Air mechanics rated.

"Enlisted men of the fourth, fifth, sixth, and seventh grades in the Air Corps who have demonstrated their fitness and shown that they possess the necessary technical qualifications therefor and are engaged upon the duties pertaining thereto may be rated as air mechanics, first class, or air mechanics, second class, under such regulations as the Secretary of War may prescribe. Each enlisted man while holding the rating of air mechanic, first class, and performing the duties as such shall receive the pay of the second grade, and each enlisted man while holding the rating of air mechanic, second class, and performing the duties as such shall receive the pay of the third grade: *Provided*, That such number as the Secretary of War may determine as necessary, not to exceed 14 per centum of the total authorized enlisted strength of the Air Corps, shall be rated as air mechanics, first class, or air mechanics, second class."

Pay provisions.

Proviso. Percentage of Air Corps enlisted strength.

Temporary rank on assignment to commands, etc.

SEC. 3. TEMPORARY RANK FOR AIR CORPS OFFICERS.—The Secretary of War is hereby authorized to assign, under such regulations as he may prescribe, officers of the Air Corps to flying commands, including wings, groups, squadrons, flights, schools, important air stations, and to the staffs of commanders of troops, which assignment shall carry with it temporary rank, including pay and allowances appropriate to such rank, as determined by the Secretary of War, for the period of such assignment: *Provided*, That such temporary rank is limited to two grades above the permanent rank of the officer appointed: *Provided further*, That no officer shall be temporarily advanced in rank as contemplated in this section unless the Chief of the Air Corps certifies that no officers of suitable permanent rank are available for the duty requiring the increased rank: *And provided further*, That no officer holding temporary rank under the provisions of this section shall be eligible to command outside of his own corps except by seniority under his permanent commission.

Provisos. Limitation.

Restriction.

Not to command outside of his corps, etc.

SEC. 4. CORRECTION OF PROMOTION LIST.—That the Secretary of War be, and he is hereby, directed to investigate and study the alleged injustices which exist in the promotion list of the Army and to submit to Congress on the second Monday in December, 1926, this study, together with his recommendations for changes, if any, in the present promotion list.

SEC. 5. AIR SECTIONS OF THE GENERAL STAFF.—That section 5 of the Act entitled "An Act for making further and more effectual provisions for the national defense, and for other purposes," approved June 3, 1916, as amended, be, and the same is hereby, amended by adding the following paragraph at the end thereof:

" That for the period of three years immediately following July 1, 1926, there is hereby created in each of the divisions of the War Department General Staff an air section to be headed by an officer of the Air Corps, the duties of which shall be to consider and recommend proper action on such air matters as may be referred to such division."

SEC. 6. FLYING PAY.—That section 20 of the Act of June 10, 1922 (Forty-second Statutes, page 632), as amended, be, and the same is hereby, amended by striking out the same and inserting the following in lieu thereof:

" SEC. 20. That all officers, warrant officers, and enlisted men of all branches of the Army, Navy, Marine Corps, and Coast Guard, when by orders of competent authority they are required to participate regularly and frequently in aerial flights, and when in consequence of such orders they do participate in regular and frequent flights as defined by such Executive orders as have heretofore been, or may hereafter be, promulgated by the President, shall receive the same increase of their pay and the same allowance for traveling expenses as are authorized for the performance of like duties in the Army. Exclusive of the Army Air Corps, and student aviators and qualified aircraft pilots of the Navy, Marine Corps, and Coast Guard, the number of officers of any of the services mentioned in the title of this Act who may be required by competent authority to participate regularly and frequently in aerial flights as defined by such Executive orders as have heretofore been, or may hereafter be, promulgated by the President shall not at any one time exceed 1 per centum of the total authorized commissioned strength of such service. Officers, warrant officers, and enlisted men of the National Guard participating in exercises or performing duties provided for by sections 92, 94, 97, and 99 of the National Defense Act, as amended, and of the Reserves of the services mentioned in the title of this Act called to active duty shall receive an increase of 50 per centum of their pay when by orders of competent authority they are required to participate regularly and frequently in aerial flights, and when in consequence of such orders they do participate in regular and frequent aerial flights as defined by such Executive orders as have heretofore been, or may hereafter be, promulgated by the President and when such flying involves travel they shall also receive the same allowances for traveling expenses as are or hereafter may be authorized for the Regular Army: *Provided*, That when officers, warrant officers, and enlisted men of the National Guard are entitled to armory drill pay, the increase of 50 per centum thereof herein provided shall be based on the entire amount of such armory drill pay to which they shall be entitled for a calendar month or fractional part thereof, and the required aerial flights may be made at ordered drills of an Air Service organization, or at other times when so authorized by the President. Regulations in execution of the provisions of this section shall be made by the President and shall, whenever practicable in his judgment, be uniform for all the services concerned."

SEC. 7. APPOINTMENT OF CHIEF OF THE AIR CORPS.—That the third sentence of section 4c of the Act entitled "An Act for making further and more effectual provision for the national defense, and for other purposes," approved June 3, 1916, as amended, be, and

---

Marginal notes (left column):

Promotion list. Investigation, etc., of alleged injustices in.

General Staff. Vol. 41, p. 764, amended.

Air sections created in, for three years.

Flying pay. Vol. 42, p. 632, amended.

Increased pay, etc., applicable to all branches of service required to participate in aerial flights.

Details of officers, other than Air Corps, etc., to aerial flights limited.

Application to National Guard, in training, etc. Vol. 39, pp. 206, 207, Vol. 42, p. 1035; Vol. 43; p. 363.

Proviso. Increased pay based on armory drill pay.

Uniformity in regulations.

Chief of Air Corps. Vol. 41, p. 762, amended.

the same is hereby, amended by adding thereto the following:

For period of 7 years, appointment of, from any grade with specified service and qualifications. "*And provided further*, That during the period of seven years immediately following July 1, 1926, any appointment as Chief of the Air Corps shall be made from among officers of any grade of not less than fifteen years' commissioned service, and from those who have demonstrated by actual and extended service in such corps that they are qualified for such appointment; and as assistants from among officers of not less than fifteen years' commissioned Assistants. service of similar qualifications: *Provided*, That the Chief of the Proviso. Chief to recommend assistants. Air Corps shall make recommendations to the Secretary of War for the appointment of his assistants."

Five-year program for increasing efficiency of Air Corps. SEC. 8. FIVE-YEAR AIR CORPS PROGRAM.—For the purpose of increasing the efficiency of the Air Corps of the Army and for its further development the following five-year program is authorized:

Personnel. Increase in number of second lieutenants and enlisted men. PERSONNEL.—The number of promotion-list officers now authorized by law in the grade of second lieutenant of the Regular Army is hereby increased by four hundred and three, and the number of enlisted men now authorized by law for the Regular Army is hereby authorized to be increased by six thousand two hundred and forty: Provisos. Allotments. *Provided*, That the increase in the number of officers and enlisted men herein authorized shall be allotted as hereinafter provided. Officers and enlisted men. The present allotment of officers to the Air Corps is hereby authorized to be increased by four hundred and three officers distributed in grades from colonel to second lieutenant, inclusive, and the present allotment of enlisted men to the Air Corps is hereby authorized to be increased by six thousand two hundred and forty enlisted Reserve officers called to active service. men. The President is authorized to call to active service, with their consent, such number of Air Corps reserve officers as he may deem necessary, not to exceed five hundred and fifty, 90 per centum of whom shall serve for periods of not more than one year, and 10 per centum for periods of not more than two years: *Provided*, That Active duty for less than six months. nothing contained in this section shall affect the number of reserve officers that may be called to active duty for periods of less than six months under existing law.

Equipment. Number of aircraft to be maintained. EQUIPMENT.—The Secretary of War is hereby authorized to equip and maintain the Air Corps with not to exceed one thousand eight hundred serviceable airplanes, and such number of airships and free and captive balloons as he may determine to be necessary for training purposes, together with spare parts, equipment, supplies, hangars, and installations necessary for the operation and mainte- Replacing obsolete, etc., craft. nance thereof. In order to maintain the number specified above, the Secretary of War is hereby authorized to replace obsolete or Provisos. Annual limitation. unserviceable aircraft from time to time: *Provided*, That the necessary replacement of airplanes shall not exceed approximately Total, exclusive of those awaiting salvage, etc. four hundred annually: *Provided*, That the total number of air- planes and airships herein authorized shall be exclusive of those waiting salvage or undergoing experiment or service tests, those authorized by the Secretary of War to be placed in museums and those classified by the Secretary of War as obsolete: *And provided* Number for National Guard and Organized Reserves training, etc., included in total. *further*, That the total number of planes authorized in this section shall include the number necessary for the training and equipment of the National Guard and the training of the Organized Reserves as may be determined by the Secretary of War.

Distribution of in- crease of personnel and equipment. METHOD OF INCREASE.—The total increase in personnel and equip- ment authorized herein shall be distributed over a five-year period beginning July 1, 1926. Not to exceed one-fifth of the total increase shall be made during the first year, and the remainder in four Estimates to be sub- mitted. approximately equal increments. The President is hereby authorized to submit to Congress annually estimates of the cost of carrying out Proviso. Supplemental esti- mate for 1927. the five-year program authorized herein: *Provided*, That a supple- mental estimate for the fiscal year ending June 30, 1927, may be submitted to cover the cost of the first annual increment.

Vol. 41, p. 765, amend- ed. SEC. 9. That section 5a of the National Defense Act, as amended, be, and the same is hereby, amended by adding at the end of said section 5a the following:

Additional Assistant Secretary of War. Appointment of, to aid in aeronautics.

" To aid the Secretary of War in fostering military aeronautics, and to perform such functions as the Secretary may direct, there shall be an additional Assistant Secretary of War who shall be appointed by the President, by and with the advice and consent of the Senate, and whose compensation shall be fixed in accordance with the Classification Act of 1923."

Encouraging Army and Navy aeronautical efficiency.

Advertising for competitive designs of aircraft, etc.

SEC. 10. (a) That in order to encourage the development of aviation and improve the efficiency of the Army and Navy aeronautical matériel the Secretary of War or the Secretary of the Navy, prior to the procurement of new designs of aircraft or aircraft parts or aeronautical accessories, shall, by advertisement for a period of thirty days in at least three of the leading aeronautical journals and in such other manner as he may deem advisable, invite the submission in competition, by sealed communications, of such designs of aircraft. aircraft parts, and aeronautical accessories, together with a statement of the price for which such designs in whole or in part will be sold to the Government.

Time for receiving designs, etc., to be specified.

Detailed information, to each applicant, of requirements of competition.

(b) The aforesaid advertisement shall specify a sufficient time, not less than sixty days from the expiration of the advertising period, within which all such communications containing designs and prices therefor must be submitted, and all such communications received shall be carefully kept sealed in the War Department or the Navy Department, as the case may be, until the expiration of said specified time, and no designs mailed after that time shall be received or considered. Said advertisement shall state in general terms the kind or aircraft, parts, or accessories to be developed and the approximate number or quantity required, and the department concerned shall furnish to each applicant identical specific detailed information as to the conditions and requirements of the competition and as to the various features and characteristics to be developed, listing specifically the respective measures of merit, expressed in rates per centum, that shall be applied in determining the merits of the designs, and said measures of merit shall be adhered to

Board to appraise and report winners of designs submitted.

throughout such competition. All designs received up to the time specified for submitting them shall then be referred to a board appointed for that purpose by the Secretary of the department concerned and shall be appraised by it as soon as practicable and report made to the Secretary as to the winner or winners of such

Public announcement, if report approved by Secretary.

If disapproved, return of papers to board, etc.

Details of announcement.

competition. When said Secretary shall have approved the report of said board, he shall then fix a time and place for a public announcement of the results and notify each competitor thereof; but if said report shall be disapproved by said Secretary, the papers shall be returned to the board for revision or the competition be decided by the Secretary, in his discretion, and in any case the decision of the Secretary shall be final and conclusive. Such announcement shall include the percentages awarded to each of the several features or characteristics of the designs submitted by each competitor and the prices named by the competitors for their designs and the several features thereof if separable.

Contracts with winners authorized.

(c) Thereupon the said Secretary is authorized to contract with the winner or winners in such competition on such terms and conditions as he may deem most advantageous to the Government for furnishing or constructing all of each of the items, or all of any one or more of the several items of the aircraft, or parts, or accessories indicated in the advertisement, as the said Secretary shall find that in his judgment a winner is, or can within a reasonable time become, able and equipped to furnish or construct satisfactorily all or part, provided said Secretary and the winner shall

Purchase of designs, etc., if Secretary decide winner can not perform contract for such aircraft, etc.

be able to agree on a reasonable price. If the Secretary shall decide that a winner can not reasonably carry out and perform a contract for all or part of such aircraft, parts, or accessories, as above provided, then he is authorized to purchase the winning designs or any separable parts thereof if a fair and reasonable price can be agreed on with the winner, but not in excess of the price submitted with the designs.

After contract with, and payment to, winner of design, etc., Government may construct the same without further compensation.
(d) After contract is made, as authorized by any provision of this section, with a winner in such design competition for furnishing or constructing aircraft, aircraft parts, or aeronautical accessories in accordance with his designs and payment is completed under said contract, and after the purchase of and payment for the designs or separable parts thereof of a winner, as authorized herein, with whom a contract shall not have been made for furnishing or constructing aircraft, aircraft parts or aeronautical accessories in accordance with his designs, then in either case any department of the Government shall have the right without further compensation to the winner to construct or have constructed according to said designs and use any number of aircraft or parts or accessories, and sell said aircraft or parts or accessories according to law as condemned material: *Provided*, That such winner shall, nevertheless, be at liberty to apply for a patent on any features originated by him, and shall be entitled to enjoy the exclusive rights under such patent as he may obtain as against all other persons except the United States Government or its assignee as aforesaid.

Sale of the aircraft as condemned material.

Proviso.
Winner may have patent for original features, etc.

Competitors to submit graduated scale of proposed prices.
(e) The competitors in design competition mentioned in this section shall submit with their designs a graduated scale of prices for which they are willing to construct any or all or each of the aircraft, aircraft parts, and aeronautical accessories for which designs are submitted and such stated prices shall not be exceeded in the awarding of contracts contemplated by this section.

No obligation to accept submitted designs not considered of sufficient merit.
(f) If the Secretary of War or the Secretary of the Navy shall find that in his judgment none of the designs submitted in said competition is of sufficient merit to justify the procurement of aircraft, aircraft parts, or aeronautical accessories in accordance therewith, then he shall not be obligated to accept any of such designs or to make any payment on account of any of them. If the Secretary of the department concerned shall decide that the designs submitted by two or more competitors possess equal merit, or that certain features embodied in the designs of any competitor are superior to corresponding features embodied in the designs of any other competitor and such features of one design may be substituted in another design, the said Secretary shall in his discretion divide the contracts for furnishing and manufacturing the aircraft, parts, or accessories required, equitably among those competitors that have submitted designs of equal merit, or he may select and combine features of superior excellence in different designs in such manner as may in his judgment best serve the Government's interests and make payment accordingly to the several competitors concerned at fair and reasonable prices, awarding the contract for furnishing or constructing the aircraft, parts, or accessories to the competitor or competitors concerned that have the highest figures of merit in said competition.

If two or more designs have equal merit, etc., contracts may be divided between competitors for furnishing the aircraft, etc.

Awarding of contract.

If unable to make contract with winner for furnishing aircraft, etc., designs may be retained and proposals for construction be advertised.
(g) In case the Secretary of War or the Secretary of the Navy shall be unable to make contract as above authorized with a winner in said competition for furnishing or constructing aircraft, aircraft parts, or aeronautical accessories covered by the whole or part of the designs of such winner, or shall be unable to agree with a winner in the competition on a reasonable purchase price for the design of such winner with whom a contract may not be made, as aforesaid, he may retain such designs and shall advertise according to law for proposals for furnishing or constructing aircraft, or parts or accessories, in accordance with such designs or combinations thereof as aforesaid and, after all proposals are submitted, make contract on such terms and conditions as he may consider the best in the Government's interests, with the bidder that he shall find to be the lowest responsible bidder for furnishing or constructing the aircraft, parts, or accessories required, but the said Secretary shall have the right to reject all bids and to advertise for other bids with such other and different specifications as he may deem proper.

Bids may be rejected.

(h) If, within ten days after the announcement of the results of said competition, any participant in the competition shall make to the Secretary of War or the Secretary of the Navy a reasonable showing in writing that error was made in determining the merits of designs submitted whereby such claimant was unjustly deprived of an award, the matter shall at once be referred by the Secretary of the department concerned to a board of arbitration for determination and the finding of such board shall, with the approval of the said Secretary, be conclusive on both parties. Such board of arbitration shall be composed of three skilled aeronautical engineers, one selected by the said Secretary, one by the claimant, and the third by those two, no one of whom shall have been a member of the board of appraisal in that competition.

(i) Any person, firm, or corporation that shall complain that his, their, or its designs hereafter developed relating to aircraft or any components thereof are used or manufactured by or for any department of the Government without just compensation from either the Government or any other source, may within four years from the date of such use file suit in the Court of Claims for the recovery of his reasonable and entire compensation for such use and manufacture after the date of this Act.

(j) Only citizens of the United States, and corporations of which not less than three-fourths of the capital stock is owned by citizens of the United States, and of which the members of the boards of directors are citizens of the United States, and having manufacturing plants located within the continental limits of the United States shall be eligible to be awarded any contract under this section to furnish or construct aircraft, aircraft parts or aeronautical accessories for the United States Government, except that a domestic corporation whose stock shall be listed on a stock exchange shall not be barred by the provisions of this section unless and until foreign ownership or control of a majority of its stock shall be known to the Secretary of War or the Secretary of the Navy, as the case may be, and no aliens employed by a contractor for furnishing or constructing aircraft, or aircraft parts, or aeronautical accessories for the United States shall be permitted to have access to the plans or specifications or the work under construction or to participate in the contract trials without the written consent beforehand of the Secretary of the department concerned.

(k) The Secretary of War or the Secretary of the Navy may at his discretion purchase abroad or in the United States with or without competition, by contract, or otherwise, such designs, aircraft, aircraft parts, or aeronautical accessories as may be necessary in his judgment for experimental purposes in the development of aircraft or aircraft parts or aeronautical accessories of the best kind for the Army or the Navy, as the case may be, and if as a result of such procurement, new and suitable designs considered to be the best kind for the Army or the Navy are developed, he may enter into contract, subject to the requirements of paragraph (j) of this section, for the procurement in quantity of such aircraft, aircraft parts, or aeronautical accessories without regard to the provisions of paragraphs (a) to (e), inclusive, hereof.

(l) The manufacturing plant, and books, of any contractor for furnishing or constructing aircraft, aircraft parts, or aeronautical accessories, for the War Department or the Navy Department, or such part of any manufacturing plant as may be so engaged, shall at all times be subject to inspection and audit by any person designated by the head of any executive department of the Government.

(m) All audits and reports of inspection, made under the provisions of this section, shall be preserved by the Secretary of War or the Secretary of the Navy, as the case may be, for a period of ten years, and shall be subject to inspection by any committee of Congress, and the said Secretaries shall annually make a detailed and itemized report to Congress of all the departments' operations under this section, the names and addresses of all competitors, and of all persons having been awarded contracts and the prices paid for aircraft purchased and the grounds and reasons for having awarded such contracts to the particular persons, firms, or corporations, and all such reports shall be printed and held subject to public distribution.

Vendor and contractor to deliver to Department a release of all claims arising out of the sale or contract.

(n) Every vendor of designs to the War Department or the Navy Department under the provisions of this section, and every contractor for furnishing or constructing for the War Department or the Navy Department, or both, aircraft or aircraft parts or aeronautical accessories, shall deliver to the Secretary of War or Secretary of the Navy, or both, when required by either or both, a release in such form and containing such terms and conditions as may be prescribed by the Secretary of War, the Secretary of the Navy, or both, of claims on the part of such vendor or contractor against the United States arising out of such sale or contract, or both.

War or Navy Department appropriations for aircraft, etc., available for purchase of designs, etc.

(o) All or any appropriations available for the procurement of aircraft, aircraft parts, or aeronautical accessories, for the War Department or the Navy Department shall also be available for payment of the purchase price of designs and the costs of arbitration as authorized by this section.

Collusion, etc., to deprive the Government of benefit of free competition, etc., unlawful.

(p) Any collusion, understanding, or arrangement to deprive the United States Government of the benefit of full and free competition in any competition authorized by this section, or to deprive the United States Government of the benefit of a full and free audit of the books of any person, firm, or corporation engaged in carrying out any contract authorized by this section, so far as may be necessary to disclose the exact cost of executing such contract, shall be unlawful, and any person, firm, or corporation that shall, upon indictment and trial, be found guilty of violating any of the provisions of this section shall be sentenced to pay a fine of not exceeding $20,000, or to be imprisoned not exceeding five years, or both, at the discretion of the court.

Punishment for violations.

Contracts authorized for quantities of aircraft, etc., from suitable designs procured hitherto.

(q) In the procurement of aircraft constructed according to designs presented by any individual, firm, or corporation prior to the passage of this Act, which designs have been reduced to practice and found to be suitable for the purpose intended or according to such designs with minor modifications thereof, the Secretary of War or the Secretary of the Navy, when in his opinion the interests of the United States will be best served thereby, may contract with said individual, firm, or corporation, at reasonable prices for such quantities of said aircraft, aircraft parts, or aeronautical accessories as he may deem necessary: *Provided*, That the action of the Secretary of War or the Secretary of the Navy, in each such case shall be final and conclusive.

Proviso. Action of the Secretary final and conclusive.

Patents and design board. Composition of.

(r) A board to be known as the patents and design board is hereby created, the three members of which shall be an Assistant Secretary of War, an Assistant Secretary of the Navy, and an Assistant Secretary of Commerce. To this board any individual, firm, or corporation may submit a design for aircraft, aircraft parts, or aeronautical accessories, and whether patented or unpatentable, the said board upon the recommendation of the National Advisory Committee for Aeronautics shall determine whether the use of such designs by the Government is desirable or necessary, and evaluate the designs so submitted and fix the worth to the United States of said design, not to exceed $75,000. The said designer, individual, firm, or corporation, may then be offered the sum fixed by the board for the ownership or a nonexclusive right of the United States to the use of the design in aircraft, aircraft parts, or aeronautical accessories and upon the acceptance thereof shall execute complete assignment or nonexclusive license to the United States: *Provided*, That no sum in excess of $75,000 shall be paid for any one design.

Duties. *Post,* p. 1380.

Offer for right to design recommended by.

Proviso. Maximum sum.

Meaning of "winner" or "winners."

(s) The terms " winner " or " winners " as used in this section shall be construed to include not more than three competitors having the highest figures of merit in any one competition.

Awarding of contracts to lowest responsible bidder.

(t) Hereafter whenever the Secretary of War, or the Secretary of the Navy, shall enter into a contract for or on behalf of the United

States, for aircraft, aircraft parts, or aeronautical accessories, said Secretary is hereby authorized to award such contract to the bidder that said Secretary shall find to be the lowest responsible bidder that can satisfactorily perform the work or the service required to the best advantage of the Government; and the decision of the Secretary of the department concerned as to the award of such contract, the interpretation of the provisions of the contract, and the application and administration of the contract shall not be reviewable, otherwise than as may be therein provided for, by any officer or tribunal of the United States except the President and the Federal courts.

Decision of Secretary reviewable only by the President and Federal courts.

SEC. 11. Under such rules and regulations as he may prescribe the President is hereby authorized to present, but not in the name of Congress, a medal to be known as the soldier's medal, of appropriate design, with accompanying ribbon, to any person who, while serving in any capacity with the Army of the United States, including the National Guard and the Organized Reserves, shall hereafter distinguish himself, or herself, by heroism not involving actual conflict with an enemy.

Soldier's medal. Awarded for heroism not in conflict with an enemy.

No more than one soldier's medal shall be issued to any one person; but for each succeeding deed or act sufficient to justify the award of the soldier's medal the President may award a suitable bar, or other suitable device, to be worn as he shall direct.

Bar for each subsequent act.

SEC. 12. Under such rules and regulations as he may prescribe, and notwithstanding the provisions of section 14 of this Act, the President is hereby authorized to present, but not in the name of Congress, a distinguished flying cross of appropriate design, with accompanying ribbon, to any person who, while serving in any capacity with the Air Corps of the Army of the United States, including the National Guard and the Organized Reserves, or with the United States Navy, since the 6th day of April, 1917, has distinguished, or who, after the approval of this Act, distinguishes himself by heroism or extraordinary achievement while participating in an aerial flight: *Provided,* That no person shall be eligible for the award of the distinguished flying cross for any act performed prior to November 11, 1918, except officers or enlisted men who have heretofore been recommended for but have not received the congressional medal of honor, the distinguished service cross, or the distinguished service medal and except those officers or enlisted men who displayed heroism while serving as instructors or students at flying schools. No more than one distinguished flying cross shall be issued to any one person, but for each succeeding act or achievement sufficient to justify the award of a distinguished flying cross the President may award a suitable bar or other suitable device to be worn as he shall direct. In case an individual who distinguishes himself shall have died before the making of the award to which he may be entitled, the award may nevertheless be made and the cross or the bar or other device presented to such representative of the deceased as the President may designate, but no cross, bar, or other device hereinbefore authorized shall be awarded or presented to any individual whose entire service subsequent to the time he distinguishes himself has not been honorable.

Distinguished flying cross. Awarded for extraordinary achievement in an aerial flight since April 6, 1917, or hereafter.

Proviso. Eligibility for acts prior to November 11, 1918.

Bar, etc., for subsequent act.

To representative in case of death prior to award.

Dishonorable service precludes an award.

SEC. 13. Each enlisted or enrolled man to whom there shall be awarded the distinguished flying cross or the soldier's medal shall be entitled to additional pay at the rate of $2 per month from the date of the act of heroism or extraordinary achievement on which the award is based, and each bar, or other suitable device, in lieu of the distinguished flying cross or the soldier's medal, as hereinbefore provided for, shall entitle him to further additional pay at the rate of $2 per month from the date of the act of heroism or extraordinary achievement for which the bar or other device is awarded, and said additional pay shall continue throughout his active service, whether such service shall or shall not be continuous.

Additional pay to enlisted or enrolled man receiving cross or medal.

Further for each bar, etc., issued.

SEC. 14. That if any section or provision of this Act shall be held to be invalid, it is hereby provided that all other sections

Invalidity of any section, etc., not to impair other provisions of Act.

No retroactive effect, etc.

Inconsistent laws repealed.

and provisions of this Act not expressly held to be invalid shall continue in full force and effect. No provision of this Act shall be retroactive and the provisions hereof shall take effect upon date of approval thereof, except as otherwise provided for herein, and all Acts or parts of Acts contrary to the provisions of this Act or inconsistent therewith be, and the same are hereby, repealed.

Approved, July 2, 1926.

ACT OF JUNE 3, 1941 F APPENDIX

[CHAPTER 167]

AN ACT

To authorize the training of enlisted men of the Army as aviation students.

June 3, 1941
[S. 1371]
[Public Law 99]

Be it enacted by the Senate and House of Representatives of the United States of America in Congress assembled, That the Secretary of War be, and he is hereby, authorized, under such regulations as he may prescribe, to cause the detail of enlisted men of the Regular Army and of other components of the Army of the United States in active Federal service for training and instruction as aviation students, in their respective grades, in such numbers and schools as he shall direct: *Provided,* That enlisted men so detailed as aviation students who are undergoing courses of instruction which require them to participate regularly and frequently in aerial flights shall be issued Government life insurance in the amount of $10,000 under the National Service Life Insurance Act of 1940 (Public, Numbered 801, title VI, part 1), except that the premiums shall be paid by the Government during the period such enlisted men are undergoing training and instruction, and upon completion of training and instruction as aviation students they shall have the option of continuing such policies at their own expense: *And provided further,* That nothing herein shall be construed as repealing or otherwise affecting existing statutory authorizations for the appointment and training of aviation students or aviation cadets.

Aviation students,
Army.

Provisos.
Government life insurance.

54 Stat. 1008.
38 U. S. C. §§ 801–818.

Existing provisions not affected.

Approved, June 3, 1941.

WAR DEPARTMENT REGULATION 615-150

G APPENDIX

"AVIATION STUDENT TRAINING."

AR 615–150
1–2

ARMY REGULATIONS }
No. 615–150

WAR DEPARTMENT,
WASHINGTON, August 1, 1941.

ENLISTED MEN
AVIATION STUDENT TRAINING

1. **Eligibility.**—*a. Who may apply.*—Applicants for training as aviation students must at the time of application be—

    (1) Enlisted men of the Regular Army or of other components of the Army of the United States in active Federal service.

    (2) Unmarried male citizens of the United States.

    (3) Between the ages of 18 and 22 years, inclusive.

    (4) Individuals who have been graduated, with not less than 1½ mathematics units credits, from a secondary school on the accredited list of the United States Office of Education and whose credits are acceptable to accredited higher institutions.

    (5) Individuals who have successfully passed such other tests as the Chief of the Air Corps may prescribe.

    (6) Of excellent character.

    (7) Of sound physique and in excellent health.

  b. Agreement required.—Each enlisted man applying for aviation student training must sign an agreement (with the consent of his parents or guardian, if a minor) by which he will agree—

    (1) To reenlist for a period of 3 years if he has less than 1 year to complete his current term of service.

    (2) Upon successful completion of pilot training (about 8 months) to reenlist again in order to serve 3 years as an enlisted pilot.

(3) To remain unmarried during the period of training as aviation student and during his first enlistment as a noncommissioned officer pilot.

c. Age limit.—No enlisted man will be detailed to aviation student training who has reached his 23d birthday.

d. Applicants who have previously received flying training at a service school.— An applicant who has been eliminated from a service flying school due to failure in flying or who has completed the course of instruction in a service flying school is ineligible for aviation student training.

2. Applications.—*a. Manner of submitting.*—Application will be made through military channels in the form prescribed in paragraph 10. It will be accompanied by—

(1) Three letters of recommendation signed by persons of recognized standing in the community in which the residence of the applicant is located or by officers familiar with his service.

(2) A certificate from the secondary school attended certifying to the subjects pursued by the applicant, the credits and grades attained by the applicant. and a statement as to whether or not the applicant was graduated.

b. To whom and how forwarded.—Applications will be forwarded through military channels to the commander of the corps area in which the unit of the applicant is located with appropriate remarks and recommendations.

c. Action upon.—In the case of an approved application of an enlisted man of the Regular Army or of other components of the Army of the United States in active Federal service, the corps area commander will issue the necessary orders for the applicant to proceed to the nearest station where examinations are held, regardless of corps area, to report to the president of examining board for examination and to return to his proper station on completion thereof. All approved applications will be transmitted by the corps area commander to the presidents of examining boards before which the applicants are to be examined. Upon completion of the examination, the papers will be forwarded by the examining board direct to the Chief of the Air Corps.

d. Change of address of applicants.—Any enlisted man who has submitted an application for training as an aviation student will inform the Chief of the Air Corps of any change of station. Failure to do this is sufficient cause for removal of his name from the list of applicants.

e. Notification of ineligibility.—Applicants found ineligible will be so notified by the authority authorized to act upon applications as soon as their ineligibility shall have been determined.

3. Examination.—*a. Examining boards.*—Applicants for aviation student training will appear before an aviation cadet examining board prescribed by AR 615–160 as modified by instructions of The Adjutant General to corps area commanders.

b. Physical examination.—Each applicant appearing before the board will first be subjected to the physical examination prescribed in AR 40–110. W. D., A. G. O. Form No. 64 (Physical Examination for Flying) will be forwarded in duplicate. Should the applicant possess defects that may be removed by simple treatment or by a minor operation, the applicant will be permitted to proceed with his examination for moral and educational fitness for pilot training with the understanding that, should he qualify in the latter, he will not be eligible for aviation student training unless and until the board shall find upon subsequent report of physical examination by a qualified examiner (not necessarily a member of the board) that he is physically qualified for flying duty.

c. Moral character and general fitness.—After the physical examination of the applicant has been completed, the board will proceed with an examination into and determination of his moral qualifications, adaptability, etc. These will be determined by means of oral questioning of the applicant, consideration of the letters of recommendation submitted by him, and by such further investigation as the board may consider necessary or desirable in this phase of the examination. The candidate will be required to measure up to the standard prescribed for aviation cadets.

d. *Educational fitness.*—The board will next proceed with the determination of the educational fitness of the applicant. Each applicant must present a certified document from a secondary school which is on the approved list of the United States Office of Education and whose credits are acceptable for entrance into accredited higher institutions. This document must show—

(1) That the applicant is a graduate from the approved secondary school.

(2) That he has credits amounting to not less than 1½ units of mathematics.

(3) The board will verify that the applicant has the required score in the General Classification Test, War Department, The Adjutant General's Office.

e. *Reports of examining board.*—The examining board will, within 5 days after completion of the examination, forward direct to the Chief of the Air Corps a separate report in duplicate for each applicant who appears before the board together with the application and accompanying papers of each applicant. The report will contain—

(1) If the applicant is physically, morally, and educationally qualified:

(a) A statement as to the applicant's moral character and general fitness.

(b) Copies of all documentary evidence presented to the board.

(c) A report of physical examination on W. D., A. G. O. Form No. 64, in duplicate.

(d) Rating in General Classification Test, War Department, The Adjutant General's Office.

(2) If the applicant is physically disqualified, report of physical examination on W. D., A. G. O. Form No. 64.

(3) If the applicant is morally disqualified:

(a) A statement as to the applicant's moral character and general fitness.

(b) Report of physical examination on W. D., A. G. O. Form No. 64.

4. Appointment.—a. *Precedence.*—In case there are more qualified candidates than vacancies, appointments will be made from eligibles in accordance with a precedence established by the Chief of the Air Corps.

b. *Method of detail.*—As a result of the examinations as prescribed above, the Chief of the Air Corps will transmit information as to the names, Army serial numbers, grades, organizations, and stations of those found qualified to The Adjutant General, with appropriate recommendations and such data as may be necessary for the preparation of orders providing for their transfer to a civil flying school for their flying training. The Adjutant General will issue the necessary orders directing the change of station and authorizing aviation student training. If the enlisted man belongs to an arm or service other than the Air Corps, the aviation student will be detailed to flying training in the grade which he holds at that time. He will be carried on detached service by his organization until he is either eliminated from aviation student training and returned to his organization or completes his aviation student training. If the enlisted man is detailed to aviation student training from the Air Corps, he will be carried on detached service by his organization until eliminated and returned to duty therein or until he has completed his aviation student training.

c. Discharge and reenlistment.—No enlisted man will be ordered to a flying school as an aviation student unless he shall have at least 1 year to serve in his current enlistment. If the unexpired portion of the current enlistment of the enlisted man is not sufficient to permit his detail under the foregoing provision, he will be discharged and reenlisted for 3 years in order to permit his detail. Such discharge and reenlistment, if necessary, will be effected at the enlisted man's station prior to his being sent to the flying school.

d. No prospective or actual aviation student will be reduced in grade because of his detail to aviation student training.

5. Training.—The scope of the training will be as prescribed in the approved program of instruction for the flying schools.

6. Action upon conclusion of training.—*a.* About 2 months before completion of advanced flying training, the faculty board at the Air Corps advanced flying school will consider the physical, moral, and professional qualifications of each aviation student due to complete his training and will render a report in duplicate containing the following:

(1) Full names and grades of aviation students (all names spelled out).

(2) Serial numbers of all aviation students.

(3) Estimated date of graduation.

(4) Statement as to whether the candidate is physically, morally, and professionally qualified for appointment to the grade of staff sergeant pilot, Air Corps, Regular Army. In case recommendation is in the negative, detailed reasons therefor will be given.

b. This report will be forwarded to the Chief of the Air Corps through the commanding general of the Air Corps training center concerned. The commanding general of the training center concerned will issue the necessary warrants effective as of date of graduation and forward same to the advanced flying school concerned. The report mentioned above will be forwarded in time to reach the Chief of the Air Corps at least 3 weeks prior to the date of graduation. Immediately upon completion of training at each elementary, basic, and advanced flying school, the commandants of such schools will submit a report on all enlisted pilots graduated to the Chief of the Air Corps. These reports will contain the number of hours devoted to and grades attained in each academic subject, flying time, and flying grades attained.

c. Upon graduation from the advanced flying school an aviation student will be discharged for the convenience of the Government and enlisted in the Air Corps for a period of 3 years. He will receive the rating of pilot and a warrant as staff sergeant pilot, Air Corps, without regard to the grade in which he received his training.

d. Noncommissioned officer pilots, Air Corps, will take precedence among themselves in accordance with the provisions of Army Regulations governing rank among noncommissioned officers.

7. Termination of status as aviation student.—*a.* If at any time the faculty board at an Air Corps elementary, basic, or advanced flying school decides that an aviation student is, for any reason, not qualified to continue his training or that he possesses traits that would render him undesirable as a noncommissioned officer in the Air Corps, the commandant thereof will forward board proceedings to the commanding general of the Air Corps training center concerned.

b. In case of approval of the faculty board proceedings referred to in *a* above by the commanding general of the Air Corps training center, he will make request to the Chief of the Air Corps for orders relieving the aviation student concerned from pilot training and his orders transferring him from the flying school concerned. The Chief of the Air Corps will, in turn, make suitable recommendation to The Adjutant General for orders returning eliminated aviation students to the organization from which they were placed on detached service.

8. **Allowances.**—*a. Clothing.*—Aviation students will be issued clothing allowances as now laid down in law and regulation for enlisted men of the grade held.

b. Other.—Allowances in rations, quarters, clothing, etc., for staff sergeant pilots, technical sergeant pilots, and master sergeant pilots will be the same as those authorized for staff sergeants, technical sergeants, and master sergeants.

9. **Promotion of enlisted pilots.**—Enlisted pilots will be promoted in accordance with eligibility requirements prescribed by the Chief of the Air Corps. Grades for enlisted pilots are staff sergeant pilot, technical sergeant pilot, and master sergeant pilot. Master sergeant pilots may, under such regulations as the Secretary of War may prescribe, be appointed warrant officer pilots.

10. **Form for application.**

Subject: Application for aviation student training.

To: Commanding General,

          _____ Corps Area,

          _____.

1. Request that I be considered for training as an aviation student in the Army Air Corps for heavier-than-air flying training with a view to pursuing the standard course of instruction prescribed by the War Department, and upon successful completion thereof, to being appointed a staff sergeant pilot, Air Corps, Regular Army.

2. My education has been as follows:

3. If this application is accepted I agree—

a. To be discharged for the convenience of the Government and be reenlisted for 3 years upon the acceptance of my application (omit if applicant has more than 1 year to serve in current enlistment).

b. That if I successfully complete my pilot training, I will agree to serve for 3 years as an enlisted pilot and for this purpose to be again discharged and reenlisted for 3 years for the convenience of the Government.

c. To remain unmarried during the period of training as an aviation student and during my first enlistment as a noncommissioned officer pilot.

3 Inclosures.

Incl. 1. Three letters of recommendation.

Incl. 2. *Evidence of educational fitness.

Incl. 3. Confirmation of paragraph 3*b*, basic letter, by parent or guardian (required only if applicant is a minor).

*See paragraph 2*a*(2).

1ST INDORSEMENT

1. Approved or disapproved.

2. Soldier was born _____, _____.
                     (Date)   **(Place)**
    Naturalized at _____ on _____.

3. Soldier's character is _____.

4. Date of current enlistment _____.

5. Army general classification test rating _____.

ENLISTED MEN

6. Height _____, Weight _____.

7. Soldier is _____.
        (Race)

8. Soldier is unmarried and has _____ persons wholly dependent and _____ persons partially dependent on him for support.

9. Previous service _____.

10. Previous civilian experience_____.

[A. G. 320.2 (7–19–41).]

By order of the Secretary of War:

G. C. MARSHALL,
Chief of Staff.

Official:

E. S. ADAMS,
Major General,
The Adjutant General.

ENLISTED PILOTS 1912–1917 H APPENDIX

The following are from "Soldier Pilots" of the Regular Army as listed in Appendix 15 of the Hennessey Study (1958).

1912
Cpl. Vernon L. Burge
Cpl. William A. Lamkey
Cpl. Samuel Katzman[1]

1914
Cpl. J. S. Krull
Sgt. William C. Ocker

1915
Sgt. Herbert Marcus
Cpl. A. D. Smith
Sgt. A. A. Adamson
Cpl. Ira O. Biffle
Cpl. S. V. Coyle
Cpl. Leo G. Flint

1916
Sgt. Felix Steinle
Sgt. B. S. Robertson
Cpl. G. D. Floyd
Cpl. H. A. Chandler
Sgt. D. M. Jones
Sgt. A. J. Ralph
Pfc. C. B. Coombs

1917
Cpl. K. L. Whitsett
Sgt. A. E. Simonin
Cpl. R. K. Smith
Cpl. H. D. McLean
Cpl. R. A. Willis

The following are from page 219 of Stephen Tillman, *Man Unafraid* (Washington, D.C.: Army Times Publishing Co., 1958). Sergeant Stephen J. Idzorek is also listed, but data on hand indicates he never acquired time as a pilot.

Thomas Boland
Wilburn C. Dodd
Samuel P. Jones

John McRae
Arnold Reuf
Wilfred G. Threader

1. The only place Sam Katzman has been found in the literature is in a newspaper article from the *Boston Evening Transcript*, Wednesday, May 2 (1928 or 1929), p. 14, pt. 3, entitled "Golden Eagles: America's Famous Old 1st Aero Squadron," by George H. Spencer.

ENLISTED PILOTS 1918–1933 ⅼ APPENDIX

The following are from page 88, in Kroll, *Kelly Field in the Great World War, 1919,* called to the author's attention by J. J. Smith, World War I researcher, and are listed as "enlisted pilots of the organization."

1st Sgt. August Ball   Cpl. Howard Culmer
Sgt. Maj. C. C. Biehl   Sgt. John Nessman
Sgt. B. B. Braley

The names of nine enlisted fliers appear on page 11 of the November 28, 1918, issue of the *Kelly Field Flyer,* headlined "Nine Receive Ratings as Enlisted Flyers." They are:

Sfc. Herbert E. Dornfield   Sgt. Linton Roberts
Sgt. Sam Friedmen   Sfc. Carleton P. Smith
Sfc. James B. Heck   Sfc. Merrill J. Tackley
Sgt. Eugene W. Martin   Sgt. Chester E. Willard
Sfc. William C. Meredith

Two more are found in another article entitled "A.S.M.S. Great Factor in Aviation," on page 3 of the *Kelly Field Eagle* (presumed to be sometime in 1918). They are sergeants, first class Oliver W. Thyfault and Charles M. Duffy, both of the Air Service Mechanics School, Kelly Field.

A photograph found at Kelly Field, dated December 14, 1918, shows eight unidentified sergeant pilots standing in front of a hangered DH-4. Printed on the back of the photo is the following information: "4884 AS—ASMS Aviation, Kelly Field, Texas. December 14, 1918." It may be that the photo includes some of those "enlisted aviators" listed above.

A 1919 Rich Field Aviation School Class book, furnished by Marjorie Waters, pictures four enlisted pilots as "Rich Field's Quartet of Enlisted Flying Instructors." They are:

M.S.E. Douglas S. Christie   Sgt. Leroy B. Gregg
Sgt. William F. Cottrell   Sgt. Rufus C. Lillard

A document furnished to the author by J. Duncan Campbell shows Sgt. Harry Thomas Wilson appointed to the grade of Master Signal Electrician-Aviator, Signal Corps, U.S.A.S., of the Regular Army on May 1, 1918. Also furnished were copies of pages from a 1919 Ellington Field publication entitled *Overseas Dreams* (Houston: Gulfport Printing Co., n.d.), in which four enlisted aviators were listed or pictured. They were M.S.E. Jack L. Popham, M.S.E. Joseph Remsen, M.S.E. Harry C. Short, and Sgt. Robert V. Thomas.

From information furnished by Col. "Rick" Glasebrook, World War I researcher, we have been able to verify the following World War I enlisted pilots:

Sfc. James R. Bandy
Sfc. Franklin P. Reynolds, Jr.
Sgt. Gerald C. Smith

From a photo found in the personal album of "Sfc. William Edward Beigel, Enlisted Aerial Pilot," and donated to the USAF Museum by Beigel's widow, Emily Beigel, six enlisted pilots are pictured standing in front of a Curtiss JN-4. A handwritten caption beneath the photo states: "Enlisted Pilots, Rich Field. *Left to right:* 'Ham Ace Sheffield,' 'Good-natured' Walter Beech, 'Happy Jack' Shealer, William F. 'Pinky' Cottrell [also listed above], 'Tail Spin' Chamlee, and 'Wild Bill' William E. Beigel." Not shown in the photograph is Sfc. pilot Harold S. Dale.

From page 82 of the "Roster of Students" of the Primary Flying Schools, Brooks, March, and Randolph Fields, September 1922–October 1932 (San Antonio: Naylor Printing Co., n.d.), copy furnished by Peg Smith, widow of former M. Sgt. pilot C.P. Smith, the following were trained in grade as pilots:

1930	S. Sgt. Maurice M. Beach	1925	Sgt. Thomas R. McComas
1933	S. Sgt. Paul S. Blair	1925	S. Sgt. Irven Mackey
1928	T. Sgt. W. M. Brees	1925	S. Sgt. S. A. Moorehouse
1927	T. Sgt. R. E. L. Choat	1923	T. Sgt. Ezra F. "Pop" Nendell
1926	S. Sgt. Richard E. Cobb	1933	S. Sgt. Thomas W. Rafferty
1925	S. Sgt. Jimmy H. Craine	1927	S. Sgt. S. J. Samson
1932	S. Sgt. Charles G. Cunningham	1933	T. Sgt. Frank J. Siebenaler
1925	S. Sgt. Boyd Ertwine	1924	M. Sgt. Stewart C. Smink
1932	S. Sgt. Arthur Hanson	1925–33	M. Sgt. Carlton P. Smith
1926	T. Sgt. Alva Harvey	1929	S. Sgt. W. L. Snowdon
1926	M. Sgt. Clarence Haymes	1932	T. Sgt. Raymond Stockwell
1931	S. Sgt. Opal Henderson	1933	Cpl. Fred O. Tyler
1927	T. Sgt. Paul B. Jackson	1927	M. Sgt. Bernard (NMI) Wallace
1932	M. Sgt. Julius A. Kolb	1929	M. Sgt. John L. Waugh
1933	S. Sgt. Gilbert E. Layman	1925	S. Sgt. Leslie L. Wells
1932	S. Sgt. Ancil L. Lovvorn	1933	Sgt. Fred H. Wilson
1932	S. Sgt. Jerome B. McCauley		

Enlisted pilots identified from aircraft accident reports of the twenties, in which they were reported as pilot in command, are listed here because they have been located nowhere else in the literature.

1918
Sgt. Robert Bratch
M.S.E. R. T. Davidson
Cpl. M. E. Porter
M.S.E. John C. Stoll

Cpl. Veserlfsky (sp ?)
Sgt. R. W. Wetsel
Sgt. Lee Willinger

1919
M.S.E. Joseph O. Burnett
Sgt. F. L. Clark
Sgt. Charles B. Copp
Sgt. H. L. Ellesier
Sgt. Gordon Gates
Sgt. F. J. Hurly (or Murphey or Murry)
Sgt. Walter Kirby

M.S.E. A. Y. Linarie
Sgt. H. G. Phillips
Sgt. Jacob Prose
Sgt. W. E. Seaton
Sgt. John P. Woodward
Sgt. S. W. Zants

1920
Sgt. Charles D. Allen
Sgt. Harry D. Glover
Sgt. Frank M. Hoover (or Hover)

Sgt. Strong B. McDann
Sgt. William J. Martin
Sgt. Thomas E. Pirtle

1921
Sgt. Jerome C. Ainis
Sgt. Paul Andart

Sgt. James E. Jones
Sgt. Carl B. McDaniel

1922
Sgt. Roland C. Blake
S. Sgt. Daniel F. Kearns
Pvt. H. G. MacLaughlin

Sgt. Wilber Rhodes
S. Sgt. Leslie Wright

1923
Cpl. L. D. Frederick
Sgt. Floyd L. Hefling
Pvt. Ross N. Hugnet

Sgt. J. G. O'Neal
S. Sgt. Duane G. Warner
Cpl. Lee C. Wilson

1924
Cpl. Claude M. Fleck
Cpl. A. Henley

Sgt. Lynnwood P. Hudson
W.O. Adam Truelie

1925
Sgt. Anderson
Cpl. Henry R. Angell
Sgt. Algot I. Bloomquist

M. Sgt. David S. Grosvenor
Sgt. Antonio Hurza

1926
Pvt. Bernard A. Bridget
Pvt. E. R. Emory
S. Sgt. Robert H. Fatt
M. Sgt. Douglas D. Johnson

S. Sgt. Fred Kelly
M. Sgt. Chester N. Kolinsky
Cpl. Lewis C. Lee

Items published in the Air Corps newsletters of November 10, 1927, March 31, 1928, and August 1, 1937, as well as the *Aviation* magazine of April 9, 1928, include the names of the following enlisted pilots:

Sgt. Edward A. Brown
Sgt. Robert M. DeWald

Sgt. Lyman R. Ellis
Cpl. Harold B. Fisher

M. Sgt. Thomas J. Fowler

M. Sgt. Albert C. Gamble

Sgt. Narry P. Gibson

M. Sgt. Joe Grant

S. Sgt. Orvil W. Haynes

Cpl. Harry C. Lewis

M. Sgt. William M. McConnell

M. Sgt. Conrad L. O'Briant

S. Sgt. Fred I. Pierce

Cpl. Maurice Riherd

S. Sgt. Warren S. Rosenberger

Sgt. Robert Travis

S. Sgt. Samuel H. Turner

S. Sgt. George Wiggs

S. Sgt. Paul L. Woodruff

Newspaper articles and photos appearing in San Antonio, Dayton, and Hawaiian newspapers of the mid thirties list the following enlisted pilots:

M. Sgt. Peter Biesiot

M. Sgt. Chester Colby

M. Sgt. Samuel Davis

M. Sgt. Cecil Guile

From correspondence, taped interviews, documents, and the personal recollections of Alva Harvey, Paul Jackson, Mrs. Peg Smith (widow of C.P. Smith), Boyd Ertwine, Julius Kolb, and others, where corroborated by the recollections of two or more persons, or other substantiating material:

Warrant Officer Leland Bradshaw may have been one of the pre–World War I enlisted pilots, but so far only post–World War I flight records have been found on which he is listed as pilot in command.

Sergeant Robert DeWald is remembered by Paul Jackson as "Gloomy Gus" and may be the Robert M. DeWald listed above. A Sergeant DeWald is also shown as an instructor on the flight log of C.P. Smith at Brooks Field in 1926.

Staff Sergeant Roy Mitchell was Alva Harvey's primary flight instructor at Brooks Field in 1924–25.

Staff Sergeant R. C. Ashley appears on Brooks Field Operations Order #39, September 14, 1923, as a primary flight instructor.

Staff Sergeant Byron Newcomb is listed as an instructor at Brooks Field in 1924. He is also shown on flight orders in 1927 as the pilot of a C-1 transport at Selfridge Field.

Sergeant Billy Winston is remembered at Carlstrom Field by Peg Smith, and also remembered by Boyd Ertwine. Winston is also mentioned on page 418 of *The Spirit of St. Louis* by Charles Lindbergh as his primary instructor at Brooks Field in April 1924.

Warrant Officer James A. Lee is listed on 1935 Air Corps list of pilots.

Sergeant Lee Q. Wasser and LeRoy Manning are known by Julius Kolb to have been sergeant pilots at Selfridge Field in 1925.

Corporal George M. Murchison is shown on the 1937 Air Corps list of personnel with aeronautical ratings on flying duty. He was rated in 1932 and was serving at Boston's airport. He is shown with 1245:55 hours of flying time.

Note: While both sergeants Carlton P. Smith and William F. Cottrell appear on two separate listings, they are only counted once for this tally.

ENLISTED PILOTS
TRAINED AS CADETS, 1923–1933

J APPENDIX

Names are furnished by the individuals themselves, from newspaper articles, photographs, lists, and documents in the files of the USAF Historical Research Center, Maxwell Air Force Base, Montgomery, Alabama. Others are from such documents as Air Service or Air Corps newsletters and from War Department Personnel Orders No. 165 dated July 15, 1935, dealing with Regular Army appointments. Most have been verified as cadets from the "Roster of Students" of the Air Corps Primary Flying Schools, Brooks, March, and Randolph Fields, 1922–1932 (San Antonio: Naylor Printing Co., n.d.).

1933	Allee, Edward Schwartz	1930	Duncan, Lawrence A.
1931	Angel, Robert S.	1929	Fisher, Charles M.
1932	Armstrong, Burton W., Jr.	1929	Fisher, Henry B.
1933	Arnold, Bob	1932	Fisher, Robert Strachen
1932	Bell, Jasper Newton	1933	Frutchey, Watson M.
1927	Blaunfuss, William	1933	Fulwider, Lawrence Scott
1932	Bordelon, Henry O.	1932	Gavin, Edwin Morris
1932	Brecht, Eugene, Jr.	1932	Gebelin, John, Jr.
1933	Brewster, Pete	1933	Glasser, Maurice E.
1931	Brown, Lawrence O.	1933	Gunn, Harold A.
1930	Byrne, Vernon M.	1932	Harris, Lester Stanford
1931	Camp, Edgar R.	1930	Harris, O. K.
1933	Cannon, Robbin C.	1931	Harvin, Charles Bennett
1932	Case, Kenneth R.	1933	Hausafus, Edward T.
1932	Classon, Clayton B.	1931	Holloway, Benjamin C.
1930	Clifton, Ray W.	1921	Holmes, George H.
1932	Cornell, Loren	1933	Holterman, Eyvind
1932	Coursey, Harry	1933	Houston, James H. C.
1932	Crutcher, Harry, Jr.	1933	Hudnell, William T., Jr.
1932	Davis, Tom S., Jr.	1932	Hunt, Jack S.
1931	Day, William Foster, Jr.	1933	Hurst, Herman E.
1931	Dennison, Howard	1932	Jarmin, Robert Edward
1933	Dennison, Junius W.	1930	Johnson, Arnold Theodore
1933	Diggs, George C.	1921	Johnson, Tracy
1930	Dorsett, Tracy	1930	Joplin, Jules
1930	Dunbar, Cornelius K.	1932	Joyce, Edwin A.

1932	Kinkle, Ross S.	1933	Powers, Duncan J.
1932	Kleinoeder, L. P.	1933	Price, John (Jack) Hughes
1932	Kreider, Harold L.	1931	Ragle, Richard C.
1933	Kryssler, John D.	1932	Renshaw, Harry Noon
1933	Laird, Russell E.	1930	Sailor, Lloyd L.
1930	Langben, Thomas Frederick	1931	Sartain, Clarence Morice
1930	Leitner, Charles Henry, Jr.	1932	Sprunger, Noble
1931	McDonald, William C.	1931	Stalder, Marvin Frederick
1933	Macintyre, George Henry	1930	Stanley, Joseph Bynum
1930	McLelland, Hamish	1931	Stephenson, Mell M., Jr.
1931	Malone, Jack Mason	1933	Stevens, Fred J., Jr.
1931	Merritt, John R.	1933	Stewart, Malcolm F.
1931	Moler, Daniel I.	1928	Swisher, Douglas
1933	Moore, Joseph Caruthers	1931	Swyter, Carl
1932	Moyers, Frank Neff	1932	Treweek, James M.
1932	Muehlesen, Dolf Edward	1932	Vavrina, Richard F.
1930	Mulvey, John J.	1932	Wackwitz, Donald Newman
1923	Murphy, Milton M.	1932	Waldron, Russell Lee
1933	Neal, John O.	1932	Ward, Fred N.
1933	Neely, Harold Lee	1933	Way, John A.
1932	Nichols, Erickson S.	1932	Weller, Richard Cole
1932	Parrish, Noel Francis	1932	Williams, Hiett S., Jr.
1933	Paul, Franklin K.	1928	Williamson, John H. "Luke"
1931	Pitman, John David	1923	Wisely, Charles
1922	Pomroy, George C.	1933	Wood, Clair Lawrence
1926	Porter, Aaron	1932	Wood, Randolph L.
1931	Poupitch, Vernet V.		

PERSONNEL (AERONAUTICAL) **K** APPENDIX

ORDERS FOR STAFF SERGEANT PILOTS

Prior to and during World War II, personnel orders were used to grant aeronautical ratings and require individuals holding those ratings to participate in regular and frequent flights. Through Class 42-H, such orders were issued by the Office of Chief of the Air Corps, War Department, Washington, D.C., under the provisions of Army Regulation 95-60 as amended through June 30, 1941. In October 1942, the authority was apparently delegated to the Gulf Coast AAF, Southeast, and West Coast training centers to grant aeronautical ratings. The Gulf Coast issued the first of such orders on October 2, 1942, followed by the West Coast Center and Southeast Center later in October and November 1942. All personnel orders shown below were furnished solely by individual former sergeant pilots.

No attempt is made in this appendix to list the aeronautical orders issued to the 226 enlisted aviators who served in the Signal Corps, Air Service, and Army Air Corps between 1912 and 1941, since most of them are documented elsewhere in the book. Nor has it been possible to adequately document the 132 Americans who were trained as NCO pilots by the Royal Canadian Air Force, and later transferred in grade into the U.S. Army Air Forces in an equivalent grade (usually that of staff sergeant), following the Japanese attack on Pearl Harbor.

With the enactment of Public Law 99 in June 1941, 2,574 enlisted men were trained as pilots and, upon graduation from advanced flying schools in 1942, were warranted as staff sergeants in the following classes, under personnel orders as indicated:

42-C (93 Graduates)
Ellington (39): Par 1, WD Personnel Order #57, 7 Mar 42.
Kelly (54): Par 24, WD Personnel Order #57, 7 Mar 42.

42-D (112 Graduates)
Ellington (56): Par 5, WD Personnel Order #102, 29 Apr 42.
Kelly (56): Par 2, WD Personnel Order #102, 29 Apr 42.

42-E (182 Graduates)
Ellington (58): Par 3, WD Personnel Order #120, 20 May 42.
Kelly (58): Par 1, WD Personnel Order #120, 20 May 42.
Luke (35): Par 5, WD Personnel Order #120, 20 May 42.
Mather (31): Par 1, WD Personnel Order #121, 21 May 42.

42-F (159 Graduates)
Ellington (56): Par 13, WD Personnel Order #149, 23 Jun 42.
Kelly (39): Par 55, WD Personnel Order #158, 3 Jul 42.

Luke (24): Par 28, WD Personnel Order #149, 23 Jun 42.
Mather (40): Par 15, WD Personnel Order #149, 23 Jun 42.

42-G (456 Graduates)
Columbus (27): Par 3, WD Personnel Order #178, 27 Jul 42.
Dothan (27): Par 5, WD Personnel Order #186, 5 Aug 42.
Ellington (90): Par 1, WD Personnel Order #186, 5 Aug 42.
Kelly (56): Par 13, WD Personnel Order #186, 5 Aug 42.
Lubbock (54): Par 7, WD Personnel Order #186, 5 Aug 42.
Luke (80): Par 1, WD Personnel Order #178, 27 Jul 42.
Moody (13): Par 11, WD Personnel Order #186, 5 Aug 42.
Roswell (31): Par 45, WD Personnel Order #178, 27 Jul 42.
Spence (26): Par 9, WD Personnel Order #186, 5 Aug 42.
Turner (13): Par 3, WD Personnel Order #186, 5 Aug 42.
Victorville (11): Par 5, WD Personnel Order #175, 23 Aug 42.
Williams (28): Par 7, WD Personnel Order #175, 23 Jul 42.

42-H (540 Graduates)
Columbus (44): Par 90, WD Personnel Order #213, 5 Sep 42.
Dothan (17): Par 88, WD Personnel Order #213, 5 Sep 42.
Ellington (98): Par 76, WD Personnel Order #213, 5 Sep 42.
Kelly (66): Par 108, WD Personnel Order #213, 5 Sep 42.
Lubbock (66): Par 106, WD Personnel Order #213, 5 Sep 42.
Luke (107): Par 25, WD Personnel Order #205, 27 Aug 42.
Moody (41): Par 86, WD Personnel Order #213, 5 Sep 42.
Roswell (1): Par ?, WD Personnel Order #???, ? ??? 42.
Spence (57): Par 92, WD Personnel Order #213, 5 Sep 42.
Turner (1): Par ?, WD Personnel Order #???, ? ??? 42.
Williams (42): Par 35, WD Personnel Order #205, 27 Aug 42.

42-I (557 Graduates)
Columbus (9): Par 56, WD Personnel Order #242, 9 Oct 42.
Craig (4): Par ?, WD Personnel Order #???, ? ??? 42.
Dothan (24): Par 41, WD Personnel Order #242, 9 Oct 42.
Ellington (113): Par 15, GCAAFTC Spl Ord #1 2 Oct 42.
Lubbock (102): Par 19, GCAAFTC Spl Ord #1, 2 Oct 42.
                Par 35 & 54, GCAAFTC Spl Ord #4, 2 Nov 42.
Luke (3): Par 12, WCAAFTC Spl Ord #233, 29 Sep 42.
Moody (68): Par 58, WD Personnel Order #242, 9 Oct 42.
Spence (67): Par 37, WD Personnel Order #242, 9 Oct 42.
Stockton (149): Par 22, WD Personnel Order #233, 29 Sep 42.
Turner (17): Par 54, WD Personnel Order #242, 9 Oct 42.
Williams (1): Par 14, WD Personnel Order #233, 29 Sep 42.

42-J (475 Graduates)
Columbus (18): Par 51, SEAAFTC Spl Ord #6, 1 Nov 42.
Craig (22): Par 53, SEAAFTC Spl Ord #6, 1 Nov 42.
Dothan (17): Par 23, SEAAFTC Spl Ord #6,[1] 1 Nov 42.
Ellington (109): Par 33, GCAAFTC Spl Ord#4,[2] 2 Nov 42.
Kelly (107): Par 60, GCAAFTC Spl Ord #4, 2 Nov 42.
Lubbock (3): Par 54, GCAAFTC Spl Ord #4, 2 Nov 42.
Luke (45): Par 4, WCAAFTC Spl Ord #284,[3] 30 Oct 42.

Moody (36): Par ?, SEAAFTC Spl Ord #??, ? ??? 42.
Spence (31): Par 29 & 59 SEAAFTC Spl Ord #6, 1 Nov 42.
Stockton (2): Par 2 WCAAFTC Spl Ord #284, 30 Oct 42.
Turner (37): Par 61 SEAAFTC Spl Ord #6, 1 Nov 42.
Williams (48): Par 6, WCAAFTC Spl Ord #284, 30 Oct 42.

1. In Southeast Army Air Force Training Center's Personnel Order #6, the early paragraphs (23-29) were issued rating the graduates as staff sergeant pilots while the later paragraphs (51-62) rated them as flight officer as of the same date. It is therefore concluded that all schools in both the GCAAFTC and SEAAFTC Class 42-J were first rated as staff sergeant pilots; then those paragraphs were revoked and new ones issued rating them as flight officers on the same date.

2. In the Gulf Coast Army Air Forces Training Center's Personnel Order #4, the early paragraphs (33-36) rated the graduating aviation students as sergeant pilots and the later paragraphs (60-61) rated graduates as flight officers as of the same date.

3. One aberration appears in the system of personnel orders when West Coast Army Air Forces Training Center issued Special Order #284 dated October 30, 1942, for rating graduates at Luke and Williams fields in Arizona rather than a personnel order.

SERGEANT PILOTS
TRAINED UNDER PUBLIC LAW 99

L

APPENDIX

Last Name	First and Initial	Advanced Class	Last Name	First and Initial	Advanced Class
Aagesen	Donald C.	42-I Moody	Allen	William S.	42-H Moody
Abbott	Frank P.	42-J Craig	Alley	Wilbur K.	42-G Ellington
Abell	Harry M.	42-J Turner	Aloi	Thomas	42-I Spence
Abernathy	Floyd H., Jr.	42-E Luke	Alsobrook	James M.	42-H Kelly
Abrahamson	Verne A.	42-I Ellington	Alvord	Stanley	42-E Luke
Achee	James B.	42-I Ellington	Alwood	James W.	42-F Kelly
Ackerman	Trent	42-I Moody	Amos	William J.	42-J Ellington
Adams	Alva T., Jr.	42-E Kelly	Anderson	B. J.	42-G Ellington
Adams	Charles M.	42-G Moody	Anderson	Charles P., Jr.	42-I Stockton
Adams	Gerald M.	42-H Williams	Anderson	Edmund B.	42-C Kelly
Adams	Hughie E.	42-I Stockton	Anderson	Eugene D.	42-I Ellington
Adams	Ira A.	42-G Luke	Anderson	Harley H.	42-H Moody
Adams	Richard L.	42-F Kelly	Anderson	Harold J.	42-F Mather
Adams	Robert W.	42-I Lubbock	Anderson	James C.	42-I Moody
Adams	William V.	42-G Spence	Anderson	James L.	42-F Ellington
Adeimy	Thomas E.	42-J Moody	Anderson	Marcus P.	42-H Williams
Aiken	Junius A.	42-G Moody	Anderson	Russell G. B.	42-H Ellington
Akin	Elgin R.	42-J Williams	Anderson	Victor A.	42-G Ellington
Albers	John H.	42-J Williams	Anderson	Wilbur M.	42-G Luke
Albertini	Herman A.	42-G Lubbock	Andrews	Charles D.	42-H Luke
Albrecht	William J.	42-G Kelly	Andrews	George L.	42-G Ellington
Aldrich	George E.	42-G Lubbock	Andrews	Gordon J.	42-H Luke
Alexander	Ernest W.	42-J Kelly	Andrews	Jimmie B.	42-J Kelly
Alexander	Jack D.	42-E Luke	Andrews	Lee H.	42-H Luke
Alexander	Jene G.	42-G Williams	Andrews	William R.	42-F Luke
Alexander	Kenneth W.	42-J Turner	Angelo	Walter L., Jr.	42-H Spence
Algee	Ulysses "Sam"	42-F Ellington	Anthony	Joseph A.	42-G Luke
Allen	Arthur G.	42-G Turner	Antrim	William P.	42-E Luke
Allen	Burke F.	42-J Craig	Applebaum	Theodore C.	42-G Dothan
Allen	Leo A.	42-J Kelly	Arbon	Leonard L.	42-F Luke
Allen	Marvin L., Sr.	42-I Moody	Arens	Urban L.	42-I Stockton
Allen	Robert C.	42-H Spence	Armagost	Edgar R.	42-D Ellington
Allen	Robert L.	42-G Moody	Armstrong	Charles H.	42-G Kelly

Armstrong	Clyde J.	42-J Luke		Barber	Chester W.	42-G Ellington
Armstrong	Gerald D.	42-I Moody		Barbour	Wesley E.	42-G Dothan
Armstrong	Glendon L.	42-D Kelly		Barclay	Charles F.	42-F Ellington
Arnold	Albert S.	42-F Mather		Barnaby	Harold T.	42-I Spence
Arnold	Robert L.	42-I Lubbock		Barnard	Dwight L.	42-J Dothan
Arnold	William C.	42-H Moody		Barnes	Floyd E.	42-E Mather
Arnot	William G., Jr.	42-G Lubbock		Barnes	Raymond J.	42-G Ellington
Arthur	Wilbert L.	42-C Ellington		Barnett	Argene	42-I Ellington
Arts	Henry F.	42-E Ellington		Barnette	Dean E.	42-G Lubbock
Ash	Harold J.	42-G Roswell		Barnette	Robert D.	42-G Columbus
Ashabranner	Davis H.	42-J Kelly		Barnwell	Royce E.	42-I Ellington
Ashberry	James R.	42-H Kelly		Barone	Salvatore T.	42-E Kelly
Ashbrook	Truman R.	42-I Lubbock		Barrett	Fred W.	42-H Ellington
Ashland	Maurice I.	42-I Moody		Barrus	Emery V.	42-E Mather
Ashley	Burl S.	42-G Luke		Barth	Richard A.	42-H Moody
Ashley	Julian B.	42-J Spence		Barton	Clinton B., Sr.	42-H Luke
Ashmore	James D.	42-G Kelly		Barton	Harold H.	42-E Kelly
Ashton	Roger G.	42-I Moody		Barton	James K.	42-G Williams
Askelson	Howard S.	42-I Spence		Barton	Rollin E.	42-H Ellington
Atchison	Frank K.	42-H Luke		Basham	John A.	42-G Kelly
Atherton	Clinton E.	42-F Mather		Baskett	Max R.	42-I Ellington
Atteberry	Lloyd E.	42-C Kelly		Bassler	Merrill G.	42-I Ellington
Aubrey	Lawrence E.	42-G Columbus		Bates	Gordon D.	42-F Ellington
Augspurger	Herschel L.	42-I Stockton		Bates	Willie L.	42-I Stockton
Autry	John B.	42-J Kelly		Batt	Standly L.	42-I Moody
Avery	Gerald E.	42-G Williams		Bawden	Robert J.	42-H Lubbock
Babb	Eugene W.	42-C Kelly		Bayless	Hubert M.	42-G Luke
Bagwell	Edward A.	42-D Kelly		Bayne	Harry C.	42-G Moody
Bahr	Gail L.	42-E Kelly		Bazin	Joseph W.	42-J Kelly
Bailer	Harold W.	42-I Spence		Beach	Paul A.	42-G Lubbock
Bailey	Boyce S.	42-F Ellington		Beach	Victor	42-J Luke
Bailey	Edward E.	42-I Moody		Beagle	Howard J.	42-G Kelly
Bailey	Joseph D.	42-D Kelly		Beall	Clyde F.	42-H Moody
Bailey	William A.	42-I Ellington		Beall	James D.	42-I Ellington
Bain	William D.	42-G Ellington		Beard	John W.	42-H Moody
Baker	Burdette H.	42-H Moody		Bearskin	Leland S.	42-H Ellington
Baker	Claude G.	42-D Kelly		Beatty	Dalton W.	42-H Ellington
Baker	DeWitt B.	42-G Turner		Beauchamp	Raymond I.	42-F Ellington
Baldry	Gordon L.	42-E Kelly		Beaulac	Edmund J., Jr.	42-G Columbus
Baldwin	Rolland "Tom"	42-D Ellington		Beaumont	Allen A.	42-F Kelly
Ball	James T.	42-J Kelly		Beaver	George W.	42-F Ellington
Ballard	Herbert J.	42-D Kelly		Beck	Charles J.	42-F Ellington
Ballard	Thomas R.	42-I Stockton		Beck	Claire	42-H Luke
Balmer	Thomas	42-G Roswell		Beck	George W.	42-F Ellington
Balmes	Fredrick N.	42-I Moody		Beck	James E.	42-H Spence
Baltezor	Jesse N.	42-H Luke		Beck	Leonard B.	42-J Kelly
Bamburg	Elby F.	42-I Spence		Beck	Lymann E.	42-I Stockton
Bansmer	Kenneth W.	42-F Ellington		Beck	Walter W.	42-H Luke
Baran	Elmer L.	42-I Moody		Beckett	Ben H., Jr.	42-D Kelly
Barber	Bernard L.	42-C Ellington		Bedell	Riley L.	42-I Ellington

Beedy	Kimmel R.	42-D Kelly
Beeler	Paul L.	42-H Spence
Belcher	Anthony W.	42-E Kelly
Bell	David V.	42-I Ellington
Bell	Jack B.	42-E Luke
Bell	Kenneth L.	42-H Kelly
Bell	Robert J.	42-J Craig
Bell	Sam O.	42-J Moody
Bell	Silas W.	42-H Ellington
Bell	Warren G.	42-F Ellington
Bell	William M., Jr.	42-J Craig
Bellefeuille	Charles I.	42-H Luke
Bellis	Carl E.	42-H Columbus
Belon	Howard M.	42-G Roswell
Bence	John W.	42-G Spence
Benedict	George J.	42-G Roswell
Benedict	Paul F.	42-I Stockton
Benedict	Ray W.	42-H Kelly
Bennett	Charles I.	42-G Lubbock
Bennion	Robert A.	42-G Ellington
Benson	Alan P.	42-G Ellington
Benson	Clarence E.	42-D Kelly
Beran	Barney B.	42-J Kelly
Berg	Howard L.	42-G Lubbock
Berg	Karl R.	42-G Kelly
Berg	Robert S.	42-I Stockton
Bergeron	Earl C.	42-G Ellington
Bergstrom	Don J.	42-E Ellington
Bergstrom	William V.	42-I Ellington
Berkenpas	Nephi	42-J Kelly
Bernard	Roger J.	42-E Ellington
Berry	Milford A.	42-H Lubbock
Bessler	Joseph F.	42-I Stockton
Beveridge	Richard F.	42-G Dothan
Bey	Otto W.	42-H Kelly
Beymer	Robey F.	42-G Columbus
Bezner	Ray W.	42-C Ellington
Biehunko	Lawrence T.	42-D Kelly
Binsley	Paul W.	42-G Kelly
Bish	Neil T.	42-J Kelly
Bishop	Charles W.	42-J Turner
Bishop	Jake S., Jr.	42-I Ellington
Bishop	Jay W.	42-I Spence
Bishop	John W.	42-F Ellington
Bishop	Lloyd A.	42-H Ellington
Bivins	Joseph L.	42-G Ellington
Black	Raymond M.	42-C Ellington
Blackburn	Wesley T.	42-H Lubbock
Blackshear	Thomas C.	42-I Lubbock
Blain	John D.	42-J Ellington
Blair	James D.	42-H Williams
Blair	John L.	42-J Dothan
Blair	Marshall F.	42-G Spence
Blair	Richard P.	42-J Ellington
Bland	George E.	42-G Ellington
Blankenship	John J.	42-E Ellington
Blanton	Paul	42-E Mather
Blickensderfer	Wendell W.	42-G Columbus
Bliss	Marvin E.	42-H Ellington
Blodgett	Robert L.	42-I Ellington
Blosel	Raymond C.	42-G Dothan
Blyth	John S.	42-G Williams
Blythe	James R.	42-H Luke
Blythe	Walter S., Jr.	42-J Ellington
Bodner	Rudolph T.	42-D Ellington
Boehm	Richard E.	42-H Lubbock
Boers	Ralph E.	42-I Ellington
Bogart	Joseph L.	42-G Ellington
Boggess	Herbert L.	42-I Ellington
Bohanon	Ray J.	42-G Columbus
Bohnert	Herbert J., Jr.	42-F Ellington
Bohns	Kenneth E.	42-G Roswell
Boise	Walter L.	42-G Roswell
Boiter	Ansel L.	42-G Roswell
Boles	James N.	42-E Kelly
Bolger	George A.	42-H Dothan
Bolling	Stephen C.	42-F Kelly
Bolton	Nelson	42-G Turner
Bombeck	Walter, Jr.	42-J Ellington
Bonnett	John W., Jr.	42-D Kelly
Boone	Mark P.	42-H Spence
Booth	Karl M., Jr.	42-J Luke
Boren	Stanley J.	42-H Ellington
Boro	William B.	42-D Kelly
Borth	Bruce W.	42-G Luke
Bosarge	Edward M.	42-G Dothan
Bosse	Carl R.	42-J Kelly
Bostick	Robert A.	42-J Kelly
Boswell	Norma L.	42-H Kelly
Botkins	William D.	42-G Kelly
Bougher	Carl L.	42-J Ellington
Bourne	Ernest E.	42-F Mather
Bowen	James F.	42-J Craig
Bowen	Joe	42-I Ellington
Bowen	Phelps C., Jr.	42-H Luke
Bowen	William D.	42-G Lubbock
Bowling	Russell R.	42-H Kelly
Boyd	Benjamin M.	42-E Ellington
Boyd	Floyd W.	42-G Luke
Boyd	Henry L.	42-I Stockton

Boyd	Joseph B.	42-G Ellington
Boyd	Robert D.	42-F Ellington
Boyd	Wilbur W.	42-F Ellington
Boyer	Raymond C.	42-J Spence
Boyers	Edward W.	42-I Spence
Bozzi	Edward M.	42-D Kelly
Braddock	Edward I.	42-C Kelly
Bradford	Leo G.	42-H Lubbock
Bradley	Edward J.	42-H Moody
Bradshaw	Samuel P.	42-C Ellington
Bramlet	John L.	42-I Ellington
Brandt	Marvin L.	42-E Ellington
Brantly	Walter F.	42-H Kelly
Brashear	Rex W.	42-G Roswell
Brazie	Charles L.	42-E Ellington
Breaud	Clifford J.	42-E Ellington
Breault	George F.	42-I Lubbock
Brennan	Joseph X.	42-G Columbus
Brensinger	Joseph R.	42-J Turner
Brentlinger	Roy W.	42-H Luke
Bridges	Merle D.	42-G Spence
Bridges	Robert M.	42-H Kelly
Briggs	Clifford A.	42-G Victorville
Briggs	Earle W.	42-J Craig
Brink	Eugene	42-J Ellington
Brisick	Edward J.	42-G Roswell
Britton	James W.	42-J Williams
Broadhead	Arthur L., Jr.	42-C Ellington
Brock	Richard S.	42-J Ellington
Brockett	William R.	42-H Ellington
Bronson	Hubert S.	42-F Ellington
Brookbank	William C.	42-H Spence
Brooke	Charles S.	42-H Ellington
Brooks	Frank E.	42-E Luke
Brooks	Roscoe J.	42-I Ellington
Brooksby	Victor V.	42-E Mather
Broome	Ira E., Jr.	42-F Ellington
Brophy	Vincent F.	42-I Stockton
Brown	Cecil A.	42-G Kelly
Brown	Cecil O.	42-G Luke
Brown	Charles H.	42-D Kelly
Brown	Eldridge W.	42-J Ellington
Brown	Ervine H.	42-J Ellington
Brown	Eugene G.	42-F Kelly
Brown	James H.	42-J Kelly
Brown	John A.	42-H Lubbock
Brown	Lewis E.	42-H Spence
Brown	Olin W.	42-G Williams
Brown	Robert D.	42-J Turner
Brown	Robert H.	42-J Moody
Brown	Russell A.	42-I Stockton
Brown	Thomas D.	42-I Ellington
Brownell	Claremont D.	42-I Moody
Browning	James L.	42-I Lubbock
Bruce	Forrest D.	42-G Luke
Bryant	Henry F.	42-J Williams
Bryant	James A.	42-H Ellington
Bryant	Robert L.	42-H Spence
Bryant	Walter A.	42-H Spence
Bryson	Eddie	42-H Ellington
Bryson	Harry W.	42-I Ellington
Bubenik	Joseph G.	42-J Turner
Buchanan	Wilbur H.	42-H Luke
Buckley	Donald W.	42-H Moody
Budnick	Michael	42-J Craig
Budris	Stanley J.	42-I Lubbock
Buersmeyer	Wilfred C.	42-E Mather
Bukovac	Thomas J.	42-I Stockton
Bull	Hubert L.	42-J Kelly
Buls	Milton R.	42-I Ellington
Bunch	Marion D.	42-G Lubbock
Burch	George E.	42-E Ellington
Burchard	Robert F.	42-G Kelly
Burchett	Weldon E., Jr.	42-J Spence
Burden	Howard L.	42-H Kelly
Burford	Dallas Q.	42-G Luke
Burgess	Eugene P.	42-J Kelly
Burgoon	Howard C.	42-J Turner
Burkhalter	Albert E.	42-G Kelly
Burns	Francis P.	42-I Lubbock
Burrell	William E.	42-I Ellington
Burris	William M., Sr.	42-E Ellington
Burt	Norman A.	42-H Moody
Burton	Arthur M.	42-I Ellington
Busenbarrick	James E.	42-J Kelly
Bush	James R.	42-G Lubbock
Bush	William B.	42-F Ellington
Bussells	Chatham P.	42-E Kelly
Butler	Heber N.	42-H Luke
Butler	James E.	42-H Luke
Butler	Owen K.	42-J Ellington
Butler	Richard M.	42-H Luke
Butler	Robert H.	42-J Williams
Butler	Robert P.	42-I Ellington
Butts	James T.	42-G Spence
Byrd	Kenneth E.	42-H Lubbock
Byron	Kenneth J.	42-I Stockton
Caffey	Norman L.	42-H Kelly
Caine	Donald F.	42-I Stockton
Caldwell	George P.	42-I Stockton

Caldwell	Wilma T.	42-H Ellington
Call	Lee R.	42-G Luke
Callahan	Joseph T.	42-H Moody
Callans	Glenn G.	42-J Luke
Cameron	George E.	42-G Roswell
Camp	Aarron B.	42-I Stockton
Campbell	Bill B.	42-H Williams
Campbell	David D.	42-H Spence
Campbell	Delbert L.	42-J Ellington
Campbell	James E.	42-I Spence
Campbell	James T.	42-G Roswell
Campbell	Joe A.	42-F Kelly
Campbell	Martin M.	42-G Dothan
Campbell	Norman C.	42-J Kelly
Campbell	William	42-I Ellington
Canham	Dick M.	42-G Luke
Cannedy	Paul J.	42-J Moody
Capin	Guy E.	42-E Mather
Capps	William W.	42-G Columbus
Cardwell	James P.	42-D Ellington
Carlson	R. Barney	42-H Lubbock
Carmack	Matt	42-F Kelly
Carneg	Harry R.	42-H Spence
Caroll	William T., Jr.	42-H Luke
Carpenter	Howard G.	42-H Luke
Carpenter	Leslie M., Jr.	42-H Columbus
Carpenter	Roy W.	42-G Turner
Carper	Robert L.	42-G Turner
Carrington	Louis H.	42-H Kelly
Carte	John F.	42-G Roswell
Carter	Cyrus F., Jr.	42-I Lubbock
Carter	Harry M.	42-I Moody
Carter	James W.	42-F Ellington
Carter	Roy T., Jr.	42-H Spence
Carter	Russell A.	42-E Kelly
Cartwright	William B.	42-J Ellington
Carver	Gerald C.	42-H Luke
Case	Rodolph	42-E Ellington
Casey	Clyde M.	42-G Luke
Casey	Durward E.	42-H Ellington
Casey	Joseph H.	42-E Mather
Casner	Edward F.	42-G Dothan
Casselberry	Donald E.	42-H Spence
Cassiday	Clyde E.	42-H Ellington
Cate	Dayton T.	42-J Kelly
Cather	William H.	42-H Moody
Cathey	Ted R.	42-E Ellington
Catlin	Richard L.	42-H Spence
Caudill	Earl W.	42-J Williams
Cecil	Ralph H.	42-I Moody
Ceronsky	Robert J.	42-H Lubbock
Cervi	Eugene A.	42-H Spence
Chaffin	Allan F.	42-H Ellington
Chamblin	Archie W.	42-E Kelly
Chance	James H.	42-H Ellington
Chancey	Norman L.	42-I Stockton
Chandler	Austin E.	42-H Kelly
Chandler	George W., Jr.	42-H Kelly
Chaney	Jack J.	42-D Kelly
Chapman	Almon C.	42-I Ellington
Chapman	Fred D.	42-J Luke
Chase	Harland G.	42-H Luke
Chase	Robert P.	41-I Stockton
Chatham	Milton E.	42-D Ellington
Check	Joseph P., Jr.	42-I Stockton
Chesley	Darvel N.	42-I Stockton
Childress	Rollin D.	42-H Ellington
Chinn	Homer W.	42-J Kelly
Choat	Vernon L.	42-D Ellington
Cholewa	Joseph S.	42-E Kelly
Christensen	Richard D.	42-D Kelly
Christman	Edward C.	42-E Luke
Christner	Winton	42-I Ellington
Churchill	Norman V.	42-G Williams
Claeys	Robert J.	42-G Williams
Clanton	Thomas R.	42-I Ellington
Clark	Arodd W.	42-J Luke
Clark	Arthur E.	42-H Ellington
Clark	Clair J.	42-H Kelly
Clark	Donald L.	42-H Moody
Clark	James K.	42-H Moody
Clark	John J., III	42-G Moody
Clark	Owen L.	42-G Lubbock
Clark	Robert L.	42-H Kelly
Clay	Leon C.	42-I Stockton
Clayton	Ramon L.	42-I Ellington
Clemens	Eugene C.	42-J Dothan
Clifford	Samuel K.	42-D Ellington
Clifton	Roy M.	42-I Stockton
Clowers	David M.	42-J Kelly
Cobb	Robert F.	42-D Ellington
Cobble	Thurman D.	42-E Kelly
Cochran	Charles F.	42-G Ellington
Cochran	Samuel W.	42-E Ellington
Coile	Henry B.	42-G Ellington
Colburn	Leo T.	42-E Kelly
Colby	Leslie W.	42-J Williams
Coldren	Clyde L.	42-J Craig
Coleman	Alfred C.	42-H Moody
Coleman	Philip E.	42-I Spence

Coleman	Ralph F.	42-I Lubbock	Crane	Roy B.	42-I Stockton
Coleman	Warren Z.	42-H Spence	Craven	Paul R.	42-E Mather
Colletti	Nicholas R.	42-I Spence	Crawford	George H.	42-G Luke
Collins	Gene A.	42-H Luke	Crawford	Howard G.	42-I Ellington
Collins	George D.	42-D Dothan	Crawford	Richard W.	42-G Luke
Collins	John J.	42-G Ellington	Crecelius	William R.	42-F Ellington
Colquitt	Robert E.	42-H Lubbock	Crepeau	Victor J.	42-J Moody
Colwell	Osburn R.	42-H Ellington	Crichton	Douglas E.	42-C Ellington
Comber	Cornelius J.	42-I Moody	Crim	James C.	42-H Lubbock
Condit	Aubrey B.	42-H Moody	Crimmins	Lloyd E.	42-D Ellington
Confer	Louis C.	42-J Moody	Crites	L. D.	42-J Kelly
Confer	Robert L.	42-H Luke	Crosby	Duane L.	42-I Stockton
Conine	William C., Jr.	42-G Luke	Crouch	John R.	42-E Luke
Conklin	Charles H.	42-I Stockton	Crowley	Elmer L.	42-E Ellington
Conley	Douglas C.	42-H Ellington	Crozier	Leslie T.	42-J Williams
Conn	Max W.	42-H Ellington	Cruncleton	Charles E., Jr.	42-E Luke
Connelly	Richard B.	42-G Ellington	Cruse	Arthur W.	42-H Ellington
Conner	William W., Jr.	42-C Kelly	Cuddeback	Thomas A.	42-J Moody
Conrad	Peter P.	42-H Moody	Culbertson	Leonard D.	42-J Kelly
Conway	Robert J.	42-J Kelly	Cummings	Robert D.	42-H Williams
Cook	Eugene D.	42-J Moody	Cummins	G. Lawrence	42-G Ellington
Cook	Howard T.	42-H Spence	Cunningham	Austin W.	42-G Dothan
Cook	James M.	42-D Ellington	Cunningham	Bruce	42-H Spence
Cook	Walter E.	42-J Williams	Curran	Francis E.	42-I Stockton
Cooley	Harry T.	42-H Spence	Currier	Wendell	42-F Mather
Cooney	Richard F.	42-E Mather	Custer	Lawrence C.	42-I Spence
Cooper	Dowd L.	42-G Ellington	Czerwiec	Edward	42-I Lubbock
Cooper	William P.	42-E Ellington	Dace	Harry L.	42-G Lubbock
Cope	Carl P.	42-G Ellington	Dailey	Harold C.	42-G Ellington
Corder	Harry D.	42-H Moody	Dalen	Mark S.	42-I Moody
Cornell	George W.	42-G Ellington	Dallas	Milburn S.	42-D Ellington
Cornell	Richard W.	42-H Luke	Darby	James F.	42-I Luke
Cornette	Charles M.	42-E Ellington	Darmody	Richard O., Jr.	42-J Craig
Cossit	James E.	42-D Ellington	Darr	Wayne L.	42-H Spence
Cote	Richard D.	42-I Spence	Davenport	Harry E.	42-I Stockton
Coughenour	Melvin H.	42-I Spence	Davenport	Mervyn A.	42-G Luke
Coulter	Jack W.	42-J Luke	Davenport	William A.	42-I Ellington
Courington	Max R.	42-F Luke	David	Laverne V.	42-C Kelly
Courson	Wesley E.	42-J Turner	Davidson	B. H.	42-J Ellington
Courtney	Johnie	42-D Kelly	Davidson	Verner K.	42-G Roswell
Couvillon	Richard E.	42-E Kelly	Davis	Allen, Jr.	42-J Kelly
Coward	James W.	42-E Kelly	Davis	Archie C.	42-H Dothan
Cowden	Clint R.	42-F Mather	Davis	Archie G.	42-J Turner
Cozby	Hubert B.	42-J Kelly	Davis	Charles L.	42-D Ellington
Craig	Robert J.	42-I Stockton	Davis	Culver O.	42-F Mather
Cramer	David	42-J Craig	Davis	Dean O.	42-H Spence
Cramer	Davis S.	42-H Williams	Davis	Ernest F.	42-H Ellington
Crane	Bradley C.	42-J Craig	Davis	George W.	42-J Moody
Crane	Carroll B.	42-I Moody	Davis	Howard L.	42-G Kelly
Crane	Joseph F.	42-I Lubbock	Davis	James	42-I Moody

Davis	James H.	42-H Ellington	Dozier	Jack B.	42-H Luke
Davis	Lavoi B.	42-G Kelly	Drake	David C.	42-I Lubbock
Davis	Leonard N.	42-E Mather	Drake	Robert O.	42-D Ellington
Davis	Ralph L.	42-J Kelly	Dreher	Alfred D.	42-G Spence
Davit	Stephen J.	42-D Ellington	Drew	Samuel F.	42-J Luke
Dawes	William A.	42-F Ellington	DuBelko	Michael M.	42-F Ellington
Dawkins	Cecil H.	42-F Kelly	Duclos	Robert A.	42-H Luke
Day	Eugene C.	42-G Kelly	Dudas	Andrew J., Jr.	42-J Ellington
Dean	Cecil O.	42-H Spence	Duff	Willard R.	42-D Kelly
Dear	Rudolph C.	42-C Ellington	Duffy	Owen M.	42-I Moody
DeBusk	Ray B.	42-I Stockton	Dunagan	Sidney W.	42-I Turner
Deckhoff	Don R.	42-I Ellington	Dunaske	John J.	42-I Ellington
Deel	Ollie I.	42-H Lubbock	Duncan	John C.	42-G Lubbock
Deere	Edward R.	42-I Ellington	Duncan	Robert E.	42-J Ellington
Deeter	Melvin M.	42-J Kelly	Dunklin	Reginald B.	42-G Dothan
Defore	Woodrow W.	42-C Kelly	Dunlap	James C.	42-H Spence
Delaney	Ronald C.	42-H Moody	Dupuy	Robert L.	42-I Stockton
Delashmutt	Everett N.	42-I Ellington	Durland	Roy H.	42-I Spence
Denman	Roger H.	42-J Ellington	Durling	Charles F.	42-G Spence
Denton	Allen W.	42-G Ellington	Durney	George P.	42-J Spence
Deroche	Earl J.	42-E Ellington	Durrett	Henry N.	42-H Luke
Deussen	Alexander	42-I Moody	Dusbabek	Joseph	42-G Ellington
Dewey	Frank M.	42-I Ellington	Dutton	Dewey A.	42-I Ellington
Dial	Irwin W.	42-F Kelly	Dvorak	Edward H.	42-H Lubbock
Dian	William	42-J Luke	Dye	Lawrence W.	42-I Spenc
Dick	Wagner W.	42-J Kelly	Dye	Thomas E.	42-I Ellington
Dickas	George H.	42-I Spence	Dyer	Fred L.	42-J Kelly
Dickson	Horace M., Jr.	42-E Kelly	Dyer	Glen E.	42-H Lubbock
Dideriksen	Robert W.	42-H Williams	Early	Nathaniel S.	42-H Luke
Diel	Harold S.	42-C Kelly	Easley	Charles D.	42-E Kelly
Dilks	Bartram H., Jr.	42-F Ellington	Easley	Leon L.	42-G Luke
Dillman	Robert C.	42-E Mather	Eaton	Frank H.	42-J Williams
Dinger	Joel A.	42-J Turner	Eaton	Lorin L.	42-H Williams
Dismukes	Roy C.	42-H Lubbock	Eaton	Wilbur B.	42-G Williams
Dixon	Jack R.	42-I Ellington	Eberhardt	Elmer	42-G Luke
Dixson	Richard B.	42-H Kelly	Eckert	Richard W.	42-G Spence
Doles	Henry A.	42-H Lubbock	Eddington	Lee B.	42-J Luke
Donahue	Joseph P.	42-G Spence	Eddleman	Kirby C.	42-J Kelly
Donnelly	Thomas E.	42-I Stockton	Eddy	James Q.	42-G Ellington
Donovan	Alsie D.	42-H Spence	Edelman	Forrest J.	42-J Williams
Dootson	Thomas C.	42-F Kelly	Edmunds	Terrence E.	42-I Luke
Doucet	Louis P.	42-G Ellington	Edwards	Francis L.	42-J Luke
Dougher	Edward E.	42-H Moody	Edwards	James R.	42-G Luke
Douglas	Logan A.	42-H Lubbock	Edwards	Leo B.	42-J Ellington
Douglas	Ralph N.	42-I Spence	Edwards	Paul H.	42-F Ellington
Douglass	Arthur T.	42-G Columbus	Edwards	Quinten E.	42-D Kelly
Downs	Thomas	42-I Ellington	Egan	John F.	42-I Spence
Doyle	Henry L.	42-D Ellington	Eggleston	Gilford B.	42-D Kelly
Doyle	Richard W.	42-E Ellington	Eichman	Frank T.	42-I Ellington
Doyle	Ula	42-J Ellington	Ekstrom	Manfred A., Jr.	42-G Lubbock

Elam	Rhodes M.	42-H Moody		Fear	Edgar A.	42-I Ellington
Eliot	Harold D.	42-E Mather		Fearing	Charles F.	42-H Williams
Ellinghaus	Fred W., III	42-H Ellington		Feistel	Robert L.	42-J Turner
Elliott	Lawrence R.	42-D Ellington		Felbab	Raymond E.	42-J Kelly
Ellis	Earl E.	42-H Williams		Fell	James "Dale"	42-G Luke
Ellis	Henry C.	42-G Ellington		Fennessey	James D.	42-J Turner
Ellyson	Milton H.	42-G Dothan		Fenwick	Dale R.	42-I Spence
Elwick	Ray D.	42-H Ellington		Ferguson	Sammy	42-J Kelly
Embrey	Ralph C.	42-C Kelly		Ferguson	William T.	42-D Kelly
Emmons	Lloyd R., Sr.	42-I Ellington		Ferrante	James D.	42-I Stockton
Engle	Charles R.	42-H Spence		Ferrato	Theodore P.	42-G Dothan
Engle	Elwin M.	42-G Ellington		Fielding	Vick A.	42-J Kelly
Engle	Richard J.	42-G Luke		Fieldson	Robert J.	42-G Kelly
Engle	Stanley L.	42-G Ellington		Fincher	Gilbert G.	42-I Lubbock
Ensminger	Robert C.	42-J Moody		Findley	James H.	42-D Kelly
Erb	William C.	42-F Mather		Finley	Harold W.	42-H Lubbock
Erickson	Arthur F.	42-G Williams		Fischel	Jay P.	42-G Luke
Erickson	Gordon B.	42-J Turner		Fish	Russell H.	42-I Stockton
Ermis	Raymond A.	42-H Kelly		Fisher	Alfred K.	42-H Columbus
Erwin	Archie T.	42-I Stockton		Fisher	Gordon E.	42-I Stockton
Escandel	Raymond W.	42-I Ellington		Fisk	Charles L.	42-J Ellington
Escandel	William N.	42-I Ellington		Fitzgerald	Emerson L.	42-J Kelly
Esser	Randolph A.	42-G Spence		Fix	Robert B.	42-G Spence
Evans	John W.	42-G Luke		Flack	Thomas V.	42-I Columbus
Evanson	Ernest F.	42-H Luke		Fleming	Dale R.	42-J Luke
Evens	Dean P.	42-H Lubbock		Fleming	George B.	42-J Williams
Evens	Fred D., Jr.	42-H Columbus		Fleming	Robert B.	42-I Ellington
Everett	Gerald C.	42-G Roswell		Floyd	Robert C.	42-G Williams
Eversull	George R.	42-E Kelly		Fontaine	Charles E.	42-G Ellington
Fahrland	Robert R.	42-J Kelly		Ford	Claud E.	42-C Ellington
Fair	Don F.	42-J Ellington		Ford	Ernest C.	42-E Luke
Fairey	John P.	42-F Ellington		Ford	Herbert E.	42-I Spence
Faithfull	William N.	42-H Lubbock		Ford	William R.	42-H Ellington
Falls	John H.	42-H Ellington		Forker	Tompson B.	42-H Columbus
Faram	Norman J.	42-J Kelly		Forrester	Walter S.	42-I Ellington
Farley	William A.	42-I Spence		Forry	Dewey J.	42-E Mather
Farmer	Roy C.	42-E Ellington		Forslund	Wayne T.	42-G Lubbock
Farness	Victor B.	42-F Kelly		Forster	Stanley L.	42-D Ellington
Farnsworth	Earl W.	42-H Luke		Fose	Rudolph H.	42-I Spence
Farr	Edgar S.	42-F Mather		Foster	George W.	42-D Ellington
Farr	Gilbert L.	42-H Kelly		Foster	James W.	42-J Luke
Farris	Randall L.	42-J Turner		Foster	Leonard R.	42-G Ellington
Farris	Russell R.	42-E Kelly		Fouty	John M.	42-G Lubbock
Farris	Walter L., Jr.	42-H Spence		Foutz	Merrill Y.	42-E Luke
Fassbender	Alexander H.	42-E Ellington		Frackowiak	Daniel S.	42-I Ellington
Faulkner	Dwight L.	42-G Luke		Frain	Martin D.	42-H Luke
Fauts	Gordon S.	42-I Turner		Fraker	Orval V.	42-G Roswell
Faux	Warren J.	42-I Turner		Framsted	Kenneth G.	42-J Kelly
Fay	James B.	42-G Ellington		Franko	Stephen	42-I Lubbock
Feagin	Luther W.	42-H Kelly		Fransen	Herbert N.	42-H Lubbock

Fredandall	Russell S.	42-H Kelly	Giddons	Charles L.	42-G Moody
Frederickson	Douglas C.	42-H Lubbock	Giese	Frank H.	42-H Kelly
Fredrickson	Raymond A	42-J Spence	Gilbert	Emmett E.	42-H Dothan
Freeman	Jacob M.	42-I Stockton	Gilbert	John W.	42-H Kelly
French	Dallas E.	42-H Luke	Gilbert	Royer W., Jr.	42-I Lubbock
French	Joseph L., Jr.	42-G Lubbock	Gilbreth	Joseph W.	42-F Mather
Frenzel	Arthur W.	42-I Lubbock	Giles	Eugene F.	42-I Lubbock
Frost	Ernest W.	42-I Stockton	Giles	Gene C.	42-F Mather
Frost	Thomas M.	42-I Stockton	Giles	Scott K.	42-C Kelly
Fruit	James A.	42-G Kelly	Gill	Paul D., Jr.	42-E Ellington
Fry	Loyal Wayne	42-G Roswell	Gillespie	Joseph H.	42-I Stockton
Frye	James E.	42-J Craig	Gillespie	Keith L.	42-I Ellington
Fugazi	John D.	42-H Luke	Gillette	George	42-E Ellington
Fuller	William E.	42-J Moody	Gilliland	Leown A.	42-C Kelly
Fullerton	Floyd B.	42-J Williams	Gilliland	Leslie D.	42-J Williams
Fulton	Henry T.	42-E Kelly	Gilliland	William R.	42-J Kelly
Furgason	Del H.	42-H Williams	Gillis	William A.	42-E Kelly
Gable	George R., Jr.	42-J Williams	Gilluly	Edwin W.	42-J Williams
Gage	James F.	42-J Ellington	Gilmer	Homer C.	42-I Spence
Gahm	Othol L.	42-I Stocton	Gilpin	Troy E.	42-I Turner
Galarneau	Francis E.	42-J Kelly	Gimblin	John S.	42-H Luke
Gall	Thomas A.	42-I Lubbock	Gipson	Guy M.	42-D Kelly
Gamble	Leslie E.	42-G Williams	Glantz	Ardell L.	42-J Kelly
Gandy	Russell N.	42-G Spence	Glasscock	Ivan	42-J Kelly
Gardner	Bob M.	42-I Spence	Glowacki	Edward J.	42-I Spence
Gardner	Jack H.	42-G Lubbock	Godfrey	Hollis A.	42-J Luke
Garrett	Charles A.	42-H Dothan	Godwin	Claude H.	42-C Ellington
Garvin	John T.	42-D Kelly	Godwin	Harlan H.	42-I Spence
Gaskins	John M.	42-H Kelly	Goldstein	Warren	42-H Dothan
Gates	Alexander J.	42-G Ellington	Gonda	John E.	42-H Spence
Gates	William M.	42-C Kelly	Goode	LeRoy D.	42-J Ellington
Gatling	William D.	42-I Spence	Gooden	Henry M.	42-I Spence
Gatski	Sam C.	42-G Lubbock	Goodman	Joseph N.	42-E Ellington
Gatti	Joseph	42-D Ellington	Goodman	Murray S.	42-J Spence
Gause	William	42-J Williams	Goodwin	Earl L.	42-G Spence
Gautier	Bill P.	42-I Stockton	Goodwyn	Roy L., Jr.	42-J Ellington
Gearhart	Fred Z.	42-H Columbus	Gordon	James T.	42-H Dothan
Gebelein	Herbert	42-I Stockton	Gorton	Ivan L.	42-I Turner
Gee	Richard A.	42-C Ellington	Gosnell	Richard J.	42-F Luke
Geer	William C.	42-H Lubbock	Gossett	Dewey L.	42-H Dothan
Gehrett	Rodney T.	42-G Ellington	Gossman	Louis R.	42-G Victorville
Geist	Lloyd J.	42-H Spence	Gower	Lorenzo R.	42-E Ellington
George	Cornelius G.	42-J Kelly	Grabenstein	Joseph L.	42-I Stockton
Gerke	Wright E.	42-J Moody	Grabowski	Victor J.	42-I Stockton
Gerrity	John J.	42-G Luke	Gradwell	Burgess	42-F Ellington
Gersch	William J.	42-C Ellington	Graham	Edward	42-J Moody
Gex	Louis	42-H Luke	Graham	Monroe W.	42-G Ellington
Gibala	Edmond J.	42-H Columbus	Graham	Nelson V.	42-I Ellington
Gibson	Ben "Hoot" S.	42-H Ellington	Graham	Oscar H.	42-J Ellington
Gibson	James P.	42-H Ellington	Graham	Robert G.	42-G Ellington

Gramling	Richard M.	42-J Ellington	Hall	Ralph J.	42-J Moody
Grams	Claire L.	42-I Turner	Halverson	Gilmore	42-G Luke
Grant	Howard K.	42-I Spence	Hamilton	Darwin R.	42-E Luke
Grant	Robert D.	42-I Spence	Hamilton	John E.	42-H Ellington
Graves	Willard E.	42-G Williams	Hamilton	Willard D.	42-J Spence
Graves	William P.	42-G Ellington	Hammersla	Robert L.	42-I Turner
Gray	Arthur M.	42-G Kelly	Hammond	Henry L.	42-I Stockton
Gray	Thomas W.	42-H Columbus	Hammonds	William H.	42-J Ellington
Grayson	Frank G.	42-G Moody	Hampson	Richard B.	42-H Columbus
Green	Augustus B., Jr.	42-I Stockton	Hampton	Hubert P.	42-G Lubbock
Green	George F.	42-H Ellington	Hampton	Winfred C.	42-I Moody
Green	Marvin V.	42-J Ellington	Hamric	Alex K.	42-C Kelly
Green	Robert D.	42-C Kelly	Hancock	Fred W.	42-I Moody
Greene	Charles A.	42-I Ellington	Hankins	Clinton E.	42-I Ellington
Greene	J. P. "Pete"	42-H Ellington	Hanley	Joseph W.	42-J Kelly
Greene	Melvin M.	42-G Ellington	Hanne	Harold F.	42-G Roswell
Greer	Fletcher P.	42-E Kelly	Hans	Charles A.	42-H Lubbock
Greer	William A.	42-G Lubbock	Hanson	Archie T.	42-F Luke
Griffith	Rockford C.	42-J Turner	Hardee	Sellers S.	42-H Dothan
Griffiths	Melvin W.	42-J Williams	Hardie	Robert L.	42-I Lubbock
Grill	Kenneth E.	42-I Lubbock	Hardin	Thomas H.	42-H Ellington
Grim	Rodney M.	42-E Mather	Harding	Claude J.	42-F Ellington
Grimes	Charles W.	42-F Ellington	Hardison	Dalton R.	42-H Lubbock
Grimes	Glenn R.	42-J Lubbock	Harlin	Charles J.	42-G Kelly
Grimes	Loy C.	42-I Turner	Harmon	Harvey L.	42-J Ellington
Grissom	Thomas J.	42-D Kelly	Harney	Raymond E.	42-I Moody
Grizzle	Howard K.	42-H Kelly	Harper	Weston W.	42-G Luke
Groce	Billy B.	42-H Kelly	Harpine	David H., Jr.	42-H Columbus
Groll	Gary J.	42-J Ellington	Harrington	Elmer E.	42-G Luke
Grovac	Donald E.	42-I Stockton	Harrington	Jack K.	42-I Stockton
Grubaugh	Neal W.	42-G Kelly	Harris	John C., III	42-I Moody
Grubb	Olin F.	42-G Turner	Harris	Joseph T.	42-G Kelly
Grucza	Joseph F.	42-G Lubbock	Harris	William J.	42-F Luke
Guess	Ellis B.	42-G Kelly	Harrison	Lynn R.	42-H Luke
Guillaum	William F.	42-J Ellington	Harry	William R.	42-J Moody
Guillotte	Robert J.	42-J Luke	Hart	Earl J.	42-J Ellington
Gunkel	Chester R.	42-J Kelly	Hartley	John A.	42-E Kelly
Gussey	Mark M.	42-I Ellington	Hartman	Elmer J.	42-G Roswell
Gwynn	Robert W.	42-F Luke	Hartzell	George B.	42-I Lubbock
Hackard	Jack D.	42-E Mather	Harvey	Douglas L.	42-J Stockton
Hacker	William E.	42-I Lubbock	Harvey	Woodrow W.	42-H Luke
Hackett	Wilbur M.	42-I Turner	Harwell	Roy D.	42-H Lubbock
Hadley	Wade H., Jr.	42-I Ellington	Hasley	Walter F.	42-I Stockton
Hagie	Douglas E.	42-G Roswell	Hass	Lawrence J.	42-H Luke
Hailes	Howard R.	42-F Kelly	Hassig	Donald K	42-E Ellington
Hairston	Richard M.	42-H Williams	Hastings	Richard H.	42-F Ellington
Halas	Anthony J.	42-E Kelly	Hatton	Phocian B.	42-H Ellington
Halbrook	John T.	42-H Ellington	Hawes	Clark J.	42-H Williams
Hale	Walter F., Jr.	42-I Ellington	Hawkes	Leon R.	42-E Mather
Haley	Raymond C.	42-G Turner	Hawkins	David C.	42-I Stockton

Hawley	Robert E.	42-F Luke
Hayes	Richard A.	42-H Luke
Hayles	Foster P.	42-G Williams
Haynes	Eugene H.	42-H Lubbock
Hazel	John H.	42-H Lubbock
Hazle	John H.	42-J Ellington
Head	John W.	42-D Ellington
Hearn	Roger V.	42-I Spence
Heaton	Robert L.	42-H Kelly
Heck	Hugh H.	42-I Moody
Hedges	Robert S.	42-H Lubbock
Hedgpeth	Louis G.	42-J Kelly
Heggem	Paul O.	42-H Ellington
Heidbreder	Kenneth W.	42-H Luke
Heinlein	Calvin S.	42-G Kelly
Hellstrom	John A.	42-G Roswell
Helminger	James C.	42-C Kelly
Helterbrand	Theodore A.	42-J Moody
Helton	Harrell B.	42-C Kelly
Hempe	Hubert G.	42-G Columbus
Hemphill	Victor J.	42-H Columbus
Hendrickson	Oscar S.	42-G Ellington
Hendry	Stuart B.	42-I Ellington
Henley	Justin O.	42-C Ellington
Henrix	George T., Jr.	42-J Kelly
Henry	Milburn B.	42-J Kelly
Hensarling	Arthur L.	42-J Ellington
Hensley	Louis E.	42-I Ellington
Hensman	Ray Van	42-E Luke
Henson	Billy M.	42-I Ellington
Herbst	Emmett A.	42-G Spence
Herles	John J.	42-H Luke
Hernandez	Manuel F.	42-G Ellington
Herrold	Leo V.	42-G Ellington
Hesler	Paul M.	42-H Spence
Hess	John R.	42-H Columbus
Hess	Robert W.	42-G Kelly
Hetzler	Harold W.	42-D Kelly
Hickman	Charles L.	42-H Luke
Hickman	James W.	42-H Lubbock
Hicks	James G., Jr.	42-H Columbus
Hicks	Joseph W., Jr.	42-J Lubbock
Higbee	Swain M.	42-H Ellington
Higgins	Malcolm H.	42-J Ellington
Higgins	Veral C.	42-G Lubbock
Hildebrand	John A.	42-D Ellington
Hiley	James H.	42-G Lubbock
Hill	Joseph G.	42-J Ellington
Hill	Kenneth K.	42-J Kelly
Hill	Wayne E.	42-I Ellington
Hillis	Asa N.	42-H Ellington
Hillman	Kenneth D.	42-G Roswell
Hinkle	Robert L., Jr.	42-I Ellington
Hinton	Charles V.	42-I Moody
Hinton	Gary F.	42-F Kelly
Hirsch	Alfred H.	42-H Luke
Hirth	Herbert H.	42-I Ellington
Hitchings	Warren C.	42-E Kelly
Hitztaler	William R.	42-E Ellington
Hochstettler	Francis L.	42-E Kelly
Hodges	Fred D.	42-J Moody
Hoff	William C.	42-G Luke
Hoffman	Lloyd J.	42-H Moody
Hofmeister	Harold E.	42-G Spence
Hogan	Jack F.	42-J Ellington
Hogan	Thomas P.	42-H Columbus
Holben	Carl R.	42-I Stockton
Holcomb	Earl L.	42-I Stockton
Holden	William S.	42-J Moody
Holder	James R.	42-I Lubbock
Holik	Horace A.	42-H Luke
Holland	Mark F.	42-E Ellington
Holland	Warren	42-H Columbus
Hollandsworth	Elwin	42-E Mather
Holley	Hazil L.	42-G Moody
Hollier	Charles E.	42-J Kelly
Holloway	Victor N.	42-G Kelly
Hollowell	Daniel J.	42-G Lubbock
Holman	Averill "Tex"	42-H Luke
Holmes	Leonard E.	42-H Ellington
Holmes	Marshall D.	42-H Spence
Hood	Lonnie C.	42-G Ellington
Hood	Lyle D.	42-H Kelly
Hoover	Jack D.	42-F Luke
Hoover	Leonard E.	42-D Ellington
Hoover	Robert A.	42-H Columbus
Hopkins	Leroy J.	42-F Kelly
Hopp	Donald K.	42-J Ellington
Hopper	Richard S.	42-H Lubbock
Horn	John D.	42-G Ellington
Horsfall	John B.	42-G Turner
Hosey	William F.	42-H Kelly
Hoskinson	Cyril J., Jr.	42-E Ellington
Houck	George D.	42-F Mather
Hough	David G.	42-E Ellington
Houghtaling	Harold A.	42-G Dothan
Houle	Joseph L.	42-I Stockton
Houp	Kenneth A.	42-J Kelly
Houston	Charles H.	42-H Lubbock
Houston	Cortez E.	42-E Mather

Houston	Jimmy B.	42-E Luke		James	William E.	42-I Lubbock
Howell	Joseph C.	42-I Lubbock		Jameson	Ted S.	42-J Ellington
Howell	Phillip P.	42-I Lubbock		Janeczko	Stanley F.	42-J Ellington
Hoye	John J.	42-F Mather		Janes	Ralph P.	42-F Mather
Hrkach	John J.	42-E Ellington		Janicki	Chester	42-H Spence
Hubbard	Van D.	42-J Moody		Jarvis	Rowan M.	42-H Williams
Huber	Fred J.	42-G Columbus		Jasmin	Leon E.	42-E Luke
Huddleston	Robert B.	42-I Stockton		Jeffers	Harold B.	42-I Lubbock
Hudson	Charles, Jr.	42-I Stockton		Jeffrey	Rayford W.	42-J Kelly
Hudson	Dock J.	42-I Ellington		Jenner	Benjamin K.	42-I Spence
Huet	Allan W.	42-H Ellington		Jennings	Hiram S.	42-E Ellington
Huey	Charles J.	42-I Stockton		Jewell	Kenneth G.	42-J Moody
Huggins	Frank W.	42-G Luke		Jewett	Raymond J.	42-H Ellington
Hughes	Malcolm Dale	42-H Williams		Job	Jesse C.	42-J Luke
Hughes	Robert R.	42-I Lubbock		Joffrion	Leonard M., Jr.	42-I Spence
Hulber	Clarence E., Jr.	42-I Stockton		Johnson	Charles I.	42-H Luke
Humphreys	Guy T.	42-F Luke		Johnson	Darwin E.	42-F Ellington
Hunt	Francis L.	42-J Williams		Johnson	David M.	42-G Moody
Hunt	Robert H.	42-H Columbus		Johnson	Doyle L.	42-I Moody
Hunter	Alva Roe	42-J Craig		Johnson	Francis R.	42-C Ellington
Huntington	Clifford	42-H Spence		Johnson	Franklin O.	42-I Lubbock
Huntsman	Clayton W.	42-J Luke		Johnson	Gerald R.	42-G Luke
Hurd	Archie W.	42-G Kelly		Johnson	Glenn A.	42-H Dothan
Hurlbut	Frank D.	42-H Luke		Johnson	Harold L.	42-I Moody
Hurst	William G.	42-G Luke		Johnson	James K.	42-G Ellington
Hutchens	Velma R.	42-J Kelly		Johnson	John C.	42-G Luke
Hutchinson	Tom	42-I Stockton		Johnson	John S.	42-I Stockton
Hutchison	Irwin C.	42-H Luke		Johnson	Lloyd B.	42-I Ellington
Hutson	Raymond C.	42-I Moody		Johnson	Quentin E.	42-G Williams
Hutson	Robert P.	42-H Columus		Johnson	Ralph M.	42-I Stockton
Hyde	Marshall E.	42-C Ellington		Johnson	Robert G.	42-G Luke
Icard	Joe W.	42-J Spence		Johnson	Robert G.	42-J Kelly
Iden	Walter M.	42-D Ellington		Johnson	Roy A.	42-J Kelly
Ineson	William L., Jr.	42-G Moody		Johnson	Russell F.	42-J Turner
Inks	Howard R.	42-J Ellington		Johnson	Thad K.	42-H Dothan
Insalaco	Vincenzo	42-I Spence		Johnston	Bernie B.	42-I Stockton
Irvin	James C.	42-E Luke		Johnston	Drexel M.	42-D Ellington
Irvine	Charles E.	42-H Columbus		Johnston	Ernest E.	42-H Williams
Irvine	Robert E. S.	42-H Luke		Johnston	Gerald W.	42-I Stockton
Irwin	William P.	42-C Kelly		Johnston	Joseph W.	42-I Spence
Iudicello	Lawrence S.	42-J Ellington		Johnston	Ramon L.	42-I Stocton
Iverson	Robert W.	42-D Kelly		Johnston	Robert M.	42-H Kelly
Jackson	Elmer R.	42-F Mather		Johnston	William E.	42-H Lubbock
Jackson	Eugene M.	42-I Moody		Jones	Charlie H.	42-I Stockton
Jackson	Floyd A.	42-J Luke		Jones	David H.	42-I Stockton
Jackson	John M.	42-I Stockton		Jones	Edwin P.	42-H Spence
Jacobs	Dan J.	42-J Kelly		Jones	Frank "Rocky"	42-G Luke
Jacobs	George D.	42-I Stockton		Jones	Graham E.	42-C Ellington
James	Robert L.	42-D Kelly		Jones	Horace B.	42-I Stockton
James	William A.	42-H Kelly		Jones	James M.	42-H Lubbock

Jones	James W.	42-I Stockton	Kerr	Gordon T.	42-J Dothan
Jones	Leonard D.	42-H Lubbock	Kerr	Jack L.	42-H Williams
Jones	Lucian P.	42-H Lubbock	Kesley	Howard N.	42-H Columbus
Jones	Morris O.	42-H Kelly	Kester	Emory J.	42-I Stockton
Jones	Nolan I.	42-J Spence	Kevan	William E.	42-J Kelly
Jones	Oscar T., Jr.	42-H Ellington	Keyes	Ed R.	42-I Lubbock
Jones	Robert W.	42-F Luke	Keyes	Woody H., Jr.	42-G Columbus
Jones	Walter D., Jr.	42-I Ellington	Keys	Joseph D., Jr.	42-J Spence
Jones	Wiley E.	42-I Lubbock	Keyser	John R.	42-I Stockton
Jones	William E.	42-J Ellington	Kibler	Irving B.	42-H Kelly
Jones	William T.	42-H Ellington	Kidd	Thedford F.	42-I Stockton
Jorda	J. Wayne	42-C Ellington	Kidder	Donald L.	42-J Ellington
Jordan	Herbert A.	42-J Ellington	Kiehm	Erdman D.	42-J Williams
Jordan	Hubert W.	42-H Luke	Kile	Allen E., Jr.	42-H Moody
Jordan	Joe B.	42-D Kelly	Kilmer	Howard L.	42-J Turner
Jordan	Marion C.	42-H Williams	Kimble	Richard E.	42-I Stockton
Joy	William R.	42-H Dothan	Kinamon	Charles L.	42-I Stockton
Juett	Clifton E.	42-I Spence	Kindle	Melvin E.	42-J Ellington
Jumonville	Benjamin R.	42-J Craig	King	James O.	42-H Kelly
Juozaitis	Elmer A.	42-J Spence	Kingrey	Jack R.	42-C Ellington
Kaffenberger	Leo W.	42-E Kelly	Kingsley	Nathan J.	42-C Ellington
Kagy	Kenneth W.	42-I Stockton	Kinsey	Claude R.	42-C Kelly
Kain	Jerry B.	42-H Luke	Kipp	Richard W.	42-J Spence
Kajor	Louis, Jr.	42-I Ellington	Kipp	Warren H.	42-G Lubbock
Kanaska	Henry G.	42-H Columbus	Kirby	Donald B.	42-H Luke
Kandarian	Haig	42-J Kelly	Kirkendofer	Donald R.	42-H Columbus
Kane	Wesley L.	42-G Kelly	Kissick	Lloyd O.	42-F Ellington
Karlberg	Eugene L.	42-E Mather	Kitchin	Robert O.	42-H Williams
Karsonovich	Joseph L.	42-E Ellington	Kithcart	Richard B.	42-G Luke
Kaspick	John A., Jr.	42-J Dothan	Klappas	Frank	42-G Luke
Kay	Gilles L.	42-G Kelly	Klass	Lewis J.	42-H Luke
Kaylor	Perry O.	42-D Kelly	Klassen	Frank J.	42-I Moody
Kazimerczak	Walter F.	42-I Stockton	Klein	John J.	42-I Spence
Keaster	William F.	42-H Columbus	Kleinke	Robert L.	42-I Lubbock
Kee	Ben R.	42-J Columbus	Klomparens	Harvey E.	42-D Ellington
Keeney	Donald A.	42-F Mather	Knapp	Gaylord A.	42-H Kelly
Keeton	Robert J.	42-I Spence	Knickerbocker	Harry G.	42-E Luke
Keith	Charles F.	42-G Columbus	Knight	Dewitt T., Jr.	42-H Columbus
Keithley	John L.	42-G Columbus	Knight	Gene C.	42-H Luke
Kelley	John P.	42-I Stockton	Knight	Robert S.	42-F Ellington
Kelley	Robert L.	42-H Lubbock	Knutson	Donald E.	42-I Ellington
Kelly	Joseph P.	42-J Ellington	Koehler	Gilbert L.	42-E Kelly
Kemp	William C.	42-I Spence	Kohlscheen	Leland C.	42-G Lubbock
Kemper	Charles L.	42-J Ellington	Koller	Clark	42-H Lubbock
Kendrick	Warren L.	42-I Moody	Koontz	Glenn H.	42-J Spence
Kent	Henry W.	42-J Spence	Korstad	Arvie P.	42-E Luke
Kenyon	Robert L.	42-E Kelly	Korth	William M.	42-F Mather
Kerlick	Carl M.	42-G Ellington	Kosko	Albert W.	42-J Turner
Kermes	William J.	42-C Ellington	Kramer	Peter A.	42-F Mather
Kern	Harold C.	42-H Dothan	Kreiser	John E.	42-I Lubbock

Linsly	Joseph P., Jr.	42-H Luke	McCallister	David F.	42-I Moody
Linzmeier	Ralph B.	42-I Lubbock	McCann	William H.	42-H Moody
Litchfield	John S.	42-C Kelly	McCarthy	Kenneth W.	42-I Spence
Little	John W.	42-H Ellington	McCarty	James P.	42-I Spence
Littorin	Irving M.	42-D Ellington	McCaskill	Oliver L.	42-I Spence
Locklear	James W.	42-F Luke	McClain	William F.	42-G Spence
Loeder	William C.	42-J Kelly	McClary	Arthur J.	42-G Columbus
Loffredo	James A.	42-G Luke	McClendon	Dennis E.	42-E Kelly
Long	Lester J., Jr.	42-H Kelly	McClure	Eugene L.	42-I Stockton
Long	Raymond W.	42-D Kelly	McClure	James H.	42-J Kelly
Long	Richard E.	42-D Kelly	McCombs	Ernest E.	42-J Ellington
Long	William F.	42-H Williams	McCracken	Howard V.	42-G Spence
Loomis	James A.	42-H Luke	McCraw	Albert R.	42-H Kelly
Lorah	Franklin A.	42-I Craig	McCrorie	Robert E.	42-G Lubbock
Loughnan	Victor J.	42-J Moody	McCue	Robert M.	42-H Kelly
Lovejoy	James C.	42-G Luke	McCullough	C. O.	42-I Lubbock
Loveland	Howard C., Jr.	42-I Stockton	McCullough	Edward C.	42-I Lubbock
Low	Carl S.	42-J Lubbock	McCurry	Charles R.	42-J Ellington
Lowe	Charles	42-G Kelly	McCutchan	James R.	42-I Spence
Lowell	Charles L.	42-G Williams	McDaniel	Howard H.	42-F Mather
Lower	Bert R.	42-J Luke	McDaniel	Lemuel D., Jr.	42-C Kelly
Lowther	Edwin E.	42-I Moody	McDaniel	Norris D.	42-C Kelly
Lubor	Jack	42-G Ellington	McDonald	Bill	42-H Kelly
Lucas	Truman	42-I Ellington	McDonald	Charles L., Jr.	42-F Mather
Luce	Richard L.	42-H Williams	McDonald	Gerald C.	42-I Ellington
Ludtke	Robert E.	42-G Victorville	McDonald	James	42-G Lubbock
Lulow	Cecil F.	42-J Moody	McDonough	Jack K.	42-G Columbus
Lumsden	Marshall E.	42-H Luke	McDonough	John E.	42-J Williams
Lund	Keith K.	42-C Kelly	McDowell	Roy E.	42-J Kelly
Luscomb	Henry K.	42-J Turner	McElhiney	Cecil R.	42-H Columbus
Lusi	Sabatino T.	42-I Lubbock	McElhiney	Thomas C.	42-G Kelly
Luther	Henry W.	42-G Roswell	McElmurry	Thomas U.	42-I Stockton
Lycan	Joseph M.	42-C Ellington	McFarland	D. H.	42-I Stockton
Lykins	George E.	42-I Ellington	McFarland	Jack H.	42-H Luke
Lykins	James O.	42-G Ellington	McFarland	Orland W.	42-F Ellington
Lyle	William H.	42-D Kelly	McGinley	Paul F.	42-I Lubbock
Lyle	William H., Jr.	42-I Ellington	McGuire	Byron S.	42-J Dothan
Lynch	Fred M.	42-G Luke	McHugh	James W.	42-H Moody
Lynch	Jack W.	42-F Ellington	McIntyre	Brandt	42-E Mather
Lynn	John H., Jr.	42-E Mather	McIntyre	Rex W.	42-G Williams
Lynn	Roland R.	42-C Kelly	McIver	Drue E., Jr.	42-I Stockton
Lynn	William H.	42-I Lubbock	McIver	Norman E.	42-H Lubbock
Lytle	Robert R.	42-H Kelly	McKeithen	Archie J.	42-H Spence
Maass	William R.	42-H Williams	Mackey	Walter J.	42-H Ellington
Mac Arthur	Howard T.	42-J Luke	McKinney	Robert M.	42-G Kelly
McBride	James G.	42-J Ellington	McKinnon	John P.	42-H Ellington
McBroom	W. B.	42-F Ellington	McLaughlin	Floyd L., Jr.	42-J Williams
McCadden	Norman L.	42-H Kelly	McLaughlin	Patrick J.	42-H Williams
McCall	Garvice D.	42-H Moody	Maclay	Robert E.	42-H Moody
McCall	Hugh E.	42-H Luke	McLean	Lloyd D.	42-I Lubbock

McMonigle	Dennis R.	42-J Kelly	Martz	Robert E.	42-D Kelly
McMullen	James A.	42-J Ellington	Maser	Howard G.	42-J Moody
McMurry	Robert J.	42-D Ellington	Mason	Frank E.	42-H Kelly
McNeil	James E.	42-H Luke	Mason	Walter L., Jr.	42-F Ellington
McPhee	John M.	42-H Luke	Massino	Edward P.	42-J Kelly
MacWilliam	James H.	42-G Williams	Masuga	Lawrence E.	42-G Columbus
McWilliams	Joseph W.	42-F Ellington	Mathis	Robert L.	42-D Ellington
Macy	Eugene J., Jr.	42-I Spence	Mathis	Vivian S.	42-H Columbus
Macy	Loran W.	42-I Ellington	Matthews	Frank C.	42-G Dothan
Madden	Edwin E.	42-J Kelly	Mattson	Frank K.	42-I Lubbock
Maddux	Walter K.	42-G Williams	Mauldin	Loyd L.	42-J Turner
Maerk	Allen E.	42-E Ellington	Maxelin	Warren I.	42-I Spence
Magee	Kenneth	42-G Luke	Maxey	John L.	42-D Ellington
Magners	Vernon S.	42-E Kelly	Maxwell	Neil D.	42-E Ellington
Magoon	Robert A.	42-G Lubbock	Mayer	Walter F.	42-J Spence
Majesky	Frank W.	42-J Ellington	Maynard	Bruce W.	42-J Luke
Majka	Fred J.	42-I Spence	Mayo	John B., III	42-F Mather
Makowski	Bernard A.	42-J Moody	Mayo	Roy F.	42-J Turner
Malenfant	Victor J.	42-H Columbus	Mayo	Watkins	42-H Spence
Mallette	Archie F.	42-C Kelly	Means	Russell E.	42-E Ellington
Mallory	Lue B.	42-J Moody	Medcalf	Rex M.	42-G Ellington
Malone	Robert C., Jr.	42-F Ellington	Medonis	Peter G., Jr.	42-G Ellington
Manahan	Eugene L.	42-E Kelly	Meek	Lewis R.	42-H Ellington
Mangarpan	Joseph L.	42-J Turner	Meeks	John R., Jr.	42-F Ellington
Manning	Harold G.	42-C Ellington	Meeks	N. V., Jr.	42-I Stockton
Manning	James H.	42-H Moody	Mellen	Henry A.	42-H Ellington
Manning	Tom C.	42-I Stockton	Melvin	John S.	42-F Luke
Manooch	Charles S., Jr.	42-H Lubbock	Menger	James M.	42-H Columbus
Marble	Ralph W.	42-I Moody	Mentzer	Lawrence L.	42-E Luke
Marcum	Everette L.	42-H Spence	Merrigan	Louis "Jack"	42-F Ellington
Maret	Paul L.	42-H Spence	Messer	John	42-J Williams
Markkanen	Howard W.	42-G Columbus	Messinger	Franklin D.	42-H Ellington
Marlaire	Lloyd L.	42-I Lubbock	Metcalf	John C.	42-G Kelly
Marrs	Loyal S., Jr.	42-I Ellington	Metheny	Frank W.	42-I Lubbock
Marsh	Raymond C., Jr.	42-F Kelly	Metsker	James W., Jr.	42-I Moody
Marsh	Russell A.	42-E Ellington	Meyer	Edward J.	42-I Craig
Marshall	Herschel W.	42-G Columbus	Meyer	George F.	42-H Luke
Marshall	William B.	42-D Kelly	Meyer	John R.	42-C Ellington
Martin	Charles W.	42-I Lubbock	Meyer	Paul E.	42-F Kelly
Martin	Edward C.	42-G Williams	Meyers	Charles A.	42-J Kelly
Martin	George F.	42-I Stockton	Michael	Leatus B.	42-G Turner
Martin	John M.	42-H Lubbock	Middaugh	Jack E.	42-H Luke
Martin	Keitt O., Jr.	42-J Turner	Middlebrooks	Berlin I.	42-G Ellington
Martin	Louis C.	42-H Dothan	Middleton	Walter O.	42-J Ellington
Martin	Louis G.	42-E Luke	Mihlfeld	Roy S.	42-I Moody
Martin	Robert C.	42-I Lubbock	Mildren	William E.	42-J Williams
Martin	Robert E.	42-H Lubbock	Miller	Arthur C.	42-J Williams
Martindale	Thomas K.	42-J Ellington	Miller	Clarence F.	42-J Ellington
Martinek	Samuel R.	42-J Craig	Miller	Earl "Dutch"	42-J Spence
Martinez	Manuel S.	42-J Spence	Miller	Gene C.	42-G Ellington

Miller	Max B.	42-F Kelly	Morgan	Emory C.	42-C Ellington
Miller	Merle D.	42-J Ellington	Morgan	Harry W.	42-E Luke
Miller	Milton P.	42-H Columbus	Morgan	John P.	42-H Ellington
Miller	Myron	42-F Mather	Morganti	Galileo J.	42-I Stockton
Miller	Ray A.	42-F Ellington	Morris	Harry R.	42-C Ellington
Miller	Roy A.	42-G Ellington	Morris	James C.	42-I Moody
Miller	Wendell D.	42-I Craig	Morris	Robert E.	42-J Ellington
Miller	William F.	42-I Lubbock	Morris	Robert L.	42-I Lubbock
Millett	Clyde L.	42-I Moody	Morris	Thomas L.	42-F Ellington
Mills	Howard E.	42-H Moody	Morrison	Gerald E.	42-H Ellington
Mills	Robert A.	42-H Luke	Morrison	Maurice	42-J Luke
Miner	Henry B.	42-J Kelly	Morrison	William J.	42-E Ellington
Minich	Lyle P. "Bud"	42-F Kelly	Morrow	David E.	42-E Kelly
Minter	Jess W.	42-F Mather	Morscher	George Q.	42-H Spence
Mitchell	Babe Ruth	42-H Kelly	Mosenthin	Harold A.	42-I Ellilngton
Mitchell	Finis A.	42-C Ellington	Moser	Willie R.	42-H Ellington
Mitchell	Judson, Jr.	42-J Kelly	Moss	Carlos W.	42-H Fllington
Mitchell	Kyle E.	42-G Ellington	Moulder	Robert W.	42-J Ellington
Mitchell	Lawton E.	42-G Ellington	Mourer	Ray S., Jr.	42-I Stockton
Mitchell	Lenyard C.	42-I Stockton	Mouser	Calvin H.	42-G Columbus
Mitchell	Rolland L.	42-I Ellington	Mousette	Alfred D.	42-I Lubbock
Mitchell	Ross H.	42-F Kelly	Mouton	Vernon J.	42-I Ellington
Mitchell	Verble	42-D Ellington	Mouzak	John N.	42-H Kelly
Mitstifer	Dayton B.	42-H Columbus	Moyer	Duane I.	42-I Ellington
Moates	John	42-H Ellington	Moyna	Robert S.	42-G Columbus
Mobley	Lucien D.	42-G Luke	Mueller	Laurin A.	42-E Mather
Moesly	Carl	42-G Lubbock	Muir	Donald W.	42-I Dothan
Moline	Siegfried L.	42-I Stockton	Mulder	Bernard A.	42-F Luke
Momberger	William H.	42-H Spence	Mullendore	Lewis A.	42-G Kelly
Momchilov	Perry	42-F Kelly	Mullins	Clayton D.	42-I Stockton
Mondt	David	42-I Ellington	Munchrath	Francis F.	42-I Lubbock
Mong	Rex E.	42-I Stockton	Munro	Thomas F.	42-J Spence
Monroe	Horace B.	42-I Stockton	Murphy	Daniel J.	42-E Ellington
Monroe	John E.	42-J Kelly	Murphy	John H.	42-H Moody
Montgomery	James H., Jr.	42-H Kelly	Murphy	Stanley W.	42-I Stockton
Montoya	Edward R.	42-G Kelly	Murray	Arthur	42-H Spence
Moon	Albert J.	42-H Spence	Murray	Robert H.	42-C Kelly
Moore	Charles R.	42-I Ellington	Murrell	Jack A.	42-H Columbus
Moore	Gene B.	42-J Williams	Muther	William N.	42-I Turner
Moore	John T.	42-G Kelly	Mutschler	Douglas L.	42-G Williams
Moore	Richard D.	42-J Ellington	Myers	Frederick L.	42-D Ellington
Moore	Robert J.	42-F Kelly	Myers	George E.	42-H Luke
Moore	Robert M	42-J Spence	Myers	James M.	42-J Ellington
Moore	Warner F.	42-G Kelly	Nabors	Jack	42-E Ellington
Moose	John L.	42-G Ellington	Nachajski	Edward J.	42-D Kelly
Moose	Marlin H.	42-I Stockton	Nachreiner	Gerald F.	42-G Dothan
Moran	Louis A.	42-I Turner	Nack	Arthur	42-C Kelly
Mordan	Merrill L.	42-J Columbus	Naftel	Stacy D.	42-G Dothan
Morehead	Barker	42-F Kelly	Naigle	Alfred J.	42-H Moody
Morgan	Edward R.	42-G Columbus	Nalder	William E.	42-H Williams

Nall	Plez T.	42-G Ellington	Olson	Vernon J.	42-G Victorville
Nance	Darell E.	42-H Luke	Olson	Victor R.	42-G Roswell
Naquin	Jules F., Jr.	42-J Kelly	O'Neal	George F.	42-I Stockton
Narramore	Roth J.	42-I Stockton	Oppreicht	John A.	42-H Luke
Natho	John L.	42-F Kelly	Orahood	Dwight H.	42-H Lubbock
Nefzger	Kenneth J.	42-G Luke	O'Reilly	Leland S.	42-I Lubbock
Neidig	William M.	42-E Ellington	Ormsby	James P.	42-J Kelly
Neidigh	Kenneth E.	42-I Stockton	Orr	Roscoe D.	42-I Lubbock
Nellor	Joseph G.	42-I Lubbock	Osborn	Calvin V.	42-I Lubbock
Nelson	Clifford W.	42-J Spence	Osborn	Clyde A.	42-G Roswell
Nelson	Elmer	42-I Turner	Osborn	Dennis L., Jr.	42-J Luke
Nelson	Harold E.	42-H Williams	Osborn	Mark A.	42-J Luke
Nelson	Lawrence R.	42-H Kelly	Osver	Sam L.	42-E Ellington
Nelson	Robert R.	42-H Williams	Otey	Walter R.	42-I Lubbock
Netzer	John J.	42-I Dothan	O'Toole	Jerome T.	42-J Ellington
Neveu	Harry K.	42-I Turner	Otten	Harold R.	42-E Ellington
Newlin	Robert V.	42-H Columbus	Owen	Clinton V.	42-H Ellington
Newman	Clovis C.	42-H Williams	Owen	Damron C., Jr.	42-G Ellington
Newquist	Weldon D.	42-F Ellington	Owen	Harold J.	42-D Ellington
Nichols	Dewey F.	42-I Ellington	Owens	Billy N.	42-F Kelly
Nichols	Max B.	42-J Williams	Owens	Harold W.	42-F Mather
Nicholson	Levi L.	42-H Kelly	Paccassi	Jerry G.	42-E Luke
Nicholson	Robert A.	42-I Dothan	Pace	Ben F.	42-I Craig
Nicholson	Thomas A.	42-I Ellington	Pace	Robert E.	42-G Ellington
Nickell	Billy V.	42-J Columbus	Pair	Jerry	42-I Lubbock
Nickum	Willard E.	42-G Lubbock	Palmer	Andrew L.	42-G Dothan
Nix	Hershel	42-F Mather	Palmer	John P.	42-H Spence
Nixon	Glynn H.	42-I Stockton	Paquette	John J.	42-I Lubbock
Nodine	Willard L.	42-D Kelly	Parent	Edmund A.	42-H Spence
Nored	Ralph R.	42-J Ellington	Parke	Benjamin F., Jr.	42-J Spence
Norell	Glen F.	42-D Ellington	Parker	Fred W.	42-G Roswell
Norman	William R.	42-J Williams	Parker	Gerald A.	42-I Dothan
Norris	Robert W.	42-G Turner	Parker	James A., Sr.	42-I Stockton
Northcott	Freeman C.	42-G Kelly	Parker	John P.	42-J Craig
Norton	James B.	42-I Ellington	Parris	Joseph E.	42-I Lubbock
Nowak	Leon J., Jr.	42-H Kelly	Partridge	Edwin C., Jr.	42-J Williams
Noxon	Donald E.	42-J Ellington	Partridge	Frederick R.	42-I Turner
Obermiller	James E.	42-C Kelly	Paschal	Thomas C.	42-G Roswell
O'Connor	William L.	42-I Stockton	Patrick	Andrew	42-I Lubbock
Odom	Stanley C.	42-I Lubbock	Patrick	William F.	42-I Turner
Ogier	Frederick C.	42-H Luke	Patterson	Claude W.	42-E Ellington
Ogle	James E.	42-H Williams	Patterson	Ernest N.	42-I Turner
Ogle	Sherman L.	42-I Stockton	Patterson	Hudson, Jr.	42-I Ellington
Ohman	Clifton P.	42-H Moody	Patterson	James H.	42-H Luke
Oholendt	Gene F.	42-D Kelly	Patton	Joseph R.	42-H Roswell
Ohrberg	George E.	42-I Lubbock	Paulson	Stanford E.	42-F Luke
Oleman	James A.	42-G Ellington	Paulson	William A.	42-H Luke
Olfson	Junior W.	42-I Moody	Pawlowski	Harry R.	42-G Luke
Oliver	Jesse G.	42-C Kelly	Peale	Robert J.	42-J Williams
Olsen	William W.	42-H Lubbock	Pearce	Cloyd T.	42-J Williams

Rasmussen	Maxwell W.	42-H Ellington	Riley	John C.	42-J Columbus
Rath	William F.	42-C Kelly	Rinker	James H.	42-H Lubbock
Rau	Edwin C.	42-J Kelly	Riordan	Jacque L.	42-G Dothan
Rauth	John F.	42-H Spence	Ripley	Bertram	42-I Moody
Rawlings	Patrick J.	42-E Ellington	Ripley	Ted W.	42-G Luke
Rawlins	Joe S.	42-D Ellington	Rise	Neil W.	42-I Dothan
Rawson	John R.	42-I Dothan	Risely	George, Jr.	42-G Ellington
Rawson	William B.	42-C Ellington	Ristau	Frank W.	42-H Luke
Ray	Shaw D.	42-G Kelly	Risvold	Mili K.	42-J Williams
Ray	Wayne S.	42-J Ellington	Ritchie	Robert K.	42-I Ellington
Rayburn	Warren D.	42-F Mather	Ritger	Frederic C.	42-I Moody
Raymond	Robert L.	42-H Luke	Ritter	Stanley L.	42-G Ellington
Rayner	Harold E.	42-J Ellington	Riverbark	Luke R.	42-I Columbus
Reagan	Allan W.	42-G Lubbock	Roach	Lloyd E.	42-D Ellington
Reagh	Grant L.	42-C Kelly	Roane	Orville R.	42-J Ellington
Reagle	Robert C.	42-I Stockton	Roane	Owen D.	42-J Ellington
Reardon	Jack D.	42-H Williams	Robbins	John B.	42-H Spence
Reas	Glen W.	42-C Kelly	Roberts	Dale C.	42-G Lubbock
Redman	Louis R.	42-G Ellington	Roberts	Gerald R.	42-I Ellington
Reed	Edward S.	42-J Ellington	Roberts	Rayford C.	42-G Dothan
Reeves	Bruce F.	42-H Ellington	Robertson	Albert D.	42-G Ellington
Reger	Ted E.	42-H Luke	Robertson	David M.	42-G Luke
Reichard	Carl F.	42-J Columbus	Robertson	Edward R.	42-J Kelly
Reimann	Robert E.	42-J Ellington	Robertson	Hugh W.	42-E Ellington
Reimbolt	James R.	42-J Luke	Robertson	William T.	42-D Kelly
Reish	John F.	42-J Moody	Robeson	Howard E.	42-F Mather
Reither	Christian W.	42-H Lubbock	Robinette	Ralph R.	42-D Ellington
Renker	Harry J.	42-F Mather	Robinette	Ross M.	42-J Columbus
Revello	Felix F.	42-I Lubbock	Robinson	Cecil P.	42-E Luke
Reynolds	Bennie E.	42-J Kelly	Robinson	Harold L.	42-J Columbus
Rhodes	James W.	42-H Luke	Robinson	Temple S.	42-G Spence
Rhodes	Thomas R.	42-D Ellington	Robison	Merle F.	42-C Kelly
Rice	Louis H.	42-G Victorville	Rockett	Marshall A.	42-G Ellington
Rich	Irving W.	42-I Spence	Rockney	Arlo D.	42-I Stockton
Richard	Wesley L.	42-H Dothan	Rodgers	Hugh M.	42-H Lubbock
Richards	Harley M.	42-H Ellington	Rodgers	John L.	42-G Lubbock
Richards	Leon A.	42-H Columbus	Roeske	Leopold A.	42-I Stockton
Richards	William F.	42-J Columbus	Rogers	Dale A.	42-I Moody
Richardson	Charles W., Jr.	42-J Williams	Rogers	Marion T., Jr.	42-J Ellington
Richardson	Herman L.	42-J Columbus	Rogers	Richard G.	42-G Luke
Richardson	Richard K.	42-I Stockton	Rogers	William H.	42-F Kelly
Richey	William R.	42-I Lubbock	Roggli	Jon W.	42-F Ellington
Richter	Denny G., Jr.	42-E Kelly	Romick	Bruce R.	42-H Ellington
Riddle	Robert L.	42-I Dothan	Roper	Hugh M.	42-J Williams
Riddle	Roy F.	42-I Moody	Rork	Cidney J.	42-G Kelly
Ridenour	John W.	42-I Moody	Rose	Richard M.	42-H Ellington
Ridley	Bill B.	42-J Ellington	Rosengrants	David	42-G Ellington
Riggan	Bedford B.	42-F Kelly	Ross	Arnold	42-I Lubbock
Riggs	Donald E.	42-F Mather	Rothey	Robert B.	42-J Luke
Rigsby	Cecil H.	42-H Williams	Rounds	Gerald L.	42-C Kelly

Routh	Jack B.	42-J Williams
Rowe	Harry C.	42-E Luke
Rowe	Scott R.	42-I Moody
Rowland	Robert R.	42-J Turner
Rowley	Fred D.	42-H Ellington
Royal	William A.	42-J Columbus
Royer	Ted G.	42-H Ellington
Rubis	Clifton L.	42-I Stockton
Ruckman	Harold W.	42-J Ellington
Rudisill	Paul B.	42-J Spence
Ruecker	Quentin C.	42-F Luke
Ruffin	Lee V.	42-I Lubbock
Rummins	Max M.	42-G Luke
Runkle	Billy B.	42-G Ellington
Runnells	Edward	42-J Columbus
Ruple	Wyman E.	42-I Lubbock
Ruse	William O.	42-I Stockton
Rush	Asbury W., Jr.	42-J Moody
Russell	Eddie R.	42-G Ellington
Rutan	James H.	42-G Spence
Ruth	Harley J.	42-G Kelly
Ryan	Robert W.	42-F Mather
Rybovich	Thomas M.	42-J Columbus
Ryerse	William H.	42-H Moody
Rymsza	Mark R.	42-F Kelly
Sabo	Paul J.	42-C Ellington
Sain	James W.	42-I Lubbock
Salman	Richard F.	42-G Lubbock
Salmon	Lloyd D.	42-I Lubbock
Salmonson	Roger N.	42-H Luke
Salomon	Lloyd R.	42-G Kelly
Salsbery	Walter E.	42-H Williams
Sammons	Willis A.	42-H Columbus
Samson	Calvin	42-H Luke
Sandberg	Robert O.	42-E Ellington
Sanders	Donald E.	42-I Lubbock
Sanders	Howard E.	42-J Williams
Sanders	Virgil L.	42-E Luke
Sauers	Dale E.	42-I Dothan
Saunders	Allan "Buck," Sr.	42-I Columbus
Savage	Irval E., Jr.	42-J Luke
Sawyer	Arthur C.	42-J Luke
Schaffer	Robert L.	42-E Kelly
Schaffner	Richard	42-J Ellington
Schalkle	Robert W.	42-H Williams
Schewel	Morton F.	42-H Lubbock
Schildt	William J.	42-C Kelly
Schlienz	Fred	42-I Ellington
Schmidt	Alexander F.	42-G Kelly
Schmidt	Emil R.	42-G Ellington
Schneider	Clarence V.	42-J Columbus
Schneiter	Edward H.	42-J Kelly
Schnerre	William O.	42-H Ellington
Schoendaler	Arsenius	42-E Luke
Schoeps	Joseph T.	42-H Lubbock
Schofield	Donald S.	42-I Dothan
Schoggins	Eugene	42-H Lubbock
Scholl	William A.	42-I Lubbock
Schonard	Ernest M.	42-H Luke
Schooley	Royden D.	42-G Victorville
Schrantz	Elmer H.	42-H Kelly
Schreiber	Frank	42-J Kelly
Schroeder	Norman C.	42-J Turner
Schroyer	Roy B.	42-C Ellington
Schultz	Arthur K.	42-J Luke
Schultz	Roy "Rocky"	42-G Ellington
Schumaker	Edelhard A.	42-I Ellington
Schwab	Raymond H.	42-J Ellington
Schweickert	Jerome G.	42-J Spence
Scofield	Earl W.	42-D Ellington
Scott	Charles W.	42-E Luke
Scott	Harvey M.	42-J Luke
Scott	Ray	42-E Ellington
Scott	Stanley V.	42-I Lubbock
Scott	Thomas K.	42-J Kelly
Scrivener	James A.	42-G Luke
Scroggins	William W., Jr.	42-G Williams
Seagraves	Mack N.	42-G Lubbock
Sears	Bert E.	42-H Williams
Sellers	Marvin H.	42-I Lubbock
Seltz	Clarence O.	42-C Kelly
Sevvertsen	Harold L.	42-H Lubbock
Sexton	Marion R.	42-H Kelly
Shaddy	James O.	42-G Lubbock
Shahan	Jesse F.	42-I Dothan
Shamel	William L.	42-G Ellington
Shannon	Joseph L.	42-I Dothan
Sharff	Walter J.	42-D Kelly
Sharpe	Thomas H.	42-G Kelly
Shaw	Donald N.	42-F Ellington
Shaw	Russell J.	42-G Lubbock
Sheely	Roy M.	42-H Lubbock
Shelby	Carroll H.	42-H Ellington
Shelly	Vern D.	42-H Columbus
Shepherd	John M.	42-E Mather
Shepherd	Thomas P.	42-J Ellington
Sheppard	Walter O.	42-D Kelly
Sherman	Brimmer W.	42-D Ellington
Sherman	Mark E.	42-J Dothan
Sherrill	John B., Jr.	42-H Lubbock

Sherry	William S.	42-G Dothan	Smith	Francis P.	42-E Mather
Shields	Richard E.	42-J Turner	Smith	Fredrick N.	42-I Dothan
Shine	Stanley S.	42-H Lubbock	Smith	Harry F., Jr.	42-J Moody
Shirey	William M.	42-I Stockton	Smith	Homer A.	42-G Luke
Shirk	Milton L.	42-H Luke	Smith	James B.	42-D Kelly
Shively	Charles F.	42-J Ellington	Smith	James C.	42-I Dothan
Shockey	Blaine B.	42-J Ellington	Smith	James F.	42-J Kelly
Shook	Abraham "Ed"	42-J Ellington	Smith	James W.	42-G Kelly
Shook	Arthur M., Jr.	42-G Spence	Smith	Jesse T.	42-E Kelly
Shook	Carmel M.	42-J Craig	Smith	John C.	42-J Kelly
Shoop	Jay I.	42-I Stockton	Smith	John C., Jr.	42-H Lubbock
Short	James H.	42-I Lubbock	Smith	Kenneth B.	42-I Dothan
Shotliff	Harley E.	42-G Ellington	Smith	Kenneth W.	42-G Lubbock
Shuck	Harold E.	42-I Stockton	Smith	Kirby E.	42-I Dothan
Shudak	Leonard E.	42-J Kelly	Smith	Leonard A., Jr.	42-G Kelly
Siegle	Torris B.	42-E Luke	Smith	Luther E., Jr.	42-E Kelly
Sigler	Donald H.	42-E Ellington	Smith	Odell K.	42-I Ellington
Silsby	Edward M.	42-E Mather	Smith	Oliver	42-F Kelly
Silverman	Kenneth M.	42-G Ellington	Smith	Richard	42-J Williams
Simenitzky	John	42-I Moody	Smith	Richard W.	42-H Columbus
Simmonds	Harold M.	42-I Dothan	Smith	Robert H.	42-I Lubbock
Simmons	Alfred C.	42-D Kelly	Smith	Ronald W.	42-H Kelly
Simmons	Claude B.	42-G Columbus	Smith	Roscoe T.	42-I Columbus
Simmons	Raymond	42-I Stockton	Smith	Thomas J., Jr.	42-J Williams
Simmons	Willison D.	42-I Ellington	Smith	Warren W.	42-E Kelly
Simon	Ted E.	42-E Luke	Smith	Wesley M.	42-I Moody
Simpson	Robert L.	42-H Kelly	Smith	Yost E.	42-I Stockton
Simpson	Talmadge J.	42-G Dothan	Snead	William E.	42-H Ellington
Singer	Alfred E.	42-I Ellington	Snedegar	John E.	42-H Ellington
Singleton	Earl H.	42-D Kelly	Snell	Irvin E.	42-J Luke
Singleton	Lester J.	42-I Ellington	Snook	Robert R.	42-I Stockton
Sjoberb	Paul J.	42-J Ellington	Snowden	Hiram M.	42-E Luke
Skaggs	William I.	42-H Ellington	Snyder	Charles B.	42-G Luke
Skelton	Earl	42-J Kelly	Snyder	Eugene P.	42-H Williams
Slater	George R.	42-H Luke	Snyder	William A.	42-J Ellington
Slattery	Bill H.	42-H Spence	Sonner	Peter J.	42-H Williams
Sloan	William J.	42-C Kelly	Sorensen	Frank H.	42-J Williams
Smail	Donald L.	42-H Ellington	Sorenson	Harry A.	42-D Ellington
Smallsreed	John W.	42-H Spence	Sorgine	Henry J.	42-I Ellington
Smidt	Robert H.	42-J Luke	Sowder	Tony R.	42-G Williams
Smith	Andrew C.	42-E Kelly	Spaargaren	John	42-I Columbus
Smith	Billy M.	42-F Luke	Spaduzzi	Robert F.	42-G Spence
Smith	Charles B.	42-I Ellington	Spafford	James R.	42-I Spence
Smith	Charles L.	42-H Lubbock	Spain	James F.	42-F Ellington
Smith	Denzil L.	42-F Mather	Sparkman	James L.	42-J Craig
Smith	Dott E., Jr.	42-J Dothan	Spaulding	Robert P.	42-I Dothan
Smith	Douglas O.	42-D Ellington	Spaven	George N., Jr.	42-H Luke
Smith	Ebert W.	42-H Spence	Speer	Robert E.	42-I Ellington
Smith	Elvin E.	42-J Dothan	Spellman	Robert R.	42-D Kelly
Smith	Francis C.	42-I Turner	Spencer	Paul N.	42-G Williams

Spencer	Robert B.	42-H Ellington	Strause	Elmer S., Jr.	42-J Moody
Spencer	Stewart R.	42-J Kelly	Streitwieser	James E.	42-I Stockton
Sperling	Charles W.	42-E Kelly	Strever	Raymond G.	42-D Ellington
Spillers	Edward C.	42-H Lubbock	Stringfellow	Donald W.	42-J Williams
Spray	Jerry O.	42-I Ellington	Stromer	Norman G.	42-H Luke
Spry	Grady C.	42-J Kelly	Strother	Donald M.	42-E Kelly
Spuhler	George W.	42-G Victorville	Stroud	Joe F.	42-F Ellington
Spurgeon	Graydon D.	42-E Luke	Stroupe	Edward P.	42-E Kelly
Spurgeon	Robert C.	42-G Victorville	Stubblefield	Clarence E.	42-I Stockton
Squire	Everett A.	42-F Ellington	Stull	Grafton W.	42-J Kelly
Stagner	Howard C.	42-J Williams	Stunkard	Millard V.	42-J Luke
Stahl	Urban F.	42-H Columbus	Sturdevant	Donald E.	42-I Ellington
Stalcup	Robert W.	42-J Dothan	Sturm	Robert L.	42-I Stockton
Stamm	Robert E.	42-J Kelly	Stutler	James O.	42-J Ellington
Standley	Carl E.	42-G Ellington	Styer	Ervine M.	42-J Luke
Stanley	Curtis H.	42-G Ellington	Su Song	Charles J., Jr.	42-G Lubbock
Stanton	William R.	42-G Lubbock	Suberg	Walter A.	42-G Columbus
Stapp	James C.	42-H Ellington	Sullivan	Donald D.	42-H Williams
Stark	Walter E.	42-H Luke	Sullivan	Gilbert J.	42-I Lubbock
Stauffer	Walter J.	42-I Moody	Sullivan	Meddie C.	42-J Ellington
Steed	Cecil V.	42-E Ellington	Summers	David, Jr.	42-H Moody
Steele	Roy R.	42-F Mather	Summers	Sherman R., Jr.	42-J Ellington
Steele	William J.	42-H Lubbock	Sumner	Earl L.	42-G Victorville
Stegink	Gerald A.	42-J Ellington	Sumner	Frederick B.	42-I Ellington
Steier	Arthur H.	42-H Luke	Sury	John J.	42-I Lubbock
Stephens	Morris G.	42-H Ellington	Swan	Guy F., Jr.	42-J Spence
Stevens	Winston J.	42-D Kelly	Swansiger	Rudy L. V.	42-H Columbus
Stewart	Alfred M.	42-G Kelly	Sway	Eugene A.	42-J Dothan
Stewart	Latimer L.	42-J Ellington	Sweeney	Walter L.	42-J Luke
Stewart	Major F.	42-H Williams	Sweet	Edward M.	42-F Kelly
Stewart	Morton A.	42-F Mather	Sweet	Leonard W.	42-J Kelly
Stewart	William F.	42-G Dothan	Swenson	Irving M.	42-C Kelly
Stine	Donald P.	42-I Williams	Swerbilow	Bernard	42-I Spence
Stoddard	Carl H.	42-H Williams	Swope	Wesley H.	42-J Ellington
Stohry	Willard B.	42-I Ellington	Szela	John J.	42-I Columbus
Stone	Jerry D.	42-G Columbus	Taback	Pincus P.	42-C Kelly
Stone	Morris M.	42-J Williams	Taber	Ernest R.	42-J Dothan
Stone	Robert A.	42-G Ellington	Tadvch	Joseph A.	42-I Spence
Stone	Robert C.	42-D Kelly	Taggart	Jack G.	42-J Kelly
Stone	Robert L.	42-J Ellington	Talbott	Louis R.	42-I Dothan
Storey	Joseph A.	42-G Luke	Talmage	Arthur L.	42-H Dothan
Story	Donald E.	42-J Williams	Tanner	Edward E.	42-J Luke
Stotts	James C.	42-E Kelly	Tanner	Edwin L.	42-G Ellington
Stout	Earl J.	42-C Ellington	Tanner	Rex C.	42-G Kelly
Stout	Richard G.	42-G Lubbock	Tauche	Walter	42-I Stockton
Stovall	C. C. "Hank"	42-E Mather	Tavernini	Lawrence A.	42-I Ellington
Stovall	Richard T.	42-C Kelly	Taylor	Bryce L.	42-H Spence
Stovall	William A.	42-J Kelly	Taylor	Donald L.	42-H Luke
Stover	Edward P.	42-E Kelly	Taylor	Frank K.	42-D Ellington
Strauch	Merle W.	42-E Luke	Taylor	Maurice R.	42-G Ellington

Taylor	Robert L.	42-H Luke
Taylor	Roger L.	42-J Kelly
Taylor	Winford D.	42-H Luke
Teague	William B.	42-F Kelly
Templeton	John S., Jr.	42-G Spence
Templin	Ronald R.	42-H Columbus
Terry	Ernest W.	42-F Luke
Terry	Robert W.	42-I Spence
Terry	William J.	42-H Lubbock
Tester	Edwin K.	42-I Dothan
Thacker	Allie A.	42-I Columbus
Thacker	Victor E.	42-C Ellington
Thames	Barney H.	42-G Ellington
Theuer	Robin H.	42-I Stockton
Thibault	Lawrence E., Sr.	42-G Columbus
Thiebsen	Richard F., Jr.	42-I Moody
Thomas	Hawley A.	42-I Moody
Thomas	Jessie J., Jr.	42-G Ellington
Thomas	Roy G., Jr.	42-H Luke
Thomas	Samuel W.	42-I Lubbock
Thomas	Walter A.	42-E Kelly
Thompson	Bernard F.	42-I Stockton
Thompson	David S.	42-G Luke
Thompson	Floyd R.	42-H Kelly
Thompson	Harold C.	42-F Kelly
Thompson	Harold W.	42-G Ellington
Thompson	Lee B.	42-C Kelly
Thompson	Paul W.	42-J Ellington
Thompson	Ralph P.	42-H Luke
Thompson	Thomas G.	42-G Ellington
Thornbury	William C.	42-G Kelly
Thornton	Harold A.	42-I Stockton
Thorp	Ernest H.	42-G Luke
Thorp	Thomas B.	42-F Mather
Throgmorton	Raymond G.	42-I Lubbock
Tichenor	Joseph H.	42-G Spence
Tierney	Thomas V.	42-E Luke
Tiger	Stanley A.	42-I Moody
Tillery	Will H.	42-G Luke
Tilley	Verle M.	42-J Luke
Tillson	Charles H.	42-H Ellington
Tomcal	Charles	42-I Spence
Toner	Luke M.	42-I Stockton
Toney	John T.	42-I Stockton
Torbett	Oscar L.	42-G Luke
Toretsky	Nathan J.	42-F Kelly
Townsend	Francis A.	42-G Luke
Towson	Louis A.	42-C Kelly
Trail	Reo C.	42-E Mather
Traylor	Edward E.	42-J Ellington
Tresvik	Victor U.	42-H Dothan
Trevisani	John J.	42-G Luke
Trott	David H.	42-I Spence
Trout	Darvin L.	42-J Ellington
Trow	Robert A.	42-I Lubbock
Truck	Harrison A.	42-D Ellington
Trujillo	Eloy H.	42-H Luke
Tucker	Claude W.	42-G Spence
Tudor	William T.	42-H Spence
Turner	Dwight E.	42-I Stockton
Turner	Glenn W.	42-J Ellington
Turner	Richard A.	42-J Moody
Turner	Wesley W.	42-H Lubbock
Tuttle	Richard F.	42-E Ellington
Tuttle	Royce E.	42-G Victorville
Tyhurst	James G.	42-H Ellington
Tyhurst	William A.	42-I Stockton
Tyndall	William C.	42-J Ellington
Uhrig	Charles E., Jr.	42-E Ellington
Ullman	Gilbert	42-G Luke
Ulsh	Arvel D.	42-F Luke
Unger	Allen L.	42-J Ellington
Uphouse	John R.	42-F Luke
Ussery	Van F.	42-H Ellington
Utes	Warren W.	42-I Moody
Vacula	Ignace L.	42-J Kelly
Vaessen	William M.	42-H Ellington
Vallery	Dean B.	42-H Kelly
Van Ausdell	Robert C.	42-D Ellington
Van Buskirk	George L.	42-I Lubbock
Van Hoy	Lonnie E.	42-H Ellington
Van Vliet	Glenn F., Jr.	42-H Luke
Vance	Richard	42-E Luke
Vandervoort	Chadwick R.	42-E Ellington
Vantrease	William T.	42-C Ellington
Varga	Joseph A.	42-H Ellington
Varley	Harold B.	42-G Luke
Vaughter	David C.	42-F Ellington
Velarde	Armando C.	42-D Kelly
Venzke	William F.	42-I Lubbock
Vermillion	Robert A.	42-H Spence
Vestal	John S.	42-H Luke
Vickers	Dorrell C.	42-J Ellington
Vickers	W. Fred	42-J Moody
Vincent	John D.	42-J Moody
Vining	Glen S.	42-H Kelly
Vinyard	Paul M.	42-I Ellington
Visscher	Herman W.	42-C Ellington
Vizi	Joseph C.	42-H Luke
Vogt	Sylvester K.	42-I Moody

Volk	Don W.	42-F Mather	Webster	Antone J.	42-J Luke
Wagner	Marion	42-I Stockton	Weed	Edgar J.	42-G Ellington
Wagner	Ralph L.	42-I Ellington	Weedin	Wilbur H.	42-E Kelly
Wagnon	Harry T.	42-J Kelly	Wegner	Robert A.	42-G Lubbock
Wahab	Thomas W.	42-I Moody	Wehrman	Kenneth E.	42-F Ellington
Walker	Billy O.	42-H Moody	Weidler	Ira J.	42-I Stockton
Walker	Harold L.	42-E Kelly	Welch	Wilford W.	42-I Stockton
Walker	Laird K.	42-J Turner	Welcome	Edwin R.	42-I Moody
Wall	Donovan S.	42-G Dothan	Welk	William J.	42-I Moody
Wall	Walter L.	42-I Moody	Welliver	Paul E.	42-G Columbus
Wallace	Jack A.	42-E Kelly	Wells	Carl W.	42-J Kelly
Wallace	John H., Jr.	42-I Spence	Wells	Charles	42-H Kelly
Wallace	William E.	42-C Kelly	Wells	Jack D.	42-D Kelly
Wallen	Nick C.	42-J Columbus	Wells	Marshall C.	42-G Luke
Walsh	Jerome J.	42-D Ellington	Welsh	Joseph S.	42-I Ellington
Walsh	Raymond M.	42-D Kelly	Welter	Ralph R.	42-F Luke
Walters	Charles A.	42-I Lubbock	Wendt	Jerold A.	42-I Moody
Walthers	William	42-J Kelly	Wenglar	Edwin F.	42-G Luke
Ward	Elmer L.	42-I Moody	Wennergren	William A.	42-J Luke
Ward	Gordon F.	42-J Moody	Wentworth	Floyd B.	42-I Stockton
Ward	Robert I.	42-I Ellington	Wernette	Eugene C.	42-I Ellington
Warlick	J. D.	42-I Stockton	West	August L.	42-J Ellington
Warner	George E.	42-E Mather	Westbrook	Oliver	42-D Kelly
Warner	Willis L.	42-I Spence	Westgate	Phillip A.	42-J Dothan
Warren	Alvin A., Jr.	42-D Ellington	Westhaver	Donald C. M.	42-J Stockton
Warren	Edwin C.	42-H Williams	Wethern	Charles D.	42-I Spence
Warren	Lewis	42-I Ellington	Weynandt	Louis M.	42-H Ellington
Warren	Robert L.	42-I Spence	Whaley	Donald J.	42-i Moody
Wasserman	Eugene J.	42-H Moody	Whayne	David M.	42-E Kelly
Wassum	Porter M.	42-J Spence	Wheat	Delton G.	42-J Turner
Waters	James D.	42-H Ellington	Wheeler	William G.	42-E Luke
Watkins	Wilbur R.	42-J Williams	Wheelhouse	Henry L.	42-I
Watson	Fred A.	42-H Kelly	White	Billy A.	42-G Kelly
Watson	Harry R.	42-G Dothan	White	Bob M.	42-J Ellington
Watson	Jack F.	42-H Ellington	White	Carrol G.	42-H Williams
Watson	Jonothan C.	42-G Ellingto	White	Charles F.	42-D Ellington
Watts	Oran S.	42-H Luke	White	Glen P.	42-E Kelly
Watts	Thomas E.	42-H Ellington	White	James E.	42-H Ellington
Wayne	Clifford	42-D Kelly	White	John R.	42-I Lubbock
Weatherman	Gerald E.	42-G Williams	White	Thomas L.	42-I Stockton
Weaver	J. L.	42-H Moody	White	Virgil S.	42-C Kelly
Weaver	Paul B., Jr.	42-I Lubbock	Whittington	Norbourne E.	42-F Mather
Weaver	William T.	42-I Moody	Wicker	Samuel J.	42-C Kelly
Webb	David W.	42-I Lubbock	Wieger	William E.	42-I Ellington
Webb	Glen E.	42-F Ellington	Wiening	Paul G.	42-I Ellington
Webb	Henry J.	42-G Kelly	Wiggins	Julius J.	42-I Stockton
Webb	Ray A.	42-F Ellington	Wilbur	Max E.	42-I Lubbock
Webber	Louis A.	42-G Luke	Wilcox	Ernest M.	42-G Luke
Weber	George H.	42-F Kelly	Wilczynski	Edwin S.	42-I Stockton

Wiley	George C.	42-H Lubbock		Wolfe	Frank W.	42-J Turner
Wilhelm	Floyd E.	42-D Ellington		Wolfe	Fred J.	42-C Ellington
Wilkerson	Fred L.	42-F Kelly		Wolfe	Merle F.	42-H Kelly
Wilkins	James W.	42-G Luke		Wolfe	Merton J.	42-H Luke
Wilkins	Paul H.	42-J Luke		Womack	Norman J.	42-F Mather
Willard	Frank H.	42-I Moody		Wood	Carl F.	42-C Kelly
Williams	Cecil R.	42-H Columbus		Wood	Herman C.	42-J Dothan
Williams	Charles K.	42-G Luke		Wood	James H.	42-I Moody
Williams	Clifton E.	42-I Stockton		Wood	William V.	42-D Ellington
Williams	Harry E.	42-J Turner		Woodall	Charles C.	42-G Kelly
Williams	Jim M.	42-J Ellington		Woodard	Floyd W.	42-J Columbus
Williams	John F.	42-J Ellington		Woods	Carroll D.	42-E Kelly
Williams	John P.	42-F Mather		Woods	Eugene D.	42-C Kelly
Williams	Marvin E.	42-J Kelly		Woods	John S.	42-J Kelly
Williams	Raymond	42-G Luke		Woodward	Melvin R.	42-G Lubbock
Williams	Robert L.	42-D Ellington		Worbs	Earl P.	42-J Ellington
Williamson	Letcher S., Jr.	42-I Spence		Word	J. C.	42-H Luke
Williamson	Loyd V.	42-H Kelly		Worthington	Rae B.	42-G Victorville
Williamson	V."Scott"	42-H Ellington		Worthington	Robert T.	42-H Luke
Williamson	William I.	42-J Kelly		Wright	Billy V.	42-H Ellington
Willis	William H.	42-H Luke		Wright	Gilbert S.	42-J Spence
Wills	Wesley J.	42-J Williams		Wright	Leslie E.	42-E Kelly
Wilmore	Billy B.	42-G Dothan		Wright	Ralph D.	42-G Luke
Wilson	Arthur D.	42-I Stockton		Wroblewski	Clayton E.	42-H Columbus
Wilson	Charles D.	42-G Luke		Wukas	John F.	42-H Turner
Wilson	Clarence E.	42-G Williams		Wunderlich	Charles V.	42-J Kelly
Wilson	Clayton R.	42-J Turner		Wyckoff	Florest G.	42-I Stockton
Wilson	Ernest W., Jr.	42-E Mather		Wylie	J. "Hal"	42-G Luke
Wilson	Harold G.	42-F Luke		Wylie	John A., Jr.	42-I Stockton
Wilson	J. E. "Jake"	42-G Luke		Wyman	Leith L.	42-H Ellington
Wilson	Jefferson D.	42-J Dothan		Wysocki	Julian S.	42-J Turner
Wilson	Ralph D.	42-H Ellington		Wyttenbach	Emmett C.	42-I Spence
Wilson	Richard L.	42-G Luke		Yahne	Verne M.	42-C Kelly
Wilson	William O.	42-J Dothan		Yancey	Don M.	42-G Dothan
Wilson	Woodrow B.	42-I Lubbock		Yaryan	Jess O.	42-C Kelly
Wingard	Walton C.	42-E Ellington		Yeargin	Oliver H.	42-H Kelly
Winkler	Winfred C.	42-I Lubbock		Yentz	Robert J.	42-E Mather
Winks	Wayne M.	42-C Kelly		Yoakam	Richard A.	42-G Ellington
Winks	William B.	42-I Stockton		Yocum	Farroll E.	42-H Ellington
Winslett	Wade B.	42-J Kelly		Yoemans	Robert B.	42-H Ellington
Wintersole	Tom J.	42-H Williams		Yongue	Leighton T.	42-J Spence
Wirkkala	Ruben R.	42-H Ellington		Yonker	William A.	42-I Spence
Wirth	Thomas F., Jr.	42-H Moody		Young	Barton R.	42-J Ellington
Wise	John F.	42-D Ellington		Young	Earl H.	42-E Kelly
Wisler	Charles H.	42-I Spence		Young	Elton C.	42-E Luke
Withers	Rudolph S., Jr.	42-G Kelly		Young	James K.	42-G Luke
Witmer	Frank D.	42-J Ellington		Young	John A.	42-I Ellington
Wofford	Drew F.	42-J Turner		Young	John M.	42-G Williams
Wolfe	Donald H.	42-I Moody		Young	Rodger D.	42-J Williams

Youngberg	Raymond A.	42-H Luke		Zeiss	Jack M.	42-H Ellington
Younger	Joseph M.	42-H Luke		Zieman	Gilbert W.	42-E Ellington
Zadra	Charles R.	42-G Luke		Zinder	Herman J.	42-G Luke
Zahora	Anthony J.	42-H Luke		Zubarik	Charles J.	42-C Kelly
Zawada	John H.	42-G Kelly		Zurney	Walter E.	42-H Ellington

RCAF-TRAINED AMERICAN SERGEANT PILOTS

M APPENDIX

A number of American volunteers were trained as NCO pilots by the Royal Canadian Air Force and later transferred to the USAAF after America entered World War II. While the total number is not yet known, 137 have been discovered to date.

Alexander, Floyd R.
Anderson, William A.
Ball, Carlos J.
Bartlett, Walter C., Jr.
Berger, Joseph S.
Bilby, Bobbie L.
Bilby, Jay
Bilby, John R.
Birminghan, Marion C.
Borell, Frank J.
Boyd, William R.
Brackius, Warren J.
Branch, Peter W.
Brandt, George W. A., Jr.
Braswell, Albert D.
Brooks, George M.
Brown, Charles R.
Brown, David W.
Browning, Troy W.
Burke, Garland W.
Cameron, William, Jr.
Capelluto, Harold A.
Carley, Wesley A.
Carroll, Harry S.
Chaufty, Paul E.
Clark, Andrew R.
Clark, Charles R.
Clark, Garth E.
Coffman, Paul H.
Combs, Robert S.
Connelly, Ralph R.
Cox, Robert M.

Craig, James D.
Crites, Loren
Crum, Charles R.
Curry, Paul S.
Daniels, Dowains C.
Davidson, George W.
Day, Richard E.
Doucet, Earl P.
Downes, William W.
Doyle, Miles M.
Dumaine, Gabriel R.
Ellis, Fredrick D.
Eno, Arthur R.
Etherington, John F. P.
Evans, Albert L.
Feeney, Thomas F.
Ferguson, John
Fitzsimmons, Robert J.
Flynt, Charles N.
Fulwider, Evan G.
Gillen, James W.
Gold, Count
Goodman, Howard L.
Graff, Warren E.
Grisanti, Victor J.
Gross, Russell L.
Hagarty, Daniel D.
Helfert, William F.
Henderson, John F.
Hendricks, Fred A.
Hind, Robert M.
Hodson, Edward G.

Hubbard, Norman K.
Hudson, Kenneth D.
Hurd, Harland F.
James, George J.
Johnson, James H.
Johnstone, David W.
Junod, Alfred E.
Kemper, Harley C.
Killian, Oliver M.
Krogh, William D.
Laird, Thomas W.
Lang, John C.
McCall, Earl G.
McCarron, James B.
McClellan, John K.
MacDonald, John C.
McMullin, Joseph W.
Martin, Jonathan S.
Mellinger, Robert H.
Miller, William A.
Montgomery, William C.
Montgomery, William J.
Morgan, Len
Moulder, Wylie R.
Myers, Bertram L.
Nagdeman, Sollie R.
Nelson, Robert F.
Newell, Donald J.
Noah, Meldon A.
O'Neal, Richard M.
Oborski, Kasimer T.
Oppenheimer, Wallace

Orrick, R. A. ("Pit")
Owen, Dean M.
Patton, Gordon A.
Percy, Louis H.
Philips, Herman A.
Pollard, Pud
Popkin, Philip
Poulton, Gene
Rice, John H.
Richards, Daniel L.
Roby, John J.
Ruddy, Warren N.
Saunders, Bert C.
Simenson, Redene W.

Singleton, James M.
Smith, Reginald A.
Stevens, Arthur L.
Stone, Wiley
Storts, Gerald E.
Stumpf, Ralph J.
Sullivan, Kenneth C.
Summers, James J.
Swathel, Ralph H.
Sweeten, David J.
Szokoly, George J.
Todd, Thomas A.
Torres, Peter A. M.
Tweed, Howard S.

Van Der Kamp, Walter P.
Wall, Vincent
Warbritton, J. D.
Warburton, Joseph R.
Watkins, William A.
Webb, Joseph B.
Webb, Rudell B.
Well, Emmitte G.
Wells, Ralph
Wheeler, Fredric W
Wilson, Charles W.
Yankee, James D.
Youngblood, Curtis N.

SUMMARY OF ENLISTED
PILOTS, 1912–1942 (INCLUSIVE) N APPENDIX

Enlisted pilots produced between 1912 and 1933	296
Staff sergeant pilots produced under Public Law 99	2,574
Flight sergeants trained in the RCAF and transferred to the U.S. Army Air Forces	137
Total	3,007

ABBREVIATIONS

AFACT	Assistant Chief Air Staff, Training
ASMS	Air Service Mechanics School
AT	Prefix for advanced training plane
BC-1	Prefix for basic combat training plane
BT	Prefix for basic training plane
Capt.	Captain
C.O.	Commanding Officer
Col.	Colonel
Cpl.	Corporal
DH-4	De Havilland-4
FAI	Federation Aeronautique Internationale
Gen.	General
GPO	United States Government Printing Office
JAP	Junior Airplane Pilot
K.P.	Kitchen Police
Lt.	Lieutenant
Lt. Col.	Lieutenant Colonel
Maj.	Major
M.P.	Military Police
M. Sgt.	Master Sergeant
M.S.E.	Master Signal Electriction
NCO	Noncommissioned Officer
Pfc.	Private, First Class
PT	Prefix for primary training plane
Pvt.	Private
R&R sheet	Routing and Record sheet
RAF	Royal Air Force
RCAF	Royal Canadian Air Force
Sfc.	Sergeant, First Class
Sgt.	Sergeant
S. Sgt.	Staff Sergeant
T. Sgt.	Technical Sergeant
USAAF	United States Army Air Forces
USAF HRC	U.S. Air Force Historical Research Center
W.O.	Warrant Officer

NOTES

PROLOGUE

1. Juliette A. Hennessey, *The United States Army Air Arm: April 1861 to April 1917* (Washington, D.C.: Office of Air Force History, 1958), p. 11 (hereafter Hennessey Study).

2. Michael F. Belcher, "The Flying Sergeants," *Proceedings* (February 1982): 74.

3. Edward C. Johnson, *Marine Corps Aviation: The Early Years, 1912–1940* (Washington, D.C.: History and Museums Division, U.S. Marine Corps Headquarters, 1977), Supt. of Documents, GPO, p. 8.

4. Comments of Maj. George E. A. Reinburg, C.O., 2nd Day Bombardment Group, in *The U.S. Air Service in World War I,* ed. Maurer Maurer, 4 vols. (Washington, D.C.: GPO, 1978–79), 2:93–94.

5. Johnson, *Marine Corps Aviation,* pp. 35–37. Discussing the 1920–29 decade, Johnson wrote:

> Throughout the decade, the authorized manpower of Marine aviation remained constant: 100 flying officers and 1,020 enlisted men. The actual number in service often fell much below these figures. In 1921, for instance, only 59 officers and 824 enlisted men were available for air duty; in 1923, the number dropped to 46 officers and 756 enlisted. Then it increased slowly and gradually during the rest of the decade . . .
>
> Even if all 100 authorized billets could be filled, however, this number fell short of the number of aviators the Marines needed to meet operational commitments. The Aviation Section could not enlarge the authorized number of flying officers because the Naval Appropriation Act of 4 June 1920 had fixed the commissioned strength of the entire corps at 1,093, and the ground forces could spare no additional officers. Accordingly, Marine aviation attempted to remedy the pilot shortage by recruiting and training enlisted aviators. This was possible because the Appropriation Act limited only the officer strength—not the pilot strength. Through this means, the Marine Corps slowly increased its force of pilots. In a wartime expansion, the enlisted men so qualified could be commissioned and assume command positions commensurate with their experienced and training.

6. William A. Riley, "The Chiefs of Fighting Two," *Journal of the American Aviation Historical Society* (Fall 1969): 145–52.

7. Al Munsch, *Marine Aviation in Nicaragua,* unpublished recollections.

8. Ken Walsh, conversation with author, October 1987.

9. From bio-sketch of W. B. "Spider" Webb, printed in the April 1984 issue and reprinted in the July 1985 issue of *Scuttlebut* (a newsletter published by the Silver Eagles Association, an association of former naval aviation pilots), pp. 10–12.

10. News item from the Associated Press in London, February 2, 1985: "Lord Cameron of Balhousie, 64, a sergeant pilot and World War II hero who became chief of the British Defense Staff and was an outspoken critic of the Soviet Union, has died in a London hospital after a long illness."

11. Harriet Fast Scott, "Red Stars in Motion," *Air Force Magazine,* March 1986, p. 62.

CHAPTER 1: America's First Enlisted Pilot

1. Col. Vernon L. Burge, transcript of Individual Record of Service.

2. Col. Vernon L. Burge, "Early History of Aviation," an unpublished personal account, a copy of which was given to author by Burge's daughter, Mrs. Marjorie Waters (hereafter cited as Burge Early History).

3. Col. Vernon L. Burge, from a personal diary, a transcript of which was given to the author by Mrs. Marjorie Waters (hereafter cited as Burge Diary), p. 34.

4. Ibid.

5. Ibid.

6. Charles de Forest Chandler and Frank P. Lahm, *How Our Army Grew Wings: Airmen and Aircraft before 1914* (New York: Ronald Press, 1943), p. 245.

7. Burge Diary, p. 35.

8. Lahm's letter to Aero Club of America:

> Fort Wm. McKinley, p. I. June 14, 1912
> The Secretary, Aero Club of America
> 297 Madison Ave., New York City, N.Y.

Sir:-

Enclosed I send application of Corporal Vernon L. Burge, Signal Corps, U.S. Army, for aviation pilot's license.

Some time ago I wrote you requesting that I be appointed official representative of the Aero Club of America in case any applicants should desire to take the test for aviation pilot's license in the Philippines.

As yet there has not been time for a reply to reach me, but if my request is granted, Corporal Burge's test is in every way regular.

He passed the test this morning and fully complied with the requirements given on page 50 of the year book for 1912. Enclosed is the barograph record of his altitude flight. It shows an altitude of about 100 meters. The center of the machine was 13 meters from the designated point on the first landing and 9 meters on the second. He shut off engine when about 8 feet from the ground the first time, and about 20 feet in the air the second time.

Corporal Burge has been under my instruction in operating the Signal Corps Wright aeroplane for over two months and I consider him fully capable to operate this machine. In addition, he is a skilled mechanic and capable of making any repairs on the machine.

Very respectfully,

Frank P. Lahm
1st Lt. 7th Cav.

9. Burge Early History, p. 9.

10. Records Group 111, General Correspondence, 1889–1917, Entry No. 44, National Archives, S.C., 30446.

11. At this time, a new rating and badge for aviators were authorized for qualified officers. Though Burge was otherwise qualified, he was not an officer, and therefore could receive neither the rating nor the badge.

12. Burge Early History, p. 1.

13. Ibid.

14. Chandler and Lahm, *How Our Army Grew Wings*, p. 78.

15. Burge Early History, p. 1.

16. Ibid.

17. Ibid, p. 2.

18. Chandler and Lahm, *How Our Army Grew Wings*, pp. 82, 71.

19. Ibid.

20. Burge Early History, p. 2.

21. James J. Horgan, "The International Aeronautic Tournament of 1907," *Missouri Historical Society Bulletin* 21, no. 3 (April 1965): 216–36.

22. Ibid., pp. 234, 235.

23. Ibid.

24. Burge Early History, p. 2.

25. Ibid, p. 3.

26. Hennessey Study, p. 16.

27. Ibid. Note: It was at this time that Burge began to keep a diary, which he continued until he soloed in the Philippines in 1912. His version of events, corroborated by Hennessey and other documents, is used here by the author to develop much of the ensuing narrative.

28. Paraphrased from Burge Diary.

29. Burge Diary, p. 11.

30. Ibid., p. 17.

31. Ibid., p. 30.

32. Eventually to wind up at the National Air and Space Museum in Washington, D.C.

33. Burge Diary, p. 30.

CHAPTER 2: The Philippine Tour of Duty

1. Burge Diary, p. 28.

2. Ibid., p. 29.

3. Robert B. Casari, *Encyclopedia of U.S. Military Aircraft: 1908 to April 6, 1917,* 4 vols. (Chillicothe, Ohio: Author, 1970–74), 2:4.

4. Burge Diary, pp. 29–32.

5. Ibid., p. 32.

6. Hennessey Study, p. 79.

7. Burge Diary, p. 32.

8. Ibid., p. 33.

9. Ibid.

10. Ibid., pp. 34, 35.

11. Letter, William C. Ocker to Frank P. Lahm, September 5, 1931, Ocker file, Call No. 16.6-63, USAF Historical Research Center (hereafter USAF HRC), Maxwell Air Force Base, Montgomery, Alabama.

12. "Who's Who in the News," *St. Louis Post Dispatch,* pt. 5, June 8, 1941.

13. Letter, Ocker to Lahm.

14. "Who's Who in the News."

15. Letter, Ocker to Lahm.

16. Charles de Forest Chandler and Frank P. Lahm, *How Our Army Grew Wings: Airmen and Aircraft before 1914* (New York: Ronald Press, 1943), p. 246.

17. The June 21, 1913, issue of the Army-Navy Register carried an article under the headline "Philippine Aviation School" with a March 1913 dateline, and reads in part: "Sergeant Burge was also instructed in handling the new duplicate control." The following is noted in the April 1913 issue of that publication: "Lieutenant Dargue flew with Sergeant Burge for a 15-minute flight." An article published in the *Rich Field Flyer* 1, no. 4 (November 21, 1918), written by M.S.E. C. C. Stevenson, an old friend of Burge's from earlier Signal Corps days, says, "In March of the same year [1912]—Burge qualified as a birdman and was granted Certificate 154 FAI, Aero Club of America. Three years were spent in the Philippines, flying and acting as flying instructor."

18. Frank P. Lahm, "Early Flying Experiences," *Air Power Historian* 2, no. 1 (January 1955): 8.

19. Ibid.

20. Casari, *Encyclopedia,* 1:31–35.

21. Ibid., p. 34.

22. Ibid., pp. 27–35.

23. Letters contained in Burge's personal effects, now in the custody of his daughter, Mrs. Marjorie Waters.

24. Burge's statement of service.

25. Casari, *Encyclopedia,* 1:35.

CHAPTER 3. North Island

1. Hennessey Study, p. 86.

2. Ibid., p. 105; and Maj. William C. Ocker, "Ante-bellum Fledglings," *The Sportsman Pilot* (August 1931): 42.

3. Casari, *Encyclopedia,* 2:37–38, 41–42.

4. Ocker, "Ante-Bellum Fledglings," pp. 14, 15, 42.

5. Elretta Sudsbury, "Jackrabbits to Jets, The History of North Island, San Diego, California" (San Diego: Neyenesch Printers, n.d.), p. 29.

6. Burge Early History, p. 5.

7. Hennessey Study, Appendix 15, p. 249.

8. "Who's Who in the News."

9. Ocker, "Ante-bellum Fledglings," p. 42

10. Ibid., pp. 14–15.

11. Undated *San Diego Union* newsclipping in Ocker's scrapbook, obviously written at the time of his FAI examination.

12. Ocker's original certificate is in the custody of the Ocker Instrument Training Center at Randolph Air Force Base, Texas.

13. Ocker, "Ante-bellum Fledglings," pp. 14–15.

14. Ibid., pp. 14, 15, 42.

15. War Department Memo for the Chief, War College Division, General Staff, "Organization and Methods of Administration of the Aviation Section of the Signal Corps," May 16, 1916, prepared and initialed by Mitchell for the signature of Brig. Gen. George P. Scrivan.

16. "An Act to Increase the Efficiency of the Aviation Service of the Army" H.R. 5304, 38 Stat. 514, 63rd Cong., 2nd Sess., chap. 186, July 18, 1914, at the USAF HRC, under File No. 167.12-2.

17. A. D. Smith, "Some Side Lights on the Early Days of Aviation," *Air Corps Newsletter* 21, no. 2 (January 15, 1938): 7–9, 15.

18. The Early Bird *Chirp,* no. 49 (August 1, 1953): 2, 8; and "Some Side Lights on the Early Days of Aviation," pp. 7–9. On the following February 10, Albert D. Smith took off at 6:50 A.M. from the waters adjacent to North Island in a Martin Hydroplane and remained aloft until 3:32 P.M., a new world endurance record for that type airplane of 8 hours and 42 minutes. Following the World War I Armistice, Smith, by then a major, led the first transcontinental round-trip flight from Rockwell Field. Between wars, he became a pilot and chief pilot for TWA, and then re-entered the service prior to World War II and rose to the rank of brigadier general.

19. Hennessey Study, Appendix 15, p. 249.

20. *San Antonio Light,* February 20, 1959. (Note: While Marcus is listed in Appendix 15 of the Hennessey Study as one of the "soldier pilots" of the period, he apparently did not become certified as such by the FAI, or rated by the Army, but Appendix 16 of the Hennessey Study includes his name on Special Order 36-24, February 12, 1915, as an enlisted man rated as an aviation mechanician.)

21. Hennessey Study, Appendix 15, p. 249.

22. Ibid., pp. 110–20, 146. Also Henry H. Arnold, "The History of Rockwell Field," 1923, File No. 7542-192.4, USAF HRC.

23. Casari, *Encyclopedia,* 3:29.

CHAPTER 4: Army Aviation Gets Involved

1. Hennessey Study, pp. 146, 147.

2. Ibid., p. 147; also Casari, *Encyclopedia,* 3:32.

3. Casari, *Encyclopedia,* 3:32.

4. Hennessey Study, pp. 149, 150.

5. Casari, *Encyclopedia,* 1:40.

6. San Diego newspaper clipping found in Ocker's scrapbook, dated July 27 (believed to be 1915 or 1916).

7. Casari, *Encyclopedia,* 3:34–46; and Hennessey Study, p. 167.

8. Hennessey Study, p. 172.

9. Ibid., Appendix 15, p. 249.

10. Ocker scrapbook, newspaper clipping, July 27, 1916.

11. Hennessey Study, Appendix 15, p. 249.

12. Ocker scrapbook, undated newsclipping from San Diego newspaper.

13. Ocker scrapbook, undated newsclipping from East Coast newspaper, believed to be January 1917.

14. "Who's Who in the News."

15. *Aerial Age Weekly,* March 26, 1917, p. 48, via Robert Casari, letter to author dated December 1984.

16. Letters contained in Burge's personal effects in custody of his daughter, Mrs. Marjorie Waters.

17. William C. Boden, "The History of Kelly Field and Its Impact on American Aviation, 1917 to 1926," pp. 31, 32. M.A. thesis, St. Mary's University, August 1967. Boden provides a glimpse of the chaos that prevailed as America tried to gear up for a war for which it was not yet prepared.

> On 28 September 1917, Lieutenant S. J. Idzorek arrived at Kelly Field from Washington, D.C., charged with the mission of organizing a mechanics training school at that airfield with a capability of training 2,500 mechanics a month. This rather lofty aim . . . was another example of the grossly exaggerated and unreal objectives conjured up in the initial heat of wartime patriotic fervor. A small, three hundred and twenty student capacity mechanics school, the "Enlisted Mechanics Training Department," was established on 1 October, 1917 in the southwest corner of Kelly Field #1. The school was comprised of eight tent-type hanger equipped with an LWF airplane, a Sturdevant airplane engine, and was staffed by an engine instructor and an airplane repair instructor.
>
> Scarcely had the first class graduated when the Kelly Field Mechanics School was closed on 29 December 1917, for being completely unsatisfactory. The unsatisfactory rating was attributed to the inexperience of the instructors, insufficient training equipment, lack of course specialization and a shortage of officers. Another more cogent reason for closing the school was that just prior to Christmas 1917, a severe wind storm literally blew the school away.

CHAPTER 5: World War I Enlisted Pilots

1. Chris Chant, *The Illustrated History of the Air Forces of World War I and World War II* (Secaucus, N.J.: Chartwell Books, 1979), p. 44, in which appears the following comment: "At first the War Office was in favor of having half the pilots commissioned, and the other

half non-commissioned, but for a variety of reasons, not all of them valid, it was decided that all pilots should be officers. The decision was reversed during World War I."

2. Hennessey Study, Appendix 15, p. 150.

3. *Kelly Field Eagle,* January 8, 1919, p. 3.

4. Boden, "The History of Kelly Field and Its Impact on American Aviation, 1917 to 1926," p. 31.

5. *Kelly Field Eagle,* January 8, 1919, p. 3.

6. *Rich Field Flyer* 1, no. 4 (November 21, 1918): 5. Rich Field, the new flying field at Waco, Texas, was named in honor of Lt. Perry C. Rich, a young student flying officer with whom Burge became acquainted in the Philippines in 1913. Similarly, Love Field in Dallas, Texas, was named in honor of Lt. Moss L. Love, the fellow student with whom Burge had learned to fly in the Philippines in 1912. Both officers perished in airplane crashes before World War I: Lieutenant Love on September 4, 1913, near San Diego; Lieutenant Rich on November 14, 1913, in the Philippines.

7. Ibid.

8. Burge's flight log, May 1918, a copy of which was given to the author by Burge's daughter, Marjorie Burge Waters.

9. Hennessey Study, p. 58.

10. J. Duncan Campbell, *Aviation Badges and Ensignia of the United States Army, 1913– 1946* (Harrisburg, Pa.: Triangle Press, 1977), pp. 11, 44–45.

11. Burge prefaces his first official flight log with the following certificate:

Rich Field, Waco Texas, May 1918 p. I. Qualified as pilot and received type B, Wright (pusher),——successfully——1914 as enlisted man at Ft McKinley, p. I., No official record kept of flying time. Many hours, did not keep any official—Diego, Calif, in 1915 this time is on——France, and not presently available. From early pusher later to tractors.

V. L. Burge, Captain, A.S.M.A.

He further certifies:

Approx 500 hours flying time prior to starting of this book. No official records kept.

He ends with this statement:

As pilot flying continuously until ordered——over one years experience flying at Corregidor, p. I. Arrived N.I., San Diego, Calif, and flew Martin continuously. Accompanied 1st Aero Squadron San Antonio, Texas for station. Ordered Flew all over northern Mexico 1916. After 3 months Ft Leavenworth detailed to Air Service.——statement in every respect.

V. L. Burge, Capt, A.S.

Returns and postings of the first Aero Squadron show him in the unit and in the appropriate place and with the appropriate company of officers and men to make it entirely possible, but more evidence is needed.

12. Rich Field Flying Department Memorandum No. 26, November 13, 1918, USAF HRC.

13. Haynes discharge certificate, USAF HRC.

14. Arthur Palmer, "Many Interesting Visitors Landing at City Airport," *North Platte Tribune,* July 16, 1929.

15. Joe C. Cline, "First Naval Aviation Unit in France," in Adrian O. Van Wyen, and the editors of *Naval Aviation News,* eds., *Naval Aviation in World War I* (Washington, D.C.: Chief of Naval Operations, 1969), pp. 10–15.

16. Maurer, ed., *U.S. Air Service in World War I,* 4:93.

17. Many World War I student aviators were trained in enlisted status, but were commissioned upon completion of the primary phase.

18. *Kelly Field Eagle,* January 8, 1919, p. 3; *The Flying Times,* Kelly Air Force Base, Texas, June 9, 1947, p. 5.

19. Ibid.

20. Telephone interview with and letter from Bandy to author, August 3, 1982.

21. From the M.S.E.-Aviator certificate issued to Harry Thomas Wilson.

22. Kroll, *Kelly Field in the Great World War,* p. 88. Additional enlisted pilots are listed in the *Kelly Field Eagle,* January 8, 1919, p. 3.

23. Aircraft Accident File No. 200.3911-1 #8, September 17, 1908–June 10, 1921, USAF HRC.

24. *Rich Field Flyer* 1, no. 9 (February 6, 1919): 8, 29.

25. Article clipped from a Brownwood, Texas, newspaper by Douglas S. Christie. No masthead or date was kept with it.

26. Letter dated January 24, 1920, from the personal papers of Sfc. William E. Beigel (cited hereafter as Beigel Papers).

27. War Department memo, January 31, 1919, from Office of the Director of Military Aeronautics, USAF HRC.

28. "Enlisted Mechanics Training Department Men to Get Flying Course at Kelly," *Kelly Field Eagle,* September 26, 1918; "Nine Receive Rating as Enlisted Flyers," idem, November 28, 1918, p. 11; "Enlisted Men May Now Do Solo Work, Washington Rules," idem, December 12, 1918; "Enlisted Men to Get Flying Instructions," idem, February 27, 1919.

29. "Flying Training of Enlisted Men," *Manual of Office and Field Administration of an Air Service Flying School with Special Reference to Flying Department,* prepared by Capt. John A. Macready, R.M.A., A.S.A., Brooks Field, San Antonio, May 1, 1919, p. 40 (see Appendix E).

30. Aircraft Accident File No. 200.3911-1 #8, September 17, 1908–April 16, 1921.

CHAPTER 6: After the Great War

1. Stencil T-138, issued by the Director of Military Aeronautics on January 30, 1919, is cited as the authority for the handling of the training of enlisted men to take flying instruction at Brooks Field, and presumably at other active flying training fields as well. The citation is contained in the Brooks Field *Manual of Office and Field Administration of an Air Service Flying School with Special Reference to Flying Department.*

2. Letter from Beigel Papers dated May 2, 1954, p. 2

3. Letter from Beigel Papers dated January 24, 1920, p. 3.

4. Ibid. The full names of those completing the Rich Field Enlisted Pilots' Course were: William E. Beigel, Walter H. Beech, Homer H. Sheffield, Harold S. Dale, Wick Chamlee, and Cleason E. Shealer.

5. Letter from Beigel Papers dated January 24, 1920, p. 3.

6. *The Fly Leaf* 2, March Field, Riverside, California, April 24, 1920, p. 7.

7. Beigel Papers.

8. From a cartoon illustration in a public relations packet furnished by the Beech Aircraft Corporation.

9. Maj. Gen. Carl McDaniel, interview by author, 1983; *Aircraft Journal,* April 17, 1920.

10. "Sergeant Sheffield Had Narrow Escape at Marlin," *Times Herald,* August 28, 1919.

11. From photo in Beigel Papers.

12. Ibid.

13. *Waco News Tribune,* November 24, 1919.

14. Beigel Papers.

15. William H. McDaniel, *Beechcraft: Fifty Years of Excellence, The History of Beech* (Wichita, Kan.: McCormick-Armstrong Co., 1982).

Beech resigned from the Swallow Airplane Company and formed The Travelair Manufacturing Corporation. Some of the aircraft produced by Travelair became legendary. The Travelair 5000 *Woolaroc* won the Dole Oakland-to-Hawaii race in 1927; the Travelair *Mystery S* racing plane won the closed-course free-for-all, beating out many of the more powerful military planes at the 1930 National Air Races. The *Mystery S* went on to win subsequent races in many other categories as well. After suffering through the Great Depression with the Travelair Corporation, Beech, together with his new wife, Olive Ann, formed the Beech Aircraft Company in 1932. The company has made aviation history ever since. In 1950, Walter Beech suffered a fatal heart attack, leaving Olive Ann as chairman of the board. She became the heart and spirit of the company and oversaw its operations until her retirement in 1984. Twenty-seven years after his death, Walter Beech was enshrined in the Aviation Hall of Fame. Olive Ann was enshrined on July 25, 1981, thus joining Charles and Anne Morrow Lindbergh as the only other husband-and-wife team to be so honored.

16. The Act of June 4, 1920 (41 Stat. 768), cited in the Moore Enlisted Pilot Study, paragraph 9, Tab B, p. 8.

17. Henry H. Arnold, "Our Army Air Corps and Its Future," *Air Corps Newsletter* 22, no. 15 (August 1, 1939): 4.

18. From the personal files of Chester Francis Colby.

19. Ibid.

20. Material on McDaniel is taken from audiotaped interview with author, from his service record, and from his unpublished autobiography.

21. Ibid.

22. From an interview conducted by Lt. Col. Joe Casey, former staff sergeant pilot, with former master sergeant pilot Boyd Ertwine.

23. From an interview conducted by the author during a 1981 visit with former sergeant pilots Boyd Ertwine and Julius Kolb in Sacramento, California.

24. *Kelly Field Newsletter* 1, no. 40 (October 16, 1920): 5.

25. Aircraft Accident File No. 200.3911-1 #8, 17 September 17, 1908–April 16, 1921, USAF HRC.

26. Ibid.

27. *Kelly Field Newsletter* 1, no. 47 (December 4, 1920).

28. McDaniel interview.

29. Ibid.

30. Ibid.

31. Ibid.

32. Ibid.

33. Ibid.

34. Par 8, Special Order Number 14, Headquarters, Tenth Group (School), Office of the Group Commander, Kelly Field, July 21, 1922, Chester Colby Collection, Edward White Museum (Hangar 9), Brooks Air Force Base, San Antonio (hereafter Colby Collection).

35. Later in his career, Byron Newcomb was transferred to the 1st Pursuit Group at Selfridge Field, Mt. Clemens, Michigan. Newcomb and Roy Mitchell later got out of the service and established an endurance record that stood for only a short while. Later on, Newcomb operated a still during prohibition days until arrested and hauled into court. He enlisted again and was killed when his BT-2 crashed while making low passes at a farmer plowing his field on a tractor.

36. In 1928 and 1929, Roy Mitchell served with the 68th Service Squadron at Kelly. He later joined American Airlines and later became the chief pilot for its southern division. By January 1941, he was the chief pilot for the entire line.

37. Par 1, Operations Memorandum No. 39, Office of the Operations Officer, Brooks Field, Texas, September 14, 1923, Colby Collection.

38. Charles A. Lindbergh, *The Spirit of St Louis* (New York: Scribner's, 1953), p. 418. Lindbergh names M. Sgt. Billy Winston as his primary flying instructor at Brooks Field.

39. There were two Fred Kellys and we don't know how to divide the accident reports between them or whether to divide them at all. Nevertheless, on August 4, 1922, a Fred Kelly made a forced landing with a DH-4 in a very small field on a mountainside near Eureka, California, collapsing the gear. On September 15, 1922, the axle on Fred Kelly's DH-4 broke on landing and flipped the plane onto its back. One year later, while at Brooks Field, Fred Kelly made a forced landing due to sediment in the carburetor. After clearing the fuel line, he took off again and snagged a fence, ending his takeoff run. And finally, on the West Coast, Fred Kelly put his DH-4 on its nose after landing when the fittings on the landing gear crystallized, causing the gear to collapse.

To further confuse the picture, both Fred Kellys later hired on as pilots with Western Air Express in its beginning days (the present day Western, now Delta/Western Airlines) and were labeled Kelly Number 1 and Kelly Number 2.

40. C. P. Smith's flight log.

41. C. P. Smith was awarded the rating of Junior Airplane Pilot (JAP) on Paragraph 4, Personnel Order No. 39, dated September 12, 1924, citing Paragraph 3, Section VIII, War Department General Order No. 55, dated December 27, 1922, for authority. Section VIII is entitled "Aeronautical Ratings." Paragraph 3 reads: "Junior Airplane Pilot: Graduation from the Air Service Primary Flying School or successful completion of such flying and technical examinations as may be prescribed by the Chief of Air Service." A roster of enlisted pilots was published in the March 31, 1928, issue of the *Air Corps Newsletter,* which included the names of ten other junior airplane pilots. These were: master sergeants Joe Grant, Douglas

Johnston, and Conrad O'Briant, T. Sgt. Leslie Wells, staff sergeants James H. Crane, Orvil W. Haynes, Fred I. Pierce, and Fred O. Tyler, Sgt. Lyman R. Ellis, and Cpl. Maurice B. Riherd.

42. *Air Corps Newsletter* 14, no. 10 (August 29, 1930): 223.

43. *Air Force Museum Friends Bulletin* 6, no. 2 (Summer 1983): 14–16, 48.

44. Ibid. Also Burges flight log, July-December 1923.

CHAPTER 7: The Sergeants Return to Flying School

1. Moore, *Enlisted Pilot Study,* Tab B, pp. 9 and 10.

2. *Roster of Students of the Primary Flying Schools, Brooks, March, and Randolph Fields, September 1922–October 1932* (San Antonio: Naylor Printing Company, n.d.), p. 11.

3. *Air Service Newsletter* 10, no. 5 (April 5, 1926): 7.

4. Col. Paul B. Jackson and Col. Alva Harvey in telephone conversations with author.

5. Col. Alva Harvey, USAF (Ret.), furnished the author with a forty-page unpublished autobiography dated 1978 (cited hereafter as Harvey autobiography).

6. Col. Paul B. Jackson, USAF (Ret.), made eight hours of audiotape available to the author which contained much anecdotal and autobiographic material on his career. (These tapes will be cited hereafter as Jackson audiotapes.)

7. Harvey autobiography.

8. Jackson audiotapes.

9. Ibid.

10. *Chicago Evening American,* May 5, 1931, cited by David G. Mayor in a short biographic sketch of Paul Jackson, published in "Bad News" (Base Air Depot) 1, no. 2 (June 1978).

11. Ibid.

12. Harvey autobiography. Corroborated by Jackson audiotapes.

13. *Roster of Students of the Primary Flying Schools,* p. 11. (Note: S. Sgt. Boyd Ertwine was ordered to Brooks Field from his unit in Hawaii by Special Order No. 34., Headquarters Hawaiian Department, Honolulu, dated February 9, 1924. The authority to enter him into flight training cited therein is: Circular No. 67, Office of the Chief of Air Service, dated July 2, 1923. Presumed that each NCO of that class entered flight training under the same authority.)

14. Interview with Maj. Gen. Carl McDaniel, USAF (Ret.).

15. Ibid.

16. Harvey autobiography.

17. Ibid.

18. Ibid.

19. Told to author during conversations with Lt. Col. Boyd Ertwine, USAF (Ret.).

20. Aircraft Accident File No. 200.3911-1 #8, September 17, 1908–April 16, 1921, USAF HRC.

21. Ertwine, in an interview with Joe Casey and the author, disclosed that he married Sergeant Mackey's widow, "Buddy," some time after she came out of mourning.

22. *History of the 12th Observation Squadron for Year 1925,* File No. 168.65011-7, USAF HRC.

23. Ibid.

24. Arnold, "The History of Rockwell Field," pp. 87–92.

25. Ronnie C. Tyler, *The Big Bend: A History of the Last Texas Frontier* (Washington, D.C.: Office of Publications, National Park Service, U.S. Department of Interior, n.d.), pp. 182–87.

26. Ibid., p. 185.

27. *Air Service Newsletter* 10, no. 2 (February 11, 1926): 21.

28. *History of the 12th Observation Squadron for Year 1925,* File No. 168.65011-7, USAF HRC.

29. Ibid.

30. Ibid

31. *Air Service Newsletter* 10, no. 3 (March 2, 1926): 16. After completing his own tour in the Philippines, Tyler left the Army and took a position as chief pilot and flight instructor for the University Aerial Service Company in Austin, Texas. He re-enlisted in 1932 and re-entered flying school as a corporal. Graduating in February 1933, he became a fully rated military pilot, his former rating of junior airplane pilot now a thing of the past. Tyler remained on enlisted status until the eve of World War II, when called to active duty as a commissioned officer. After the end of World War II, Tyler was assigned to the southwest Pacific where, in a second irony, while taking off from an island base with a very heavy load, his plane lost power on an engine. He could not maintain sufficient speed or altitude to return to the field and was forced to put the plane down, not on his familiar American desert as he had so often in earlier days, but in an alien sea. Tyler perished in the attempt.

32. Haynes personal papers.

33. Newsclip from an unidentified and undated newspaper in Haynes's scrap book.

34. A second article clipped from an undated and unidentified newspaper found in Haynes's scrap book.

35. Aircraft Accident File No. 200.3911-1 #8, September 17, 1908–June 10, 1921, USAF HRC.

36. *Air Service Newsletter* 10, no. 1 (January 19, 1926): 19, V-5524-AS.

37. *Air Service Newsletter* 10, no. 2 (March 19, 1926): 8.

38. Roy Mitchell later went with the airlines and later still became the chief pilot for the southern division of American Airlines.

39. Telephone conversation between author and Alva Harvey.

40. Telephone conversation between author and Paul Jackson.

41. *Chicago Evening American,* May 5, 1931, cited by Mayor.

42. Ibid.

43. Jackson audiotapes.

44. Ibid.

45. Jackson audiotapes and flight logs.

46. Ibid.

47. Ibid.

48. Ibid

49. Ibid.

50. Jackson telephone interview with author, October 1985.

51. Jackson audiotapes and *Air Corps Newsletter* 19, no. 24 (December 15, 1936): 13–15.

52. Jackson audiotapes.

53. Operations Order No. 69, Headquarters, Albrook Field, Canal Zone, July 21, 1934.

54. Col. Julius Kolb, letter to author, August 13, 1981.

55. Col. Kolb, interview with Joe Casey, transcripts made available to author.

56. Telephone conversations with Col. Julius Kolb in 1981 and 1982.

57. Moore Study, Tab B, Par. 29, p. 22.

58. *Air Service Newsletter* 10, no. 5 (April 5, 1926): 7. A paragraph in the *Air Service Newsletter* just cited tells of Sgt. Sam Nero's extraordinary skill as a bombardier. It was the reason he was on duty at Phillips Field. To the personnel at Phillips Field, Nero was a legend. To the citizens of nearby Havre de Grace, he was unknown—until February 1926—when they became the beneficiaries of his special skill. As the winter ice on the Susquehanna River began to break up, it accumulated against the bridge, forming an ice dam that threatened to back the river over the city. Nero hung two one-hundred-pound demolition bombs in racks beneath a DH-4, and with Lieutenant Bond as pilot, headed for the river. After several dry runs over the icy target they turned back toward the bridge and made their live run. Nero released the bombs which fell true, breaking the ice jam without putting a scratch on the bridge.

59. Letter from Chief of the Air Corps to the War Department Adjutant General, dated September 14, 1928, Subject: *Enlisted Pilots, Bombers and Gunners.*

60. Reply by endorsement from Adjutant General to Chief of the Air Corps, November 21, 1928.

61. *Roster of Students of the Primary Flying Schools,* p. 82

62. Ibid., p. 39.

63. In a post–World War I article headlined: "ASMS Great Factor in Aviation History" published in the *Kelly Field Eagle,* January 8, 1919, p. 3. Sergeant 1st Class Carlton P. Smith is listed as one of the Air Service Mechanic School's "Enlisted Aviators." His service record lists the authority for his rating as a junior airplane pilot as Peronnel Order 39, Paragraph 4, September 12, 1924. His rating as an airplane pilot is shown as Personnel Order 149, Paragraph 2, June 29, 1933.

CHAPTER 8: A Different Breed of Cat

1. Col. Lloyd Sailor, USAF (Ret.), letter to author dated December 1, 1980.

2. *Air Corps Newsletter* 15, no. 14 (December 4, 1931): 425.

3. Moore, *Enlisted Pilot Study,* Tab D.

4. Col. Lawrence O. Brown, USAF (Ret.), audiotape interview with author.

5. Reprinted from DeWitt S. Copp, *A Few Great Captains* (New York: Doubleday, 1980), p. 171; copyright by the Air Force Historical Foundation.

6. Brown audiotape.

7. Ibid.

8. Col. Harry Hines, USAF (Ret.), audiotape interview.

9. Ibid.

10. Maj. Gen. Russell L. Waldron, USAF (Ret.), audiotape interview by Lt. Col. Joseph H. Casey, USAF (Ret.), and transcribed for author.

11. *Air Corps Newsletter* 19, no. 5 (March 1, 1936): p. 7.

12. Col. Lloyd Sailor, USAF (Ret.), letter to author, December 1, 1980.

13. Brown audiotape.

14. Col. Loren Cornell, USAF (Ret.), audiotape interview with author.

15. Brig. Gen. Noel Parrish, USAF (Ret.), conversation with author during September 1982 enlisted pilot reunion at Colorado Springs. General Parrish died on April 7, 1987, at which time the Pentagon published a photograph of the funeral ceremony at Ft. Myer, Virginia, in its April 16, 1987, edition of the *Pentagram* stating: "Parrish had organized and directed the training during World War II of the black combat pilots known as the Tuskegee Airmen."

A more personal and heartfelt tribute to the courage, fairness, and integrity of this unusual man is contained in an article by T. J. McDowell entitled "The Tuskegee Airmen" in the October 1981 issue of *Sergeants* magazine, part of which follows:

> Parrish had been a flying instructor at a school in Illinois before coming to Tuskegee, and seemed to have a feel for the problems the black men were facing. During his tour as commander of Tuskegee, Parrish earned the reputation for being a fair, professional officer.
>
> To this day, the Tuskegee Airmen treat Parrish, now a retired general, with warmth and genuine affection.
>
> "There are not enough good adjectives in the dictionary to describe this man," O'Neal says fondly. "He's beautiful." To a man, the airmen describe Parrish as being the force that motivated them to excel during the war. Parrish, they say, knew more about them than they knew about themselves.

16. Col. Harold Kreider, USAF (Ret.), audiotape interview with author.

17. Brown audiotape.

18. Col. Paul Jackson, USAF (Ret.), telephone conversation with author.

19. Sailor, letter to author.

20. Ibid.

21. Moore, *Enlisted Pilot Study,* Tabs J and I.

22. Letter from Col. Ray Clifton, USAF (Ret.), to Lt. Col. Russell Shaw, USAF (Ret.), and made available to author.

23. Waldron-Casey transcribed audiotape interview.

24. William McDonald, "The Chennault I Knew," *Air Power Historian* 6, no. 2 (April 1959): 88–92.

25. Sailor, letter to author

CHAPTER 9: In Search of a Niche

1. Paraphrased from an interview conducted by Lt. Col. Joe Casey, October 28, 1980, with Col. Julius Kolb, USAF (Ret.)

2. Col. Julius Kolb, letter to author, February 18, 1981.

3. Jackson audiotapes, and additional conversations with author.

4. Ibid.

5. *Dayton News,* July 9, 1933.

6. M. Sgt. Ralph W. Bottriell, letter to Surgeon General, U.S. Army, July 16, 1920.

7. Aircraft Accident Reports File No. 200.3911-1, September 17, 1908–June 10, 1921, USAF HRC.

8. Lt. Gen. Lewis H. Brereton, *The Brereton Diaries* (New York: Morrow, 1946), p. 309.

9. Jackson audiotapes.

10. Lt. Col. Joe Casey, USAF (Ret.), to author following interview with Boyd Ertwine dated August 5, 1982.

11. Lt. Col. Ertwine's response to questionnaire.

12. Gen. Carl McDaniel in interview with author.

13. Transcription of Lt. Col. Boyd Ertwine's audiotaped interview by Lt. Col. Joe Casey.

14. Jackson audiotapes.

15. Ibid.

16. "Who's Who in the News."

17. Ocker and Crane, *Blind Flight in Theory and Practice* (San Antonio: Naylor, 1932).

18. "Who's Who in the News"; *Air Corps Newsletter* 14, no. 10 (August 29, 1930): 202.

19. Brig. Gen. Maurice Beach, "The Saga of an Average American Boy," unpublished autobiography, p. 8.

20. Biographic material of Col. Paul Blair was compiled from information contained in correspondence with author, together with numerous telephone conversations and personal visits with author. Specific date of transfer to 3rd Transport Squadron is contained in *Air Corps Newsletter* 19, no. 24 (December 15, 1936): 24.

21. *National Geographic Society Magazine* 58, no. 3 (September 1930): 330, 333, 339.

22. Col. Frank Graves, USAF (Ret.), audiotaped conversation with author (hereafter cited as Graves audiotape).

23. Col. Charles W. Johnstone, USAF (Ret.), audiotaped conversation with author.

24. Ibid.

25. Graves audiotape.

26. Elfin Wallace, widow of Bernard Wallace, interview with author.

27. Col. Paul Blair, USAF (Ret.), letters and responses to questionnaire.

28. Maurer Maurer, ed., *Air Force Combat Units of World War II: History and Ensignia* (Washington, D.C.: Zenger, 1961), pp. 52–53.

29. Blair letters.

30. Col. Paul Blair, letter to Col. Jack Price of the office of the Air Inspector, Headquarters, Army Air Forces and dated October 10, 1945. Colonel Blair served as commanding officer at Kelly Field from April 28, 1943, to July 15, 1944.

31. Blair letters.

32. Jackson audiotapes; and *Air Corps Newsletter* 20, no. 22 (November 15, 1937): 25.

33. Blair letters.

34. *Air Corps Newsletter* 21, no. 13 (July 1, 1938): 10.

35. *Air Corps Newsletter* 21, no. 6 (March 15, 1938): 6.

36. Jackson audiotapes.

37. Blair, notes penned to author on April 23, 1987.

38. Col. Jerome B. McCauley, individual flight records (Form 5), November 1934–February 1938.

39. Col. Kolb, letter to author, April 24, 1981.

40. McCauley, individual flight records.

41. Letter of commendation from Maj. Clayton Bissell, C.O. of the 18th Pursuit Group, Wheeler Field, T.H., to McCauley and Kolb, dated February 14, 1938. Also, *Air Corps Newsletter* 21, no. 6 (March 15, 1938): 11. Both of these accounts say that water from the thermos bottles was the fluid used to refill the hydraulic reservoir. However, the author, while flying as copilot to then Lt. Col. McCauley on a flight from Nouvion, Algeria, to Malta for pre-Sicilian invasion briefings heard of that event firsthand. We had just taken off from a fighter field near Sfax when our hydraulic pressure line coming into the selector valve ruptured and sprayed a heavy mist throughout the crew compartment. Our crew chief quickly repaired the line and refilled the system from spare fluid routinely carried aboard for such emergencies. It was then that Col. McCauley told his version of the incident in Hawaii.

42. Col. Kolb, letter to author, May 14, 1981.

43. Moore Study, Tab K.

44. Maurer, *Air Force Combat Units of World War II,* pp. 123–31.

CHAPTER 10: The Approaching War

1. Moore Study. Tab I, pp. 1–3.

2. Transcription of Col. Kolb interview by Lt. Col. Joe Casey, October 28, 1980.

3. Brig. Gen. Maurice M. Beach, "The Saga of an Average American Boy," unpublished autobiography, pp. 8–9.

4. Maurer Maurer, ed., *Air Force Combat Units of World War II: History and Ensignia* (Washington, D.C.: Zenger, 1961), pp. 123–31.

5. Ibid.

6. Kolb, undated letter entitled "My Comments," in response to questions on author's roster of enlisted pilots.

7. Moore Study, Tab I, pp. 1–3.

8. Lt. Col. Ertwine audiotape interview by Lt. Col. Joe Casey.

9. Burge personal 201 file.

10. Ibid.

11. "Who's Who in the News." (Note: From personal conversations with Mrs. Doris Ocker Osborn, Ocker's only child, it was learned that Ocker's delayed retirement date was cut short by his death by cancer at Walter Reed Hospital on September 15, 1942.)

12. Early Bird *Chirp,* no. 49 (August 1, 1953): 2, 8. Smith became a brigadier general by the end of World War II.

13. War Department Special Orders No. 234, October 7, 1941.

14. Final entry in Burges's flight record (Form 5), October 1941.

15. Associated Press news release, March Field, California, July 6, 1942.

16. Moore Study, p. 10.

17. Brandt, letter to author dated June 4, 1989.

18. Office of the Chief of the Air Corps, Memorandum on Enlisted Pilots, December 18, 1940, prepared for the War Department Chief of Staff.

19. Undated memorandum for the Chief of the Air Corps from Military Affairs Branch of the Judge Advocate General, 211, Subject: "Training of Enlisted Men in Grade as Aviation Students."

20. War Department General Staff Memorandum for Chief of Staff, January 25, 1941, Subject: "Enlisted Pilots."

21. War Department Letter, Bureau of Public Relations, June 4, 1941, "Enlisted Pilots" (National Archives).

22. National Archives record group 18 of the Army Air Forces.

23. Routing and Record sheet from Lieutenant Colonel Carter to Executive of Plans. Subject: "Legislation to Authorize Training of Enlisted Pilots in Grade," April 5, 1941.

24. Public Law 99, 55 Stat. 77th Congress, 1st session—CHS. 167, 168— June 3, 1941 (chapter 167). See Appendix F.

25. War Department Bureau of Public Relations press release entitled "Enlisted Pilots," dated June 4, 1941. See Appendix G.

26. Army Regulation 615-150, entitled "Aviation Student Training," August 1, 1941, Par. 6, C, and Par. 1, b, p. 3.

27. Article in *Air Corps Newsletter* 24, no. 13 (July 1, 1941), entitled "Enlisted Pilots Begin Training in August. Gulf Coast Training Centers Get First Students—Use of Pilots Undetermined, Ferry Duty Anticipated. What Kind of Ensignia?"

28. Routing and Record sheet from Stratemeyer, Training and Operations, to Air Corps Ferrying Command, September 27, 1941. Subject: "Plans For Utilization of Enlisted Pilots." Subsequent comments occur in following order.

29. Borum letter, August 11, 1941. National Archives.

30. Ibid., comment 2, Robert Olds's reply.

31. Ibid., comment 4, Stratemeyer to Exec, Chief of Air Corps.

32. Ibid., comment 5, from Chief of Air Corps to Air Corps Ferrying Command.

33. Ibid., comment 6, Olds's reply.

34. Ibid., comment 7, Stratemeyer's order.

35. Maurer, *Air Force Combat Units of World War II,* pp. 52, 53, 154, 188, 196.

36. Ibid., pp. 192, 193.

CHAPTER 11: The Sergeant Pilots Join the Battles

1. Lt. Col. J. Wayne Jorda, USAF (Ret.), and former sergeant pilot with Class 42-C, in audiotaped interview with author.

2. Robert Haynes Murray, former sergeant pilot with Class 42-C, *The Only Way Home* (Waycross, Georgia: Brantley Printing Company, 1986), pp. 11, 12.

3. File No. GP-82-HI, February 9, 1942–March 1943, Folder No. 5667-46, *History of the 82nd Fighter Group* 00080876, USAF HRC.

4. Lt. Col. Jesse Yaryan, USAF (Ret.), and former sergeant pilot with Class 42-C, in videotaped interview with author, cited hereafter as Yaryan interview.

5. Telephone interview with Col. Robert E. Kirtley, USAF (Ret.), squadron commander

of the 95th Fighter Squadron, 82nd Fighter Group, at the time the sergeant pilots of Class 42-C reported for duty.

6. Yaryan interview.

7. Murray, *The Only Way Home,* pp. 18–19.

8. Headquarters Army Air Forces Routing and Record sheet from office of AF DMR to AFACT, Subject: *Enlisted Pilots,* dated March 21, 1942.

9. Comment 2, dated March 28, 1942, from Hoyt S. Vandenberg in response to the Routing and Record sheet cited above.

10. Comment 4, dated April 6, 1942, which was Vandenberg's final comment on the Routing and Record sheet cited in n. 9 above.

11. Yaryan interview.

12. *History of the 82nd Fighter Group.*

13. Yaryan interview.

14. Col. Robert E. Kirtley, December 13, 1986, telephone conversation with author.

15. Extracted from *USAF Historical Study No. 85,* "USAF Credits for Destruction of Enemy Aircraft during World War II," and "American Fighter Aces Album," Library of Congress Catalog No. 78-65455.

16. Paragraph 5, Special Order No. 262, Hamilton Air Base Squadron, Hamilton Field, California, September 19, 1942.

17. Lt. Col. James Obermiller, USAF (Ret.), and former sergeant pilot with Class 42-C, in response to letter from author dated March 14, 1988.

18. John Kingsley, former sergeant pilot with Class 42-C, audiotape comments supplied to author in January 1988 (cited hereafter as Kingsley audiotape).

19. Obermiller, response to letter from author dated March 14, 1988.

20. Kingsley audiotape.

21. Routing and Record sheet from AF PMP, subject: *Assigment of Enlisted Pilots,* dated July 31, 1942, National Archives.

22. Memorandum for the Assistant Chief of Staff, G-1, Subject: *Retention of Noncommissioned Grade by Enlisted Pilots,* June 26, 1942.

23. As told to author by Robert C. Van Ausdell, sergeant pilot of Class 42-D, Ellington Field, Houston.

24. Comments written by William Cather, May 3, 1980, in response to sergeant pilot questionnaire, File No. 167.6-63, USAF HRC.

25. "Do You Recall," *Sergeant Pilot's Newsletter* 7, no. 2 (June 1986): 12

26. William Cather's comments on questionnaire dated May 3, 1980.

27. "Do You Recall," p. 12.

28. *Sergeant Pilot's Newsletter* 7, no. 1 (February 1986): 5.

29. AAF Training History, *History of Training in the U.S. Army Air Force 1939–1944,* pp. 3, 4.

30. Author's own experience.

31. Christopher Shores, Hans Ring, and William N. Ness, *Fighters over Tunisia* (London: Neville Spearman, 1975), p. 330.

32. Special Order 328, Headquarters Air Force Eastern Defense Command and First Air Force, Mitchell Field, New York, dated December 1, 1942.

33. Ira Over, memorandum, "The Odyssey of the 27th Fighter-Bomber Group (Formerly 27th Bombardment Group [L]) from Hunter Field, Ga., to Camp Shanks, N.Y.," p. 7.

34. French, German, Italian, British, and American sergeant pilots are cited throughout two books that give chronological accounts of air battles over the deserts of Egypt, Libya, and Tunis. They are Christopher Shores and Hans Ring, *Fighters over the Desert* (New York: Arco, 1969), and Christopher Shores, Hans Ring, and William N. Ness, *Fighters over Tunisia* (London: Neville Spearman, 1975).

35. Maurer Maurer, ed., *Air Force Combat Units of World War II: History and Ensignia* (Washington, D.C.: Zenger, 1961), p. 194.

36. Alexander G. Clifford, *The Conquest of North Africa, 1940–1943* (Boston: Little, Brown, 1943), p. 346. Clifford, a British war correspondent with the Eighth Army at the time, describes the importance of transport aircraft in exploiting the battle at El Alamein.

> Somehow 2400 tons of supplies had to be got up to the [British Eighth] army every day. It was a very highly motorized army, and whereas a World War I division would live and move on 300 tons a day, these desert divisions needed 420 tons each day, including water, and just maintaining them was not going to be enough. They had to be given a surplus of everything so that they could be ready to launch another offensive at once.
>
> The men handling the job started with this knowledge; that the road would be blown up, the water pipe severed, the railway broken in many places, that every well would be salted or oiled, that every harbor would be dynamited. So immediately behind the front they collected piles of railway metals, bulldozers, well borers, new sections for the pipeline, cranes, harbor equipment, engineers to deal with booby traps, other engineers to repair every form of destruction the enemy could devise. They found, much as they expected, that the railway had been blown up 40 times between Alamein and Daba, 67 more times before Matruh and a good hundred times between there and Capuzzo. Yet in the month after the army reached Capuzzo, 133,000 tons of supplies were unloaded at the rail head. The water pipe was actually mended while it was flooded by heavy rains. New wells were bored. The navy kept putting stuff ashore on beaches and little harbors, despising nothing because it was too small. Four ships were being unloaded in Tobruk within a couple of days of taking the place. Benghazi had now been five times deliberately dynamited, and bombed almost nightly for two years. It was thought that 800 tons a day would be the extreme limit of its capacity; but before the end of December 3000 tons had been handled in a single days work.
>
> And there was another thing . . . something which was nothing new to the Germans, but which no British army had ever done before. In this campaign for the first time air transport was used on a serious scale. Great fleets of American Douglases and Lockheeds began to fly low over Cyrenaica, bringing up aviation spirits and spare parts and personnel and any small but urgent thing that the army needed. The air force supply lorries almost disappeared from the road. Nothing remotely resembling it had ever been seen before on our side of the front."

37. From author's diary, and from author's individual flight record (Form 5) relating to that campaign.

38. Col. Robert E. Pace, USAF (Ret.), former sergeant pilot, autobiographical audiotape.

39. Marshall C. Wells, former sergeant pilot and copilot on that fateful mission, videotaped interview conducted by Lt. Col. John J. Hoye, USAF (Ret.).

40. John P. Williams, former sergeant pilot, audiotaped interview supplemented with duplicate documents from his file made available to author.

41. Ibid. Paraphrased from conversations with John P. Williams and the citation for his Distinquished Flying Cross.

42. Brig. Gen. Edwin F. Wengler, USAF (Ret.), and former sergeant pilot, telephone conversation with author.

43. From an article entitled "A Unique 'Trash Hauler' Squadron," in the USAF *Museum Friends Bulletin* 7, no. 3 (Fall 1984): 8–13. Also Steve Birdsall, *The Flying Buccaneers: The Illustrated Story of Kenney's Fifth Air Force* (Garden City, N.Y.: Doubleday, 1977), p. 30.

44. Lt. Col. Forrest Bruce, USAF (Ret.), and former sergeant pilot, in conversations with author.

45. *22nd Troop Carrier Squadron History from 3 April 1942 to 31 January 1944,* report dated March 8, 1945, p. 7, USAF HRC.

46. *21st Troop Carrier Squadron History from January 1942 to January 1944,* report dated May 24, 1945, p. 3, USAF HRC.

47. Lt. Col. Sammy Pierce, USAF (Ret.), and former sergeant pilot, in videotaped interview with author, and Warren Z. Coleman in telephone conversations with author.

48. George Johnston, *Morseby to Manila via Troop Carrier* (Sydney, Australia: Angus and Robertson, Halstead Press, 1945), p. 13. Johnston describes the fight:

> Down the green slopes of the Bulolo Valley came the full-scale Japanese attack against the important gold-field airport of Wau. The small Australian garrison, outnumbered five to one, was pushed back almost to the outskirts of the landing field. It was then when it seemed impossible that the vital little tropic town could be held, that the "bully-beef" bombers were again rushed in to save the day. They rushed to and fro across the great jagged peaks of the Owen Stanleys, bringing everything else needed to stem the waves of Japanese troops that swarmed across the low rounded hills of the mountain valley. They came under the patrolling top cover of P-38's and P-40's in which every pilot's finger was itching on the gun button.
>
> Once the Japs decided to smash the resistance and fracture our aerial supply by launching a fierce "blitz" on Wau airfield with scores of zeros and dive bombers. The sky was black with aircraft and pocked with the gray and white puffs of bursts from anti-aircraft guns. Plane after plane came crashing down, trailing black smoke and red flame. A Douglas transport on the field was disintegrated. Another Douglas raced up the valley with two zeros chasing it, guns and cannons blazing. But out of the sun came the P-38's, and the Zeros went smashing straight into the great green mountain wall, belching oily smoke into the sky as they hit. Altogether 40 Japanese planes were destroyed in that wild melee. The rest were driven off. Natives on the Wau drome bent their backs to their shovels as they filled in the bomb craters. Within an hour the Douglas transports were streaming in again.
>
> Twenty-four hours after the beginning of the Japanese attack on the Wau airfield the enemy was in full retreat, leaving a thousand enemy dead.

49. Lt. Gen. William H. Tunner, USAF (Ret.), *Over the Hump* (Washington, D.C.: Office of Air Force History, 1964), p. 59.

50. Maj. Monzell J. Phipps, USAF (Ret.), "Staff Sergeant Pilots Flew China Airlift—The

Hump," in *China Airlift—The Hump,* 2 vols. Vol. 1 ed. James F. Brewer, Vol. 2 ed. Harry G. Howton (Dallas: Taylor Publishing, 1980), 2:62–65.

51. From conversations with Bob Lay, former sergeant pilot and Hump pilot.

52. Ibid.

53. Ibid.

54. *China Airlift—The Hump,* Vols. 1 and 2.

55. From conversations with Bob Lay.

56. Public Law 658, July 8, 1942 as cited in AAF HS-166, p. 45, USAF HRC.

EPILOGUE

1. They are: Claude E. Ford (5), Alva Roe Hunter (5) Frank D. Hurlbut (9), Joe W. Icard (5), J. Wayne Jorda (5), Jack Lenox (5), Claude R. Kinsey (7), Lawrence P. Liebers (7), Sammy S. Pierce (7), Peter E. Pompetti (5), Gerald L. Rounds (5), William J. Schildt (6), William J. Sloan (12), Herman W. Visscher (6), Oran S. Watts (5), Samuel J. Wicker (7), Charles J. Zubarik (6).

2. They are: major generals Charles I. Bennett, Jr., William T. Hudnell, Jr., Carl B. Mc-Daniel, and Russell L. Waldron; and brigadier generals Harry C. Bayne, Maurice M. Beach, Harold Neely, Noel F. Parrish, Albert D. Smith, Edwin F. Wengler, and Rodger D. Young.

3. Maj. Harry Mamaux, III, Air Command and Staff College Report 84-1655: *The Enlisted Pilot Program in the USAAF 1941-1942: Was It Successful?,* p. 30.

4. Lt. Col. Carl M. Putnam, *Armor,* July-August 1973, pp. 46–48

BIBLIOGRAPHY

BOOKS AND BOOK-LENGTH REPORTS

Arnold, Henry H. *Global Mission.* New York: Harper & Brothers, 1949.

———. "The History of Rockwell Field." 1923. File no. 7542-192.4, USAF HRC.

Bekker, Cajus. *The Luftwaffe War Diaries.* Trans. and ed. Frank Ziegler. New York: Ballantine Books, 1973.

Bell, Dana. *Air Force Colors.* Vol. 1, *1926–1942.* Carrollton, Tex.: Squadron/Signal Publications, 1979.

Brereton, Lewis H. *The Brereton Diaries.* New York: Morrow, 1946.

Brinson, William L. *Three One Five Group.* Lakemont, Ga.: Copple House Books, 1984.

Caidin, Martin. *Air Force: A Pictorial History of American Air Power.* New York: Rinehart, 1957.

Casari, Robert B. *Encyclopedia of U.S. Military Aircraft: 1908 to April 6, 1917.* 4 vols. Chillicothe, Ohio, 1970–74.

———. *Encyclopedia of U.S. Military Aircraft: The World War I Production Program.* 3 vols. Chillicothe, Ohio, 1972–75.

Chandler, Charles deForest, and Frank P. Lahm. *How Our Army Grew Wings: Airmen and Aircraft before 1914.* New York: Ronald Press, 1943.

Casey, Louis S. *Curtiss: The Hammondsport Era, 1907–1915.* New York: Crown, 1981.

Copp, DeWitt S. *A Few Great Captains.* New York: Doubleday, 1980.

Craven, Wesley F. and James L. Cate, eds. *The Army Air Forces in World War II,* Vol. 4, *The Pacific: Guadalcanal to Saipan.* Chicago: University of Chicago Press, 1950.

———. *The Army Air Forces in World War II.* Vol. 5, *The Pacific: Matterhorn to Nagasaki.* Chicago: University of Chicago Press, 1953.

———. *The Army Air Forces in World War II.* Vol. 6, *Men and Planes.* Chicago: University of Chicago Press, 1951.

Deighton, Len. *Fighter: The True Story of the Battle of Britain.* New York: Alfred A. Knopf, 1978.

Fahey, James C., ed. *U.S. Army Aircraft (Heavier than Air), 1908–1946.* New York: Ships and Aircraft, 1946.

Glines, Carroll V., Jr. *The Compact History of the United States Air Force,* rev. ed. New York: Hawthorn Books, 1973.

Goldberg, Alfred, ed. *A History of the United States Air Force, 1907–1957.* Princeton, N.J.: Van Nostrand, 1957.

Hardesty, Von. *Red Phoenix: The Rise of Soviet Air Power, 1914–1945.* London and Melbourne: Arms and Armour Press, 1982.

Hennessey, Juliette A. *The United States Army Air Arm: April 1861 to April 1917.* Washington, D.C.: Office of Air Force History, 1958.

Holmes, Donald B. *Air Mail: An Illustrated History, 1793–1981.* New York: Clarkson N. Potter, 1981.

Johnson, Edward C. *Marine Corps Aviation: The Early Years, 1912–1940.* Washington, D.C.: History and Museums Division, U.S. Marine Corps Headquarters, 1977.

Kroll, H. D., ed. *Kelly Field in the Great World War, 1919.* 2nd ed. San Antonio: San Antonio Printing, 1919.

Lindbergh, Charles A. *The Spirit of St Louis.* New York: Scribner's, 1953.

Maurer, Maurer, ed. *Air Force Combat Units of World War II: History and Ensignia.* Washington, D.C.: Zenger Publishing, 1961.

———. *Aviation in the U.S. Army, 1919–1939.* Washington, D.C.: Office of Air Force History, 1987.

———, ed. *Combat Squadrons of the Air Force: World War II.* Washington, D.C.: Albert F. Simpson Historical Research Center and Office of Air Force History, 1982.

McDaniel, William H. *Beech: Fifty Years of Excellence, The History of Beech.* Wichita, Kan.: McCormick-Armstrong Co., 1982.

Mosley, Leonard. *Lindbergh: A Biography.* Garden City, N.Y.: Doubleday, 1976.

Murray, Robert Haynes. *The Only Way Home.* Waycross, Georgia: Brantley Printing Co., 1986.

Office of History, San Antonio Air Logistics Center, Kelly Air Force Base, Texas. *A Pictorial History of Kelly Air Force Base, 1917–1980.* Air Force Logistics Command, 1984.

Saint-Exupery, Antoine de. *Airman's Odyssey.* New York: Harcourt Brace Jovanovich, 1984.

Shelby, Carroll. *The Cobra Story: A Man, His Dream and His Automobile.* New York: Trident Press, 1965.

Shiner, John F. *Foulois and the U.S. Army Air Corps, 1931–1935.* Washington, D.C.: Office of Air Force History, 1983.

Shores, Christopher, and Hans Ring. *Fighters over the Desert.* New York: Arco, 1969.

Shores, Christopher, Hans Ring, and William N. Hess. *Fighters over Tunisia.* London: Neville Spearman, 1975.

Van Wyen, Adrian O., and the editors of *Naval Aviation News,* eds. *Naval Aviation in World War I.* Washington, D.C.: Chief of Naval Operations, 1969.

Wolk, Herman S. *Planning and Organizing the Postwar Air Force, 1943–1947.* Washington, D.C.: Office of Air Force History, 1984.

LEGISLATION

55th Stat., 77th Congress, 1st session, Chapter 167, June 3, 1941, S.1371, Public Law 99. An Act *To Authorize the Training of Enlisted Men of the Army as Aviation Students.*

WAR DEPARTMENT MEMORANDA

Moore, Capt. A. L., Office of the Chief of the Air Corps, February 15, 1940. Subject: "Enlisted Pilots."
Office of the Chief of the Air Corps, December 18, 1940. Subject: "Enlisted Pilots." This study is a reconsideration of Captain Moore's earlier enlisted pilot study.
Personnel Division G-1, January 25, 1941. Subject: "Enlisted Pilots."

REPORTS

Mamaux, Harry O., III. Student Report 84-1655. "The Enlisted Pilot Program in the USAAF, 1941–1942: Was It Successful?," Air Command and Staff College, Air University, Maxwell AFB, Ala.

STUDIES

Boden, William C. "The History of Kelly Field and Its Impact on American Aviation, 1917 to 1926." M.A. thesis, St. Mary's University, San Antonio, Texas, August 1967.
U.S. Army Historical Studies No. 7. "Legislation Relating to the AAF Training Program, 1939–1945." USAF Historical Archives, Maxwell AFB, Ala., pp. 58–96, and appendixes 5 and 8.

REGULATIONS

Army Regulation 615-150, August 1, 1941. "Aviation Student Training."

PERSONAL FILES

Beach, Maurice M. "The Saga of an Average American Boy." Unpublished autobiography.
Beigel, William E. *My Career in Aviation.* Unpublished autobiography.
Burge, Vernon L. "Early History of Army Aviation." Unpublished memoirs.
———. Diary maintained from May 1909 through May 1912; flight logs dated May 20, 1918–October 1941, including a recap of flying time between 1912 and 1918.
Harvey, Alva L. Unpublished autobiography, 1978.

INDEX